Multinationals in Latin America

Multinationals in Latin America
The Politics of Nationalization

Paul E. Sigmund

A TWENTIETH CENTURY FUND STUDY

The University of Wisconsin Press

Published 1980

The University of Wisconsin Press
114 North Murray Street
Madison, Wisconsin 53715

The University of Wisconsin Press, Ltd.
1 Gower Street
London WC1E 6HA, England

Printings 1980, 1982

Printed in the United States of America

ISBN 0-299-08260-1 cloth, 0-299-08264-4 paper; LC 80-5115

The Twentieth Century Fund is an independent research foundation which undertakes policy studies of economic, political, and social institutions and issues. The Fund was founded in 1919 and endowed by Edward A. Filene.

Contents

Foreword

In these days of crisis management, successive administrations have been preoccupied with one foreign policy issue at a time; during the 1960s, the war in Vietnam was paramount, while in the 1970s the Arab-Israeli conflict was preeminent. Meanwhile, of course, other problems are left unresolved and frequently fester. Such has been the case with relations between the United States and Latin America. To be sure, from time to time Cuba has been the focus of crisis management, but since the abandonment of the Alliance for Progress, inspired in part by Fidel Castro's revolution, little attention, comparatively speaking, has been paid to events in Latin America.

Because of the Twentieth Century Fund's long-standing interest in United States-Latin American relations and its commitment to policy analysis of the economies of the developing world, the Trustees decided to support a proposal by Paul E. Sigmund of Princeton University. His study deals with the implications of the nationalization of United States corporate enterprises in Latin America for the future of foreign investment and for our relations with the Third World. Isolated take-overs of American private and corporate holdings in Latin America had taken place in the past — they were central to United States reactions to the early Mexican revolution and to Cuba under Castro. While American foreign policymakers were directing their attention to other areas, nationalization became a trend in Latin America, and corporations, as well as the United States government, went on the defensive. These nationalizations caused a deterioration in American relations with Peru and contributed to the Central Intelligence Agency's intervention in Chile. Moreover, nationalizations seemed likely to increase since Latin American theories of *dependencia* and of state sovereignty over foreign investment, incorporated into the New International Economic Order, were being advanced by Third World states.

For these reasons, the Trustees of the Fund saw merit in Sigmund's proposal to examine nationalization in five major Latin American countries, ranging from the still unsettled take-overs in Cuba to the negotiated take-over of foreign-owned petroleum companies by the democratic government of Venezuela. Sigmund's primary objective was to identify the political and economic conditions underlying the demands for nationalization, to evaluate the arguments for and against such nationalizations, and to analyze the difficulties encountered in the management of nationalized industries and the solutions adopted to overcome them. These case studies were also designed to test the ideology of both the proponents and the opponents of nationalization against historical realities.

When the Fund undertakes the sponsorship and supervision of policy research, it expects its authors to study past events mainly in terms of their implications for the future. Sigmund has met this test. He has looked beyond the take-overs to the future of private investment in Latin America and in other developing countries. In Latin America, where the nationalization movement has had the most momentum — leading to the take-over of the major enclaves in mining, communications, and banking — he has concluded that the trend may well have climaxed. Latin American governments, having exerted their sovereignty in those areas regarded as critical to national development, have come to accept and even welcome foreign investment, subject to specific economic and political restrictions. At the same time, multinational enterprises have also learned from recent experiences the ways and means of accommodating to the new investment environment and protecting themselves from political challenges. In this new equilibrium, as Sigmund sees it, the United States public interest in foreign investment has changed significantly, calling for changes in the role of the United States government in protecting and promoting such investment.

We are grateful to Paul Sigmund for his clear, sober, and balanced examination of a critical aspect in United States-Latin American relations. His study, which carefully avoids argumentative and sterile assessments of blame, is an important contribution to understanding the forces at work in the world economy. His reasoned approach will lead policymakers and the public to devote some thought and concern to the future problems posed by the nationalization movement.

M. J. Rossant
Director

The Twentieth Century Fund, Inc.
January 1980

Multinationals in Latin America

1

The International Debate
on Nationalization

*Private investment as a carrier of technology, of trade op-
portunities, and of capital itself . . . becomes a major factor in promoting industrial and agricultural development.
Further, a significant flow of private foreign capital stimu-
lates the mobilization and formation of domestic capital
within the recipient country. . . . Unfortunately for all
concerned, these virtually axiomatic views on the beneficial
role of . . . private capital have been challenged in recent
and important instances. U.S. enterprises, and those of
many other nations, operating abroad under valid contracts
negotiated in good faith and within the established legal
codes of certain foreign countries, have found their contracts revoked and their assets seized with inadequate compensation or with no compensation. Such actions by other
governments are wasteful from a resource standpoint,
short-sighted considering their adverse effects on the flow
of private investment funds from all sources, and unfair to
the legitimate interests of foreign private investors.*

—Richard M. Nixon, *Economic Assistance and
Investment Security in Developing Nations,*
1972

. . . Each State has the right . . . to nationalize, expropriate, or transfer ownership of foreign property, in which case appropriate compensation should be paid by the State adopting such measures, taking into account its relevant law and regulations and all circumstances the State considers pertinent. In any case where the question of compensation gives rise to a controversy, it shall be settled under the domestic law of the nationalizing State and by its tribunals. . . .

Charter of Economic Rights and Duties of
States, United Nations General Assembly
Resolution 3281, 1974

A central and seemingly irreconcilable issue between the United States and the developing world is the conflicting view of the rights of foreign investors. On the one hand, the capital-importing nations, with the support of the communist world, have asserted their right to "full sovereignty" in the treatment of foreign investment located in their territories and have used the United Nations and other international forums to support their claims. On the other hand, the United States government and, in a less doctrinaire way, other capital-exporting countries have insisted that, under international law, investors possess certain contractual rights; the capital-exporting countries have buttressed their position with the argument that private foreign investment should be encouraged because it is the most convenient and beneficial way to achieve rapid development.

The dispute is an old one. Since the nineteenth century, analogous arguments have been used by Latin Americans to defend the inclusion of a clause in investment agreements in which the foreign investor specifically gives up the right to resort to international or foreign arbitration in case of disputes and agrees to abide by the decisions of national courts. Similar views were expressed in a draft provision prepared by the Economic Committee of the League of Nations in 1929, which only provided for "national compensation" in cases of expropriation, rather than the "fair compensation" requested by the British delegation. The debate on this subject has received much more attention in recent years because of the escalation in the number and magnitude of nationalizations of foreign property in Asia, Africa, and Latin America and of the adoption of resolutions, by lopsided majorities at international meetings, in support of an absolute right of developing countries to take over foreign enterprises with little or no compensation.

On December 12, 1974, for example, the United Nations General Assembly adopted a Charter of Economic Rights and Duties by a vote of 120 in favor, 6 opposed, including the United States, and 10 abstentions. As the discussions before the vote revealed, the negative votes were directed at the charter's section on nationalization (quoted at the beginning of this chapter), particularly the omission of any reference to an obligation to compensate in accordance with international law standards. By a vote of 71 to 20, with 18 abstentions, the General Assembly rejected a proposal put forth by fourteen developed countries that a provision be added requiring nationalizing states to pay "just compensation in the light of all relevant circumstances" and "fulfill in good faith their international obligations." By a vote of 87 to 19, with 1 abstention, it also defeated a provision that "undertakings relating to the import of foreign capital" should be "observed in good faith."

Seven months earlier, on May 1, 1974, the Sixth Special Session of the General Assembly endorsed a declaration of principles of the New International Economic Order, which included the claim that "the full permanent sovereignty of every State over its natural resources and all economic activities" involved "the right to nationalization or transfer of ownership to its nationals." The resolution omitted any reference to a duty to compensate, and it called upon the agencies of the United Nations to assist developing countries "with the operation of nationalized means of production."

The near unanimity in the General Assembly and the quasi isolation of the American representatives reflected a marked shift in the balance of power within the United Nations. Twelve years earlier, following an intense struggle between an American effort to secure endorsement of the principle of "prompt, adequate, and effective" compensation for nationalized property and a Soviet attempt to secure support for "the inalienable right of peoples and nations to the unobstructed execution of nationalization and expropriation," the General Assembly adopted Resolution 1803 on Permanent Sovereignty over Natural Resources, which called for "appropriate compensation in accordance with the rules in force in the State taking such measures . . . and in accordance with international law." While repeatedly referring to permanent state sovereignty over natural resources, the resolution concluded that "Foreign investment agreements freely entered into, by, or between, sovereign states shall be observed in good faith." The vote on the resolution was 87 to 2 (France and South Africa voted no), with 12 abstentions (the Communist countries plus Ghana and Burma). In accepting the expression "appropriate compensation," the United States representative stated that his delegation "was confident" that it "would be interpreted as meaning under international law, prompt, adequate, and effective compensation."[1]

Before 1962, however, comparatively few nationalizations had taken place in the Third World, and when they had they frequently had produced international crises of varying degrees of seriousness. In 1946, Juan Domingo Perón bought out the British-owned Argentine railroads on generous terms, and in the next decade, Burma, India, and Indonesia took over British- and Dutch-owned property with little conflict. However, Iran's seizure of British-owned petroleum in 1951, Guatemala's nationalization of United Fruit's holdings in 1953, Egypt's and Iraq's expropriation of European property in 1956 and 1957, Guinea's seizure of all French holdings after it achieved independence in 1959, and the Cuban expropriations of American property in 1959 and 1960 — all caused serious disputes with the major powers.[2] As the Iranian and Guatemalan situations demonstrate, it was still possible in the 1950s for the Western powers to intervene successfully to defend the property of their citizens, and they were particularly likely to do so if a case could be made that their security interests in the cold war would be adversely affected. The failure of the Anglo-French intervention in 1956 against Gamal Abdel Nasser's nationalization of the Suez Canal was an indication, however, that the weapons of the age of "gunboat diplomacy" in defence of economic interests might no longer be appropriate.

Beginning in the late 1960s, there was a notable increase in the number of nationalizations of foreign-owned concerns in Asia, Africa, and Latin America. While these take-overs did not result in military intervention, they were usually surrounded by considerable contention, and the affected enterprises often sought the assistance of the United States government in their disputes with the nationalizing governments. By 1974, the State Department could identify 106 investment disputes involving American property in 39 countries. It estimated that the amount in dispute could run as high as $3.5 billion out of a total of $25 billion in the book value of United States investment in Asia, Africa, and Latin America. Three years later, an updated State Department list identified 78 new cases of investment disputes between February 1975 and February 1977. While there was an increase in petroleum nationalizations in other parts of the world, nearly half of the new cases involved Latin American countries and two-thirds were in the area of natural resources.

THE UNITED STATES POSITION

The United States government has always recognized the right of foreign governments to nationalize foreign property, but it has consistently maintained that international law requires that it be carried out for a public purpose on a nondiscriminatory basis and that prompt, adequate, and effective compensation be paid. The issue of compensation has been a particularly difficult and ambiguous one. On its face, the traditional standard appears to demand immediate or almost immediate payment of full market value in internationally convertible currency. In fact, of course, there is no known case where this standard has been fully applied. First, it is very difficult to ascertain full market value when there is no real market for many of the investments in the Third World. The alternative, the value on the company books for tax purposes (net book value), usually results in a figure that companies regard as unfair, and it is subject to dispute because of differing tax laws.[3] Second, most countries do not have the wherewithal to provide immediate compensation. Even the oil-rich members of the Organization of Petroleum Exporting Countries (OPEC) have other uses for the revenue bonanza that they have acquired. Third, the majority of the nationalizing countries have chronic balance-of-payments problems and large international debts; it is difficult, if not impossible, therefore, to produce the internationally convertible currency demanded by the traditional standard.

Nevertheless, the United States government has continued to insist on prompt, adequate, and effective compensation. Indeed, after being faced with repeated violations of that standard in nationalization agreements between the oil companies and the OPEC countries, the State Department, on December 30, 1975, issued a formal statement reaffirming its commitment to the "prompt, adequate, and effective" formula and stating that it, "wished to place on record its view that foreign investors are entitled to the fair market value of their interests. Acceptance by U.S. nationals of less than fair market value does not constitute acceptance of any other standard by the United States Government. As a consequence the United States Government reserves its rights to maintain international claims for what it regards as adequate compensation under international law for the interests nationalized or transferred."

In support of its position, the State Department has gone well beyond normal diplomatic representations or protests to nationalizing governments. In Latin America, from the time of the Mexican nationalization of oil in the late 1930s through the nationalization disputes with Chile and Peru in the 1970s, United States policymakers have considered using or have employed economic pressures, boycotts, the denial of aid, and concerted action with other creditor nations to back up their insistence on full compensation.

Congress has even gone a step farther by legislating quasi-automatic sanctions against governments that nationalize American holdings without full compensation. In 1962, reacting to the 1960 Cuban nationalizations and to the expropriation of the International Telephone and Telegraph Company (ITT) subsidiary in southern Brazil, Congress enacted the Hickenlooper Amendment, mandating the termination of all United States aid to any country that nationalizes American-owned property and does not, within six months, "take appropriate steps . . . to discharge its obligations under international law toward such citizen or entity, including speedy compensation for such property in convertible foreign exchange, equivalent to full value thereof, as required by international law." While the State Department was sympathetic with its intent, it opposed the amendment because the automatic character of its sanctions left little room for negotiation, and, indeed, was likely to produce nationalistic reactions that might hamper prospects for a settlement. Nevertheless, the amendment has been reenacted with each new Foreign Assistance Act, although in 1973 a provision was added permitting the president to waive the application of the amendment if he considered such action to be in the national interest.

Two years after passage of the Hickenlooper Amendment, a Supreme Court decision led Congress to take further action in the field of expropriation. In *Banco Nacional de Cuba* v. *Sabbatino* in 1964, a case involving the seizures of American property in Cuba in 1960 by the Castro government, the Court asserted that "there are few if any issues in international law today on which opinion seems to be so divided as the limitations on a State's power to expropriate the property of aliens." Citing the nonjusticiability of "acts of state," the Court decided that "the Judicial Branch will not examine the validity of a taking of property within its own territory by a foreign sovereign government, extant and recognized by this country at the time of the suit . . . even if the complaint alleges that the taking violated customary international law" (84 S. Ct. at 940).

Reacting strongly to the Court decision, Congress adopted what is sometimes referred to as the Second Hickenlooper Amendment to the 1964 Foreign Assistance Act, providing that, "no court in the United States shall decline on the ground of the federal act of state doctrine to make a determination on the merits giving effect to the principles of international law in a case in which a claim of title or other right to property is asserted . . . based upon or traced through a confiscation or other taking after January 1, 1959, by an act of that state in violation of the principles of international law . . . " The amendment, however, included an escape clause. The president could still invoke the act of state doctrine by a formal submission to the Court stating that it was required in a particular case because of "the foreign policy interests" of the United States.

In January 1972, Congress went still further. The González Amendment, passed as part of a bill providing funds for international financial institutions, provided that in the case of the nationalization of American property *unless* the president determined that "a) an arrangement for prompt, adequate, and effective compensation has been made, b) the parties have submitted the dispute to arbitration. . . . or c) good faith negotiations are in progress aimed at providing prompt, adequate, and effective compensation under the applicable principles of international law," the United States representatives to the World Bank, the International Development Association, the Inter-American Development Bank, and the Asian Development Bank are required to vote against any loan or any other utilization of the funds of the bank for the benefit of the nationalizing country. The congressional action coincided with a statement by President Nixon to the same effect. The statement had been worked out after elaborate negotiations among the White House, the State Department, and the Treasury Department. It resulted in the creation of a special Inter-Agency Group on Expropriation whose function was to review such cases in light of the antiexpropriation legislation and to recommend courses of action for the government.

The work of that group, which includes representatives from the White House, Treasury, Commerce, and State departments, was substantially expanded with the insertion of an antiexpropriation clause into the Trade Act of 1974. The Trade Act establishes a Generalized System of Preferences (GSP) on import duties for the benefit of developing countries, but in Section 502, it denies GSP eligibility to any country that has expropriated the property of a United States national without prompt, adequate, and effective compensation. Again, there is a provision for a waiver of the application of this section by the president, but only if he determines that such a waiver is consistent with "U.S. national economic interest."

As a result of this legislation, the United States government must now engage in a day-to-day monitoring of every country in the Third World to determine whether it can be certified as eligible for tariff preferences. Before 1962, the United States government's involvement in investment disputes was a matter for discretionary decision by the State Department. It decided whether and how it would aid American companies involved in investment disputes with other nations. Now the government is mandated to take action or to give reasons why such action is not taken, and, because of GSP, those reasons must be economic rather than political.

The insistence on prompt, adequate, and effective compensation might appear to be a blind adherence to the absolute and universally binding nature of property rights. However, the United States government has also argued that adherence to these standards is in the best interests of the developing nations and of world economic welfare. According to President Nixon's 1972 statement, it was "axiomatic" that private investment promotes development by aiding in the transfer of technology, by providing access to international markets, and by accelerating capital formation in areas that lack domestic sources of capital. Nationalization of foreign investment is viewed by American spokesmen as interfering with this process in at least two ways. On the one hand, if full compensation is paid, scarce capital resources are diverted from the creation of new productive capacity. On the other, if little or no compensation is paid, the flow of new investment capital is diminished or terminated because of the adverse "investment climate"—and development again suffers.

Proposals have been put forth suggesting that compensation be financed from international sources on concessional terms. The United States government reply has been that there are better uses for the capital of international financial institutions. Moreover, if the financing of expropriations were to become a major concern of such institutions, contributions from the developed countries would cease, and those institutions would not be able to secure loans from the international credit market.

Besides negative sanctions against expropriation, the United States Congress has also taken positive steps to encourage the flow of American investment to the Third World. The Investment Guarantee Program, originally established in 1948 as part of the Marshall Plan's aid program to Europe, gave government insurance to United States investors abroad against risks from war, inconvertibility, and, in 1950, expropriation. It was replaced in 1969 by the Overseas Private Investment Corporation (OPIC), an organization initially financed by tax money which offers insurance to United States private investors overseas, principally in the Third World. Foreign investment is also encouraged by the tax system. Credit is given against United States taxes for taxes paid elsewhere. United States taxes are deferred on a part of unrepatriated profits of overseas subsidiaries until they are brought back to the United States. In addition, until 1980, there were specific tax advantages for Western Hemisphere Corporations that invested in the Americas.

Congress and the State Department have tried to encourage the use of international arbitration agencies as a way to resolve investment disputes. In 1966, the American government supported the creation of the International Centre for the Settlement of Investment Disputes (ICSID) within the World Bank, and in 1974, Henry Kissinger, secretary of state, proposed the establishment of an Inter-American Investment Tribunal to investigate questions of fact connected with investment controversies and to promote their peaceful settlement. For many years, the United States also tried to internationalize investment insurance programs through an International Investment Insurance Association designed to coordinate, regularize, and depoliticize the various investment insurance programs of the capital-exporting nations. In May 1976, at the Nairobi meeting of the United Nations Conference on Trade and Development (UNCTAD), Secretary Kissinger made another attempt to establish an international framework to encourage investment flows when he proposed the creation of an International Resources Bank that would both assist in financing investment in the development of raw material production in the developing nations and, because of its international sponsorship, reduce the risk of expropriation.

Official United States government opposition to the Third World proposals on the subject of nationalization was matched by criticisms of those proposals by American writers from both the left and the right. The liberal *Washington Post* pointed to the contradiction between the desire of the Third World for more investment by the rich countries and the claim that "the poor (countries) can take over the plants as they please for whatever they want to pay," while a conservative critic attacked the New International Economic Order as an attempt by the representatives of a large assortment of minor or major tyrants to "initiate a transition into a socialist world."[4] The most telling criticism of the Third World proposals was that they would sharply reduce living standards in the developed countries, while only benefiting the wealthier income groups in less developed areas. Thus, the resulting international redistribution of income would amount to taking from the poor in the rich countries to give to the rich in the poor countries.[5]

THE VIEW FROM THE THIRD WORLD

The emergence in the mid-1970s of the proposals for a New International Economic Order was one of many indications of the development of a consensus among the less developed nations on North-South economic relations. The UN General Assembly, UNCTAD, and related institutions provided the arena in which that consensus was developed, and it was shaped principally by writers and diplomats from Latin America.

UNCTAD first met in 1964 in Geneva, where it established a permanent secretariat. Before the next meeting at New Delhi, in 1968, the representatives of the Third World countries, known unofficially as "the Group of 77," held a preparatory meeting in Algiers and adopted a common program, the Charter of Algiers. Similar meetings were held at Lima, in October 1971 before the 1972 Santiago UNCTAD meeting, and in Manila, in February 1976 before the May 1976 meeting in Nairobi. From the documents adopted at these meetings, as well as from speeches of the representatives of "the 77" at the UNCTAD meetings that followed, and from the Sixth and Seventh Special Sessions of the UN General Assembly, it is clear that there is almost total disagreement with the United States position on nationalization, compensation, and the virtues of private, foreign investment.

The first area of disagreement concerns the respective spheres of national sovereignty and property rights. In the promotion of national development, indeed, in the very establishment of nationhood, the developing nations have asserted the right of "the State" (significantly, the word is capitalized in UN documents) to modify property relations in accordance with national priorities. In the resolution on the New International Economic Order asserting the state's right to nationalize, no mention is made of a duty of the nationalizing government to pay compensation. In other documents, such as the UN Charter of Economic Rights and Duties of States, compensation is supposed to be "appropriate," although the decision on how much to pay is left up to the nationalizing government, and no provision is made for outside arbitration unless the states concerned "freely and mutually" agree. The demand made by the United States for "prompt, adequate, and effective" compensation has been repeatedly defeated when it has been proposed. Third World writers cite European writers on international law, such as Samy Friedman and Konstantin Katsarov, to support their claim that neither in the theory of international law nor in the practice upon which it is based is there a recognized duty to full compensation.[6] Resistance to full compensation and opposition to outside tribunals are not restricted to representatives of the political left, but they have consistently characterized the attitudes of less developed nations, representing a variety of political perspectives.

A new, significant element, however, has been added to the debate. Now, the developed countries' belief in the benefits of foreign private investment has also come under attack. It is no longer considered "axiomatic" that such investment is always beneficial to host countries. The supposed benefits to be derived from private investment in the transfer of capital, technology, and managerial expertise have been subject to increasingly critical scrutiny in the present decade. Capital is not transferred from the developed countries, the critics assert, since the foreign investor borrows most of his funds locally, thus distorting the local capital market. Foreign investors take far more in profits out of the country than they bring in through new investment, thus exacerbating the chronic balance-of-payments problems of the less developed countries. Profits are inflated through the manipulation of royalty and licensing payments and transfer pricing between subsidiaries, and the use of tax havens and accounting devices to avoid paying local taxes. The technology that the foreign investor introduces is obsolete and/or inappropriate because it is capital-intensive rather than labor-intensive.

A "favorable investment climate" often seems to require an authoritarian—usually military—government that imposes policies of political repression and economic austerity, justifying them as prerequisites for economic growth. Regressive and inequitable patterns of income distribution are reinforced and even exacerbated because the benefits of foreign investment go primarily to upper income groups. Thus, Third World countries are being "undeveloped" through the expanding "global reach" of the large multinational corporations based in the United States and Europe, and the benefits claimed for foreign investment—technology, marketing, capital, industrialization, and economic growth—turn out to be fallacious on all counts.[7]

A number of solutions have been proposed to control the adverse effects of foreign investment and to increase the likelihood that the multinational corporation will benefit the host country. They include the establishment of codes of conduct, investment screening, joint ventures, and forced divestment on a fixed timetable, as well as legislation regulating profit remittances, technology transfers, the employment of nationals, and the expansion of exports. Another alternative, however—to be used as a threat in bargaining with the multinationals and, in the view of some, a preferable way to promote accelerated development, increased equity among nations, and national control of economic decisionmaking—is nationalization.

Nationalization forms an integral part of the proposals for a New International Economic Order as one of the ways to correct the inequities produced by a framework of international economic relations, which has been developed by, and for, the wealthy and powerful nations. Government take-overs of foreign holdings are seen as necessary to assure that economic activities within the nation are directed toward national goals. Economic decisions will then be made for the nation, it is argued, rather than in the interest of the foreign corporation, and maximum benefit can be secured from the nation's natural and human resources. In addition, nationalization makes it easier for the less developed countries to take common action to secure a distribution of the returns from international economic relations that is more favorable to the producing country and its citizens.

However, the debate on nationalization and on the costs and benefits of foreign investment has raised questions about the official United States position, which require a critical evaluation of the point of view of the advocates of nationalization. At the same time, it is also necessary to take account of the countercriticism that lays part of the blame for the economic problems of the Third World on the readiness of those leaders to resort to attacks on foreigners as a substitute for a serious effort to remove the internal obstacles to economic development, especially the discouragement of capital flows through "confiscatory" nationalizations. Apart from questions of morality or international law, it is appropriate to ask if there are significant costs to national development that should be weighed against the advantages of nationalization, even when the international context has shifted to make such nationalization easier. More generally, the question of whether the necessarily substantial role of the government in less developed economies should be exercised through direct ownership and control of economic activity must be examined.

Observers of the debate over nationalization and the rights of foreign investors are inevitably reminded of an earlier argument in Europe and America concerning the right of the state to interfere with the property of its citizens in the interest of social justice or economic planning. Then, as now, it was asserted that such intervention would have adverse economic effects, that the market system was the most efficient way to promote economic growth, and that the poor were responsible for their own plight. The difference between the two situations, however, is that there is no generally accepted system of international legislation or morality; nor is there a compulsory judicial and coercive system to develop or apply a community consensus on the limitations on the exercise of the property right. There are only the overriding claims of national sovereignty being made by a majority of less developed nations in the United Nations, the practical limits that are imposed by the economic interdependence of rich and poor, and the moral debate over the conflicting interpretations of international law and morality.

Is the assertion of an "inalienable" right to nationalization with "appropriate" compensation simply another way of saying "Soak the rich," or is it a call for the international recognition of the right of societies and governments to organize their economic and social institutions in accordance with the contemporary demand for state action to promote economic growth and social justice? If, indeed, North-South differences are becoming as important as the East-West conflict that has dominated world politics for the last thirty years, those differences ought to be studied in the hope of helping to resolve, or at least assuage, the confrontation that seems to have developed in the area of the nationalization of foreign enterprise. Both sides have economic, philosophical, and ideological arguments concerning the respective advantages and disadvantages of nationalization and private foreign investment. Recognizing that some differences involve irreconcilable value conflicts, it is useful to examine and evaluate the positions of the two sides and to attempt to separate out what is self-serving rhetoric and what is effective argumentation supported by convincing evidence.

Is the American and Western resistance to the efforts to assert state control of the foreign-owned sectors of the economies of the Third World simply an ideological and egoistic reflex of the rich against the poor? Or is there a basis for the assertion that the statist and expropriatory course of the Third World nations is damaging for their own welfare and that of the world as a whole? What are the costs and the benefits of nationalization to national development in comparison to, or combined with, alternative approaches? What does the record of American defense of private investment show about the motivation and direction of United States foreign policy in the past, and what should that policy be in the future? Conversely, what does the record of Third World nationalizations indicate about the possible pitfalls of government take-overs? What are the lessons that can be drawn from the experience of nationalization thus far? Which is "at bay" in the last quarter of the twentieth century, the multinational corporation or the sovereignty of the nation-state? These are among the questions that this book will attempt to answer.

2

The Development of Economic
Nationalism in Latin America

*The eyeglasses through which the Third World is coming to
view the United States have been ground by Latin American oculists.*

> —Kenneth Coleman, *The American Political
> Science Review,* 1977

*It is certain that foreigners who are located in a given country
have the same right to protection as its nationals but
they cannot lay claim to a protection which is more extensive.
. . . To admit [this] would be to create an excessive and
dangerous privilege essentially favorable to the powerful
states and injurious to weaker nations—to establish an unjustifiable inequality between nationals and foreigners. . . .*

> —Carlos Calvo, *Le Droit International,*
> paras. 1280, 257, 1896

*It not infrequently happens that under the rules of international
law applied to controversies of an international aspect,
a nation is required to accord to aliens broader and
more liberal treatment than it accords to its own citizens.
. . . It is not a question of discrimination but a question of
difference in their respective rights and remedies. . . .*

> —United States-Mexican General Claims Commission, Case of George W. Hopkins, 1927

If the "invisible hand" of Adam Smith ever was valid, it is completely inapplicable to Latin America and other underdeveloped regions, which need a government's firm guidance.
— Victor Urquidi, *The Challenge of Development in Latin America,* 1964

The conflict described in chapter 1 in not new to Latin America. Although until recently resort to nationalization has not been frequent, the continent has a long history of controversies over the relation of territorial sovereignty and independence to the claims of foreign investors and governments. Consequently, Latin America has become the leader among the developing countries in developing the theory and practice of economic nationalism.

Since the middle of the nineteenth century, foreign investment has played a leading part in Latin American development. Initially, the principal investors were British, but by the beginning of this century, American capital began to flow into Latin America in increasing quantities, growing from 20 percent of all foreign investment in 1914 to 74 percent in 1965. Direct foreign investment has been the principal method of transfer of capital in recent years, but in the nineteenth century it often took the form of loans by banks or private citizens to Latin American governments, usually at very high interest rates. When Latin American governments defaulted on those loans, threatened or actual intervention by European powers followed. These interventions were justified by the principle enunciated a century earlier in a treatise on international law by Emmerich de Vattel: under the law of nations, a state may intervene to seek redress for wrongs done to its citizens, if those citizens are not protected by the state in which the offense was committed.[1]

THE CALVO DOCTRINE AND NONINTERVENTION

The Latin American response to European and American intervention was the so-called Calvo Doctrine. Carlos Calvo (1824–1906) was an Argentine diplomat who wrote a treatise on international law, which went through five editions in Spanish and French between 1868 and 1896. The Calvo Doctrine, drawn from his work, is the first of many Latin American contributions to the development of international law embodying the point of view of the less developed (in Calvo's terms, "weaker") nations. It asserts that foreigners are to be treated on a plane of absolute equality with the nationals of a given country. Foreigners should not lay any claim to diplomatic protection or intervention by their home countries since this would only provide a pretext for frequent violations of the territorial sovereignty and judicial independence of the less powerful nations.

From the first Pan-American Conference in 1889, the Calvo Doctrine was repeatedly put forward at inter-American meetings by the Latin American states. Just as often, however, it was rejected by the United States as contrary to international law, which required all states to maintain a certain minimum international standard in the treatment of foreigners and enabled foreign governments to extend diplomatic protection to their citizens if they were being mistreated. The doctrine also was the basis for the inclusion in many investment contracts of a so-called Calvo Clause, by which foreign investors specifically renounced any appeal beyond the national courts of the host country. Like the doctrine, the Calvo Clause has been rejected or modified in international litigation, but it continues to appear in Latin American investment contracts.[2]

In 1902–3, Great Britain and Germany blockaded the Venezuela coastline in order to force a settlement of the financial claims of their citizens. The reactions to the blockade from Latin America and the United States demonstrated their continuing disagreement over intervention. The Argentine Foreign Minister, Luis M. Drago, proposed that the United States subscribe to the principle, later to be known as the Drago Doctrine, that "public debt gives no place for armed intervention, and less still to the material occupation of the soil of American nations by a European power." Instead, in a message to Congress in 1904, President Theodore Roosevelt announced the Roosevelt Corollary to the Monroe Doctrine, providing that "in the Western Hemisphere the adherence of the United States to the Monroe Doctrine may force the United States, however reluctantly, in flagrant cases of [Latin American] wrongdoing or impotence, to the exercise of an international police power."

Following the announcement of the Roosevelt Corollary, the United States repeatedly intervened in the Caribbean "to maintain order," to ensure payment of debts to European countries, and to protect American persons and property. Interventions took place in the Dominican Republic in 1904; in Cuba in 1906; in Panama in 1908, 1912, and 1918; in Nicaragua in 1912; in Mexico in 1914 and 1916–17; in Haiti in 1915; in Cuba in 1916; in the Dominican Republic in 1916; and in Nicaragua in 1926. It was not until December 1933, with the adoption of Franklin Roosevelt's Good Neighbor Policy, that the United States formally gave up its unilaterally declared right of armed intervention and, in 1934 and 1936, relinquished its treaty rights of intervention in Cuba and Panama. But even in so doing, Roosevelt was careful to note that "the whole continent in which we are all neighbors" had a common concern in the maintenance of "orderly processes of government" in the hemisphere.

When the Organization of American States (OAS) was created at the Ninth Inter-American Conference in Bogotá in 1948, the United States specifically endorsed the principle of nonintervention when it agreed to Article 15 of the OAS Charter, which declares: "No State or group of States has the right to intervene, directly or indirectly, for any reason whatever, in the internal or external affairs of any other State. The foregoing principle prohibits not only armed force but also any other form of interference or attempted threat against the personality of the State or against its political, economic, or cultural elements." The Bogotá conference also adopted an Economic Agreement, which included a provision that "Any expropriation shall be accompanied by payment of fair compensation in a prompt, adequate, and effective manner." However, the provision immediately provoked formal reservations by eight of the Latin American states, which reasserted the Calvo principles of the primacy of national law in such cases. Neither the United States nor most of the Latin American states have ratified the economic agreement.

The existence of Article 15 in the OAS Charter did not prevent the United States government from landing the marines in the Dominican Republic in 1965, nor did it deter the Central Intelligence Agency (CIA) from intervening in Latin American politics. However, it did provide a moral and legal standard to which the weaker Latin American states have been able to appeal. Along with the right of asylum and, more recently, the assertion of a 200-mile coastal zone of patrimonial waters, nonintervention is a distinctive Latin American contribution to international law. Moreover, it is now in the process of becoming an international norm that is binding on the great powers. Twenty years ago, it could be asserted that "the Calvo Doctrine has failed to receive recognition as a principle of international law and as such is now dead," and "The so-called Drago Doctrine . . . is unfounded, and has not received general recognition. . . . "[3] but the principle of nonintervention that underlies both is very much alive today. With the advent of a Third World majority in the United Nations, what was a continuing demand of Latin American countries has now been extended worldwide through the adoption of the Charter of Economic Rights and Duties of States.

THE STATE AND PRIVATE PROPERTY
IN LATIN AMERICAN THOUGHT

In contrast to the Latin American opposition to *international* intervention for the protection of property, Latin American tradition and practice have been much more favorably disposed to intervention by the government in the *domestic* economy to limit or abolish property rights. While Anglo-American law has recognized the principle of eminent domain, which permits the taking of property for public purposes with fair compensation, it has generally placed a greater value on the individual's right of private property than have Latin countries with a Roman law tradition and a Catholic cultural heritage. From Article 39 of the Magna Carta, adopted in 1215, to the Fifth and Fourteenth Amendments to the United States Constitution, the requirement of "due process" in the taking of property has been interpreted to mean that not only must correct legal procedures be used, but that a substantive vested right inheres in private property, which gives rise to a demand for compensation when such property is taken by the state. Latin America, on the other hand, is heir to a Spanish tradition that vests property rights primarily in the royal patrimony within the framework of a heirarchical and organic concept of society. In contrast, the American contractualist political tradition, drawn from John Locke's *Second Treatise of Civil Government,*[4] emphasizes the rights of the individual against the state, in particular the "natural right" of property. While one can exaggerate the differences between the two traditions, both of which emerged from the same medieval European roots, the facts that the Spanish Empire was organized in a centralized and bureaucratic fashion that contrasted strongly with the tradition of local self-government in the English colonies, that the religion of Latin America was Roman Catholicism rather than Protestantism, and that the Latin American legal system was based on a predominantly absolutist Roman law rather than an evolving common law based primarily on judicial and jury decisions have influenced Latin American institutions and attitudes in a statist direction. Even when the Spanish and Catholic traditions were rejected, as in the Mexican Revolution of 1910–20, the discussion on agrarian reform and mineral rights during the 1917 Mexican constitutional convention demonstrated the general acceptance of a "concession" theory of property. It adhered to the principle that all property comes by grant of the central government as successor to the Spanish monarch. Subsoil rights, in particular, remain the property of the nation—a point that was to be the source of continuing dispute with the United States. Catholic views on "the social function" of property, influenced by the writings of St. Thomas Aquinas and recent papal encyclicals on the social obligations of property holders, also affect Latin American perceptions of the limits on private property. The phrase "social function" itself was used in the debates during the 1960s over agrarian reform in Chile, Colombia, and Venezuela, and it appears in the Colombian and Venezuelan agrarian reform laws. While there is continuing disagreement over the relevance of the various elements in what William Glade calls "the neo-Iberian institutional framework," it is difficult to deny that from colonial times to the present Latin Americans have been accustomed to much greater degrees of state regulation of property rights than have Americans.[5]

The historical influences in the Latin American tradition favoring state intervention have been reinforced by the dominant role of the state in contemporary Latin American political thought. Not only the Marxists, but also Social Democrats, populists, Christian Democrats, and even conservatives accept the need for a strong state role in the economy. The left calls for nationalization of foreign and domestic industry and agrarian reform. The center espouses a mixed economy, which includes substantial government intervention, through fiscal and monetary policies, state control, and sometimes ownership of "strategic" industries — especially if they are in foreign hands.

What is strikingly different from the ideological pattern in the United States is the readiness of right-wing groups to accept a strong state role in the economy. In the nineteenth century, the principal political parties in most of Latin America were the Liberals and Conservatives. While the liberals generally endorsed laissez faire in economics, the conservatives, like their European counterparts, were in favor of state action to promote economic development — an attitude that could be explained, in part, by the fact that they controlled or strongly influenced most governments. In the twentieth century, with the development of welfare liberalism and the decline of the church-state issue as a source of division, liberals and conservatives no longer have substantial differences. (In the case of Chile the two parties fused in 1966.) The right generally agrees on the importance of state intervention to facilitate, rather than limit, private economic activity, particularly by providing investment capital in a situation in which the private sector is unwilling or unable to do so. Laissez faire, never very powerful as an ideology in Latin America, has almost no support today. The issue is not whether the state should have a strong role in the economy, but who will control or influence state economic policy, in what directions, and to whose benefit.[6]

STATE INTERVENTION
IN INDUSTRY AND AGRICULTURE

The theoretical justification for state intervention has been accompanied by a considerable expansion in the role of government in economic life. State-sponsored import substitution, that is, the establishment of domestic industries to produce goods formerly imported from abroad, has become an economic necessity since the depression; during World War II and continuing thereafter, balance-of-payments problems have compelled Latin Americans to abandon their previous pattern of exchanging primary products and raw materials for manufactured goods from the developed countries. Whether the ensuing industrialization was carried out by foreigners invited by generous tax and import duty benefits granted by the government, or by domestic capitalists with loans from state financial or development agencies, or by the state itself, the government took a decisive role in the promotion of economic growth — long before the development theorists wrote about the need for government action to promote development in the Third World. This expansion of the state's economic role was welcomed by middle-class groups because it provided bureaucratic positions and political power in the state sector. It was supported by low-income groups (or those who claimed to speak for them) since it offered industrial jobs and welfare programs. And it was favored by the new technocratic elite of economists, engineers, and social planners who began to emerge in the 1960s to guide and direct the state's expanding economic and social activities.

It was only after the import substitution policy had been pursued for many decades that it was discovered that the policy did not have the favorable impact on the national balance of payments that had been expected. Industrialization led to massive immigration to the cities. The growth of the cities, in turn, increased demand for food, which the neglected agricultural sector could not produce, and foodstuffs had to be imported from abroad. The new and often inefficient industries also required imports of capital goods as well as replacement parts leading to further balance-of-payments problems. Finally, in the 1960s, greater emphasis began to be placed on export promotion, but here, too, government subsidies, tax benefits, and the like were utilized to promote "nontraditional" exports.

The state role in agriculture also has expanded in recent years. As the population moved into the cities and domestic food production failed to keep up with rising demand, Latin American governments began to take an interest in a sector that they had heretofore ignored. That interest was intensified in the early 1960s as the challenge of the Cuban Revolution and the propaganda surrounding the Kennedy-sponsored Alliance for Progress combined to make agrarian reform a central issue in nearly every Latin American country. The debates surrounding the adoption of agrarian reform laws showed the degree of acceptance of state action to alter property-holding patterns. The quasi-confiscatory compensation provisions contained in some of those laws were an indication that the so-called international standard of "prompt, adequate, and effective" compensation was not and could not be applied to the reform of the agricultural sector since it would require vast government expenditures that no country could afford.[7]

In most cases, the agrarian reform programs did not affect foreign holdings. An early exception, however, was the Mexican agrarian reform program, which was begun in the 1920s. In fact, the "prompt, adequate, and effective" formula for compensation first appeared in official United States government documents on July 21, 1938, when Cordell Hull, secretary of state, protested Mexican seizures of American-owned property in Mexico under its agrarian reform program. As Latin American critics of the agrarian reform programs of the Alliance for Progress were wont to point out, no such concern over property rights was demonstrated by American ambassadors and Agency for International Development (AID) mission directors when the rural landholdings of Latin Americans were taken over in the 1960s.

State intervention in restructuring the economy received further support from a number of Latin American sources during the 1960s. Beginning around 1960, the United Nations Economic Commission for Latin America (ECLA or, in Spanish, CEPAL), located in Santiago, Chile, became a major source of theories of development, which were based on the Latin American experience but had a general application to the developing countries. In a series of influential reports, speeches, and books, Raúl Prebisch, the Argentine executive secretary of ECLA who had held that position since its creation in 1948 until 1962, blamed Latin America's development problems on "structural" problems in agriculture and industry. In addition, he argued that development was hampered by the declining terms of trade between the prices paid for the raw materials and primary products produced by Latin America and the prices that it was compelled to pay for the manufactured goods it imported from the United States and Europe. The solutions that he suggested—Latin American regional integration, agrarian reform, international commodity price support programs, and sharply increased taxation of upper income groups—all involved increased state intervention in the economy. When Prebisch moved from Santiago to Geneva in 1964, to become secretary general of the newly formed United Nations Conference on Trade and Development (UNCTAD), he brought his ideas to a wider forum. Thus, the discussion of the adverse impact of the terms of trade became part of the bill of particulars in the criticism of the developed nations by the Third World.[8]

A similar movement from Latin America to the rest of the Third World took place with the development of state-run commodity producer cartels—one of the solutions proposed by ECLA for the declining export earnings of Latin America. In September 1960, Juan Pablo Pérez Alfonzo, the Venezuelan minister of mines, persuaded the Middle Eastern oil producers to form the Organization of Petroleum Exporting Countries (OPEC) for the purpose of stabilizing oil prices through the regulation of production—a project of particular concern to Venezuela since its costs of production were higher and known reserves limited in comparison with those of the Middle Eastern oil producers. In the mid-sixties, a similar but less successful effort was made by Third World copper producers led by Chile, and agreements on the production of coffee and tin have also been made, at the initiative of Brazil and Bolivia, respectively. Thus, Latin Americans have taken the lead in forming a common front with the less developed states in Africa and the Middle East. UNCTAD, under Manuel Pérez Guerrero of Venezuela, who succeeded Prebisch as secretary general from 1969 to 1973, became the vehicle through which ECLA and associated ideas on state-promoted development were transmitted to the rest of the developing world.

ECLA's support of economic integration led to a number of attempts by Latin American countries to cooperate on a regional basis. The first two efforts along these lines, the Central American Common Market (1959) and the Latin American Free Trade Area (1960), had only limited success. However, in May 1969, the countries of the west coast of Latin America — Colombia, Ecuador, Peru, Bolivia, and Chile (joined in 1973 by Venezuela) — signed the Andean Pact of Regional Integration. The pact provided for automatic reductions of import duties among its signatories on a phased basis, which would eventually lead to the abolition of tariffs and the creation of an Andean Common Market. It also established a headquarters in Lima, staffed by young *técnicos*, and a Pact Commission (*Junta*), with the power to make additional decisions to promote regional development and integration.

Calculating that there was a danger that foreign investors would move into the new Common Market and eventually dominate it economically unless the Andean group took action, the Commission, on December 31, 1970, adopted Decision 24, which established a Standard Regime for the Treatment of Foreign Capital. New foreign investment was excluded from the areas of public utilities, the mass media, advertising, and banking, and existing foreign firms in these areas were given three years to sell 80 percent of their stock to local nationals. The profit rate on invested foreign capital was limited to 14 percent for repatriation purposes and 5 percent for reinvestment. New foreign enterprises wishing to take advantage of the tariff reductions were required to sell 51 percent ownership to national investors or states over a period of fifteen to twenty years. The decision reflected a shift in the goals of Latin American economic policymakers — from regional integration to the promotion of domestic investment — and the assertion of national control over the direction and extent of foreign investment. Although it appeared to be aimed at stimulating investment by the domestic private sector, its practical effect has been to increase the role of state development and financial agencies in applying and facilitating the "fadeout" of foreign capital.

DEPENDENCY THEORY

The Andean Pact's shift from a focus on internal structural change to control of external influences was related to a change of emphasis in Latin American thought from ECLA-influenced structuralism to Marxist-influenced dependency theory. Despite the weakness of organized Communist parties in all Latin American countries except Chile and Cuba, Leninist theories of imperialism had long evoked a favorable response. Their appeal was understandable, for they provided an easy explanation for Latin American underdevelopment. According to these theories, despite their formal independence the Latin American economies had functioned from the beginning of their history until the present day to serve the interests of the developed countries. Foreign capital, far from assisting in the development of Latin America, had had a negative effect since foreign investors had exploited Latin American raw materials and agriculture for the needs of the European and American economies for markets, raw materials, and profitable investments in a way that benefited only a tiny Latin American elite linked in interest, ideology, and culture to the developed countries.[9]

The Leninist notion that the interests of foreign capital and of Latin America were inevitably opposed was criticized as long ago as 1936 by the Peruvian leader of the Aprista party, Victor Raúl Haya de la Torre. He argued that imperialism was the *first* stage of capitalism in Latin America, which created economic and social effects, such as urbanization, industrialization, and an organized working class that could form an anti-imperialist alliance with the middle class "as controlling forces in the state." This alliance would bring about the economic independence of Latin America "based on equality in the exchange of raw materials and finished products and the investment of capital according to the principle of progressive nationalization of the sources of production under the control of the state."[10] Haya de la Torre's belief that the government could act to control the effects of "imperialism," as a result of economic and social changes produced by foreign investment, had some of the dialectical quality of Marxist-Leninist thought, but it did not adhere to the Leninist solution — an inevitable violent revolution against imperialist capitalism. In contrast to Lenin, Haya's analysis inclined his party, like other "populist" Latin American parties formed in the 1940s and 1950s, to endorse reformist solutions by Latin American governments to the problems that both reformers and radicals attributed to foreign economic interests. One of those solutions was nationalization, but as Haya explained, it could also involve joint ventures with foreign capital and control of foreign investment through state development corporations.

The revolutionary/reformer dichotomy with regard to the theory of imperialism was also evident in the various versions of its more influential successor, the various theories of dependency. By the late 1960s, dependency theory had replaced ECLA structuralism as the prevailing orthodoxy among Latin American development theorists. Dependency theorists attributed Latin America's economic problems to the fact that its development had been "conditioned" or limited by, and subordinated to, the economies of the major capitalist countries. This had led to the "distortion" of the Latin American economies through "the development of underdevelopment," which had resulted from their dependent condition.

The dependency analysis seemed to allow more scope for existing Latin American governments to alter or diminish the dependent relationships than did the theory of imperialism. Presumably, there could be degrees of dependency; imperialism however, argued for complete control (etymologically it is derived from the Latin verb, *imperare* — to command) of Latin America by external forces. For the more radical dependency theorists, however, only a thoroughgoing socialist revolution of the Cuban variety could resolve the problem of Latin American economic dependence. Thus, these theorists recommended the nationalization of all foreign investment as part of a general program to eliminate exploitation by foreign economic influences. In this respect, although the focus of their analysis was on the economic evolution of Latin America rather than of Europe or the United States, they did not depart from the Leninist prescription, although their emphasis was different. However, there was also a reformist wing of the dependency writers who, while they agreed on Latin America's dependent condition, argued that dependency could be reduced by the control or selective nationalization of foreign investment, the promotion of Latin American industrialization by state or private efforts, and a lessening of cultural and economic ties with the capitalist West. Both wings of the dependency school, however, were prepared to use nationalization as a major element of Latin America's struggle to overcome its dependence.[11]

Latin American dependency theories, like the other positions described above, were also diffused to other parts of the Third World as African and Asian writers adopted the terminology and methods of the Latin Americans. A common vocabulary was formed among Third World thinkers. It changed the self-definition of many Latin American representatives in international organizations from members of the West committed to democratic and libertarian values (even when they were not able to implement them in practice), to leaders of the less developed "South" struggling against the developed "North" in the name of international equity and social justice. An indication of the depth of the shift was the attempt by the outgoing president of Mexico, Luis Echeverría Álvarez in 1976, to use his sponsorship of the Charter of Economic Rights and Duties of States and support for the New International Economic Order as a platform for an abortive campaign to become secretary general of the United Nations, despite the fact that his strident anticapitalist and anti-American rhetoric had ensured the opposition of the American and Western European representatives.

The broad appeal of the dependency analysis lay in its mixture of Marxist tools of analysis with nationalist goals of self-determination and a greater share in the benefits of economic development. It gave a form and direction to the generalized resentment by Latin Americans of their underdevelopment, and in both its radical and reformist versions it identified foreign, especially United States, economic influence as the principal obstacle to Latin American development. Thus, both groups of *dependentistas* were agreed on a conflictual model as a description of existing economic relations between Latin America and the major exporters of capital, especially the United States, although they differed on its resolution.

UNITED STATES WILSONIAN LIBERALISM

It was just this inherent conflict of interests that the American view had always denied. From the time of Latin American independence, United States-Latin American relations were considered by Americans to be based on a coincidence of interest of the two areas. No matter that the Monroe Doctrine left the United States as the paramount power in the Western Hemisphere, its purpose was to ensure the independence of the new Latin American states. Woodrow Wilson's liberalism did not prevent him from landing troops in Mexico, but American intervention, Wilson said in 1914: "was actuated by no other motives than the betterment of the conditions of our unfortunate neighbor, and by the sincere desire to advance the cause of human liberty [by] helping them compose their differences, starting them on the road to continued peace and prosperity, and leaving them to work out their own destiny, but watching them narrowly and insisting that they shall take help when help is needed."[12] The Organization of American States (OAS) too, was justified by an appeal to the common interests of the nations of the Western Hemisphere. Part of their common interest was opposition to "the political system of an extra-continental power," as the OAS Caracas Conference of 1954 put it (just before the CIA assisted in the overthrow of the Communist-influenced Arbenz government in Guatemala). Similarly, appeals to self-determination and democracy for the Cuban people were used to justify American intervention against the Castro regime in the early 1960s. The Dominican intervention of 1965 was also defended as necessary to prevent the establishment of a communist government in the Western Hemisphere.

The same Wilsonian liberalism has, until recently, permeated American views of inter-American economic relations. American investors were to provide the capital that Latin America needed for its development—and this was to the mutual benefit of the host nation and the investor. Inter-American economic relations, as indeed the whole postwar structure of international economics established at Bretton Woods, were to be governed by free trade and the free flow of capital to the mutual benefit of all. Even when the need for structural reforms in Latin America was recognized in the Alliance for Progress in 1961, private investment was supposed to provide half of the $20 billion that, it was estimated, Latin America would need over the next decade. The development of a vigorous private sector in Latin America was seen as desirable because it would both stimulate economic growth and promote the socioeconomic conditions for the development of liberal democracy—and foreign investment would assist in the process. When Latin Americans urged special economic concessions from the United States, they were warned of the dangers of relying on "political" criteria rather than the neutral arbiter, the world market.[13] Free trade and the free movement of capital would benefit both the United States and Latin America.

An essential requirement for the international market system to operate, however, was that property rights and contracts be respected. And here American liberalism and Latin American statism and economic nationalism seemed to be in direct opposition to one another. The Latin Americans insisted on the right and, indeed, the necessity for the state to intervene in private economic relations in the interest of development—including those involving foreigners. The United States perceived this intervention as likely to be discriminatory, confiscatory, and inimical to economic growth and world welfare. While abjuring the resort to force in inter-American relations (with two exceptions in the 1960s, Cuba and the Dominican Republic), the United States was prepared to use diplomatic and economic pressure to defend the property rights of its citizens, and it justified this position as in no way opposed to the rapid economic and social development of Latin America—indeed as essential to it.

The conflicting positions became more evident in the 1960s as political, economic, and military assistance programs involved the United States more deeply in Latin America than ever before. At the same time, American investment increased from $8.3 billion in book value in 1960, to over $12 billion in 1970. On the other hand, Latin American policymakers were becoming better trained; the role of the government was expanding; and ECLA structuralism and dependency theory became the accepted way to describe Latin American economic relations, not only among radical intellectuals but among commentators, government officials, the military, and politicians. The rising tide of economic nationalism could no longer be described as the result of Communist influence or the machinations of Fidel Castro, as country after country set limits on, or took control over, foreign economic activity.

THE NEW WAVE OF NATIONALIZATIONS

Nationalization of foreign enterprises now became commonplace, whereas before the sixties such actions had been exceptional and had evoked strong sanctions. As described in chapter 1, all three branches of the American government were compelled to respond to the challenge, as American utilities, mines, oil companies, banks, and, in a few cases, manufacturing plants were taken over in many Latin American countries. The increase in the number and size of the nationalizations of American enterprises in Latin America during the last twenty years is evident in table 1, which describes the type and claimed value of expropriated American holdings and the compensation later paid.

NATIONALIZATION ISSUES

Certain conclusions and queries already emerge from the nationalizations listed. The overwhelming majority involved extractive industries, banking, or utilities — and only in the cases of Cuba under Castro and Chile under Allende were significant American investments in manufacturing and trade taken over. The question that arises, then, is whether there are special char-

Table 1. Nationalizations of American enterprises in Latin America, 1900-1977

Year	Country	Enterprise	Claim	Year of and amount of settlement
1900	Nicaragua	Timber	$1,048,154.*	*1909* $600,000.
1928	Guatemala	Chicle	$561,800.	*1930†* $225,468.
1917-41	Mexico	Landholdings, 1917-27; 1927-41		
		National Railways minority stock, 1937	$75,000,000.	*1941* $40,000,000.
1937	Bolivia	Standard Oil properties confiscated— company accused of fraud	$3,000,000.	*1942* $1,729,375.
1938	Mexico	Six oil companies	$262,000,000.	*1940* $13,000,000. *1942* $23,995,911.
1952	Bolivia	Patîno Tin—U.S. investors reported to have 27 percent of shares		*1960* $6,000,000.
1953-54	Guatemala	United Fruit land: 1953—234,000 acres 1964—174,000 acres	$15,854,849.	*1954* Land returned after overthrow of government
1958	Argentina	American & Foreign Power Co.	$60,000,000.	*1961* $53,632,000. arbitral award
1959-62	Brazil	American & Foreign Power Co. subsidiaries in 3 Brazilian states	$32,700,000.	*1963* $135,000,000. for subsidiaries in ten Brazilian states
1959-60	Cuba	Cattle ranches; sugar lands and mills; two oil refineries; three banks; nickel plant; manufacturing plants; public utilities; hotels; etc.	$3,346,000,000.‡	Pending

36

Table 1 *cont.*

Year	Country	Enterprise	Claim	Year of and amount of settlement
1960	Mexico	American & Foreign Power Co. subsidiary	Negotiated	*1960* $70,000,000.
1962	Brazil	ITT subsidiary in Rio Grande do Sul	$6,000,000.– 10,000,000.	*1963* $7,300,000.
1963	Argentina	All foreign oil contracts, including nine U.S. companies	$300,000,000.– 395,000,000. for all companies	*1965* $51,700,000. for five companies
1967	Chile	Kennecott copper mine with 51 percent interest; Anaconda new mine with 25 percent interest; Cerro Corp., new mine with 30 percent interest	Negotiated	$92,900,000. $3,750,000. $18,600,000.
1968	Peru	International Petroleum Company (Exxon)	$120,000,000.	*1974* $23,100,000. and $4,400,000. in interest
1969–73	Peru	Grace Company's sugar plantations; fishmeal companies; three factories	Negotiated as part of global settlement	*1974* $35,000,000.
1969	Chile	Anaconda, two copper mines with 51 percent interest, option to buy full ownership	Negotiated	$203,000,000.
1969	Bolivia	Cancellation Gulf Oil contract	$118,000,000.	*1970* $78,662,171.
1970	Peru	ITT 69 percent interest Peruvian telephone	$18,500,000.	*1970* $17,900,000.
1970	Peru	Chase Manhattan Bank shares in Peruvian bank	Negotiated	$6,300,000.
1970	Ecuador	ITT subsidiary	$5,000,000.– $7,500,000.	*1971* $600,000.

37

Table 1 *cont.*

Year	Country	Enterprise	Claim	Year of and amount of settlement
1971	Chile	Bethlehem Steel sub-sidiary; Armco Steel subsidiary	Negotiated	*1971* $31,000,000.
1971	Chile	Bank of America and First National Bank branches	Negotiated	*1971* $5,000,000.
		Anglo Lautaro Nitrate	Negotiated	*1971* $4,000,000.
		Remaining interests of Anaconda, Kenne-cott, and Cerro	$325,000,000. $276,000,000. $ 37,500,000.	*1974* $253,000,000. $ 68,000,000. $ 41,800,000.
		ITT subsidiary inter-vened (formally ex-propriated in 1974)	$153,000,00.0	*1974* $125,000,000.
1971–73	Chile	Subsidiaries of Du-Pont; Coca-Cola; General Motors; Northern Indiana Brass; Parsons and Whittemore; Ralston Purina; RCA; many other companies intervened but re-turned after Sep-tember 1973 coup	Negotiated	*1971–73* $30,000,000.
1973	Peru	Four fishmeal subsidi-aries; three road construction compa-nies; branch of Standard Oil of California	Negotiated as part of global settlement	*1974* $7,000,000. in un-remitted profits to fishmeal companies plus $3,500,000.
1973	Argentina	Four banks		*1974* $16,500,000.
1973	Peru	Cerro de Pasco Mining	$145,000,000.	*1974* $8,000,000.– 10,000,000. plus $67,000,000. in unremitted profits

Table 1 cont.

Year	Country	Enterprise	Claim	Year of and amount of settlement
1974	Argentina	ITT subsidiary, Exxon, and Cities Service gas stations	Negotiated	*1976* Returned with compensation
1974	Venezuela	Bethlehem Steel and U.S. Steel mining subsidiaries	Negotiated	*1975* $101,400,000.
1974	Ecuador	Texaco, Gulf subsidiaries, 25 percent interest	Negotiated	$148,000,000.
1975	Peru	Gulf Oil subsidiary	$2,000,000.	*1977* $1,540,000.
		Marcona Iron Mines	$167,000,000.	*1976* $61,400,000.
1975	Colombia	Foreign banks given three years to sell 51 percent interest to Colombia		*1976* Citibank sells its 51 percent interest
1976	Venezuela	Twenty-one oil companies	$5,000,000,000. (informal estimate)	*1976* $1,010,000,000. (minus $134,000,000. for equipment deficiencies in 1978)
1976	Venezuela	Owens-Illinois Glass subsidiary	Negotiated	*1979* Nationalization proceedings discontinued
1977	Ecuador	Forced sale of Gulf holdings	$122,000,000.	$82,000,000.

Sources: U.S., Library of Congress, Legislative Reference Service, *Expropriation of American-owned Property by Foreign Governments in the Twentieth Century,* Report to the House Foreign Affairs Committee, July 19, 1963 (Washington, D.C.: Government Printing Office, 1963); U.S., Department of State, Bureau of Intelligence and Research, "Nationalization, Expropriation and Other Takings of United States and Certain Foreign Property Since 1960," Research Study (mimeo.), 30 November 1971; U.S., Department of State, Bureau of Intelligence and Research, "Disputes Involving U.S. Foreign Direct Investment: July 1, 1971 through July 31, 1973," Research Study, 28 February 1974; U.S., Department of State, Bureau of Intelligence and Research, "Disputes Involving U.S. Foreign Direct Investment: August 1, 1973–January 31, 1975," Research Study, 20 March 1975; U.S., Department of State, Bureau of Intelligence and Research, "Disputes Involving U.S. Foreign Direct Investment, February 1, 1975–February 28, 1977," Report No. 855, 19 September 1977; *New York Times, passim; Wall Street Journal, passim.*
*Actual claim was $1,048,154.28.
†Actual settlement was $225,468.38.
‡U.S. Foreign Claims Settlement Commission recognizes $1,769,000,000.

acteristics of the enterprises that were taken over that led them to be nationalized, or, of those that escaped such a fate, that protected them against nationalization. Is the recent effort by Latin American governments to take over "the commanding heights" or essential industries in their economies coming to an end, or will there be a new wave of take-overs in the areas of manufacturing and trade? Alternatively, is there a stage of development or a "nationalization situation" that some Latin American countries have experienced and others may still go through in the future?

Second, in all cases except that of Cuba, some sort of compensation was paid, although often it was far below the companies' claims. This raises several additional questions: Was the payment of compensation the result of pressure by the United States government, or are there other factors that induce nationalizing governments—even Communist governments—to pay compensation? Is there a possible alternative international law standard for the payment of compensation other than the American-supported "prompt, adequate, and effective" formula that might provide the basis for an equitable and mutually agreeable settlement?

Third, how have the numerous nationalized industries fared under state ownership? Have the predictions of inefficiency, bureaucratization, and politicization of domestic and international economic relations been borne out by the experience of Latin America to date? Are there less costly alternatives to nationalization, such as joint ventures or different tax policies? Are there certain areas for which nationalization is a desirable arrangement and others in which it would be counterproductive? If the experience of nationalization is to be evaluated, what standards should be used: national autonomy, economic growth, or social justice; international equity, economic efficiency, or world welfare; or the national interest of the United States as defined in any number of alternative ways?

This would seem to be an appropriate time for such a review and analysis because the American and Latin American positions appear to be coming closer together. In the United States, the assumption of an automatic harmony of interest between American investment overseas and national welfare is now widely questioned. At least since the time of the oil crisis of 1973, Americans have become increasingly aware that the large multinational corporations have their own interests and that legislation may be necessary to assure that those interests coincide with the national interest. Proposals for the nationalization of the petroleum industry are being seriously considered. Increasing foreign investment in the United States has elicited demands for stronger legislative control of foreign economic interests. Government policy in the area of communications, transportation, health, energy, and raw materials has departed widely from the laissez faire model. The tax provisions encouraging overseas investment have come under increasing attack, as has the quasi-governmental Overseas Private Investment Corporation (OPIC), which gives government-guaranteed insurance to United States investments in the less developed world. The revelations of the role of American-based companies in the "destabilization" of the Allende government in Chile and of massive bribery by American firms of foreign politicians and businessmen have further eroded the image of American investment abroad. At the same time, other interest groups besides those representing business have acquired an increasingly important influence on the formation of United States policy toward Latin America.[14] The wisdom of measures such as the Hickenlooper Amendment, which commits the American government to intervene on behalf of expropriated American businesses, and of the requirement that OPIC continue to attempt to secure compensation from expropriating governments even after it has paid the insurance claims of the companies involved ("subrogation"), is now widely questioned. Moreover, it is recognized that there is a national interest in continued access to the raw materials and trade of the less developed countries. The question that is raised is, what form should that new relationship take, and how would it resemble, or differ from, the proposals of the New International Economic Order? Part of that answer clearly involves United States policy concerning the protection of, or guarantees for, American investment overseas.

On the Latin American side, there have also been some important changes in the 1970s. In regimes as diverse as Mexico, Peru, Brazil, and Argentina, there has been increasing concern over the dangers of excessive state centralization of economic activity. The strict controls on foreign investment established by the Andean Pact countries have been evaded or partially eased, and Chile has left the pact because its terms seem to discourage foreign investment. In Mexico, the first Latin American country to nationalize American investment, new methods for the control and direction of foreign investment through taxation and investment screening have been developed, which may make resort to nationalization obsolete. Discussions of foreign investment by Latin American policymakers and social scientists are becoming more technical and less ideological — as detailed economic analyses of the costs and benefits of such investment replace the "Yankee, Go Home" attitude. The dialogue between Latin America and the United States on nationalization and foreign investment is likely to be less confrontational as the earlier polarization between Wilsonian liberalism and economic nationalism is replaced by a common desire for an assessment of the interests of the United States, of Latin America, and of the multinational corporations to determine where they conflict and where they coincide.

Such an assessment has not taken place so far. The writing on nationalization and foreign investment has not directly compared nationalization and direct foreign investment as alternative development policies or combined a consideration of United States policy interests with those of the Third World and of the multinational corporations. It would seem, therefore, that it is time to attempt to integrate the various approaches that have been taken to the problem in order to analyze and evaluate nationalization policy as it relates to the objectives of the capital-exporting and capital-importing nations, as well as to world welfare and development.[15] Latin America is the most fruitful area for this kind of study since nationalization and economic nationalism have a longer history there than in any other area of the Third World. Moreover, both Latin American and North American social scientists and historians have long been engaged in research that is directly relevant, and as indicated above, Latin American theory and practice have had an important "demonstration effect" on other developing countries.

THE FIVE CASE STUDIES

Excluding the Latin American agrarian reform programs that, with the important exception of the nationalization of the holdings of United Fruit in Guatemala in 1953–54, have not been primarily aimed at American property, five Latin American countries have carried out nationalizations of American enterprises with significant domestic and international effects. The take-over of the American- and British-owned oil industry by the Mexican president Lázaro Cárdenas in 1938 demonstrated that an underdeveloped country can challenge the large international oil concerns and successfully operate a state-run concern — so successfully, in fact, that when writers speak of the failures of state petroleum companies they make a specific exception for Pemex (Petróleos Mexicanos). In addition to its international ramifications, the Mexican oil nationalization had important domestic economic and political effects: it promoted Mexican industrialization by providing cheap energy and the development of Mexican technical capacity, and it constituted the core of what has become, in recent years, a large public sector in the Mexican economy.

Castro's Cuban Revolution is the next major case of nationalization. American property, worth nearly $2 billion, was taken over in 1959 and 1960, both exacerbating the deterioration of United States-Cuban relations and constituting a major obstacle to the improvement of relations between the two regimes. The Cuban case was influenced by the Mexican example, as well as by the hostile United States reaction to the Guatemalan land expropriations.

The case of Chile is particularly useful to compare and evaluate various policies toward foreign investment. Over the last twenty years successive Chilean governments have pursued sharply differing programs ranging from primary reliance on taxation and fiscal instruments between 1955 and 1964; through a mixed economy model pursued by the Frei government until 1970; to Allende's nationalization of the copper mines and the take-over of nearly five hundred other enterprises by purchase, intervention, or requisition; and finally, to the policies of rapid denationalization and strong encouragement of foreign investment pursued by the Pinochet regime.

Nationalization was also a central feature of the Peruvian military regime under General Juan Velasco Alvarado, which came to power in the October 1968 coup and announced that it would pursue a "third way" between capitalism and communism. Velasco engaged in a number of innovative experiments in the relation of the state to the economy and to private and foreign investment. The extension of nationalization to new companies was halted with Velasco's removal in August 1975, and some of his more radical economic experiments were de-emphasized, but the experiences of his regime in the areas of worker participation and of alternative compensation schemes merits close study.

Finally, those who organized the relatively conflict-free and carefully planned nationalization of the oil industry in Venezuela in 1976 attempted to apply what they had learned from the mistakes of earlier nationalizations. The Venezuelan example, based on careful calculation of relative bargaining strength and the costs and benefits of nationalization, may provide a new model for nationalization policy elsewhere.

Each of the five countries studied has a particular relevance for the student of public policy in a developing nation, and each has influenced policymakers outside its borders. The Mexican model of a mixed economy, combining a substantial state sector in mining, transportation, and energy with an active domestic private sector and substantial foreign investment engaged primarily in manufacturing, has been widely discussed and imitated elsewhere. The Cuban case, involving wholesale nationalization, has provoked reactions of admiration and rejection on the part of Latin American intellectuals, students, and policymakers for a decade and a half. The Chilean example, in particular the policies pursued by the Allende government, seems to offer important lessons in how *not* to nationalize, while Peruvian nationalization policy followed a more pragmatic and experimental course, which, however, has had only mixed results. Venezuela appears to be unique because of its oil wealth, but on closer examination, it too can provide important insights for policymakers elsewhere. In particular, Venezuela set a good example of how to bargain with the multinationals and to receive the benefits of foreign technology and marketing skills after nationalization.

In each of the five cases, American policy has differed. The Mexican nationalizations provoked some initial hostility on the part of the American government, but for a variety of reasons, especially foreign policy considerations, the United States finally compelled the oil companies to accept compensation that was far from "prompt, adequate, and effective." The cold war reinforced United States opposition to the expropriations in Cuba, and the compensation question continues to be one of the most important obstacles to improved United States-Cuban relations, especially since the amounts due have been formalized by the United States Foreign Claims Settlement Commission. Fearing the extension of the Cuban example, the United States supported the Alessandri and Frei governments in Chile and strongly opposed that of Allende. In the Allende case, the compensation question was one reason, but not the only one, for United States government hostility. In Peru, the same question was at the root of a "little cold war" between the two governments between 1968 and 1974, but it was finally settled amicably, as was a later dispute over the nationalization of the Marcona iron mines in 1975. In Venezuela, a compensation settlement was quickly arrived at between the government and the oil companies, making the United States government intervention unnecessary despite the fact that the agreement fell considerably short of the officially endorsed standard.

It should be possible to draw some lessons from the experience of nationalization of American enterprises in Latin America. Which nationalizations may be described as successful and which unsuccessful, and why? From the point of view of Latin American development, what are the effects of nationalization on economic growth and social justice? Which sectors benefit and which lose, and how does the whole political and economic system change as the result of the creation of a large state sector? What are the costs and benefits of different mixtures of public and private investment (both foreign and domestic), and which sectors are more appropriate for public ownership?

Because the pattern of American economic presence in Latin

America has been altered as a result of the nationalizations of the last two decades, the case studies should provide some indications of the future of private foreign investment in less developed areas. Alternatives to nationalization, such as joint ventures, service contracts, and gradual divestment, will be discussed as well as possible defense strategies by investing companies, especially in areas that are most prone to expropriation.

The case studies should aid in the evaluation of United States policy concerning the protection and encouragement of American investment in less developed countries, including the standard of compensation for expropriated property and possible new initiatives for the promotion of investment in natural resources. Similarly, the effectiveness in resolving disputed cases of the various United States government responses to nationalization on a continuum from diplomatic protest to coercive intervention will also be considered. It should then be possible to discuss alternative future policies for investors, host countries, and home countries in a world of economic nationalism and growing interdependence.

The book will conclude with a discussion of the shape of the emerging new international economic relationships and the ways in which they may contribute to the professed goal shared by the proponents of both the new and old international economic orders: how best to achieve a peaceful and mutually beneficial transfer of real resources—especially capital and technology—from the wealthy to the poor areas of the world.

3

Nationalization and the
Mexican Model of Development

*Poor Mexico, so far from God and so close to the United
States.*
—Attributed to Porfirio Díaz

*Ownership of the land and waters within the boundaries of
the national territory is vested originally in the nation which
has the right to transfer control over them to private individuals, thus establishing private property. Expropriations
may only take place by reason of public utility and with
compensation. The nation shall forever have the right to
impose upon private property the limits which the public
interest may dictate. . . . In the nation is vested direct ownership of all minerals . . . such as petroleum and all hydrocarbons, whether solid, liquid, or gaseous. . . . Only Mexicans by birth or naturalization and Mexican companies
have the right to develop mines, waters, or mineral fuels in
the Republic of Mexico. The state may grant the same right
to foreigners provided that they agree . . . to be considered
as Mexicans with respect to such property, and accordingly
not to invoke the protection of their governments regarding
the same . . .*
—Constitution of Mexico, Article 27, 1917

The role of the state-managed enterprise in Mexico is not to make a profit but to serve the community by promoting production, consumption, employment, and investment within a framework of social justice.
— Antonio Dovali, Director, Pemex, 1972

Mexico does not have an expropriatory mentality.
— José Campillo, *Mexican Newsletter,* 1973

Any discussion of nationalization in Latin America must begin with the case of Mexico. The Mexican take-over of the foreign-owned petroleum industry in 1938 was important for two reasons. First, the United States developed its policies toward nationalization and formulated its "prompt, adequate, and effective" standard for just compensation in response to the Mexican expropriation of American-owned oil companies. The intermittent negotiations with Mexico between 1911 and 1941 concerning the status of American property in that country resulted in the development of a body of doctrine and precedent that has conditioned United States attitudes and responses to the present day. Second, the Mexican nationalization of a basic mineral resource proved that a less developed country could take control of a key economic sector over the opposition of its foreign owners, could operate it successfully, and thereafter, could continue to attract foreign investment to other sectors of its economy. The Mexican example altered the perceptions and subsequent relationships between host countries and foreign investors.

American responses to revolutionary nationalism in Mexico were ambivalent and divided. But when sympathy for the revolutionary goals of social justice and equity came into conflict with a concern for the protection of American property rights, the defense of property usually won out. When property interests were sacrificed, it was because national security and foreign policy interests, not ideology, overrode the narrower objective of the diplomatic and political protection of American property.

American property interests were jeopardized by two goals of the Mexican Revolution. Those who owned agricultural land were adversely affected by the revolutionaries' efforts to carry out an extensive agrarian reform, and the large holdings of the American oil companies stood in the way of achieving what the revolutionaries called the "recovery" of control of the nation's mineral resources. Both goals were contained in the Mexican constitution of 1917, but they were resisted by American property owners and companies who successfully enlisted the United States government in their defense. The pressures that the American government was able to exert on Mexico — involving diplomatic, political, and economic sanctions as well as the implicit or explicit threat of military intervention — only postponed but did not prevent the eventual take-over of the petroleum industry.

In 1938, a combination of favorable factors, including the sympathy of the American ambassador and the impending conflict in Europe, enabled Mexico to carry out what in retrospect appears to have been a successful nationalization. Nationalization was not an overnight success, however. Mexico first had to overcome serious postnationalization problems — an attempted blockade by the oil companies, threatened domination of the oil industry by the petroleum workers' union, inefficiency and bureaucratization in the industry, and a serious shortage of investment capital for new exploration.

When the issue of compensation had been resolved as a result of United States government initiatives, Mexico began to encourage American investment in other areas where it needed capital, technology, and modern methods. Efforts were made to use other means besides nationalization — negotiated purchase, differential taxation, and screening of foreign investment — to alter the existing pattern of foreign investment so that the national economy would benefit. The result was a successful development model involving a mixed economy with a powerful and expanding state sector; the virtual elimination of foreign ownership in mining, utilities, and transportation; a substantial but increasingly controlled foreign presence in the areas of manufacturing and processing; and the growth of an increasingly influential Mexican private sector. And just when the model seemed to be getting into difficulties because of increased government indebtedness, the discovery of large new oil reserves brightened the prospects for Mexico's economic future.

This chapter will center around three principal topics: (1) the development of American diplomatic doctrine and practice as it emerged in the course of the negotiations among American companies, government policymakers, and the Mexican government concerning the expropriation of United States holdings in Mexico; (2) an analysis of the circumstances surrounding the 1938 nationalization of the American petroleum holdings in Mexico and its consequences; and (3) an evaluation of the foreign investment policy of Mexico between the 1940s and the present, viewed as a case study for other less developed countries.

THE ESTABLISHMENT OF THE PETROLEUM INDUSTRY AND THE CONFLICT OVER SUBSOIL RIGHTS

Mexico shares with other Latin American countries the common heritage of Spanish law. As early as the fourteenth century, that law included provisions that all mines and their products were the property of the crown and could be worked only by virtue of a royal license or grant. In the sixteenth century, those provisions were extended to the Spanish colonies, allowing the exploration and development of mines provided that they were registered with the crown and that a royalty was paid. Spanish legislation also provided that mines not worked for four months were to be declared abandoned. In 1783, the Spanish legislation was specifically applied to Mexico.

In 1884, contrary to the earlier laws, Mexico adopted a new mining code that included a provision specifically stipulating that "petroleum and gaseous springs" were to be the "exclusive property of the owner of the land." Subsequent Mexican legislation, in 1892 and 1909, confirmed the 1884 law.

The legislation adopted between 1884 and the beginning of the Mexican Revolution in 1910 was designed to promote economic development by opening Mexico to foreign capital as advocated by the *científico* advisors of the Mexican strong man, Porfirio

Díaz, who ruled that country from 1876 until 1911. The Díaz policy was so successful in attracting foreign investment that, by 1911, foreigners owned half the total wealth of the country and dominated every economic activity except agriculture. As much as a quarter of the agricultural land was also owned by foreigners. While a few thousand Mexican *hacendados* controlled over half the arable land, 90 percent of the rural population was landless.[1] Many of the large landholdings were obtained by government sale of confiscated church lands while others were acquired by questionable legal maneuvers that permitted taking land that had been in the possession of small holders, villages, or Indian communities.

The Porfirian legislation granting title over subsoil petroleum to owners of the surface under which it was located was in effect shortly after the turn of the century, at the time that British and American investors began to develop the Mexican oil industry. An Englishman, Weetman D. Pearson (later Lord Cowdray), and an American, Edward L. Doheny, secured an exemption from all Mexican taxes except for a small stamp tax. Under British and American auspices, oil production expanded from 10,000 barrels in 1901 to 12,552,000 barrels in 1911, with a continued increase throughout the next decade.[2]

Oil production was not adversely affected by the Mexican Revolution of 1910-20. The oil companies were able to make judicious payments to those in local control, and the oil fields suffered only minor damage. The oil industry was affected, however, by the demands for social justice, land reform, and control over national resources that were added to the original political program of "effective suffrage, no reelection" espoused by those who overthrew the Díaz dictatorship. In 1916, the Mexican Congress established a Committee on Nationalization of Petroleum, but it was evident that Mexico did not have the economic resources nor the technical capacity to take over the oil industry. It did need more revenue and tried to increase the oil tax. But whenever the oil taxes were raised, and this happened regularly after 1912, the foreign oil companies would complain of "confiscation," and the American and British ambassadors would then lodge formal protests. Those protests were part of the continuing efforts by both embassies to protect the property of their citizens or to secure compensation when the properties had been taken over by one or another revolutionary government. The two issues — land reform and control of national resources — were thus fused despite their clear distinction in earlier Spanish and Mexican law.

Both issues were discussed in the same article of the Mexican constitution as drafted at the constitutional convention of Quere-taro in 1916-17. Article 27 of the 1857 constitution provided that private property could be expropriated "with prior compensation" when public utility required it. However, the delegates to the constitutional convention were determined to expand the government's powers — both to validate the agrarian reform that had become a central objective of the revolution and to regain control over the nation's natural resources now being exploited by foreigners. In an attempt to meet the latter objective, the 1917 constitution eliminated the Díaz mining laws, which granted mineral and petroleum rights to the owner of the surface, and re-asserted the direct ownership (*dominio directo*) by the nation of natural resources in the subsoil. In cases of compensation for ex-propriation, the new constitution omitted the requirement that payment be made prior to the take-over of the property involved. Pastor Rouaix, a central figure in the drafting of the constitution because of his position as confidant of both President Venusti-ano Carranza and the more radically oriented delegates, explained the meaning of *dominio directo* as follows: "That is to say, the complete proprietorship that it [the state] has had over these products is inalienable and imprescriptible, and only by means of concessions and subject to determined conditions may it cede the use of these to private individuals."[3]

Article 27 of the 1917 constitution was seen by the oil compa-nies as a threat to their established property rights, and they en-listed the United States embassy in support of their position. As soon as the provisions of Article 27 became known, the embassy asked for assurances from President Carranza that its principles would not be applied retroactively and made this a condition of the United States grant of *de jure* recognition of his government. The embassy had other weapons with which to pressure the Mex-icans. It could withhold or impose embargoes on the flow of arms from the United States (an arms embargo had been used in Carranza's favor earlier). It could influence the granting of loans from United States sources — and Carranza was repeatedly given to understand that only with firm guarantees for United States propertyholders would any loans be forthcoming. The most important threat, however, was armed intervention. There is evidence that a declaration of war on Mexico was actively considered by the Wilson cabinet in 1919, and that, in the same year, Republican senators in league with the oil companies unsuccessfully attempted to secure Wilson's support for an invasion of Mexico.[4] During World War I, Mexico was a principal supplier of oil for the allied forces in Europe, and Carranza was aware that armed intervention was not unlikely if there were any interruption of that oil.

The oil companies repeatedly rejected Carranza's demands that they apply for permits for new drilling. A principal weapon used by the companies was the threat to withhold petroleum taxes, which in 1918 already accounted for 10 percent of the central government's revenue and by 1922 accounted for 33 percent of its income.

In succeeding administrations, the United States government continued to defend the oil companies. As a condition for United States recognition of the government of President Álvaro Obregón (needed to prevent arms shipments from the United States to Obregón's rivals), American and Mexican representatives signed the Bucareli Accords in 1923, named after the house at 85 Bucareli Street in Mexico City where the informal negotiations were carried on. Under the accords, Mexico promised that Article 27 would not be applied to oil companies that had carried out "positive acts" in developing their properties, and it gave present owners preference to exploit undeveloped holdings. In 1925, the new government of Plutarco Elías Calles demanded that the oil companies convert the titles to their oil lands to fifty-year concessions. The companies refused to do so, and in 1926 and 1927, the United States government actively considered withdrawing recognition and, once again, using armed intervention. (The military commander in the petroleum-producing areas who was ordered by President Calles to blow up the oil fields in the event of an American invasion was the future president General Lázaro Cárdenas, who expropriated the fields in 1938.) In 1927, through the good offices of the new American ambassador, Dwight Morrow, the companies agreed to a compromise formula. Their holdings were described as "confirmatory concessions," but the fifty-year limit was not included, and the guarantee for areas in which "positive acts" had been carried out was reaffirmed.

The picture that emerges from the disputes of the 1920s and 1930s is a rather consistent one. A weak Mexican government continually threatened by internal revolts was attempting to reassert the principle of national ownership of mineral resources, which it viewed as a fundamental law that had been violated by Porfirio Díaz. The oil companies, on the other hand, took advantage of the financial and political weakness of the government to prevent new government controls on their operations or the establishment of the principle that the oil wells were in any sense national property. They were able to enlist the support of the United States government in their behalf, both because they could point to the Porfirian laws under which their original investments had been made and because American diplomats considered it their duty under international law to extend diplomatic protection to the property of American citizens, whether agricultural or mineral. In defense of American property, the United States possessed a powerful battery of weapons, including denial of diplomatic recognition, control over the flow of arms, withholding of loans, and *in extremis* armed intervention. Government support of the oil companies was reinforced by strategic considerations, not only during World War I, but thereafter as concern mounted over what was believed to be the likely depletion within a generation of United States oil reserves. (This argument became less compelling in the 1920s as new, cheaper oil sources were discovered in Venezuela and Venezuela replaced Mexico as the world's second ranking oil producer.) With such powerful support, the companies could be intransigent. For example, in 1922 they rejected outright a Mexican proposal that would have established joint ventures with the Mexican government to carry out oil explorations.[5] At that time, the question of nationalization was rarely brought up, except by some of the more radical members of the legislature. Instead, the controversy centered around the issues of taxation, drilling permits, and the replacement of fee-simple titles by concessions. The oil companies refused to yield on these issues as well, and they were supported in their intransigence by American diplomatic representatives.

CÁRDENAS AND THE NATIONALIZATION OF OIL

It was only in the next decade that new circumstances made nationalization feasible. The Mexican government's institutional capacity had been improved by the creation of an official government party in 1929 and the adoption of a labor code in 1931 that included provisions for the direct intervention of the government in labor disputes. In 1934, a state-owned petroleum company, Petromex, was created, consciously following the example of Argentina, which had long had a state oil company, Yacimientos Petrolíferos Fiscales (YPF). Once again, feelers were put out as to possible joint ventures between the government and the foreign oil companies, but again they were rejected. Efforts to attract Mexican investors in Petromex were not successful either. Thus, lacking capital, the state company did not expand its activities. Owing to the discovery of new fields in the British-owned area, petroleum production increased in the early 1930s (production had fallen steadily since early in the previous decade), but the new government company produced only a miniscule share. In 1935, 99 percent of Mexican oil production, 98 percent of mining, and 100 percent of electricity were owned by foreigners.

In 1934, the official government candidate, General Lázaro Cárdenas, indicated in his presidential campaign speeches that the Calles-Morrow agreements would no longer form the basis of government policy. After he took office, Cárdenas secured adoption of a Nationalization Law, which, although primarily aimed at facilitating his expanded program of agrarian reform, was broad enough to be applied against the foreign mining and petroleum interests as well. Among the reasons that could be used to fulfill the requirement of "public utility" for an expropriation were "maintenance of the supply of food and articles of basic necessity to cities and population centers . . . the establishment, development, and preservation of an enterprise for the public good . . . [and] the necessary means to avoid the destruction of natural resources. . . ." Compensation was to be based on declared tax value and could be paid for a maximum of ten years.[6]

The Cárdenas labor policy included an effort to group all labor unions under a single confederation that formed a constituent part of, and could be controlled by, the government party. In 1935, the various petroleum workers were first joined into a single Syndicate of Petroleum Workers of the Republic of Mexico (STPRM), and in the following year, the STPRM joined the Mexican Labor Confederation (CTM). Beginning in 1936, the petroleum workers, with Cárdenas's support, demanded increased wages and the unionization of the industry's white-collar workers. When the foreign companies rejected the union's demands, the government appointed a joint negotiating committee, which was unable to arrive at an agreed solution. In June 1937 at the request of the labor union, the government declared the dispute an "economic conflict" within the terms of the 1931 Labor Code, and the Federal Conciliation and Arbitration Board appointed a committee of three experts to recommend a settlement. After an extensive, although not impartial, study of the wage dispute, the committee produced a 2,700-page report that declared that the companies had been making profits that were 2.5 times greater than their official figures owing to transfer pricing and bookkeeping devices. The report recommended wage increases totaling 26 million pesos and called for all white-collar personnel to be unionized, except for 1,100 confidential employees. The oil companies appealed the committee's recommendation, and on March 1, 1938, the Mexican Supreme Court ruled against the companies. The companies assumed that the worst that could now happen would be a temporary government "intervention" of the oil fields; they offered the government a 22 million peso wage increase combined with 4 million pesos in increased investment. The government rejected the compromise and demanded fulfillment of the court's decision. On March 16, the companies gave in on the 26 million peso figure but refused to accept the limit on confidential employees. After another fruitless meeting on

March 18, Cárdenas decided on the expropriation of the petroleum industry—a decision that he had been considering for ten days. His decree cited Article 27 and the provisions of the Nationalization Law concerning essential supplies, national defense, and damage to natural resources.[7]

There had been other nationalizations in Latin America before this one. Indeed, Mexico had taken over what remained of foreign ownership of its railroads only a year before. However, this was the first time that an underdeveloped country had suddenly taken control of a major foreign enclave in the area of mineral resources despite united opposition of the companies involved. When so many of his predecessors had not dared to touch the companies, why did Cárdenas take such an unprecedented step?

One way to answer this question is to contrast the relationships among the Mexican government, the oil companies, and the United States in 1938 with those relationships one or two decades earlier. As noted in chapter II, United States policy toward Latin America changed early in the Roosevelt administration with the adoption of the "Good Neighbor Policy." Roosevelt formally eschewed treaty rights such as the Platt Amendment, which allowed United States intervention, and the general practice of "dollar diplomacy" and the use of armed force in inter-American relations. He sent a close personal friend, Josephus Daniels, to Mexico as ambassador, and his New Deal administration was much less sympathetic toward the claims of United States business interests than were its Republican predecessors. Thus, the threat of armed intervention, always present in earlier negotiations, became remote. In addition, the international situation—the approach of World War II and the threat of fascist expansion—made it advisable for the United States to rally the support of its neighbors against a possible Axis threat.

Internally, too, Cárdenas was in a stronger position than were his predecessors. Although there was one armed outbreak at the end of his administration, he was not threatened by genuine rivals in 1938, and he had built up important institutional sources of support in his party and among the peasantry and organized labor. The party's relationship to labor was crucially important since it meant that there were ways to control the petroleum workers union, which had been the instigator of the conflict in the first place. Moreover, there was now a group of trained Mexican petroleum technicians, since Mexican legislation required the hiring and technical training of Mexicans, limiting the use of foreign personnel. While the economic consequences of a decline in oil production would still be serious, they would not paralyze the country—and even the decline in tax revenue would not be catastrophic since, despite recent increases in production and taxes, oil income provided only 12 percent of the government's income in 1937. In addition, from a legal point of view, the Nationalization Law clearly applied to this case, and it provided for deferred compensation. Ideologically, expropriation was as important as the economics of the issue. Recovery of natural resources had been a central element of the revolutionary program since the adoption of the 1917 constitution.

Whether Cárdenas considered all these factors is difficult to ascertain. The expropriation was discussed in the cabinet at least once in March before the action was taken, but Cárdenas and others have denied that any conscious plan had been developed earlier to take over the oil industry. The Cárdenas administration had decided to exert tighter control over the oil industry, but it seems likely that if the companies had been willing to compromise earlier they would have avoided, or at least postponed, nationalization.

Why did Cárdenas not resort to temporary "intervention" as the companies had expected? Clearly, the belief in national ownership of subsoil rights, a long history of oil company arrogance, the claim of the experts' report that the companies were making and concealing large profits, combined with the recent law prescribing procedures made nationalization an obvious solution.

Thus, in retrospect it appears that the Mexican situation in 1938 was unusually suited to nationalization. There had been a dramatic improvement in the political and institutional capacity of the Mexican government, the organizational and legal structure had been clarified, and Mexican technical capacities had improved. The external constraints, which had limited earlier governments, were reduced because of the ideological orientation of the Roosevelt administration and the change in the international situation that limited the abilities of foreign governments to exert pressure. The oil companies, too, contributed to the situation. The discoveries of alternative Venezuelan fields and a long history of Mexican weakness had developed a habit of intransigence in negotiation. The stage was thus set for a "nationalization situation," and Cárdenas was able to take an action that was almost unthinkable for his predecessors.

Politically, nationalization produced an outpouring of national solidarity. Even the Roman Catholic church, which had been feuding with the regime for twenty years, expressed its support. Collections were taken up, and wealthy matrons donated their jewels to cover the cost of nationalization. The compulsory textbooks used in all Mexican schools began to teach that "The act of expropriation . . . will convert Mexico from a poor country to a rich and prosperous nation, losing the characteristics of a semicolonial country in which its wealth never benefitted its own people, but only a few capitalistic companies, usually of a foreign nationality."[8]

Far from making Mexico rich, the short-run economic effect of the oil nationalization was extremely negative. Fearing that the Mexican expropriation might inspire other Latin American governments to follow suit, the oil companies, which controlled 90 percent of world petroleum marketing, instituted a boycott of Mexican oil. They also attempted to prevent Mexico from securing tankers to transport its oil, from purchasing machinery and spare parts, and even from buying ethyl for refining purposes. Mexican oil production declined from 4 million barrels in February 1938 to 2.1 million barrels in April, although it experienced a slow recovery thereafter, reaching 4 million barrels again in mid-1939.

Much of the production was consumed internally. The domestic share of Mexican oil, which had amounted to 43 percent during the preceding year, rose to over 50 percent in 1938 and 1939, reaching 66 percent by 1941. In addition, the Mexicans were able to evade the boycott by selling to Italy—and to a limited degree to Germany and Japan—as well as to independent producers in the United States who were willing to evade the boycott in exchange for cheaper crude oil.

UNITED STATES POLICY – PROMPT, ADEQUATE, AND EFFECTIVE COMPENSATION

The United States government was divided in its response to the Mexican take-over. The soft line, critical of the oil companies and sympathetic to the desires of the Mexicans, was represented by Ambassador Daniels and, to a considerable degree, President Roosevelt. Cordell Hull, secretary of state, in pursuit of a long-standing State Department policy based on Mexico's expropriation of American agricultural holdings, vigorously defended American property rights. In contrast to its conduct in later cases of expropriation, the Treasury Department was not actively committed to defending the companies. The reason for this was that the secretary of the treasury, Henry Morgenthau, was concerned that American intransigence might move the Mexicans closer to the Axis powers or even encourage a profascist coup. (Rightist opponents of Cárdenas are known to have sought financial support from the oil companies, but the United States National Archives reveal that the government rejected all suggestions of possible aid to rebel groups.)[9]

In his public statements and his communications with Roosevelt and Hull, Ambassador Daniels argued against a hard line with Mexico. According to Daniels, a hard-line position violated the Good Neighbor Policy and repeated the errors of Woodrow Wilson, which both he and Roosevelt had been able to observe firsthand as secretary and assistant secretary of the navy in Wilson's administration. Roosevelt himself, interviewed about the Mexican situation two weeks after the nationalization, was quoted by the Associated Press as saying, "As for the American oil companies whose properties were taken over when they failed to abide by a Mexican court decree ordering wage increases . . . they were entitled to damages equivalent only to actual investment, less depreciation." Citing New Deal domestic policy, Roosevelt added that indemnification "should not include prospective profits" – a point on which the oil companies were adamant since the subsoil controversy had centered around the ownership of the oil still in the ground.

On March 26, the Department of State hardened its position.

Hull sent Cárdenas a strong note insisting that Mexico pay "just compensation . . . having a present effective value . . . " to the oil companies. He stated: "This does not mean that the [Mexican] government may later pay, as and when it may suit its convenience. . . . My government directs me to inquire . . . what specific action with respect to payments for the properties in question is contemplated by the Mexican government, what assurances will be given that payment will be made, and when such payments may be expected. . . ."[10]

The tone of the letter was regarded as excessively harsh by both the Mexicans and Ambassador Daniels, who agreed with the Mexican foreign minister to consider the note as "not received." Daniels also wrote to Hull warning him that pressure on Cárdenas might lead to a right-wing coup. He urged Hull to propose to the oil companies that they work out with Cárdenas a production-sharing arrangement on the oil produced in Mexico, while awaiting an evaluation for compensation purposes. Hull's reply was to issue a public statement insisting on the necessity of fair compensation based on "assured and effective value."

The Treasury Department was also involved in the dispute. For the past three years, it had been purchasing practically all newly mined Mexican silver as well as much of the Bank of Mexico's accumulated supply. As a result, Mexican silver production had expanded, and taxes from the silver industry now accounted for 15 to 20 percent of the Mexican government's tax income. In December 1937, the Treasury agreed to a State Department request to stop its silver purchases in order to pressure Mexico to settle American land claims. This decision was subsequently reversed by Secretary Morgenthau. After the oil expropriation, however, the Treasury publicly announced that it would "defer continuation of the monthly silver-purchase arrangements with Mexico until further notice." The effort to exert economic pressure on Mexico abounded in contradictions: (1) the majority of the Mexican silver production came from American-owned mines; (2) Secretary Morgenthau was seriously concerned with the effects of an economic crisis on the stability of the Cárdenas government; and (3) a considerable fluctuation in the price of silver would affect the price of the United States Treasury's large silver holdings. While the State Department forced the Treasury to announce, on March 27, 1938, that it was stopping the regular bilateral monthly purchases of Mexican silver, after a three-week drop in purchases the Treasury began to buy similar amounts of Mexican silver on the world market. The result was that in 1938 Mexico actually exported 50 percent more silver to the United States than it had in 1937. Thus, except for a period of three weeks, the announced embargo on Mexican silver was never actually imposed.

However, the reaction of foreign and domestic capital to the uncertainties associated with the nationalization produced a general flight of capital from Mexico, a decline in the Bank of Mexico's reserves, and a drop in the exchange rate of the peso from about 3.6 to the dollar to a little over 5 to the dollar in 1939. (In 1940, it was valued at 4.85, where it remained until 1949.) The Treasury Department produced a study arguing that Mexico could make full compensation if given some short-term assistance; it even proposed that Mexico be given a low-interest loan in return for the settlement of outstanding Mexican-American disputes. The proposal was opposed by the State Department. Despite some fear by Hull that Mexico might turn to the Axis powers to sell its oil, he continued to back the oil companies. In 1938, the State Department vetoed the financing of five Mexican projects by the Export-Import Bank. In 1939, it substantially reduced the amount of Mexican oil that was imported at a 50 percent reduction in tariff rates, and as late as 1941 it forbade the Navy to purchase Mexican oil.

The intransigence of the State Department was based on a long history of negotiation with the Mexicans. The issue of compensation was first raised in 1915, when American-owned agricultural properties were taken over as a result of the Mexican agrarian reform. The Mexican government promised to pay for the lands in bonds at the declared tax value. But American negotiators objected to payment in bonds and demanded "just" compensation. For several decades, little progress had been made in the discussions. In mid-1938, Mexico proposed a partial settlement, with an initial payment of $1 million on one set of claims. Again, the

State Department insisted on an overall settlement, and this time it linked together the agrarian and oil claims. In July, after denying to the press that the United States government was putting financial pressure on Mexico (*New York Times*, July 1, 1938), Secretary of State Hull went to Morgenthau and asked him to lower the world price of silver by one cent, explaining, "The President and Daniels have given the Mexicans the impression that they can go right ahead and flaunt everything in our face. Daniels is down there taking sides with the Mexican Government and I have to deal with these Communists down there; I have to carry out international law." Morgenthau, however, refused to go along with Hull's request. A week later, Hull handed the Mexican ambassador a note, which was also released to the press, in which he asserted that "the taking of property without compensation is not expropriation. It is confiscation. It is no less confiscation because there may be an express intent to pay at some time in the future." While expressing sympathy for "the desires of the Mexican Government for the social betterment of its people," Hull demanded "prompt and just compensation . . . as prescribed by international law." When he discussed American agrarian properties later in the note, Hull described a just settlement as based on "prompt, adequate, and effective compensation" — the first time that the famous formula was used in an American diplomatic document.[11]

As Secretary Morgenthau noted in his diary at the time, both the State Department and the companies were concerned about the effect that the Mexican expropriation would have elsewhere. A year earlier during a tax dispute, the Bolivian government took over the Standard Oil subsidiary — and the question of compensation had not yet been settled. After the Mexican action, Cuba, Colombia, Brazil, Ecuador, Chile, and Uruguay all adopted laws limiting or forbidding exploitation of mineral resources and/or petroleum by foreign companies. While these actions were, in part, the result of a general increase in economic nationalism spawned by the problems induced by the depression, there is no doubt that the Mexican example encouraged similar actions elsewhere.

The companies were determined to resist the wave of economic nationalism which threatened their holdings, and they pressed the United States government to reject the Mexican nationalization as invalid and illegal. But from the beginning, the State Department accepted the principle that a state has the right to nationalize, provided that it gives full compensation. United States government pressures on Mexico, as in later cases, were exerted behind the scenes and were aimed at inducing Mexico to agree to an overall financial settlement.[12] The State Department apparently reasoned that if the pressure was sufficiently great and the settlement sufficiently expensive, similar actions might be discouraged elsewhere. The State Department was particularly concerned about Mexico's influence on Venezuela, which had replaced Mexico as the major foreign source of oil for the United States. On the other hand, security considerations in Mexico discouraged the application of extreme pressure for fear that it might lead either to a right-wing coup against Cárdenas or to increasingly close commercial—and perhaps political—relations with Germany, Italy, and Japan.

It is interesting to contrast the actions of the British and American governments with regard to the Mexican expropriation. Because of new discoveries, the production of the British Shell subsidiary in Mexico now substantially exceeded that of the American-owned companies. Since the 1920s, the British had been deferring to the American lead in defense of the petroleum companies, but in this case they took quite a different course from that pursued by the Americans. As a consequence of the expropriations, diplomatic relations with Mexico were broken by the Chamberlain government and not restored again until after World War II. For a combination of ideological and strategic reasons, such harsh action was not contemplated by the United States. Diplomatic action centered on securing adequate compensation. While economic pressures were exerted, they were limited by internal divisions within the American government and by fear of counterproductive effects.

Without direct United States enforcement, the company-organized boycott was unsuccessful. Indeed, within a matter of months, Mexico was able to sell some of its oil in the American market by pricing it 12 to 15 percent below posted prices. In August 1938, the first contract for shipment to the American market was signed with Eastern States Petroleum for 360,000 barrels a month. Overall, Mexico exported 15 million barrels in 1938 as compared with 24 million barrels in 1937, and its 1938 export income, in depreciating pesos, was less than half that of the preceding year. The Mexicans first attempted to sell their oil to France, but British pressure forced the French to refuse. They then turned to the Axis powers. In September 1939, Ambassador Daniels reported that over half of Mexico's oil exports since the expropriation had gone to Germany and Italy, while 16 percent had been exported to the United States, mostly for refining and reexport. Other sources indicate that Germany bought nearly 2 million barrels, or about 13 percent of Mexico's oil exports in 1938 and 1.5 million barrels, or 8 percent in 1939, while Italy's share of Mexican oil exports rose to 25 percent in 1939. (Shipments to Germany stopped in September 1939 with the outbreak of World War II.) The first oil shipment after the expropriation went to Japan, and Mexican trade with that country nearly quadrupled between 1938 and 1940. By 1939, total Mexican petroleum exports reached 19 million barrels, and by 1940, with the failure of the company boycott, Mexico shipped 16 million barrels to the American market, as compared with 7.3 million barrels in 1937 and 3.3 million in 1938.[13]

The attempted boycott by the oil companies was not limited to sales and purchases in the United States, however. The companies also tried to prevent Mexico from securing oil tankers in which to ship petroleum abroad, and they initiated lawsuits to prevent Mexican oil sales in the United States as well as in France, Holland, Belgium, and Sweden. Except for one case that kept a tanker in Mobile, Alabama, for six weeks, none of those suits was successful, although they delayed some oil deliveries and probably had the effect of discouraging some potential buyers. In addition, the companies carried out an anti-Mexican propaganda campaign in the United States in an attempt to discourage tourism. Mexican tourist income, in fact, declined by one-third in 1938, although the reasons for that decline are unclear.

THE COMPENSATION AGREEMENT

The Mexican government repeatedly offered to negotiate the terms of a compensation settlement. The Mexicans offered a down payment with subsequent payments to be made out of petroleum export revenues to the amount of the declared tax value of the company installations, plus additional expenditures that had been incurred for investment. The oil companies, however, demanded either immediate return of their properties or immediate full payment, including the value of the oil in the ground. The State Department suggested an agreement by which the companies would take over exporting the oil for the Mexican government. In 1939 a negotiating team tried to establish a joint venture between the companies and the Mexican government, but talks broke down over the question of compensation. Finally on May 1, 1940, the solid front of the oil companies was broken. The Mexicans concluded an agreement with Sinclair Oil which, having fewer overseas operations, was less concerned that the Mexican nationalization would encourage such actions elsewhere. The compensation for Sinclair's holdings, representing 40 percent of American oil holdings in Mexico, was in excess of $13 million—$8 million in cash over three years and the remainder in petroleum purchases at a discount over four years. After the Sinclair agreement, it was clear that the companies could no longer hope for return of their oil holdings.

With the likelihood of American involvement in World War II increasing, the Department of State gave up its support of the oil companies. In an effort to develop hemispheric solidarity and military cooperation against the threat of external attack, and finding a favorable response from the new Mexican president, Manuel Ávila Camacho, the State Department informed the oil companies, in September 1941, that, in the national interest, they should arrive at an overall settlement with Mexico. In November 1941, the long-standing dispute over compensation for expropriated American land was settled. The agreed compensation for American land, amounting to $40 million over fourteen years, was matched by an American "peso stabilization" loan of exactly the same amount. Other steps were also taken. Official silver purchases amounting to $25 million a year were begun again, a military assistance program was initiated, and an Export-Import Bank loan of $30 million for road construction was arranged. According to the memoirs of Mexico's finance minister at the time, the prospect of an Export-Import Bank loan was one of the reasons that Mexico was willing to negotiate a compromise. The Mexicans also agreed to make an initial cash payment of $9 million to the oil companies and to participate in a joint commission to work out the full compensation arrangement.

According to the Department of Commerce, the 1938 book value of the American oil investments was $69 million, although after the nationalization the companies estimated the value of their holdings at $262 million. Between January and March 1942, a joint American-Mexican board of two experts worked out an agreement that set the final compensation for American oil companies at just under $24 million plus about $5 million in interest. (The earlier payments to Sinclair should be added to this figure to determine total compensation paid by Mexico to United States companies.) With additional interest, the payments amounted to $30 million paid out over five years. In 1947, a similar agreement was made with the British, amounting to $80 million in principal and $50 million in interest paid over a period of fifteen years.[14]

The Mexican-American General Agreement of November 19, 1941 and the oil compensation settlement that followed marked a turning point in United States-Mexican relations. The settlements were motivated on the American side by a desire to cooperate more closely with the Mexicans to secure hemispheric defense. The Mexicans, on the other hand, were interested in securing public and private capital from the United States for Mexican development. In analyzing the conflict, Mexican historian Lorenzo Meyer sees the Mexican move to the right, in the sense of a slowdown in agrarian reform and a more favorable attitude to foreign investment, as the price paid by Cárdenas for the expropriation. However, both before and after the nationalization of petroleum, Cárdenas publicly expressed his desire for foreign investment in areas such as manufacturing, and at the end of 1939, the Mexican legislature passed a law giving guarantees to foreign investment in specified industries. Although Manuel

Ávila Camacho, Cárdenas's successor, is generally held responsible for a diminution in the pace of the Cárdenas reforms, the petroleum issue was not a contributing factor since the Sinclair settlement, which was agreed on before he took office, demonstrated that the compensation question would be resolved, and preliminary negotiations for an overall bilateral diplomatic settlement had already been initiated.

What lessons on nationalization can be drawn from the Mexican case? First, it seems to provide an illustrative example of the interaction of strategic and economic interests in the making of American policy. When strategic interests required an assured flow of oil during and after World War I, the oil companies were able to get strong support from the United States government, but when foreign policy interests before and during World War II dictated otherwise, the companies' desire for government action to aid them in their dispute with Mexico was overridden by broader considerations. On the question of compensation, the companies received considerable support from the State Department. Ignoring the subsoil rights issue, the State Department, which was still negotiating compensation for the agrarian expropriations, linked the petroleum and agricultural cases and negotiated on behalf of both interests. However, the department admitted from the outset that the Mexicans had the right to nationalize, although it insisted initially on immediate payment and coupled this insistence with the application of overt and covert economic pressures that were designed, ostensibly, to make the Mexicans more amenable to a settlement but in fact weakened their capacity to pay. The companies' position was weakened, however, by the State Department's unwillingness to give them unconditional support by the ineffectiveness of the company-organized boycott and by the willingness of other countries, especially the Axis powers, to buy Mexican oil. The Mexican case does not confirm the charge that United States foreign policy is dominated by powerful corporate interests, but there is enough evidence of official cooperation with those interests to support the view that company interests will be assisted unless broader foreign policy goals interfere.

That support, however, will not extend to the point of rejecting the right of governments to nationalize, provided full compensation is forthcoming. The definition of full compensation appeared at the outset to mean immediate payment in convertible currency, but when the United States decided to press for a settlement, it agreed to payment in installments, and it also relieved the strain on Mexico's balance of payments by extending various types of economic assistance.

POSTNATIONALIZATION PROBLEMS

In conversation with the Mexican ambassador three days after the nationalization in 1938, the undersecretary of state, Sumner Welles, asserted that it was "a notorious fact" that Mexico could not operate the oil wells at a profit or pay the workers as well as the companies had paid them. Welles warned the ambassador that in view of the companies' control of the world market, the Mexicans would be able to sell their oil only "at ruinous prices" to countries to which it was ideologically opposed, such as Germany, Italy, and Japan. Similarly, Josephus Daniels also expressed fears that Mexico would "be drowned in oil."

In fact, although April 1938 production was only half that of January, by September crude oil production had reached 82 percent of the January figure and refining had reached 92 percent. The April drop in production was thus related more to the decline in exports (from 200,000 barrels in March to 15,000 barrels in April) and to inadequate storage facilities than to a lack of technical capacity by Mexican oil workers. Over the next decade domestic consumption increased by an average of 8.9 percent a year, accounting for 91 percent of Mexico's production in 1947. Initially, however, there were problems with transportation from the refineries, most of which had been oriented to the external market.[15]

In June 1938 a new state oil company, Petróleos Mexicanos (Pemex), was organized under a board of directors of nine, three of whom were to be named by the petroleum workers union. The workers received a wage increase that was 8 to 15 percent below the amount ordered by the court in March, although full implementation of the court award was promised for the future. The court's ruling that certain employees were to be exempt from unionization was ignored, and nearly all white-collar employees became union members. Despite declines in production, the number of workers and administrative employees rose from nearly 16,000 in April to nearly 18,000 in July and to 23,000 in October 1939. In March 1940, Cárdenas made use of the Federal Conciliation Commission to reduce the number of employees.[16]

The government also attempted to replace the union-controlled managers and supervisors but only acquired effective control of the white-collar workers after 1942. In December 1946 when President Alemán took office, the entire administration was reorganized, and a cost-accounting system was introduced. Moreover, a new chief executive of Pemex, Antonio Bermúdez, succeeded in establishing order and efficiency in what had been an anarchic, corrupt, union-dominated organization.[17]

While the boycott was effective for only a few months after the expropriation, the lack of technology, of modern refineries geared toward the internal market, and of capital for exploration and development of new wells continued to plague the nationalized oil industry during the 1940s. Added to these problems were union corruption and featherbedding. By any account — whether it was payment of taxes equal to those that the companies had been paying before expropriation, operating to produce a profit, or even covering costs of depreciation — the industry was in deep trouble. One writer estimates that between 1941 and 1947 the amount in default to the government was between 40 million and 194 million pesos.[18]

At one point, Pemex could not even pay the government the gasoline tax that it was charged with collecting. While it is true that the war limited the possibilities of export to countries other than Cuba and the United States, even after the war's end only a relatively small proportion of Mexico's production was exported, and certain types of refined oil continiued to be imported in increasing quantities. In 1943, as part of the cooperative hemispheric defense effort of the United States and Mexico (and only over State Department objections), the Export-Import Bank granted a credit for the construction of a high octane refinery.

Yet as late as 1949, the bank refused further assistance for oil exploration purposes because the State Department did not want it to compete with private capital. Since the end of the war, negotiations over a possible reentry of the oil companies into Mexico on a joint venture basis had been taking place. But they foundered over company insistence that the Mexican legislation be changed to allow complete company control of operations. Despite nationalist opposition, Bermúdez authorized risk contracts for exploration with the Cities Service Company in 1948 and with another American company in 1949. The Cities Service contract provided that drilling was to be carried out under the direction of Pemex and that the company could purchase 50 percent of the oil discovered at a considerable discount. In return, Cities Service was to make a $10 million loan to Pemex. The contracts were terminated in the late 1960s, and no further exploration contracts were signed after 1950.[19]

PRICING POLICY

The figures on production are a more reliable indication of the effectiveness of Pemex's operation than are those on profit and loss; the latter figures were adversely affected by a deliberate government decision to keep the price of oil, gasoline, and kerosene low. Despite continuing inflation, the price of kerosene dropped from seventeen centavos a liter in 1938 to fourteen centavos in 1945, and the price of gasoline and other products increased at a rate that was far below the increase in the cost of living. Except for the price of fuel oil, this policy continued after Bermúdez took over in 1946. By 1958, according to Bermúdez's own estimate, the real price of kerosene had dropped by 81 percent in twenty years, that of gasoline by 46 percent, and that of diesel oil by 50 percent.[20] Under the system of administered prices, gasoline prices remained fixed from 1958 until December 1973, when a 55 percent increase was authorized. Subsidized low prices continued to be maintained for kerosene and diesel bus fuel.

Pemex's pricing policy illustrates a problem that reappears in other Latin American nationalizations — the conflict between applying conventional business methods based on the profit motive to nationalized industries and the desire of government policymakers to secure "uneconomic" social and political benefits from the nationally owned enterprise. The administered price for kerosene could be viewed as a subsidy for the poor, but the low price of gasoline helped the upper and upper middle classes; the low diesel price aided farmers and truckers, and cheap transportation helped the industrialists. While socially beneficial, the policy was never measured against possible alternative applications of the hidden subsidy. Bermúdez argues that if it had not been for the government pricing policy Pemex would have shown a profit under his administration and could have secured capital for investment and exploration out of earnings rather than through long-term loans and service contracts.

By the late 1950s, Mexico had become a net importer of oil. Exploration expenditures increased in the 1960s, although the number of new wells drilled was still far below the comparable United States figure. But in the 1970s, an expanded exploration program paid off handsomely. In 1973, just when Mexico was beginning to import substantial quantities (110,000 barrels a day) of high-priced OPEC oil to keep up with rising domestic consumption, Pemex made several large finds enabling it to become a net exporter once again. In 1978, Mexico's proven oil reserves rose to 40 billion barrels and estimated potential reserves of oil and gas to over 200 billion barrels. By 1980, Mexico expects to export over 1 million barrels of oil a day, earning $6 billion a year in foreign exchange.

By the mid-1960s, Pemex was being cited as the exception to the rule that government-run enterprises were bound to be inefficient, bureaucratic money-losers. It financed its investment programs with substantial borrowing from abroad (including a loan in the mid-1960s from the Export-Import Bank), and its earnings were sufficient to cover both costs of operation and taxes to the government, a considerable improvement over the government-subsidized operations of the earlier period.

In the mid-1960s, the number of Pemex employees was estimated at two to five times the number employed in comparable activities by American oil companies of comparable size. In the 1970s unfavorable comparisons were made between Pemex's 100,000 employees and the work force of 25,000 in the much larger Venezuelan petroleum industry. Wages, while among the best in Mexico, were far below those paid in the United States. It is no secret that down to the present day securing a job in the oil industry involves a sizable "kickback" to union officials, and union corruption continues to be a fact of life. Yet there was no longer any doubt about the financial soundness of Pemex or the competence of its administrators, who were directing the largest Latin American-owned corporation in the world.[21] Anticipating an expected bonanza in the 1980s, the Mexican government has drawn up plans to use the oil revenues to promote agricultural development, increase employment, and expand Mexico's industrial base.

FOREIGN INVESTMENT IN MANUFACTURING

For twenty years after the expropriation of the oil wells, there were no further nationalizations in Mexico. With the accession of Miguel Alemán to the presidency in 1946, Mexico began to promote industrialization by encouraging domestic entrepreneurs and attracting foreign — mainly American — investment to the manufacturing and consumer sectors, where Mexico lacked both capital and technology. Foreign investment had constituted 66 percent of all Mexican investment in 1910, and it was heavily concentrated in mining, oil, and utilities. By 1940, that figure had dropped to 9.5 percent, and only 6.5 percent of that amount was located in the manufacturing section. Beginning around 1950 however, American manufacturers, attracted by Mexico's proximity, political stability, low-wage costs, the availability of raw materials, the absence of restrictions on profit remittances, and the prospect of access to a large potential market protected by tariff and import quota barriers, established Mexican subsidiaries at such a rate that Mexico became the largest recipient of United

States investment in the Third World. By the late 1960s, 75 percent of all foreign investment was in manufacturing, 80 percent of it by United States companies, and total United States investment in manufacturing in Mexico had risen from $10 million in 1940 to $1.6 billion in 1970.

The movement out of basic industries and into manufacturing was accelerated by government decisions in 1958 and 1960 to nationalize the foreign-owned telephone company and several electric companies. In 1967 the government, through a combination of strong-arm tactics and serious negotiation, acquired a controlling interest in the leading American-owned sulphur company in 1967, and it purchased the remainder in 1972. Accompanying the purchase of foreign interests in basic industries was legal pressure to force "Mexicanization," that is, the establishment of joint ventures in which Mexican nationals held majority control. Mining, although theoretically subject to the same provisions as petroleum with respect to subsoil rights, had been left in the hands of private owners, most of them foreign, until 1961. At that time, a new mining law provided that "when the federal executive deems it advisable" mixed state-private mining companies were to be established, with a majority of the shares owned by the national government. New mining concessions were to be restricted to Mexican citizens or companies that were primarily Mexican owned. Existing foreign-owned mining companies were permitted to continue operating for twenty-five years, but a 50 percent reduction in taxes given to mining companies that were majority-owned by Mexicans provided a powerful incentive to Mexicanization. By the mid-1970s, 99 percent of mining production was carried on by Mexicanized companies, and Mexico had considerably expanded its processing, refining, and marketing of iron ore, copper, lead, zinc, and sulphur. A new mining law passed in 1975 reserved phosphates and sulphur for state ownership, assigned iron and coal to mixed state-private companies, and extended the power of the state to regulate the fertilizer, steel, and energy industries.[22]

In the early 1970s, the government entered the steel industry in a major way. It secured foreign loans, including a loan from a consortium of foreign banks that involved the World Bank and the Inter-American Development Bank, to develop a mammoth steel complex at Las Truchas, and it expanded its majority-controlled Altos Hornos steel mill. Through the government development bank, *Nacional Financiera*, it assisted the Mexicanization process with loans and direct participation. Thus by the mid-1970s, a whole host of government-owned trusts (*fideicomisos*) and mixed companies with majority-state ownership was engaged in mining, banking, and the production of 95 percent of the country's fertilizer, 90 percent of its buses, 80 percent of its tobacco and sisal, 40 percent of its sugar, and the marketing of 28 percent of its cotton.[23]

Having successfully moved foreign investment out of mining and into manufacturing, the Mexican government began to place stronger legislative restrictions on the direction, composition, and financing of investment in the manufacturing area as well. In the late 1960s, there was increasing criticism of the concentration and character of foreign investment in manufacturing. Mexican and American critics of United States investment in Mexico argued that American firms were buying out existing Mexican firms, raising money for expansion on the Mexican credit market, and contributing to Mexico's balance-of-payments problem by importing foreign machinery and making excessive payments to foreign companies for profits, technology, licensing, and royalties. The response to these criticisms emphasized the benefits of foreign investment from outside capital brought in, of new industries created (replacing imports and saving foreign exchange), of technology introduced, of Mexican personnel trained, of exports expanded, and of general economic growth increased.[24]

The critics did not wish to eliminate foreign investment; they only wanted to control it. Thus the solution adopted was not nationalization but legislation that could be applied in a way which extracted maximum national benefits from the foreign investor but left him with enough incentives to persuade him to continue to invest. In 1973, a Law on the Promotion of Mexican Investment and the Regulation of Foreign Investment was enacted. The law reserves exclusively for the state the areas of petroleum, electricity, telephone and telegraph communication, and rail transportation. It requires that radio and television, highway, air, and maritime transportation, and gas distribution be Mexican-owned. It limits foreign investment in new companies or new products to 49 percent ownership (40 percent in petrochemicals and automobiles and 34 percent in mining) and foreign acquisition of existing companies to 25 percent of capital. It also bans the use of dummy Mexican shareholders (*prestanombres*) by foreigners, and it requires that all foreign investment register with the government. A National Commission on Foreign Investment can grant exceptions to the law based on a long list of criteria, including the investment's effects on employment, the balance of payments, and the development of Mexican technological capacity. Other recent legislation requires registration and review of contracts for payments to foreigners for technology, patents, and royalties; limits patent rights to ten years and allows for their expropriation; and mandates the Mexicanization of trademarks.[25] Foreign investors protested against the new legislation, claiming it would discourage foreign investment in Mexico. Although in 1974 new American investment increased, it declined in 1975, and in 1976 except in the area of trade, it dropped very sharply. However, this was probably caused by the uncertainties associated with devaluation and the presidential succession. In 1977 and 1978 there was a recovery in reinvested earnings and new investment, as the National Commission on Foreign Investment interpreted the law's provisions more liberally, allowing 100 percent control for firms that increased exports, raised local content of their products, or built labor-intensive factories elsewhere than Mexico City. The principal result of the law seems to have been a considerable increase in the number of joint ventures, often involving Mexican banks or government agencies as part owners. Mexico may also have lost some access to foreign technology because of the reluctance of foreign investors to accept the legal requirement that the Mexican licensees acquire full ownership of the technology on the expiration of the contracts.[26] However it has also acquired knowledge of the pattern of foreign investment in Mexico, as well as instruments with which to direct it into areas of national interest, e.g., the acquisition of modern technology and the promotion of exports.

EXPANSION OF THE STATE SECTOR

At the same time that the Mexican government was placing further controls on foreign investment, it was also substantially increasing its role in the economy. In 1946 the Secretariat of National Properties *(Patrimonio Nacional)* was established and charged with the principal responsibility of supervising Pemex and programs of public works. In 1970, the parastatal sector comprised 92 agencies, most of them under *Patrimonio.* By the end of Luis Echeverria's administration in December 1976 that number had increased to over 740 agencies. Besides electricity and petroleum they included such vital areas as banking, steel, phosphate, fertilizer, sugar, and food processing. Controlling their expenditures and coordinating their activities had become such an administrative nightmare that one of the first acts of the new Lopez Portillo government in early 1977 was an administrative reorganization, which included the division of parastatal organizations into sectors and the establishment of stricter controls on expenditures.[27]

By the mid-1970s, Mexico combined a greatly expanded state role in the economy with a large domestic private sector, and an important foreign investment sector, which was increasingly associated with Mexican firms and limited and directed as to its range of activities. It had taken more than half a century, but the goal of Mexican control of the subsoil, enunciated in the 1917 constitution, had been largely achieved. The expropriation of petroleum was a major step in the implementation of that goal, and the oil industry provided the central core around which the state sector was built. With the large new oil discoveries in the 1970s and the readjustment of its price structure, the oil industry no longer acted as a drain on public finances. Rather, it made a major contribution to the Mexican budget and to the balance of payments. The expansion of the public sector raised fears in the private sector that further nationalization would occur. The fears were accentuated at one point in 1972 when the minister of national properties threatened the use of expropriation against recalcitrant industrialists. However, if the reasons for the expansion of state economic activity are analyzed, it seems that except for the nationalization of oil, telephones, and electricity, there has not been a conscious policy of socialization of industry. The increase in state ownership has been piecemeal and in response to specific situations and needs. Thus for example the sugar industry was taken over through a process that one writer has called "nationalization by inertia" — the increasing indebtedness of the sugar processors to the government as a result of its refusal to authorize any increase in the price of sugar between 1958 and 1970. As the treatment of the mining and manufacturing sectors indicates, the Mexican government now recognizes that there are less costly ways to achieve national control over the foreign sector than wholesale expropriation.

In 1970, a new law requiring an independent external audit of all state enterprises was established. Yet the law does not seem to have restrained the rapid increase in government expenditures. The deficit of the public enterprises in Mexico rose from 8 billion pesos in 1969 to 65.5 billion pesos in 1975 (twice the budgeted amount) — despite a 57 percent increase in the income of Pemex in 1974 and a 20 percent increase in 1975.[28] The general rise in government spending, especially by public enterprises (from 17 percent of gross domestic product in 1970 to 36 percent in 1976), was not balanced by a corresponding increase in taxes, and the overall government deficit rose from 3 percent of the gross domestic product in 1972 to 5 percent in 1974, 9 percent in 1975, and 12 percent in 1976. Mexico's foreign borrowing soared, increasing the public debt from $3 billion in 1970 to $20 billion by the end of 1976, with additional $3 billion increases in 1977, 1978, and 1979. (Foreign financial institutions were willing to lend, usually through multibank syndicates, because the new oil discoveries made Mexico a good risk.) The inflation rate increased significantly — almost 25 percent in 1974 and 40 percent in 1976. After a suitable delay to permit the election of the next president — José Lopez Portillo in July 1976 — two successive devaluations occurred in the fall of 1976, which resulted in a drop in the value of the peso in relation to the dollar from 12.5 to 22.5.

THE LESSONS OF MEXICO

Critics of the 1938 expropriation cite its negative effects — the ensuing drop in foreign investment, the lack of capital for exploration and refining, and the drain on national resources because of the necessity of subsidizing Pemex in the early years. They note that excess employment, union corruption, and reliance on expensive foreign loans to finance exploration and investment continued to hamper the Mexican oil industry. The defenders of Cárdenas's action reply that it is not at all clear that the American and British owners of the oil fields would have done much investing or expanding of producing and refining capacity in Mexico since they could secure greater profits in their Venezuelan and Middle Eastern operations. They would also have been less concerned with expansion of internal consumption, and in all likelihood the desire for substantial profits would probably have raised the price of energy far more than did Pemex. Research and development would have been carried out elsewhere, and the Mexican oil industries would have been subject to the vagaries of the world market, instead of being directed toward national purposes.[29]

It is difficult to come to a conclusion concerning this controversy since, in part, that conclusion depends on how one evaluates the tradeoff between economic efficiency and autonomy in national decisionmaking. One might speculate about an alternative policy for the oil industry similar to that pursued in the rest of the mining sector, such as the use of legislation and taxation to compel divestment to Mexican investors or to the state. Even the goal of cheap energy could have been achieved by legislation requiring the sale of a certain amount of production at a controlled price. Thus, nationalization was not the only alternative, and its goals might have been achieved more gradually and in a less painful fashion. Yet just because the oil industry was exposed and isolated and a different policy was followed with manufacturing it is doubtful that the nationalization was as costly in foreign investment as its critics indicate. In terms of the reinforcement of national self-confidence, the development of technical expertise, and increased ability to deal with foreign economic interests, there is no doubt that the nationalization of petroleum was a net plus. Nationalization also permitted the government to keep the domestic price of oil and its products at artificially low levels — although the wisdom of this policy is questioned by some economists. With the discovery of vast new reserves in the 1970s, just after a huge increase in the international price of petroleum, even the earlier delay in exploration and development seems to have been to Mexico's advantage.

For policymakers in other countries facing similar situations, the Mexican model provides a number of useful lessons. The complex of factors that enabled Mexico to carry out the expropriation successfully and, eventually, to operate the industry efficiently was rather special. Yet when similar "nationalization situations" developed in other countries, leaders could look to Mexico as an example of an underdeveloped country that defied the large companies and did not succumb to pressure from the major powers. They could learn other lessons — that there is a need to establish control over the labor unions in the nationalized enclave in order to avoid the creation of a "labor aristocracy" or even a state within a state. Policymakers must be aware of the political pressures that will seek to increase employment and discourage price increases even when there are increased costs.[30] It might also be concluded from the Mexican case that in the absence of a cartel, such as OPEC, nationalization is not likely to provide a bonanza by keeping the profits that formerly had been remitted abroad in the host country. At least partial compensation is necessary if the nationalizing country wishes to attract continuing foreign investment in other fields or to obtain loans from abroad, and even if the take-over is confiscatory the losses resulting from the decline in efficiency, production bottlenecks, etc. are likely, at least initially, to more than balance the economic gains from confiscation.

Perhaps the Mexican model as it developed after 1946 would be of greater interest to a developing country today. The careful assessment of how to attract foreign investment and then exploit and direct it once it has come into the country, plus the use of tax incentives and other inducements to force gradual divestment to national investors or the state, provides a more subtle alternative to choosing between a complete open-door policy for foreign investment and the confrontational expropriation of foreign holdings. However, the Mexican experience also seems to indicate that government promotion of industrialization and control of foreign investment requires a considerable increase in state intervention and manipulation of the economy. This in turn can produce financial and political problems similar to those that often follow nationalization – bureaucracy, politicization, and large government deficits. An important difference however, is that foreign capital would not be rejected but only controlled and persuaded through financial incentives to move in directions that the government sees as beneficial to development. This movement away from confrontational nationalization toward a more flexible bargaining relationship with foreign capital, which first became evident in Mexico in the 1940s, has been followed in recent years by many other Third World governments. The most important lesson of the Mexican example is the continuing need of the less developed countries to secure, on improved terms, access to technology, investment capital, and credit.

For the American investor, Mexico seems to typify the political sensitivity and vulnerable character of investments in natural resources, wherein the foreigner is seen as exploiting the national patrimony. On several occasions the foreign owners were given opportunities to replace their holdings in the extractive industries with joint ventures between Mexico and the foreigner – and this could have mitigated the Mexican feelings of exclusion – but these were rejected, leaving nationalization the only alternative. The Mexican case also seems to indicate that no matter how strong the legal position of the foreigner he will not be able, legally, to resist a government that is determined to nationalize, as long as some token compensation is made, since domestic law can be changed and international law is ambiguous. Extralegal measures are also likely to fail, for there is no certainty of United States government support or of unanimity among the members of the industry. Investment in the mining sector, therefore, is particularly risky. This risk is increased in the case of the oil industry because the return on investment is unusually high, much higher today because of the actions of OPEC, and the host country will wish to retain those profits.

In terms of American foreign policy, the Mexican case raises questions concerning the continued insistence of the United States government on "prompt, adequate, and effective compensation" — a standard first developed in response to Mexican nationalization but not adhered to in the final settlement, which involved both an overall lump-sum agreement and an American loan to Mexico. If "prompt" means "immediate," as Hull initially interpreted it, the standard is unworkable, unless the nationalizing country has access to substantial credit from the United States, international banks, or lending institutions. If full compensation includes in-ground deposits, it will not be accepted by any country. The most likely commonly agreed standard is declared tax value or book value — and although this may result in some loss for the companies, that possibility should have been considered at the time of investment.

The Mexican case also shows that responses to nationalization within the United States government will differ according to an individual's position, personality, or bureaucratic interest. These differences are likely to be intensified, at least under Democratic administrations, by a basic tension in American thought between sympathy for reform in Latin America, as evidenced in statements by Wilson and Roosevelt, and resistance to possible American property losses. Differences also exist between the perceived national interest in the protection of investment from confiscatory expropriation, as a part of the duty of diplomatic protection and because of its adverse effect on international trade and investment, and the broader strategic concerns, such as maintaining political or military cooperation that might be jeopardized by strong United States government sanctions. The crucial lesson that should have been learned from the Mexican experience was that the national strategic interest may be distinct from the economic interest of United States investors. It is clear in the next case — the expropriation of American companies in Cuba — that the United States was not as conscious of that distinction as it had been in Mexico.

4

Cuba — Nationalization
with Soviet Support

*The government of Cuba shall never enter into any treaty
with any foreign power which will impair or tend to impair
the independence of Cuba. . . . The Cuban government
consents that the United States may exercise the right to intervene for the preservation of Cuban independence, [and]
the maintenance of a government adequate for the protection of life, property, and individual liberty. . . .*

> — Platt Amendment to the Army Appropria-
> tion Bill of 1901

*Is the United States wise in pledging itself, as it has pledged
itself, to complete abstinence from the use of force in dealing with the states of the New World? . . . Suppose, for example, a full-fledged Communist regime should some day
be established in Cuba, a regime which definitely asserted its
acceptance of the Communist faith, and which formed close
relations with the USSR? . . . A thoroughly Communist regime in Cuba would, in practice, not only involve American
property interests to a very substantial degree; but it would
also present a very definite threat to the security of the
United States itself.*

> — Dexter Perkins, *The United States and the
> Caribbean*, 1947

I personally have come to feel that nationalization is, at best, a cumbersome instrument. It does not seem to make the state any stronger, yet it enfeebles private enterprise. Even more importantly, any attempt at wholesale national-ization would obviously hamper the principal point of our economic platform — industrialization at the fastest possi-ble rate. For this purpose foreign investments will always be welcome and secure here.

— Fidel Castro, 1958

Our revolution is neither capitalist nor Communist. . . . we are making a humanist revolution. . . . Capitalism sacri-fices man. The Communist state sacrifices man. . . . Our revolution is not red, but olive green.

— Fidel Castro, 1959

I am a Marxist-Leninist, and I will be a Marxist-Leninist until the last day of my life.

— Fidel Castro, 1961

The proletariat took power in Cuba through the conversion to Marxism-Leninism of a government of lawyers. . . . Through Castro who is the Cuban Soviet, the workers dis-cover their own interest and participate in the direction of society by ratifying his initiatives.

— J. P. Morray, *The Second Revolution in Cuba*, 1962

The great problem from the viewpoint of the U.S. Govern-ment is how Cuba can arrive at a just compensation agree-ment for the $1.8 billion plus claims adjudicated by the Foreign Claims Commission in 1966. This does not include interest or various U.S. Government claims. Before these claims are on the path to settlement, that natural develop-ment of trade which rightly should occur from geography cannot take place or proceed very far.

— Culver Gluysteen, spokesman for the State Department, 1977

After World War II, the United States possessed new instru-ments for the promotion of its policies around the world. Not only was American economic power beyond challenge outside the Soviet bloc, American prestige and ideological predominance was backed up by its military might, which proved itself in the victory over fascism and reestablished its strength at the time of the Korean War, and by a string of mutual assistance pacts agreed to around the world, the first of which was the Rio Treaty, signed in 1947. In addition, the United States had established the Central Intelligence Agency (CIA), a powerful intelligence agency that not only gathered information about other governments but also developed a capability to influence — and even to subvert — governments through its covert action operations.

While the CIA's capability was initially directed at countering Soviet propaganda and front group activity in Western Europe, it could be used against Third World governments which might take actions against American interests — including those of an economic nature — which were seen as detrimental to national security. As this capability expanded it led to an extension of CIA activities and a willingness to make use of the agency that were evident in the next major confrontation between the United States and a Latin American government involving the nationalization of United States enterprises — the only such confrontation which still remains unresolved — the case of Castro's Cuba.

The Cuban case deserves detailed analysis for three reasons. First, the debate over the causes of and responsibility for the breakdown of relations between the United States and Cuba has produced a large and controversial literature. Part of that literature maintains that the primary cause of the mutual hostility was a fundamental conflict between Castro's reform plans and the United States insistence that American-owned property in Cuba must be protected. It is useful, therefore, to examine the period leading to the rupture of diplomatic and economic relations in order to assess the role that American investment played in that rupture. Second, the rapid socialization of the Cuban economy and the economic policies which were adopted following the take-over of American property in 1960 provide us with a useful case study of the problems and prospects of wholesale nationalization in a Third World country. Castro has been frank to admit that Cuba made mistakes in its economic policy. Thus, the Cuban experience illustrates the difficulties that such a policy may encounter, and it provides a partial explanation as to why Cuban strategies have not been followed elsewhere. Third, the change in United States-Cuban relations in the mid-1970s may suggest that the United States should reevaluate the battery of legislative and administrative measures that were enacted as a result of the conflict with Cuba.

THE IRANIAN AND GUATEMALAN PRECEDENTS

In 1951, Iran became the first government since 1938 to nationalize foreign petroleum, when Premier Mossadegh took over the holdings of the Anglo-Iranian Oil Company after it refused to accept his demands for a larger share in profits and government review of company books. The British company secured the help of the other six members of the "Seven Sisters," the major oil companies, in measures to oppose the Iranian nationalization, and together the oil companies imposed a boycott of Iranian oil that, since there were no alternative markets (the Soviet Union had its own petroleum) and because Iran did not have the necessary transportation and marketing networks, cut off Iran's principal source of foreign exchange. Mossadegh was able to hold out for a few years, but he finally succumbed to a CIA-assisted military coup in 1953.

After the coup, the United States encouraged the establishment of a petroleum consortium in Iran that included the "Seven Sisters," the French national oil company, and a 5 percent share for small United States companies. The CIA involvement and the inducements to the companies (many companies already had access to cheaper oil elsewhere in the Middle East) were seen as necessary for security reasons – the Russian threat to northern Iran, the possibility of interruption of oil supplies to Europe if the Iranian example were followed, and the need to maintain a stable pricing system for friendly Middle Eastern states such as Saudi Arabia. An antitrust suit against the American oil companies was called off at the time, and, as it had done earlier in Saudi Arabia, the Internal Revenue Service ruled in 1954 that the oil companies could credit their Iranian taxes against their United States tax bills up to the United States tax rate.[1]

The success of the Iranian operation appears to have encouraged the CIA to involve itself in another covert effort at subversion in 1954 in Guatemala. The Guatemalan government, under Jacobo Arbenz Guzmán, had followed an increasingly leftward course since Arbenz came to power in 1951. In 1953, the government had "intervened" (temporarily seized) the Guatemalan Electric Company and the railroad owned by the United Fruit Company, and had expropriated 234,000 acres of United Fruit land, offering 25-year bonds in compensation at the value listed on the Guatemalan tax rolls. Guatemalan landholders were also affected by the measure, but two-thirds of the land taken over was owned by United Fruit. Another 172,000 acres were expropriated in February 1954. True to form, the State Department protested the compensation as neither prompt, adequate, nor effective and entered a claim on behalf of the company for nearly $16 million — far in excess of the Guatemalan bonds that, because of failure to update tax assessments, amounted to only $627,000 for the 1953 expropriations and in excess of $500,000 for those made in 1954. In June 1954 the Arbenz government was overthrown as a result of an invasion by a CIA-assisted force under Col. Carlos Castillo Armas and pressure on Arbenz by the Guatemalan Armed Forces.

The relation of the United Fruit expropriations to the overthrow of Arbenz is a source of continuing controversy over the relation of security and economic factors to the Guatemalan intervention. Already under the Truman administration, with the cold war at its height and the Korean War still going on, American policymakers were disturbed by the increasing influence of the Guatemalan Communist party in the Arevalo and Arbenz governments, particularly the establishment of Communist control of labor and peasant organizations. In mid-1952, prior to the United Fruit expropriations, President Truman authorized the shipment of arms to Nicaragua to support anti-Arbenz efforts. He subsequently countermanded the order on the insistence of the State Department, but in early 1953 the State Department was suggesting that, "Unofficially we can support well-organized counter-revolutionary operations mounted from neighboring countries." Participants in the CIA operation have placed the date of the official decision to support the overthrow of Arbenz in the summer or early fall of 1953.[2] When the Organization of American States, (OAS) at the initiative of John Foster Dulles, secretary of state, passed a resolution in March 1954 stating that, "the domination or control of the political institutions of any American State by the international Communist movement, extending to this hemisphere the political system of an extra-continental power, would constitute a threat to the sovereignty and political independence of the American States," it was clear, not least to the Guatemalan representative, that the resolution was aimed at the Arbenz government.

After the overthrow of Arbenz, members of his government who fled into exile made much of the fact that Dulles's former law firm acted as legal counsel to United Fruit, that the families of John Moors Cabot, assistant secretary of state for Latin America, and of Henry Cabot Lodge, United States representative to the UN, were prominent stockholders in United Fruit, and that John Foster Dulles's brother, Allen Dulles, was the head of the CIA, which masterminded the overthrow of Arbenz. They described in detail the prominent role of the American ambassador following the overthrow of Arbenz in the reorganization of the Guatemalan government, the reversal of Arbenz's reforms, and the reopening of Guatemala to American investment. The lesson that they drew was a simple one: the Arbenz government had been overthrown because it had carried out reforms which hurt American economic interests.[3]

Why begin a discussion of Cuban politics with an analysis of United States policy toward Iran and Guatemala? The overthrow of Mossadegh, and especially the overthrow of Arbenz, had a direct impact on the thinking of the principal actors—the United States, the Soviet Union, and Cuba—and in particular, upon Fidel Castro and Ernesto "Che" Guevara.

The impact on Guevara was direct. After finishing his medical studies in Argentina in 1953, Guevara took his second trip through Latin America. He observed firsthand and criticized the aftermath of the 1952 Bolivian revolution. Moving on to Ecuador, he then traveled by United Fruit banana boat to Central America. In Costa Rica, which had become a haven for the democratic left in exile, he met Costa Rican President José Figueres Ferrer, as well as Rómulo Betancourt and Juan Bosch, the future presidents of Venezuela and the Dominican Republic. Guevara developed an immediate personal hostility toward Betancourt, but he got along better with Juan Bosch, who later said that his discussions with Guevara at that time gave no indication that he was sympathetic to Communism.[4]

When he reached Guatemala, Guevara met other left-wing Latin Americans who had also been attracted to Guatemala by the Arbenz reforms, among them members of Fidel Castro's 26th of July Movement. When the Arbenz regime was attacked, Guevara attempted to organize resistance but finally was compelled to take refuge in the Argentine embassy. Radicalized by his experience in Guatemala, Guevara fled to Mexico, where in the summer of 1955 he met Fidel Castro. Castro had just been given amnesty by the Cuban dictator, Fulgencio Batista, from a prison sentence imposed after his attack on the Moncada Barracks on July 26, 1953. Guevara joined the group of eighty-two Cuban exiles, who landed in the Sierra Maestra in Cuba in December 1956 and began a guerrilla war that ended in victory over Batista two years later. In Mexico and in the Sierra Maestra, Guevara developed a close personal relationship with Fidel Castro and his brother, Raúl. He cited the example of Guatemala in discussions with Castro and in his book, *Guerrilla Warfare* (1960), to show how "the monopolists" will react to a government that attempts to engage in social reform.

CASTRO, THE UNITED STATES, AND COMMUNISM

In Castro's public statements during this period, he did not indicate that he felt there was an inevitable conflict between the revolution that he intended to carry out and all foreign investment. At his trial after the attack on the Moncada Barracks on July 26, 1953, he only mentioned the need to nationalize the telephone and electricity "trusts". Even these industries were omitted in later versions of his program, for example, in the Declaration of Sierra Maestra in 1957 and in a magazine interview in 1958, quoted at the beginning of this chapter. Earlier, Castro had been a member of the *Ortodoxo* party, whose program called for tariff protection for Cuban industry and an agrarian reform to be carried out chiefly through the distribution of idle land. Like other *Ortodoxos*, he was opposed to the Cuban Communist party (Partido Socialista Popular—PSP), which had been discredited by its earlier support of Batista. (In the early 1940s, two leading members of the PSP had served in Batista's cabinet.) The PSP had repeatedly denounced Castro as a bourgeois "putschist" and only began to cooperate with Castro six months before Batista's overthrow. Thus, there is no reason to believe that sympathy with Communism led Castro to take the actions he did after he came to power. What one can perceive is an abiding mistrust of the intentions and purposes of the United States government, in particular of its close relationship with and support for United States business interests. For anti-Batista Cubans, this relationship was symbolized most dramatically by a ceremony at the Presidential Palace in March 1957, which took place one day after an unsuccessful assassination attempt on Batista's life resulted in the death of twenty-five leaders of the Revolutionary Student Directorate. In the presence of Arthur Gardner, the American ambassador, Batista received a golden telephone from the American-owned telephone company in gratitude for his grant of a rate increase. Published pictures of Ambassador Gardner embracing the chief of staff of the Batista army further symbolized United States support of the dictator.[5]

THE UNITED STATES AND BATISTA

In mid-1957, Ambassador Gardner was replaced by Earl Smith. Because of the importance of the American ambassador, described by Smith as "second only to the President of Cuba," the change of ambassadors was taken as a sign that United States support might possibly be withdrawn from Batista. Smith described his policy as one of nonintervention but, as he noted in his book on his experience as ambassador, "for a power as great as the United States, it is nearly impossible not to intervene in a country as closely associated with us as Cuba has been." Smith was strongly critical of the State Department decision of March 1958 to suspend arms shipments to Batista and to enforce the congressional proviso requiring Cuba to consult with the United States before using its American-supplied arms for purposes other than hemispheric defense. Under the Military Assistance Program begun at the time of the Korean War, the United States had been supplying Cuba with arms. But because of the rising intensity of the guerrilla war and the publicity of brutal treatment and repression by the Batista government was receiving stateside, the United States government suspended the program. Yet the United States Military Mission was not withdrawn from Havana, and the guerrillas were still being killed by American weapons. (Guerrilla armament and financing also came from the United States, principally from anti-Batista Cuban exiles in Miami.) Reflecting his exaggerated view of the importance of United States policy, Smith's book attributes the Castro victory to the cutoff of military aid to Batista.[6] In fact, the United States action was only one of many factors. The major reason for Castro's success was the massive opposition to Batista from nearly every sector of Cuban society.

CASTRO AND THE UNITED STATES – FIRST PHASE

Once Castro came to power on January 1, 1959, it was clear that Smith, whom the guerrillas accused of being "neutral in favor of Batista," could not remain. On January 7, the United States recognized the new government, noting "with satisfaction the assurances given by the Government of Cuba of its intention to comply with the international obligations and agreements of Cuba." Smith resigned three days later without meeting Castro. He later wrote that any such intention on his part was quickly dispelled after Castro publicly stated, "if the United States intervened to protect its investments there would be 200,000 dead gringos in the streets."

The comparatively rapid United States recognition of the post-Batista government was facilitated by the broadly based character of the new cabinet, which included in key posts middle-class economists and lawyers with previous political affiliations to the reformist parties of the center-left. Castro himself became commander-in-chief of the armed forces, and the post of prime minister was given to Jośe Miro Cardona, a well-known lawyer who had opposed Batista. (In late February, Castro became prime minister.) The largely ceremonial post of president went to a judge who had publicly defended the guerrillas, Manuel Urrutia. Cuban businesses offered to pay their taxes in advance, the American Chamber of Commerce indicated its support, and when asked if the United States had offered aid, Castro replied that all aid would be welcome. Except for the adverse publicity in the United States concerning the drumhead war crimes trials of Batista collaborators, it seemed that "the Robin Hood of the Sierra Maestra" would follow the lines of reformist populist nationalism similar to those being pursued by contemporary democratic leaders elsewhere in Latin America. Although the Batista legislature was dissolved, the judiciary was purged, and political parties were dissolved, Castro announced that elections would be held in fifteen months, and the press and trade unions operated free of government interference.

Yet Castro was at least considering a more radical policy. In February, he made a triumphal trip to Venezuela, and President Betancourt later revealed that Castro approached him when they were alone and asked for a possible loan and a guaranteed supply of oil since he was thinking of "having a game with the gringos." Betancourt replied by saying that he supported "evolution not revolution."[7]

Castro was determined to lessen United States domination of the Cuban economy, but it was not obvious that this would necessarily lead to a confrontation with the United States government. It is true that American firms owned one-third of the Cuban sugar mills; the two nickel refineries (one built with United States government money); large tracts of land including 300,000 acres owned by the hated United Fruit, which would be affected by the projected agrarian reform; the telephone and electric companies mentioned in Castro's 1953 speech; and a railroad, a cement plant, banks, hotels, and many manufacturing and marketing firms. However, Castro's economic advisors, and the parties with whom they had been affiliated, saw foreign investment as a useful source of capital and technology that could, by appropriate tariff, exchange controls, and tax laws, be directed toward national development. Judging by his contradictory statements, however, Castro seemed to have been ambivalent on the subject.

Why, then, was the Cuban economy transformed within two years from a predominantly capitalist system dependent on the United States for 65 percent of its imports and 75 percent of its exports, into a self-proclaimed Marxist-Leninist system, in which the Communist world supplied 70 percent of its imports including nearly all its oil, and bought 75 percent of its exports? There are two polar positions that attempt to explain this transformation. One theory holds that, because of his Communist sympathies, Castro was determined from the outset to move Cuba into the Soviet orbit, while the other claims that there was an inherent, and thus unavoidable, contradiction between Castro's plans for social justice and national independence and the United States commitment to the defense of the status quo. Even if both theories are rejected as too simplistic, some assessment of the interaction of American and Cuban policy during these crucial two years is needed, along with some attempt to allocate responsibility for what two pro-Castro writers have called a "tragedy in the hemisphere." To what extent did United States policy encourage Castro to align himself with the Soviet Union? To what extent was Castro's decision to do so dictated by motives other than a response to American opposition? Finally, for the purpose of this study, what role did the United States defense of American investments play in contributing to this process?[8]

It was clear from the start that Castro was extraordinarily sensitive on the question of United States-Cuban relations. An inherent part of the political doctrine that Castro adhered to during and after his university years was the belief that after the overthrow of the dictator Gerardo Machado in 1933 the United States, through its "proconsul" Sumner Welles, had prevented the nationalist and reformist regime of Ramón Grau San Martín and his supporters in the *Directorio Estudiantil* (Student Directorate) from carrying out their program of labor legislation, social justice, and nationalism. They attributed United States nonrecognition of the Grau regime, during the four months before it was overthrown by Fulgencio Batista, to fears that his government would adversely affect United States investments.[9] A more important influence on Castro's attitude toward the United States was the CIA intervention in Guatemala, which he viewed, purely and simply, as an exercise in defense of American economic interests—United Fruit. His right-hand man, Che Guevara, also attributed the turn to the right after 1958 of the government in Bolivia, the National Revolutionary Movement (MNR), to American influence there.

On March 4, Castro had lunch with the new American ambassador, Philip Bonsal, who wrote that his impression after the lunch was that "there was a chance of working with him." Nevertheless, when José Figueres gave a speech in Havana on March 22, in which he called on the Cubans to stand with the United States and the West in the event of an East-West conflict, Castro attacked Figueres and asserted that Cuba was confronted by a conspiracy of vested interests, and that the American "trusts" had killed ten times more Cubans than Batista's tyranny.

THE UNITED STATES TRIP

Yet in April, when he went to the United States on the request of the American Society of Newspaper Editors, Castro still did not seem to have decided on a course of action toward the United States. Before he left, he told the Cubans that he intended to seek credits from the World Bank and, perhaps, from the International Monetary Fund. He took along his principal economic advisors, and plans were made to develop forty new industries in which United States investors might be interested.

The trip resulted from the invitation of a private group, and when Castro arrived in Washington, President Eisenhower was "out of town," playing golf. Castro met alone with Vice-President Nixon, and he later recalled that, "I simply limited myself to explaining the realities of my country and . . . demonstrating that the measures which we were going to take, some of which affected North American interests, were just." After the meeting, Nixon wrote a memo indicating that he was convinced that Castro was "either incredibly naive about Communism or under Communist discipline." Three months later, Nixon began to urge the arming of Cuban exiles to overthrow Castro.

When Castro returned from the meeting with Nixon, he told one of his economic advisors that, "we have to stop the executions and the infiltration" (of Communists), and in May, he told a Havana newspaper that his "personal impressions were good." In 1977, he told an American newspaper editor that the interview had concluded with a Nixon promise that, "We will work together."[10]

In his speech to the newspaper editors, Castro denied that he had any intention of confiscating foreign private industry since Cuba sought foreign investment as a source of increased employment. His economic advisors held conversations with the State Department and the secretary of the treasury, but on Castro's direct instructions (he seems to have changed his mind on this), they did not ask for economic assistance—although Castro's treasury secretary later claimed that the assistant secretary of state had offered aid. Raúl Castro was not on the trip, nor was Guevara, but Castro's brother telephoned him during the trip warning him not to be seduced by the Americans. After a triumphal tour of the East Coast, Fidel met Raúl in Houston and flew to South America for the meeting of the Organization of American States (OAS) in Buenos Aires.[11]

In Buenos Aires, Castro suggested that the United States initiate a ten-year, $30 billion program of economic assistance to Latin America, insisting that, "we are not opposed to private investment." He indicated, however, a preference for investment by domestic firms. International investors, he maintained, would tend to avoid areas in which profits were less secure because uncertainties could result from social conflicts "that stem from hunger, poverty, and unsatisfied need."[12] The $30 billion figure was seen as astronomical by the American delegation, and those suspicious of Castro assumed that he had proposed it in order to provoke an American rejection. That figure, however, was not far out of line with the $20 billion figure proposed at the Alliance for Progress meeting less than two years later (although only half of it was to come from governmental sources). Castro's proposed program seemed to indicate a willingness to accept American investment and aid – but only on his own terms.

THE AGRARIAN REFORM LAW

Ambassador Bonsal met Castro on his return to Havana in early May, and they had a friendly talk. They did not see each other again until a month later, and in the interim one of the decisive factors in the deterioration of United States-Cuban relations emerged – the adoption of the 1959 Agrarian Reform Law, which directly affected large tracts of American-owned land.

Some American property had already been adversely affected by the Castro reforms. In March, the Cuban government canceled the 1957 telephone rate increase and appointed an "intervertor" to investigate the company's economic affairs. The American-owned electric company was also ordered to reduce its rural rates by 50 percent. However, neither the companies nor the State Department interpreted these actions as justifying an official protest.

The Agrarian Reform Law, adopted on May 17, 1959, was stronger than the one Castro proposed in 1953, promising distribution of land titles in small plots to sharecroppers, tenants, and squatters. Yet it was not collectivist in its content. The 1959 law set an upper limit of 995 acres on landholding by any one person, but allowed exceptions of up to 3,300 acres for particularly productive sugar and rice plantations and cattle ranches. Compensation was to be based on the 1958 declared value for municipal tax purposes and was to be paid in twenty-year bonds at 4.5 percent interest. Expropriated lands were to be transformed into agrarian cooperatives under the administration of the Institute of Agrarian Reform (INRA) or distributed as family-sized holdings of 66.4 acres. The law also provided for the expropriation of lands under the 995-acre maximum, if necessary, to provide previously promised land for squatters and tenants. One provision, aimed directly at the American-owned sugar lands, specified that corporations could not own sugar plantations unless every stock-holder was a Cuban citizen. However, it was later announced that the expropriation of the sugar lands would be delayed until the middle of 1960, after the sugar harvest for the following year was completed. Thus, the principal American-owned agricultural properties initially affected were in activities other than sugar.

Early in June, Senator Smathers of Florida first raised the question of the possibility of cutting the United States quota for the import of Cuban sugar. Under the quota system (established, as Castro pointed out, to make it economically possible for United States cane and sugar beet producers to supply part of the American market), the United States was currently allocating 38 percent of its sugar imports to Cuba at a support price of 5.25 cents a pound—well above the world market price of about 3 cents. The quota amounted to a subsidy of sugar producers in Cuba (one-third of them American), and in return, Cuba gave preferential tariff rates to American imports. The guaranteed price also provided a steady and secure income for Cuba in a world market characterized by violent price oscillations.

On June 11, the State Department sent a note to the Cuban government. Although it expressed sympathy for "the objectives which the Government of Cuba is presumed to be seeking," and recognized that "under international law a state has a right to take property within its jurisdiction for public purposes," and that "soundly conceived and executed programs for rural better-ment, including agrarian reform in certain areas, can contribute to a higher standard of living, political stability, and social prog-ress," the note reminded the Cubans that international law re-quired "payment of prompt, adequate, and effective compensa-tion," observing that the wording of the Agrarian Reform Law gave the United States government "serious concern with regard to the adequacy of the compensation to its citizens whose prop-erty may be expropriated." In addition, the note recalled that the 1940 Cuban constitution, under which the investments had been made, required prior payment in cash for expropriated land and the establishment of its value by a court. (The final section of the Agrarian Reform Law made the law a part of the constitution, thus repealing the constitutional requirement of compensation in cash.) The reference to the 1940 constitutional provision in the State Department note is the basis for later assertions that the United States demanded cash payment for all expropriations of United States property. However, Ambassador Bonsal has stated that the United States embassy discussed the compensation question with Cuban officials, including the possibility of payment in "long-term bonds that would be marketable and would be payable in dollars if desired." Bonsal had been trying to see Castro for over a month, and finally, as a result of the note, a meeting took place in which Castro indicated that he still felt that American investment could contribute to Cuban development. A Cuban reply to the State Department note, delivered a few days later, was principally devoted to a defense of compensation in bonds rather than in cash. The reference to cash compensation, in the note of June 11, may have had an important impact on Castro, for he later remarked that the American reaction to the Agrarian Reform Law persuaded him that "there was no possibility of accommodation with the United States." However, aside from the fact that a protest referring to payment in cash was sent *before* the expropriations had even begun (possibly as a means of securing an interview with Castro), the United States reaction did not seem to be excessive. Castro had never concealed his intention to carry out an extensive agrarian reform — and United States policymakers were well aware of those intentions. But the tradition of the demand for "prompt, adequate, and effective" compensation and of American paternalism toward Cuba led the State Department to issue a statement that appears to have confirmed Castro's suspicions that the United States was exclusively concerned with protecting the property of its nationals, which would be affected by his reforms. Whether it was a result of his trip or of the United States reaction to agrarian reform, after May Castro never again publicly criticized Communism and the Cuban Communist party, as he had done in previous months.[13]

The take-over of land was carried out enthusiastically by members of INRA, with little or no regard for the provisions of the law. The bonds that had been authorized were never printed, and when Ambassador Bonsal met the new Cuban Foreign Minister on July 23, he complained of the "hostile atmosphere" surrounding the relations of the government and the American-owned telephone and electric companies. In late June, citing Communist infiltration of the revolution, Major Pedro Díaz Lanz resigned as head of the Cuban Air Force and fled to Miami. Two weeks later, he repeated his charges of Communist infiltration before the United States Internal Security Committee in Washington. During the same week, Castro attacked the Cuban president, Manuel Urrutia, accusing him of "fabricating the legend of Communism," and feigned resignation of his post as prime minister in order to force Urrutia out of office. He followed this with a mass rally on July 26, attended by 500,000 people, that he described as "pure democracy," and superior to the electoral process.

Despite Bonsal's repeated efforts to see him, Castro's next meeting with the ambassador, after their first discussion in early June, did not take place until September 3. Bonsal, once again, brought up the land seizures and the problems of the American-owned utilities (electricity rates had been reduced by 30 percent during the summer and the American and Foreign Power Company protested that the new rates would lead to a loss of $13 million by its Cuban subsidiary). Bonsal described Castro as "reasonable and friendly" but noncommittal and noted that, in response to the ambassador's complaint about his difficulties in seeing him, Castro promised that he could have an interview at any time on twenty-four hours' notice. Bonsal was optimistic after the interview. He found that the Cubans were making an effort to improve relations. Castro renewed his promise to hold elections in four years, and in a speech delivered on September 17, he specifically referred to Cuba's need for private enterprise and its desire to discuss with the United States the problems produced by the land reform. On the part of the State Department, Bonsal later wrote, "there was a disposition to continue a policy of patience, or, as some put it, to give Castro more rope." The latter description was used by those who believed that Castro was dangerous but favored postponing action against him until other Latin Americans came to the same conclusion. At the same time, continuing pressure was put on the State Department by Americans affected by the Castro reforms to take a stronger anti-Castro line; and important policymakers responded to those pressures. One of the affected interests was the King Ranch of Texas, whose $3 million worth of cattle ranching properties were being taken over. Key policymakers, such as R. Richard Rubottom, assistant secretary of state for Latin America, Thomas C. Mann, undersecretary of state for economic affairs and Rubottom's successor in 1960, and Robert B. Anderson, secretary of the treasury and close confidant of President Eisenhower, were all from Texas and sympathetic to the King Ranch complaints. Rubottom later recalled that the discussion of possible actions against Castro began after the Agrarian Reform Law was adopted and American protests went unheeded. According to Rubottom, in September 1959, serious consideration began to be given to cutting the Cuban sugar quota and arming the anti-Castro exiles.

THE REORIENTATION OF THE REVOLUTION

On October 11, three firebombs were dropped on a Cuban sugar mill by a plane that had departed from Florida. As early as March 1959, the Batista exiles had formed an anti-Castro organization in Miami, but the October flights represented the first real effort by anti-Castro Cubans using military equipment. The flights must have reminded Castro of the Guatemalan affair, particularly since, like Arbenz, he was having trouble acquiring arms owing to United States opposition. Ironically, on the next day, October 12, the United States delivered a reply to the Cuban government's June 15 defense of the Agrarian Reform Law. The United States repeated its claim that Cuba was obligated to pay full compensation under international law and its own constitution; it rejected Cuba's comparison of its reform to the United States-imposed agrarian reform in postwar Japan under which payment had been made in bonds. The United States thus seemed, once again, to be insisting on payment in cash.[14]

On October 15, Raúl Castro was named minister for the armed

forces, and a pro-Communist army captain was appointed head of the agrarian reform in the province of Camaguey. Reacting to these appointments, Huber Matos, military governor of the province, resigned his post, and in a public letter to Castro "as one of your comrades of the Sierra — as one of those who set out determined to die in carrying out your orders," warned him of Communist infiltration of the revolution. Matos's resignation coincided with another bombing flight from Florida, and Castro reacted to it by going personally to Camaguey to arrest Matos "as a traitor who had obstructed the Agrarian Reform." (In December Matos was sentenced to twenty years in jail for treason after a trial in which Castro himself delivered a seven-hour speech for the prosecution.) The next day, two more Florida-based planes flew over Havana dropping leaflets signed by Díaz Lanz accusing Castro of being a Communist. At a mass rally in Havana, Castro denounced the foreign aggression, implying that the United States government had supported the bombing of the Cuban capital. The Cuban government also published a pamphlet entitled *Cuba's Pearl Harbor*, with a doctored photograph on the cover purporting to show an air battle over Havana. The United States protested the anti-American campaign, arrested Díaz Lanz, and announced strict measures to prevent such flights in the future.

The arrest of Matos led to the resignation, in November, of three of the moderate members of Castro's cabinet (a fourth, the treasury minister, resigned four months later), and the appointment of Che Guevara as head of the National Bank. Seizure of foreign-owned land was stepped up, often ignoring the provisions of the Agrarian Reform Law, and a 60 percent royalty was imposed on foreign oil companies. The government seized the records of the oil companies and required them to drill on their concessions or lose them. In addition, a law was promulgated allowing the government to take over, through intervention, any companies that were in financial difficulties or had reduced production. In November, contacts were made in Mexico with the Soviet vice-premier, Anastas Mikoyan, and in December a correspondent for the Soviet news agency, TASS, arrived in Havana.

LOST OPPORTUNITIES

The cabinet reorganization led Ambassador Bonsal to conclude that there was no "further possibility of rational dialogue between our two governments." However in January an effort was made at a rapprochement. It began badly. The State Department issued a press release on January 11 summarizing a note that had been delivered to the Cuban Foreign Ministry protesting the Cuban seizure, confiscation, and occupation of American-owned land, buildings, and equipment "without any sanction in Cuban law, without written authority . . . and without court orders." The next day incendiary bombs were dropped by Florida-based planes on seven sugarcane fields. On television on January 21, Castro denounced the United States note in such extreme terms that the ambassador was recalled to Washington for consultation. While there, he drafted a statement of United States policy toward Cuba which Eisenhower delivered on January 26. It expressed the United States government's hope that its citizens could continue to make constructive contributions to the Cuban economy through their investments and insisted that the United States would "continue to bring to the attention of the Cuban government instances in which the rights of its citizens under Cuban law and international law have been disregarded and in which redress under Cuban law is apparently unavailable or denied." The note concluded that the government "has confidence in the ability of the Cuban people to recognize and defeat the intrigues of international Communism."

In late January, discussions concerning improved relations were initiated, through the mediation of the Argentine ambassador to Cuba. However, they foundered when the United States rejected Foreign Minister Roa's precondition that no unilateral measures against Cuba were to be taken by the United States while the negotiations were in progress. Roa was referring, of course, to a possible cut in the Cuban sugar quota, which Secretary of State Herter had mentioned in December and a number of United States senators favored. In mid-March, a final behind-the-scenes effort at mediation was made. It centered around a

United States offer of technical assistance and military aid to protect Cuba from the Florida-based flights. On March 17, it was rejected by President Dorticos on behalf of Castro.

THE SOVIET TRADE AGREEMENT

The American attempt to improve relations with Cuba may have been related to United States knowledge of the impending arrival in Havana of Anastas Mikoyan for trade talks. After ten days of negotiations, on February 13, 1960, the Soviet Union announced that it had agreed to buy from Cuba 425,000 tons of sugar in 1960 and 1 million tons of sugar each year for the four following years at the world price of three cents a pound, paying 20 percent of the purchase price in dollars and the rest in Soviet goods. The Soviet Union also granted Cuba a $100 million credit at 2.5 percent interest, to be repaid over twelve years, that was to be used for the purchase of machinery, equipment, and raw materials, including crude and refined petroleum. Cuba had found an alternative market for part of its sugar crop, in the event that the United States sugar quota was cut, and a source for petroleum.

Cuba also needed a supplier of arms to defend itself from the invasion that Castro seems to have decided, now and probably earlier, was likely. Whether an arms deal was discussed in the negotiations with Mikoyan is not known, although Che Guevara urged such an agreement and in *Guerrilla Warfare,* written at about this time, he advocated such a course. The joint communiqué issued at the end of Mikoyan's visit also referred to the intention of both governments "to collaborate actively in the UN." It did not discuss the possibility of opening diplomatic relations. On February 15, the United States embassy concluded that the visit was a "long step toward putting [Cuba] definitely in the Soviet camp" and that "there is little further hope that the United States will be able to reach a satisfactory relationship with the Cuban government as presently constituted." Although it opposed "drastic measures at this time," the embassy recommended that the United States "concentrate on devising a means to correct the present intolerable state of affairs."[15]

THE DECISION TO OVERTHROW CASTRO

The Assassination Report of the Senate Select Committee on Intelligence Activities, published in 1975, pinpoints the exact date when the Eisenhower administration decided to adopt drastic measures—the overthrow of the Cuban government. Some have speculated that the flights from Florida, which began in October 1959, were provoked or assisted by the Central Intelligence Agency. However, the Assassination Report indicates that "apparently" the CIA Special Group first discussed the overthrow of Castro on January 31, 1960. According to the minutes of the meeting, Allen Dulles, the head of the CIA, "suggested that covert contingency planning to accomplish the fall of the Castro government might be in order." Yet as late as March 9, Secretary of State Herter stated at a press conference that President Eisenhower "had repeatedly rejected" the cutting of Cuba's sugar quota.[16] One day later, however, the National Security Council (NSC) discussed the adoption of an American policy to "bring another government to power in Cuba." The NSC was informed that a plan "to effect [sic] the situation in Cuba was being worked on" by the CIA, and in fact, on March 14, a plan was discussed by the CIA Special Group that involved "sabotage, economic sanctions, propaganda, and training of a Cuban exile group for possible invasion."[17] On March 17, without Ambassador Bonsal's knowledge, President Eisenhower approved the CIA plan. The arming and training of Cuban anti-Castro exiles was begun. On March 30, Castro accused the United States of attempting to overthrow his government, using the same methods it had used in Guatemala, and on May 1, he correctly noted that the training of an exile invasion force had been initiated.

Why did the United States change its Cuban policy at this time? The trade pact with the Soviet Union may have influenced the decision, but the USSR had bought sugar from Cuba before, and the Russians had been careful to limit their commitments to Cuba. In fact, diplomatic relations were not established between Cuba and the USSR until May. The Russian reluctance to get embroiled in a Cuban-American conflict may have been related to the "spirit of Camp David" and the upcoming Summit Conference. It may simply have been a recognition that Cuba lay in the United States sphere of influence and the expectation that if Castro went too far the United States would act as it had in Guatemala — it would eliminate a hostile government from the Caribbean.

The Guatemalan precedent seems to be relevant in explaining United States policy. The arming of exiles and economic pressure had worked before, and it was assumed that it would work again. The reasoning behind the plan, however, ignored the important differences between the situations of Arbenz and Castro — it did not recognize Castro's enormous popular support and his control of the armed forces.[18] In addition, the United States believed the Russians would not move to support Castro because of their interest in improved American-Russian relations. In addition, anti-Castro stories related by Cuban exiles in Miami and the American talk of "giving Castro enough rope to hang himself" or "putting him through the wringer" made it easy to believe in the possibility of his overthrow as a result of economic pressures and external and internal discontent.

What was the relation of Castro's expropriations to the United States actions? The Assassination Report quotes a memorandum dated December 11, 1959, from the head of the CIA's Western Hemisphere Division, that refers to the dangers to United States holdings in other Latin American countries if the "far left" dictatorship in Cuba remained in power. Government policymakers, both publicly and privately, seem to have been motivated by opposition to communism rather than the threat to American property, but key individual policymakers were influenced by the take-overs of American-owned agricultural properties without compensation. In the few meetings between the United States ambassador and Castro, the principal topic seems to have been the defense of American property interests. When the Florida-based planes began to appear over Cuba and Castro found it difficult to secure arms as a result of American pressures, this seemed to confirm his belief that American policy was dominated by the "trusts." When he aligned himself increasingly with the USSR in order to defend himself against a possible invasion, his actions produced precisely what he was attempting to avoid. The conclusion is, therefore, that United States policy in defense of American investments was a contributing factor to Castro's decision to seek Soviet support, which, in turn, helped to produce a United States decision to overthrow him.

THE SUGAR QUOTA CUT

If the decision to overthrow Castro was made in March, it was not immediately evident from United States actions. However, the decision made in July to cut the sugar quota was based on the policy adopted in March of using economic pressures to force Castro out of power. It was hoped that popular discontent, with or without an exile intervention, would lead to his overthrow.

In April, the first shipments of Soviet oil arrived under the February trade agreement. Some of it could be refined in the small Cuban refinery, which had been taken over by the Castro government because the owner had collaborated with Batista. However, the Cuban government, citing the savings from the lower price at which the oil was acquired, also ordered the Esso, Texaco, and Shell refineries to refine the oil. The companies argued that they had no legal obligation to do so and that the quality of the Soviet oil was such that expensive alterations would have to be made in the refineries. Although Ambassador Bonsal assumed that the oil companies would eventually accede under protest, he was informed in early June by an Esso executive that the companies had been told by the Treasury Department, with the agreement of the State Department, that a refusal to refine the oil was "in accord with the policy of the United States government," and that this information was also being transmitted to the Shell Company in London. On June 7, the three companies formally refused to refine the Soviet oil. A few days earlier, the State Department had also announced that the United States programs of economic assistance and military training for Cuba were being terminated.

The Cuban government "intervened" the three refineries three weeks later, following a trip by Raúl Castro to Czechoslovakia to secure arms and presumably after they had been assured of adequate oil supplies by the Soviets. They proceeded to refine the oil without the technical difficulties that had been predicted by the companies. Earlier congressional opposition to giving the president the power to cut the Cuban sugar quota now evaporated, and the appropriate committees quickly approved an administration bill giving the president the power. The final version passed both houses on July 5 — four days after *Wall Street Journal* wrote an editorial which compared Cuba's Castro with Iran's Mossadegh and predicted a similar fate for him.

On July 6, President Eisenhower eliminated virtually the entire balance of the Cuban sugar allotment for 1960, claiming that future sugar supplies were uncertain because of Cuban commitments to the Soviet Union. Why he took such a drastic step, a step that the *New York Times* found "more severe than had been generally expected," appeared puzzling at the time. It becomes more comprehensible within the context of the earlier NSC decision to attempt Castro's overthrow which was made in the belief that the USSR was unlikely to supply Cuba with enough petroleum for its needs. It is true that the Soviet Union did not have enough oceangoing oil tankers to supply Cuba, but it bought or leased tankers from other countries and expanded its own tanker fleet.[19] The estimate that the USSR would not be willing to make the kind of massive economic commitment that would be required to save Cuba from economic collapse may have been correct in March, when the initial decision to attempt Castro's overthrow was made, but by July, after the breakdown of the Paris Summit Conference over the U-2 incident and in the midst of a polemic between the USSR and China, it was no longer valid. The cut in the sugar quota followed the take-over of the oil refineries but seems to have been more than simply a reprisal for the refinery seizures. It was an act of economic warfare aimed at "a change of government" in Cuba.

NATIONALIZATION LAW 851

Castro's reaction was to make good on his June 29 threat to retaliate against a sugar quota cut by seizing "all Yankee property down to the nails in their shoes." The Moa Bay nickel refinery had been intervened in March because it had announced that it was ceasing production. Two American-owned hotels had experienced a similar fate in June, American-owned agrarian and cattle-raising properties belonging to United Fruit, the King Ranch, and others had been taken over under the agrarian reform, and the American-owned sugar lands were scheduled to be expropriated imminently. Yet there had been no indication up to this point of the wholesale nationalization of American industrial and commercial properties in Cuba. However, just before Eisenhower announced the cut in the Cuban sugar quota, the Cuban cabinet adopted Law 851 authorizing the nationalization, if "convenient to the national interest," of all American-owned property in Cuba. It established payment in bonds from a fund that was to be created by depositing in a special dollar account 25 percent of all dollar income accruing from sales to the United States in excess of 3 million tons at a price of no less than 5.75 cents per pound (the current United States support price). Since the Cuban quota had been almost completely eliminated, and since before the cut the quota had only been 119,000 tons above the 3 million mark, it was clear that no compensation would be forthcoming for the expropriated properties. As in the agrarian reform, the compensation bonds (the law provided for 30-year bonds at 2 percent interest) were never printed. The law, however, was not totally without significance because it left open the possibility for a negotiated settlement of the compensation for expropriated property — particularly since in the 1970s world sugar prices rose well beyond the 1960 United States support price.

The decision to take over the vast United States properties in Cuba appears to have been a personal one on Castro's part since no one else in Cuba, including the Communist party — which often urged prudence in extending nationalization[20] — is on record as favoring such a drastic course of action at that time. But once that decision was made and assurances of Soviet economic and military support (including a promise made on July 9 by Khrushchev of "figurative" support by Soviet rockets, if necessary) had been received, the socialization of the Cuban economy proceeded rapidly. In late July, lands belonging to three large American-owned sugar mills were taken over, and, in early August, thirty-six American-owned sugar mills, the intervened United States oil refineries, American-owned marketing systems, as well as the two utilities were nationalized. In September, three American-owned private banks were expropriated; the remaining private banks were taken over in October. (The two Canadian-owned banks were exempted and later paid for in cash because Castro wished to remain in the good graces of the Canadians.) On October 13, 1960, Law 890 expropriated 382 enterprises, including subsidiaries of Procter and Gamble, Swift, Du Pont, Sherwin-Williams, and sixteen other United States companies. A day later, an Urban Reform Law was promulgated that canceled all existing mortgages on urban real estate, many of them held by American-owned financial institutions.

THE EMBARGO AND FURTHER NATIONALIZATIONS

The State Department responded to Nationalization Law 851 by sending a formal protest asserting that it was in violation of international law because of its "discriminatory, arbitrary, and confiscatory" character in singling out the property of United States nationals for expropriation with no provision for a legal appeal. It said that the measure failed to meet "the most minimum criteria to assure payment of prompt, adequate, and effective compensation." On October 20 the United States imposed an immediate embargo on all American exports to Cuba, except for medicine and certain foods, declaring that this action was a response to Cuba's discriminatory policies against United States exports and to its seizures of American property. In retaliation, the Cubans nationalized 166 more American-owned hotels and insurance companies, the Nicaro Nickel plant (partly owned by the United States government), subsidiaries of Sears, Roebuck, Woolworth, International Harvester, Coca-Cola, and many other companies. Although this surge of nationalization began as retaliation against the United States, it was soon extended to other foreign-and Cuban-owned properties. By early 1961, 75 percent of Cuban industry and 30 percent of its agriculture were state-owned.[21]

In December President Eisenhower fixed the Cuban sugar quota for the first quarter of 1961 at zero, and in early January, when Castro demanded that the embassy staff be reduced to eighteen members, diplomatic relations were broken by the United States. Castro made some tentative overtures to President Kennedy at the time of his inauguration, but Kennedy did not respond favorably. His reaction was based on several factors: his public support of the Cuban "freedom fighters" during the 1960 election campaign, a deep, personal animosity against the Caribbean *caudillo* who had called him an "illiterate millionaire," and his father's intense hostility toward Castro. Most important, Kennedy knew that the CIA-sponsored Bay of Pigs invasion was in the final stages of preparation.

The Cuban invasion of April 17, 1961, described by Theodore Draper as "one of those rare politico-military events – a perfect failure," enabled Castro to destroy what remained of the domestic resistance to his rule, and in a public speech after the invasion he proclaimed for the first time that the Cuban revolution was "socialist."[22] In April, the United States announced that the American market was closed to Cuban exports, and in June it placed further restrictions on the shipment of foodstuffs to that country. In June, Castro took over all the private schools in Cuba, including those operated by American religious orders. In February 1962 a total American embargo on trade was imposed, and in 1963 Cuban assets that remained in the United States were frozen, and all dollar transactions with Cuba were prohibited. The break with Castro was complete.

NATIONALIZATION AND UNITED STATES-CUBAN RELATIONS

The Cuban case poses most dramatically some of the central problems involved in the conflict over nationalization of foreign investment. The defense by the American government of the claims of its investors to prompt, adequate, and effective compensation was a contributing factor in the deterioration of relations between the two countries between 1959 and 1961. In assessing its role in that process, one must attempt to determine the relative weight of strategic and economic considerations on the American side. Correspondingly, on the Cuban side, the relative roles of ideology and power politics in Castro's decision to radicalize his revolution and to align Cuba with the Soviet Union must be examined.

In considering American motives, it might be useful to ask whether United States policy would have been different if there had been no American investments in Cuba. If we look at the overthrow of Mossadegh in Iran in 1953 for instance, the record, as documented by policy papers and testimony published in 1974 by the Senate Subcommittee on Multinational Corporations, indicates that strategic interests predominated. No United States property was involved; indeed, the American oil companies needed special inducements to enter Iran after Mossadegh's overthrow. In Guatemala, as well, although motives seem to have been more mixed, a Communist-dominated regime in Guatemala was seen as a strategic threat to the Panama Canal, particularly if its weak and unstable neighbors followed suit. It seems likely that, even if United Fruit lands had not been taken over by Arbenz, the United States, at the height of the McCarthy period, would have worked against a government in which there was an increasingly strong Communist role in an area considered to be of vital interest to the United States.[23]

The Cuban case is more complex. While there were anti-Castro pressures within the foreign policy establishment as early as the summer of 1959 after the implementation of the Agrarian Reform Law, American policy did not shift to outright hostility to Castro until March 1960. And in March, the defense of American property interests was of less concern than were Castro's increasing reliance of the Cuban Communist party and his emerging alliance with the Soviet Union.

However, Castro's decision to forge that alliance appears to have been made earlier, probably in October 1959. In making that decision his perception, based on the Guatemalan precedent, that United States policy was dominated by the defense of property interests and that the United States government would attempt to subvert any government that threatened United States property, became a self-fulfilling prophecy. The 1959 Agrarian Reform Law, then, becomes important because the State Department protest, which followed almost immediately, however diplomatic and even sympathetic its wording, was seen by Castro as the beginning of a reenactment of the Guatemalan experience. When that protest was coupled with the continuing arms embargo, and, in October the initiation of firebombing and leaflet raids from Florida, it seemed that the parallel was too perfect. It is true that the protest was standard diplomatic procedure for the State Department, that the arms embargo was an effort to discourage Castro's continuing forays in the Caribbean, and that the flights were not part of official policy — although conceivably, despite the lack of evidence turned up by the Senate Select Committee, there may have been CIA connivance at the local level — yet this is not how Castro viewed United States actions. One element in the tragic escalation of tension between the two countries was thus the continuing insistence by a conservative American administration upon prompt, adequate, and effective compensation for expropriated property. The United States made this the most important, if not only, item on its Cuban policy agenda.

A number of other points in the initial State Department response to the agrarian reform are also open to criticism. First, it *appeared* to be insisting on compensation in cash — even if it was not actually doing so. The reference in the note to the Cuban constitution of 1940 seemed to repeat the arguments made to the Mexicans that investors should be guaranteed that the legal context in which their investments are made would remain immutable. In addition, the note alluded critically to the provisions for compensation on the basis of past tax declarations. However, if the investors have benefited by low tax assessments, it may be argued that they should be satisfied with lower compensation in the event of nationalization. In any case, the "prompt, adequate, and effective" formula seems once again to have been unworkable.

For the Cubans, the move to the Soviet Union seems to have been both a strategic and an ideological shift. Castro could have continued to play the nationalist game, as he did in his first six months in power,[24] but then he could not count on Soviet support against the United States. By October 1959 he seems to have been convinced that only an alignment with the USSR would supply him with the arms and petroleum he needed in the event that the United States tried to overthrow him. If there had been no American property in Cuba, he might not have made the same calculation — but, given Cuba's strategic location, if for geopolitical reasons he had made the decision to align Cuba with the Soviet Union, it seems likely that American hostility and opposition would have been just as great.

United States opposition to the nationalization of American companies was thus an important contributing factor to the increasingly anti-American stance of the Cuban Revolution, which in turn produced an American decision to attempt Castro's overthrow. Most of the Cuban nationalizations, however, were the result rather than the cause of the worsening of relations between the United States and Cuba, since the bulk of American property was taken over in the last half of 1960 in reprisal for the sugar quota cut in July and the trade embargo in October. The cut in the sugar quota (which, at the time, appeared to be an overreaction by Washington to Castro's intervention of foreign oil refineries) was based on an earlier decision to attempt to overthrow Castro, which was itself a response to Castro's moves to seek Soviet support rather than to his economic reforms. Ironically, the resulting take-over of over $1 billion in American property accelerated the movement toward Communism and the socialization of the Cuban economy that the American policy had been trying to prevent. The process was much more rapid than it had been in either the Soviet Union or China, and United States policy was partially responsible.

POSTNATIONALIZATION PROBLEMS

From an economic point of view, the first eighteen months of the revolution had been a success. The redistribution of income resulting from the measures limiting rents and utility charges and from agrarian reform produced additional purchasing power that stimulated the depressed Cuban economy. The foreign exchange problems that developed in 1960 were resolved through Soviet economic assistance, especially in the supply of oil and in the purchase of sugar.

Running the newly nationalized economy, however, was and continued to be a problem. Since its inception, INRA, the agrarian reform agency, had been operated without any attempt at cost accounting. If a zonal chief needed money he applied for and received credits from the central office. Young and inexperienced managers took over the nationalized firms. When the Freeport Sulphur Company withdrew its personnel from the Moa Bay nickel plant, the new manager of the plant was a twenty-two-year-old former student of engineering at Tulane University, and the chief engineer was 28. The new head of the former Procter and Gamble plant was a physician who knew some chemistry. As the embargo took effect, replacement parts became impossible to obtain, except from Europe or Canada. Processing equipment for Russian oil and wheat had to be altered, and raw materials that had been obtained from the United States had to be secured from the Eastern-bloc countries. Rice, a staple of the Cuban diet, was now imported from China, rather than New Orleans. Thus, there were serious management, technical, and supply problems as a result of the sudden transformation of the economy.[25]

CONTROL OF LABOR

Since the state was the chief employer, the labor unions, accustomed to making demands (*reivindicaciones*) on their employers, had to be brought under control. The process had already begun in November 1959 with the imposition of a Castro-dictated unity slate at the Confederation of Cuban Workers (CTC) congress. Thereafter, "anti-unity" labor leaders were purged from the unions. In May 1960, the general secretary of the Confederation, David Salvador, was removed and later imprisoned. At the next CTC congress in November 1961, a single list of candidates was presented to all unions, headed by Lázaro Peña, an old-time Partido Socialista Popular (PSP) member who, ironically, had been CTC chief during the period in the 1940s when the Communists had supported Batista. In June 1961, Che Guevara announced that workers did not have the right to strike. In August, a new labor law stated that the duty of labor unions was to fulfill the production plans of the nation and to organize and carry out political education activities. At the next CTC Congress in 1966, new responsibilities were added to the list of duties: the organization of "socialist emulation," voluntary labor, and the strict application of work quotas, wage scales, and labor discipline. By 1969, Carlos Rafael Rodríguez, a member of Castro's cabinet, could admit that "the unions are transmission belts of the Party directives to the workers but have insufficiently represented the workers to the Party or to the Revolutionary Government."[26]

CENTRALIZED ECONOMIC DECISIONMAKING

Following the nationalizations, the government proceeded on a course of rapid centralization of economic decisionmaking. A Central Planning Board (Junta Central de Planificacion, JUCE-PLAN) was established in February 1961, with Fidel Castro its chairman and Raúl Castro its vice-chairman. Che Guevara was placed in charge of a newly created Ministry of Industries that was to direct a four-year plan to industrialize the country and eliminate its dependence on sugar. Exchange controls had only been imposed in late 1960, and the first shortages of consumer goods and food, created by an increase in consumer demand, the rapid economic changes, and the United States embargo, began to appear in mid-1961. When basic foodstuffs were affected by the shortage in early 1962, rationing was introduced. As a result of the rationing system, the upper and middle classes, including the urban workers, probably ate less well, but those in the countryside and small children (who were allowed a liter of milk per day) benefited.

It soon became apparent that the hastily drawn up industrialization plan was completely unworkable. Cuba's balance-of-payments deficit jumped to $238 million in 1962 and $323 million in 1963, while its sugar crop dropped to 4.8 million tons in 1962 and 3.8 million tons in 1963. Part of the problem was attributable to the conversion of the sugar cooperatives into state farms in 1961. The Second Agrarian Reform in 1963, which extended the area of state ownership to 70 percent of Cuban agriculture, did not help. When Castro returned from a visit to the Soviet Union in May 1963, he announced that the industrialization drive was to be postponed and renewed emphasis was to be placed on the production of sugar and tobacco. Since the deficit in the Cuban balance of trade was made up almost entirely by credits from the Soviet Union, the Soviets seem to have made it clear that a reversal of economic policy was a precondition for further economic assistance.[27]

MORAL INCENTIVES AND BUREAUCRATIC CENTRALISM

The ensuing period, from 1963 to 1970, was characterized by an emphasis on moral incentives and "socialist emulation" as the spur to production in industry and agriculture. This plan was combined with continued centralization of decisionmaking and planning in the government ministries in Havana and, especially, in the person of Fidel Castro. But sugar production did not improve, and despite a massive investment effort estimated in the late 1960s at 31 percent of gross national product (GNP), the economy stagnated—indeed, on a per capita basis it declined—and Cuba slipped from fourth to twelfth among the Latin American nations in per capita GNP between 1960 and 1972. Sympathetic socialist visitors from other countries were critical of the excessive centralization, bureaucratization, and militarization of the economy, but Castro continued to pursue a policy that he proclaimed would outstrip the Soviet Union in arriving at Communism. In the mid-1960s, Castro engaged in a polemic with the other Communist parties of Latin America and criticized the Soviet Union for its assistance to "the Latin American oligarchies." However, when the Soviet government reacted by slowing down oil deliveries in late 1967 (leading to the introduction of gasoline rationing in Cuba in January 1968) and by delaying the signature of a new economic agreement, Castro muted his criticisms and a few months later gave public support to the Soviet invasion of Czechoslovakia that was criticized by Communist leaders in Western Europe. No clearer evidence could be given of the dependence of Cuba on Soviet economic assistance.[28]

The pattern of bureaucratic centralism modeled on the Soviet Union was intensified in 1968, when 56,000 small service, repair, retail, and handicraft private businesses were nationalized. Street vendors were eliminated and lines at food shops lengthened, while absenteeism in industry increased as moral incentives and peer pressure provided insufficient motivation to come to work.

The emphasis on moral incentives reached its culmination in 1970, with the failure of a massive countrywide campaign to reach Castro's announced goal of a 10-million-ton sugar harvest. In a remarkably detailed and frank analysis of the problems of the Cuban economy, Fidel Castro's speech of July 26, 1970, gave graphic illustrations of the inefficiency and disorganization produced by the overcentralization of the economy. Castro took personal responsibility for the failure of the harvest to reach its goal.[29] While the concentration on the sugar harvest ultimately produced 8.5 million tons, a new record, it also led to massive dislocations in the rest of the economy and a sharp drop in economic growth.

ECONOMIC AND POLITICAL INSTITUTIONALIZATION

In September 1970, an "antiloafing" law was passed to deal with the mounting problem of absenteeism, estimated at 20 percent of the work force. Efforts were initiated to mechanize the sugar harvest, rather than to rely on the mobilization of "volunteers" for the harvest which had proved wasteful and inefficient. In early 1971, following a visit by the head of the Soviet Planning Agency (Gosplan), a system of enterprise cost accounting was introduced. As a result, Cuban state enterprises received limited autonomy in investment decisionmaking and control over certain associated activities such as transport. In addition, factories were permitted to run their own housing construction programs through the so-called minibrigades of workers detached from the factory to carry out specific construction efforts, material incentives were reintroduced with payment for overtime and hazardous work, and consumer durables, such as refrigerators, television sets, and washing machines, were distributed on the basis of need and merit as determined by one's fellow workers. In November and December 1970, union elections were held, and in many cases, more than one candidate was nominated for each position. In 1973, the first CTC Congress since 1966 approved (by 99 percent) a program providing for increased worker participation in the discussion of draft labor laws and, through monthly "production assemblies," in decisions on production—although not on salaries, hiring, and investment. The Congress also formally approved the use of material incentives as an application of the socialist principle, "To each according to his work." (This later became part of Article 19 of the 1976 Cuban constitution.) Between the 1970 elections and the 1973 CTC Congress, the unions were reorganized with a single union under each central agency or ministry.[30] The institutionalization of the labor movement was followed by political institutionalization as well. The first Congress of the Communist Party of Cuba was held in December 1975, and elections for local Organizations of People's Power and approval of a constitution took place in 1976. At the end of 1976, the indirectly elected Assembly of People's Power met and elected a Council of State, with Fidel Castro as its president.

THE SOVIET SUBSIDY

The attempt to organize and institutionalize the Cuban economy was the result both of the lessons of the 1970 sugar harvest and of continued Soviet pressure. The reasons for that pressure are evident, considering the extent of the Soviet subsidy to Cuba. The Soviet Union made up the Cuban trade deficit which, except for 1974 (when sugar prices averaged thirty cents a pound, reaching a high of 65 cents a pound in November), never dropped below $180 million and in some years reached $500 million. Between 1960 and 1975 the USSR also provided Cuba with free military equipment, worth somewhere between $1.5 and $3 billion.

In December 1972, it refinanced a Cuban debt of about $5 billion, agreeing to forego payments of principal and interest until 1986. The Soviets also buy Cuban nickel at 40 percent above the world price, and they buy sugar at a regularly renegotiated fixed price, which is usually above the world market price (eleven cents a pound from 1964 to 1970, rising in the 1970s to thirty cents a pound for the 1976–80 period with the possibility of higher payments if world market prices for Cuban imports rise). In addition, in 1973 and 1974 the Soviet Union sold oil to Cuba at a price that was about one-half the OPEC price, although it has readjusted the oil price upward each year, based on the world market price for the previous four years.

Since Soviet aid to Cuba is tied to the purchase of Soviet goods which may be overpriced, it is difficult to compute the total amount of the subsidy to Cuba. However, if the balance of trade subsidy, the sugar, oil, and nickel subsidies, the military aid, the nonpayment of interest, as well as earlier subsidized interest rates are added together, it would not be difficult to come up with a figure of about $12 billion for the total subsidy of the Soviet Union to Cuba between 1960 and 1977.[31] Some estimates placed the 1978 subsidy alone well in excess of $1 billion.

Cuba has attempted to lessen its dependence on the USSR by signing trade agreements with Japan, Canada, Western Europe, and Latin America. It continued to trade with Canada, Mexico, and Spain throughout the 1960s, and trade with Japan rose from 4 percent of Cuban trade in 1969 to 12 percent in 1974. Since 1973, Cuba has received loans and credits from non-Communist countries totaling $3.5 billion, but doubts about capabilities for repayment may limit the use of those credits. For example, the expenditure of $300 million of a $1.2 billion credit extended by Argentina in 1973 was delayed in 1976 for economic reasons. While the percentage of Cuban trade with socialist countries has dropped from 75 percent to 60 percent, dependence on the USSR continues. Nickel exports to Western Europe have increased, but sugar remains the principal source of foreign exchange (about 75 percent of exports), and the USSR is the most advantageously priced buyer.[32]

Cuba has been able to carry nationalization about as far as it can go, but in the process it has incurred certain costs. It continues to be dependent, economically and politically, on the Soviet Union. The political nature of the relationship has enabled Cuba to continue to receive a large subsidy — on a per capita basis the largest aid program in the world and considerably greater than United States aid programs to similarly dependent Latin American states, such as the Dominican Republic. However, as Castro's support of the 1968 Soviet invasion of Czechoslovakia demonstrated, the Soviet Union can compel Cuba to support its policies if it wishes to do so.

Another cost of nationalization has been massive inefficiency owing to the rapidity of the establishment of state control, centralization of decisionmaking, bureaucratization, and, in cases like the 1970 sugar harvest, distortion of the economy in obedience to the will of Fidel Castro. In the mid-1970s, the cost-accounting systems, which had been introduced in state enterprises, began to distinguish between economic and "social" costs. By 1981, economic decisionmaking is to be decentralized on an enterprise basis, using the *calculo economico* system that requires each enterprise to make a profit and to pay interest on central bank credits. It still seems, however, that if the Soviet subsidy were ended the regime would face serious economic difficulties. The twin problems — Cuba's dependence on the export of sugar, a product in oversupply on the world market, and its need to import half its food and nearly all its petroleum, the world price of which has been set at a high level by OPEC — have not been and cannot be solved by nationalization.

On the positive side, the central control of the economy has permitted the Cuban government to make impressive social gains. Medical care is free and life expectancy has been extended from 56 to 71.8 years; social security coverage is universal; illiteracy has been cut from 23 percent (40 percent in the countryside) to an official figure of 3.9 percent, and in 1978 a campaign was waged to secure a universal sixth-grade literacy level; unemployment has been virtually eliminated (although the Cuban equivalent of "featherbedding" has not); and in the 1970s a program of housing construction by minibrigades of factory workers helped to solve a critical housing shortage. Most significant, development and investment have been shifted from Havana to the countryside and smaller cities—in marked contrast to the nearly universal pattern elsewhere in Latin America.

An additional but intangible cost of nationalization is its effect on political and personal freedom. The state controls all aspects of the economy, and at least until recently it was difficult for the ordinary citizen in Cuba to express any complaints or needs, not to mention political views opposed to the government. The new system of workers' assemblies in the factories, the 1976 election of the 10,000 representatives to the municipal assemblies, and the local Organizations of People's Power provide a framework for some communication, but it is too early to judge the effect of these changes. In any case, the individual citizen has little or no choice concerning where he or she works. (The defenders of the Cuban system reply that at least he or she has a job.) In addition, by Castro's own estimate in interviews with American journalists, the regime still had over 3,000 political prisoners in 1978 and over 15,000 in the early 1960s. (In late 1978, Cuba began to release political prisoners and to permit the emigration of those who had relatives abroad. All except 700 are expected to be released.)

UNITED STATES-CUBAN RELATIONS AND THE QUESTION OF COMPENSATION

In late 1974 and the first part of 1975 following Richard Nixon's resignation, the United States and Cuba began to move slowly toward improved relations. In the summer of 1974, Castro granted interviews to a number of American journalists and stated that the lifting of the "blockade" (the Cuban misnomer for the embargo on *American* trade) was his only condition for the initiation of negotiations with the United States. Senators Javits and Pell, one a Republican and the other a Democrat, visited Cuba. In October 1974, a group of distinguished American academics and business leaders argued that "the embargo indiscriminately and adversely affects the lives of innocent Cuban men, women and children. Far from weakening the present regime the embargo . . . makes it easier for the Cuban government to justify and prolong its tight control over the intellectual and political activities of the Cuban people." In March 1975, following a series of secret meetings between United States officials and Cuban envoys, Henry Kissinger announced that the administration "sees no virtue in perpetual antagonism between the United States and Cuba." and in the Organization of American States, the United States dropped its opposition to the ending of the OAS embargo. The United States ended its boycott of ships that engaged in trade with Cuba in August 1975, and it was announced that American subsidiaries in other countries would be granted permission to trade with Cuba "when local laws or policies" favor such trade. Hearings held in mid-1975 by subcommittees of the House International Relations Committee chaired by congressmen Jonathan Bingham and Donald Fraser seemed to indicate that there was considerable support for lifting the embargo. Finally, in September the assistant secretary of state for Latin America, William D. Rogers, announced the administration's readiness to begin negotiations.[33]

Whatever progress had been made was seriously set back by the Cuban intervention in the Angolan civil war in the fall of 1975. There was no further effort to negotiate until after the inauguration of President Carter in January 1976. At that time, the two nations again began a process of signaling to one another regarding the preconditions for serious negotiations. The rapprochement was accelerated in September 1977 when "interest sections" of the two countries were opened in Havana and Washington but was halted in late 1977 with the evidence of an expanded Cuban military presence in several African countries.

Even if the embargo were lifted, the question of compensation for the expropriated American properties in Cuba would be a major obstacle to the improvement of United States-Cuban relations. This is particularly true in the area of trade between the two countries, which is presumably the reason that Castro is interested in ending the embargo. In the absence of "good faith negotiations" or arbitration aimed at providing "prompt, adequate, and effective compensation" for expropriated United States property, the 1974 Trade Act forbids tariff exemptions under the Generalized System of Preferences, the Hickenlooper Amendment prevents economic aid unless the president formally invokes a national interest waiver, and the González Amendment mandates United States opposition to any loans from international financial institutions. (Cuba is not now a member of any such institution.) Cuban exports could also be subject to attachment by United States courts in the settlement of claims arising out of the expropriations of American-owned property. This condition applies unless the United States trading partners take possession in Cuban ports or the president makes use of the escape clause in the 1964 Foreign Assistance Act allowing him to invoke the "act of state" doctrine to remove the dispute from the courts.

Furthermore, imports from Cuba would suffer from a serious competitive disadvantage if they did not benefit from Most Favored Nation tariff status which requires congressional action. As in most of its trade with Western nations, Cuba would also desire government-subsidized or -guaranteed credits from the Export-Import Bank and the Commodity Credit Corporation to finance its trade with the United States. In both cases, the 1974 Trade Act requires that in order for a "nonmarket economy" country to receive credits or tariff advantages it must enter into a bilateral agreement with the United States. That agreement must include provision for the settlement of commercial disputes and must be approved by both houses of Congress. The president must also certify that the recipient country allows freedom of emigration to join close relatives in the United States and does not require the payment of more than a nominal exit or visa tax. In late 1978, Cuba began to allow political prisoners to emigrate to the United States and elsewhere, but there are still restrictions on emigration by others. There is also specific congressional legislation, adopted in 1962 and incorporated by reference in the 1974 act, that forbids granting "benefits of any concessions contained in any trade agreement" unless "the President proclaims that he has determined that Cuba is no longer dominated or controlled by the foreign government or foreign organization controlling the world Communist movement."[34] Finally, the issue of human rights in Cuba has been raised in Congress in opposition to any aid to Cuba.

There are, therefore, a large number of legislative hurdles to be surmounted, by congressional action or executive finding, before Cuba can enter into mutually beneficial trade relations with the United States. The compensation question is further complicated by congressional action directing the predetermination of the value of the disputed claims by American citizens and corporations. In 1964, Congress authorized the Foreign Claims Settlement Commission to assess the "amount and validity of the claims for property losses as a result of official actions by the Cuban government after January 1, 1959." In 1972, the commission completed its work on a total of 8,816 claims. Although 1,195 of the claims were dismissed, the final total amount of claims recognized came to $1.8 billion, of which well over $1.5 billion was in corporate claims and $270 million was in individual claims. The United States government also has $200 million in claims against Cuba. If, as the commission suggested, a 6 percent interest charge should be added, covering the period from the 1959 and 1960 nationalizations down to the settlement, the amount owed rose to over $4 billion as of 1979.

The Cubans, of course, do not recognize the Claims Settlement Commission figures as binding. Cuban Law 851 of 1960, however, accepts the principle of compensation on the basis of declared value for local tax purposes (estimated at about $900 million) out of 25 percent of surplus earnings from sugar sales to the United States. The sugar quota system was ended in 1974, and the world price is well above the 5.75 cents per pound figure in the 1960 legislation. (The 1977 International Sugar Agreement is aimed at stabilizing the world price at eleven cents per pound.) However, the total United States sugar imports in 1976 were only 4.5 million tons, and there may be hesitancy to arrive at a special arrangement with Cuba that will hurt suppliers such as Brazil, the Philippines, the Dominican Republic, Peru, and Mexico. In addition, Cuba has normally supplied over 3 million tons of sugar annually to the USSR, Eastern Europe, and China at prices well above the world market price. Its sales to the non-Communist world are limited by the International Sugar Agreement, and its annual production of sugar for export in recent years has only ranged between 5 and 6.5 million tons. Thus, it is clear that Cuba would not have the 3 million ton minimum for export to the United States that the 1960 law mandates.

That law could be changed by Cuba or the United States could increase its sugar imports, but Cuba would still have to recognize that some compensation was owed. In 1975, in conversation with United States visitors, Carlos Rafael Rodríguez, the most knowledgeable and authoritative Cuban official on foreign trade, told a visiting American delegation that the compensation question would also have to involve United States payments for damages done to the Cuban economy by the Bay of Pigs invasion, the embargo, and the exile attacks. In 1977, Castro said that Cuba would have to be compensated for "aggression" before it would pay compensation for American property.[35] No estimates of these amounts were given, but presumably they are in excess of the amounts certified by the Foreign Claims Settlement Commission.

Resolution of these problems could come only after the trade embargo is lifted — a requirement that Castro has made as a precondition to serious negotiations. Article 25 of the 1976 Cuban constitution explicitly recognizes a right to "due compensation" for expropriated property, "taking into account the interests and the economic and social needs" of the former owner. It is clear that a settlement of the compensation question will not be easy, particularly because of the large amounts involved. While some large corporations with recent investments in Cuba were able to write off many of their losses as tax deductions, many others, including most of the small claimants, either had no income against which to offset the losses or could take only small proportions of their losses because of United States tax law restrictions. The members of the Joint Corporation Committee on Cuban Claims (see table 2), for example, who only recovered about 12 percent of the value of their properties set by the Foreign Claims Settlement Commission, have expressed their opposition to the recognition of Cuba and the opening of trade relations without a compensation agreement.

The Commerce Department has estimated a potential trade of $300 million with Cuba if trade relations are normalized, but since the prospect for subsidized credits is limited by restrictions in current trade legislation that trade is not likely to expand rap-

Table 2. Major corporate claims against Cuba
as certified by the United States Foreign Claims Settlement Commission, 1972

Corporation	Amount of claim
*Cuban Electric Company (Boise-Cascade)	$267.6 million
International Telephone and Telegraph	130.7 million
*North American Sugar Industries (Borden)	109.0 million
Moa Bay Mining Company (Freeport Minerals Co.)	88.3 million
*United Fruit Sugar Co. (United Brands)	85.1 million
West Indies Sugar Co.	84.9 million
*American Sugar Company (Amstar Corp.)	81.0 million
Standard Oil Co. N.J. (Exxon Corp.)	71.6 million
*Bangor Punta Corp.	53.4 million
*Francisco Sugar Company	52.6 million
Texaco, Inc.	50.1 million
*Manati Sugar Company	48.6 million
Nicaro Nickel Company (Freeport Minerals Co.)	33.0 million
Coca Cola Company	27.5 million
*Lone Star Cement (Lone Star Industries, Inc.)	24.9 million
New Tuinueu Sugar Co., Inc.	23.3 million
*Colgate-Palmolive Co.	14.4 million
*Braga Brothers	12.6 million
*Boise-Cascade Corp.	11.7 million
American Brands Inc.	10.6 million
Atlantic Richfield Company	10.2 million
*Burrus Mills, Inc. (Cargill, Inc.)	9.8 million
Pan American Life Ins. Co.	9.7 million
*United States Rubber Co., Ltd. (Uniroyal, Inc.)	9.5 million
*F. W. Woolworth and Co.	9.2 million
Havana Docks Corp.	9.0 million
*Continental Can Co., Inc.	8.9 million
*Firestone Tire and Rubber	8.3 million
International Harvester	8.3 million
*Owens-Illinois	8.1 million
General Motors Corp.	7.7 million
Chase Manhattan Bank and Assoc.	7.3 million
IBM World Trade Corp.	6.4 million
First National City Bank	6.2 million
*Swift and Co. (Esmark, Inc.)	6.0 million
*First National Bank of Boston	5.9 million
General Electric Company	5.9 million
Libby, McNeil and Libby	5.7 million
*Goodyear Tire and Rubber	5.1 million
Sears, Roebuck and Co.	3.7 million
*Lykes Bros., Inc. (Lykes-Youngstown Corp.)	3.4 million

Table 2. *cont.*

Corporation	Amount of claim
*Reynolds Metals Co.	3.4 million
*Sherwin Williams Company	3.4 million
*Gillette Japan, Inc.	3.3 million
Dupont Inter-American Chemical	3.0 million
*King Ranch Inc.	2.9 million
*B. F. Goodrich	2.8 million
W. R. Grace and Co.	2.5 million
University of Chicago	2.5 million
International Standard Electric (ITT)	2.2 million
*Hilton International Co.	1.9 million
Pepsico, Inc.	1.9 million
Olin Mathieson (Olin Corp.)	1.8 million
Warner Lambert, S. A.	1.6 million
*E. R. Squibb and Sons Interamerica	1.5 million
*Standard Brands, Inc.	1.4 million
Sterling Drug, Inc.	1.3 million
*International Paper	1.0 million
USM Pan America, Ltd.	1.0 million
*General Dynamics Corp.	1.0 million
*Phelps Dodge Corp.	0.9 million
*Standard Fruit and Steamship Co. (Castle and Cook Inc.)	0.7 million

Source: Cuban Desk, U.S., Department of State, mimeographed list.
*Member of Joint Corporate Committee on Cuban Claims.

idly,[36] although such credits are available and have been extended by Argentina, Mexico, Canada, and many European countries. On the other hand, Castro has repeatedly emphasized Cuban interest in United States agricultural machinery (especially sugarcane cutters), replacement parts, foodstuffs, fertilizers, and medicine. An agreement would improve Cuba's credit rating (and hence interest rate) on the Eurodollar market. For the United States, in addition to sugar, Cuban exports of nickel, tobacco, chrome, shellfish, and rum would be of interest to importers. American companies have also discussed with the Cubans possible joint ventures or service contracts in tourism or the construction of manufacturing plants. Conceivably, some of this trade could be carried out on a barter basis or could be financed by private United States bank credits, although the banks might require some resolution of the compensation question as a pre-condition. (The two might be tied together so that the loans are made as the compensation process begins to go into effect.)

The compensation issue is not insoluble, but it is likely to take some time to resolve and will impede improved trade relations between Cuba and the United States, especially where tariff concessions are involved. A trade and compensation agreement of the type that was signed by Cuba with Switzerland in 1967 could be employed, earmarking a percentage of Cuban sales to the United States to finance bonds issued as compensation, but this would require the Cubans to drop or lessen their claim to countercompensation. In any event, the total sum agreed to by the Cubans is likely to be no larger than the various lump-sum compensation agreements between the United States and Communist countries which average about 40 cents on the dollar. An agreement is likely to be accompanied by or related to other economic incentives, such as United States loans and credits. It is clear that the bargaining will be lengthy and difficult.

CONCLUSIONS

The Hickenlooper Amendment and other legislation adopted in reaction to the Cuban nationalizations cumulatively constitute a formidable barrier to normal trade relations between the United States and Cuba. They commit the United States to exercise the instruments of state power, whether through economic coercion or the withholding of benefits, to discourage or punish those who take over United States property without compensation. The question that arises then is whether this legislation, based on conflicts that were initiated twenty years ago, is still appropriate today.

Besides discouraging others from imitating the Cuban example, the United States legislative sanctions, especially the trade embargo, were designed to make the support of Cuba as expensive as possible for the Soviet Union. The large cost to the Soviet Union of subsidizing Cuba probably accounts for Soviet reluctance to become involved in similar subsidies elsewhere in Latin

America, notably Allende's Chile. By now, the Cubans have been able to undercut most of the effects of the United States embargo by trading with other countries, but their balance of payments continues to be negative, requiring a considerable Soviet subsidy. The conclusion that a radical nationalist may draw from the Cuban example is that wholesale nationalization is a risky and expensive business, unless one is assured of substantial external support and authoritarian control of internal consumption.

The costs of nationalization include inefficiency and bureaucratization, which many observers have noted about the Cuban economy. Some decentralization of decisionmaking, cost accounting, and increased worker participation, as well as a considerable reliance on material incentives, have alleviated part of the problem. The Cubans have made substantial advances in education, welfare, equity, and social justice, but this has been done at the cost of an inefficiently organized economy and the sacrifice of political liberty. In addition, the socialization of industry and agriculture does not seem to have brought Castro to the goal of economic independence, a prime motive for the original break with the United States. Castro may prefer dependence on a power 6,000 miles, rather than 90 miles away, but that dependence is not likely to end in the foreseeable future.

The trade embargo has outlived its usefulness, if it ever had any. It is not likely to lead to the overthrow of Castro, it does not seem to increase significantly the cost to the Soviet Union of supporting Cuba, and it is ineffective in preventing other countries from trading with Cuba. If the considerable hurdles created by the United States Congress, many of them related to the compensation issue, can be successfully overcome, the removal of the embargo can help to produce an atmosphere that can, at the very least, improve the possibilities of resolving the many other issues that still divide the two countries. It may also lead to a compromise on the issue of compensation. Perhaps, then, new patterns of cooperation between American business and the Castro government can be established, and the bitter disputes of the early 1960s, which brought the world to the brink of destruction, can finally be put to rest.

5

Chile and Nationalization: Four Approaches to Foreign Investment

The Chileanization program must be considered a failure.
> —Keith Griffin, *Underdevelopment in Spanish America,* 1969

The Frei Chileanization program . . . was, by any but the most stingy standards, clearly a success.
> —Theodore Moran, *Multinational Corporations and the Politics of Dependence,* 1974

The uncompensated expropriation of the U.S. copper mining investments [by the Allende government] . . . was a game that had no winners.
> —Eric Baklanoff, *Expropriation of U.S. Investments,* 1975

The multinational enterprises and the national economies of [the] Third World are characterized by very divergent structures, objectives, and strategies. . . . From the point of view the countries involved, the logical conclusion of the attempts to reconcile the irreconcilable is to eliminate the conflicts completely by nationalization.
> —Norman Girvan, "Las Corporaciones Multinacionales del Cobre en Chile," 1974

131

*Allende's brand of socialism failed to recognize Chile's most
important idiosyncrasy: an inadequate, distorted, inefficient, noncapitalistic capital accumulation process.*
>—Markos Mamalakis, *The Growth and Struc-
ture of the Chilean Economy,* 1976

*The official U.S. policy that brought security to Anaconda
and Kennecott brought death to Orlando Letelier.*
>—Eulogy, Memorial Service after assassination
of Allende's former United States ambassador,
Princeton University, 1976

The events in Cuba finally convinced American policymakers
of the need for new initiatives toward Latin America. Shortly after taking office, President Kennedy proposed an Alliance for
Progress between the United States and Latin America. The program was designed to demonstrate that social reform and economic development could be carried out without resorting to
communist methods or allying oneself with the Soviet Union.
With a planned expenditure of $20 billion over ten years, the Al-
liance sought to underwrite reforms in areas such as housing, tax
collection, education, and land tenure. Half of that amount was
supposed to come from private sources in the United States.
Thus, at the very outset, the problem was raised of a potential
conflict between the maintenance of a favorable investment climate and the need for social, economic, and political changes in
Latin America which might adversely affect foreign economic
interests.

The Kennedy administration did not think that this conflict
was insuperable. In order to calm fears of losses from expropriation and insurrection, it promoted the extension of the Agency
for International Development (AID) Investment Guarantee
Program to Latin America. It encouraged the larger American
investors to coordinate and expand their investments in Latin
America through the Business Group for Latin America. Hoping
to show that cooperation between American business, the United
States government, and development-minded Latin Americans

could demonstrate that the interests of the United States and Latin America were mutually reinforcing rather than in conflict, it sought a "showcase" where the ideas behind the alliance could be put into practice.

A leading candidate for that showcase role was Chile. With about the same population and gross national product as Cuba, it possessed a 130-year history of almost unbroken adherence to the norms of constitutional democracy. Its population was articulate, intelligent, and politically aware, and it was an open, free society. Like Cuba, Chile was largely dependent for its foreign exchange upon the export of a single commodity—copper. It, too, had an active Communist party that, in cooperation with a Marxist-oriented Socialist party, was making a strong bid for power in the 1964 presidential elections. Part of the platform of the Communist-Socialist coalition was the nationalization of the American-owned copper mines, the utilities, the nitrate industry, iron mines, insurance companies, and private banks.

The two principal presidential candidates were Salvador Allende Gossens, the Socialist-Communist candidate, and Eduardo Frei Montalva, the candidate of the centrist Christian Democratic party. During the campaign, Frei proposed the Chileanization of the copper industry, that is, the purchase by the Chilean government of majority ownership of the copper mines with the purchase price to be invested by the American companies in the expansion of production. In April, when a special election to fill a congressional vacancy revealed that there was little electoral support for the right-wing parties, the rightist parties threw their support to Frei in an effort to stop Allende. The United States government also gave both overt and covert assistance to Frei.

Frei was elected by a 54 percent absolute majority, a rarity in Chile's multiparty politics, and he proceeded to implement his Chileanization program through a series of agreements with American companies. The Chilean state acquired 51 percent control of the Kennecott subsidiaries in 1967. In 1969, after extended negotiation, in which the American ambassador played an active role, the principal Anaconda mines were also "Chileanized." The investments that the companies made as part of the Chileanization scheme were covered by AID investment insurance, which was assumed by the Overseas Private Investment Corporation (OPIC) that replaced the AID Investment Guarantee Program in 1969.

The Chileanization program did not last long. In 1970, Salvador Allende, in a three-way race, was narrowly elected president with 36 percent of the vote. He then proceeded to nationalize the copper mines and many other sectors of the economy. In the case of the copper companies nationalization was achieved by amending the constitution, but in the other cases forced purchases, "temporary" requisitions, interventions, and other loopholes in the law were used to take over industrial and agricultural properties. The excessively rapid expansion of state ownership, the resulting decline in production, runaway inflation, and the breakdown in the observance of the constitutional "rules of the game" by both the pro- and anti-Allende forces produced a military coup on September 11, 1973.

After the coup a military junta, headed by General Augusto Pinochet Ugarte, reversed the Allende nationalization policy. It returned seized industrial and agricultural properties, sold most of the state companies (although not the copper mines), and attempted to entice new foreign investment into Chile through a liberalized Statute of Foreign Investment. The United States government, which had overtly and covertly opposed Allende, was ambivalent to the new regime, chiefly because of the international publicity given to the repression that followed the coup.

The nationalization and foreign investment policies of the Frei, Allende, and Pinochet governments, as well as those of the regimes that preceded them, provide an opportunity to evaluate the major alternative approaches to foreign investment. These include the various taxation schemes applied between 1955 and 1964; the joint venture approach between the government and the foreign copper companies adopted by the Frei government; nationalization with little or no compensation as implemented by Allende; and the open door policy to foreign investment pursued by the Pinochet government.

The study of recent Chilean politics also requires an analysis of United States foreign policy. The deep and continuous overt and covert involvement of the United States government in Chilean affairs from 1963 to 1973 has been investigated by the Senate Intelligence Committee and has been analyzed in its report, *Covert Action in Chile*. In addition, the links between the State Department, the United States embassy, the CIA, and large American corporations with substantial interests in Chile, especially the copper companies and the International Telephone and Telegraph Company (ITT) have been amply documented.[1] The AID Investment Guarantee Program and its successor, the Overseas Private Investment Corporation (OPIC), were heavily committed in Chile, and the Chilean case has raised serious questions concerning the desirability of government-backed insurance programs for United States investment overseas. The Chilean nationalizations, along with those in Peru, also had a direct influence on the antiexpropriation policies adopted by President Nixon and Congress in the early 1970s. However, the changed attitude toward foreign investment of the Pinochet government as well as of many other Latin American governments may suggest that such United States government activism in defense of American investment is no longer necessary or desirable.

THE DEVELOPMENT OF A COPPER ENCLAVE

The fact that the military junta in Chile, which took power in 1973, did not denationalize the copper mines indicates that copper has a strategic character that differs from other industries. Copper is Chile's principal export, accounting until very recently for 75 percent of its foreign exchange earnings. Yet until 1967, Chile's major copper mines were 100 percent American owned. Large-scale copper mining using modern methods was only begun in Chile in the first decade of this century, when William Braden, an American entrepreneur, built a car road, and later a railroad, into an enormously productive mountain of ore at El Teniente, to the south of Santiago. Braden received the financial support of the Guggenheims, who bought the mine from him in 1908. In 1911 they also bought control of what was to become the largest open-pit copper mine in the world, Chuquicamata, in the northern desert of Chile. In 1915, the Guggenheims bought control of the Braden Copper Company and combined it with their American copper mines to form the Kennecott Copper Corporation. However, in order to finance other ventures, in 1923 the Guggenheims sold a majority interest in the Chuquicamata mine to the Anaconda Copper Company, which was already developing a smaller Chilean mine at Potrerillos. Anaconda was interested in increasing its control of copper production because it was in the process of vertical integration—that is, acquiring control of all steps in copper production from mining to smelting, refining, and production of finished products. In the 1950s, the Potrerillos mine was exhausted, and Anaconda replaced it with a new mine at El Salvador. The four American-owned mines comprised the large-scale mining sector (Gran Mineria) of the Chilean copper industry, amounting to 80–90 percent of Chilean copper production.

In 1922, the Chilean government began to tax the Gran Mineria with a levy on profits of 6 percent. The rate was increased by another 6 percent in 1925, and during the depression an artificially low exchange rate was imposed for a portion of the dollars they brought into Chile—the so-called legal costs of production. A further 6 percent was imposed in 1934, and by 1939 the total copper tax amounted to 33 percent. Part of the tax was used to finance the new Chilean Development Corporation (Corporacion de Fomento de la Produccion, usually referred to as Corfo), which was established to promote import substitution, that is, the establishment of new Chilean industry in order to diminish the necessity for imports. By the early 1950s, as a result of increased taxes and the pegged exchange rate, the Chilean government was receiving 86 percent of gross profits from copper, but the American companies were reluctant to invest in new production. The lack of new investment meant that the Chilean share in world copper production dropped from 20 percent in the 1930s to 11 percent. Following a public outcry over an agreement between the United States government and the American companies to hold down the price of copper during the Korean War, the Chileans attempted to take control of copper marketing. However, when the bottom dropped out of the copper market in 1954 following the war's end, control was returned to the companies. The following year, the Chilean Congress adopted new legislation that marked the beginning of meaningful and informed government regulation of the copper industry.

THE 1955 "NEW DEAL"—
DIFFERENTIAL TAXATION AND
GOVERNMENT REGULATION

The 1955 *Nuevo Trato* (New Deal) legislation established a regulatory agency to deal with the copper companies. It also eliminated the artificially low compulsory exchange rate (now about one-sixth the free rate) that had led the companies to keep their expenditures in Chile to a minimum. In addition, the *Nuevo Trato* legislation reorganized the previous jumble of copper taxes into a single 50 percent tax and a 25 percent surtax, the latter to be reduced in proportion to increases in production, disappearing altogether when output reached a level which was two times average production between 1949 and 1953. The new Department of Copper was directed to collect statistical information on costs, sales, pricing, marketing, and the like in order to make government regulation less dependent on reports from the companies. It was further authorized to monitor imports by the copper companies so as to assure the maximum use of domestic components. The legislation also allowed an accelerated depreciation rate for new investments, a provision that was particularly beneficial to Anaconda's new investment at El Salvador, designed to replace its exhausted holdings at Potrerillos. (The need for substantial investment from abroad, in order to avoid a drop in copper production as a result of the exhaustion of Potrerillos, was one of the reasons for the liberal investment provisions of the law.)

It soon became apparent, however, that the base production figure had been set too low. Because of a large unused production capacity, it was possible for the companies to take advantage of the tax incentives by expanding their production with little increase in investment. The reduction in taxes and expanded production greatly increased profits for the companies, both in absolute terms and as a percentage of book value. (In cases like

El Salvador that percentage was inflated because of the accelerated depreciation system.) When it turned out that, ironically, the two companies appeared to be using their Chilean profits to expand their American operations — Kennecott built a refinery in Baltimore and Anaconda increased its domestic ore base in copper and aluminum — the Chilean nationalists were outraged. Once the El Salvador mine was completed Anaconda did little new investing in its Chilean operations. The other American copper company, Kennecott, only increased its gross investments from $8 million between 1950 and 1955, to $13 million between 1955 and 1960. While Chilean tax revenues increased almost 300 percent, the companies' profits doubled. All that Chilean observers could see were the lack of new investment and what appeared to be windfall profits that amounted, according to some computations of average book value, to 37.9 percent a year for Kennecott and 22 percent a year for Anaconda.[2]

By the early 1960s, dissatisfaction with the government's copper policy had become widespread. On the left, the Communist and Socialist parties, whose electoral alliance had come close to capturing the presidency in 1958, denounced the exploitation of Chile by the copper companies and called for nationalization of the mines. In the center, a dynamic new party, the Christian Democrats, proposed Chileanization or part ownership by the state. Even on the right, leading members of the Conservative party attacked the foreign companies, resulting in a negative decision by the Kennecott Company on a contemplated investment program at El Teniente.

During the 1950s, Chile's sluggish economy had grown at a per capita rate of less than 1 percent a year, inflation was rampant, its inefficient agriculture necessitated substantial imports of food, and the economy was characterized by gross inequities in the distribution of income and land tenure. For the competing political parties in Chile's multiparty system, the foreign copper companies were an easy target. Even conservative President Alessandri's supporters began to favor more drastic measures. It became clear then that the *Nuevo Trato* agreements were a classic case of the "obsolescing bargain." At the time the agreements were drawn up, they appeared advantageous to Chile in attracting new investment, but once those investments were made they looked much less attractive as the companies secured handsome profits at minimal costs. As Chilean experts and politicians began to compute the possible gains that could have been made under alternative arrangements, it was evident that the 1955 arrangement would not last. The problems that had arisen with the 1955 tax scheme seemed to indicate that reporting requirements and tax inducements to expand production would not produce sufficient "returns" to assuage the growing nationalist feelings. Specifically, Chileans wanted increased production, domestic refining, and a larger national share in profits, and these goals seemed to require a much larger degree of national control of the industry than the 1955 agreements offered. Yet despite Chile's increased technical capacity, nationalization posed the threat of loss of markets, management skills, and technology, and Chile was chronically short of the investment capital needed to expand production and refining capacity. The program offered by the Christian Democrats, "Chileanization," or the purchase of 51 percent ownership with the purchase price to be reinvested in the expansion of production and refining, seemed to provide the best of both worlds.

THE JOINT VENTURE— FREI'S CHILEANIZATION PROGRAM

After Frei's election, President Johnson appointed Ralph Dungan, one of President Kennedy's White House aides, United States ambassador to Chile. Dungan immediately identified himself and the United States with the Christian Democratic reform programs, including a radical redistribution of agrarian land. Chile began to receive more United States aid per capita than any other country in Latin America. The AID Investment Guarantee Program also began to insure new American investments in Chile, and twenty-two such contracts were written in the 1965 fiscal year.

Frei immediately entered into negotiations with the copper companies for partial ownership of existing mines. Anaconda was more resistant to the proposal than was Kennecott since it was more dependent on the profits from its Chilean subsidiary. However, Anaconda agreed to spend $130 million (a little less than half of which would come from an Export-Import Bank loan) on investments to expand production and refining in return for a reduction in taxation from an average of 62 percent to about 52 percent. To give the appearance of participation in the Chileanization program, Anaconda also agreed to a 25 percent Chilean share in La Exotica, a small new mine near Chuquicamata. The Cerro Corporation agreed to develop its first Chilean copper mine at Rio Blanco, under an arrangement that involved a 70 to 30 percent split between Cerro and the Chilean state. Again, the Export-Import Bank was to provide part of the financing, and a group of Japanese firms, interested in guaranteed access to the new copper production over the next fifteen years, also participated in the financing. The Chilean state guaranteed a portion of both loans.

The most spectacular and controversial part of the Chileanization program was the arrangement worked out with the Kennecott Corporation. The basic outlines were agreed to within six weeks after Frei took office, and he was able to announce it as a "Christmas present" to Chile on December 21, 1964. The reason that the negotiations took so little time was that the Kennecott executives already had been contemplating selling off part of their Chilean holdings. The agreement appeared to offer a mutually satisfactory arrangement for both Chile and the company. However, it later became clear that, in fact, the company received the lion's share of the benefits.

The agreement basically involved the sale of 51 percent of the Kennecott equity at El Teniente to the Chilean state, with the proceeds from the sale to be reinvested in the expansion of output from 180,000 to 280,000 metric tons a year. This was to be combined with a reduction in the copper tax to a straight 44 percent rate, replacing the 1955 sliding scale of 50–75 percent, plus a surtax of about 10 percent imposed in 1961. Kennecott was also to receive a management contract for ten years. What made the deal suspect, however, from the point of view of the Chilean economic nationalists, was that the 51 percent purchase price was to be computed after a revaluation of the book value of El Teniente, to be based on present "replacement value." As a result, the book value was raised from $69 million to $160 million. Codelco (*Corporación del Cobre*), the successor to the Copper Department, thus acquired a debt obligation to Kennecott of over $81.6 million. Kennecott further protected this loan by insuring it with the AID Investment Guarantee Program. Chile also invested $27.5 million of its own funds and guaranteed repayment of an additional loan of $110 million from the Export-Import Bank. Finally, Kennecott secured a loan on future production of $45 million from European and Asian copper consumers and sold collection rights on the loans to banks in those areas.

As Theodore Moran has pointed out, as a result of the Chileanization of its mines Kennecott received a larger book value and a much lower tax rate on its remaining 49 percent than it had had on the wholly owned mine before the Chileanization. In addition, without investing any new money of its own (it used the Chilean compensation funds), it was assured that the Chilean government would be in deep trouble with the United States government and financial institutions on three continents if it decided to expropriate.[3]

Chilean dissatisfaction with the copper agreements was expressed in the congressional debates surrounding their approval. The left objected to the agreements, claiming that nationalization was a preferable alternative. The right began to use the copper question to wring concessions from the Frei government on a pending agrarian reform bill. The final approval for the Chileanization agreements was made possible only by a series of maneuvers in the Chamber of Deputies that involved reneging on an understanding with the centrist Radical party—one of several factors contributing to the Radicals' subsequent shift to the left in support of the Allende candidacy in 1970.

The Kennecott agreements were based on the assumption that the price of copper would average around 29 cents per pound. In fact, escalating United States involvement in the Vietnam War created a shortage of the metal, and as a result by 1967 the price of copper reached 90 cents per pound on the London Metals Exchange. Only a relatively small share of world copper is sold on the London Metals Exchange, and the companies were able to keep American prices within a much lower range. But when prices began to rise in 1966, the sale of 90,000 tons of copper to the United States strategic reserve stockpile at 36 cents per pound, as compared to the London price of 60 cents, particularly aroused the Chilean ire. In 1967, the Chilean government took over copper pricing directly, basing it on the London price. The Chileans also promoted the formation of a would-be copper cartel, the Intergovernmental Council of Copper Exporting Countries (CIPEC, after its Spanish title) involving Peru, Zambia, Zaire, and Chile. Together these nations accounted for about 35 to 40 percent of world production and 70 percent of the copper traded internationally. Chile also took the lead in the creation of the Andean Pact, an agreement to form a common market on the west coast of South America.

The increase in price, the expansion of production, and especially the decrease in the effective tax again raised the profits of the copper companies in a spectacular fashion. Profits doubled between 1965 and 1966 and increased by another 50 percent in 1967. By 1969, a British scholar, Keith Griffin, could argue that the Chileanization had been a mistake. According to Griffin, if the companies had been nationalized in 1964, compensation could have easily been paid out of the high profits made later in the decade, and Chile would have owned its copper mines.[4] The problem with Griffin's analysis is that it ignores the important fundraising abilities of the copper companies. The companies had been able to secure large amounts of capital from the Export-Import Bank and other foreign sources which were then invested in the expansion of production and refining. More significant, however, is the fact that Chile was able, while maintaining access to the marketing and technology of the copper companies, to secure control of pricing policy and, finally in 1969, to capture in taxes most of the windfall profits from high international prices.

NATIONALIZATION BY AGREEMENT

Chile was able to capture those profits by renegotiating, under duress (threat of nationalization), the arrangements it had worked out with the copper companies only three or four years earlier. Arguing that the Chileanization agreements had been signed on the assumption that copper prices would remain stable, Chile imposed a new sliding scale of taxes on all the copper companies. The taxes ranged from 54 percent to 78 percent on all income generated by any "overprice" (*sobreprecio*) in excess of 40 cents per pound. President Frei, under pressure from members of his own party to nationalize Anaconda's holdings, whose profits were now said to be between 25 and 28 percent of book value, suddenly announced in May 1969 that he was initiating negotiations for the Chileanization of the Anaconda mining companies at Chuquicamata and El Salvador, which the company had refused to include in the earlier Chileanization agreements. After a month of negotiations in which the American ambassador, Edward Korry, exerted strong pressure behind the scenes to persuade Anaconda to agree, Frei was able to announce that Chile would have majority ownership of the mines with payment on the basis of 51 percent of book value to be paid out of the projected profits of the mines over the next twelve years. He also announced an arrangement with Anaconda for an "agreed-upon nationalization" (*nacionalización pactada*). Once 60 percent of the payment for the initial 51 percent had been completed, the Chilean state would have the option to purchase the remaining 49 percent at a price based on recent earnings. Through a complex voting procedure, Anaconda was to retain management control until that point, and it also received a three-year marketing contract at a fee of 1 percent of sales — features that were immediately attacked by the opposition.

Following the agreement, Chile's participation in copper profits took an immediate jump, rising from $200 million in 1968 to $353 million in 1969. On balance, then, the verdict on the Frei Chileanization joint venture program must be favorable. Although the financial arrangements of the earlier agreements were not as advantageous as in 1969, the negotiators established the legal basis for national control of the industry and attracted the investment of outside capital that would permit Chile to double production and triple refining. The assumption that subsequent tax income from the increased capacity would be more than sufficient to pay for the rise in Chilean indebtedness depended on whether the world market demand for copper would absorb the additional capacity—but in the 1960s optimistic assumptions for the future of the world economy did not seem unwarranted.

The program also gave the Chilean government ultimate, or at least eventual, control in crucial areas of production and refining without interrupting the flow of technology and managerial expertise. Whether the government could exert such control initially is debatable, but it is clear that over time—three years for marketing and probably a somewhat longer period for management—it would have been able to do so. The mines were being run by Chileans, and even the top management of the Chilean subsidiaries, with very few exceptions, were Chilean. (In 1971, Kennecott claimed that only 2 of its 10,000 employees in Chile were American.) If Chile nationalized, there was no guarantee that those Chileans would work for the Chilean state—or that the flow of technological innovations or new methods, as well as spare parts and replacements for specialized machinery, would continue. Under the Chileanization program, there was no interruption of this kind, while there were serious problems in these areas after the copper mines were taken over by the Allende government.

Chileanization also assured Chile of continued access to export markets. While opponents of the agreements were critical of the continued control of sales by the marketing organizations of the American companies, this arrangement, too, could be terminated after three years by the "Chileanized" companies' boards of directors if circumstances warranted it. After the Allende government nationalized the copper mines in 1971, it was able to find alternative marketing channels abroad, even using the European or Asian sales agents of the American copper companies. However, the lack of difficulty in marketing after nationalization was related to worldwide supply shortages at the time, and knowledgeable and sympathetic observers warned that nationalization could bring with it serious problems in selling copper on the world market.[5]

The Frei government successfully secured United States government support for the Chileanization agreements, an especially important factor in the 1969 Anaconda negotiations. The 1969 agreements, extending Chilean ownership to the Anaconda mines and eliminating the excessively generous tax terms of the earlier arrangements, corrected the weaknesses of the earlier Chileanization agreements and probably would not have been concluded without active American embassy involvement.

The claim has been made, however, that the 1969 agreements, which based the purchase price after 1972 on recent profits, gave Anaconda an incentive to extract only the most easily available, high-quality ore and not to take conservation measures for the future. After nationalization in 1971, the Allende government cited such practices as the basis for one of the deductions that it made from the compensation due to Anaconda.

NATIONALIZATION AND IDEOLOGICAL DIFFERENCES

The arguments over specifics, however, were only superficial manifestations of a fundamental ideological division between those who saw the interests of the multinationals opposed to those of the host countries and those who felt that agreements were possible based on the mutual interests of both parties. For the leftist parties, given their basic emphasis on the national and international class struggle, there was no question that nationalization with little or no compensation was the only solution. For some members of the center parties and a few representatives of the nationalist right, the increasing appeal of the theory of the *dependencia* of the Third World on the capital-exporting nations fulfilled the function that Marxism exercised for the left. Dependency theorists argued that nationalization was the appropriate way to assure national control of policy in vital areas, such as Chilean copper, that were easily identifiable because of their enclave character, that were volatile and unpredictable because of the price fluctuations on the world market, and that were crucial for the national economy because of their overwhelming impact on the balance of payments as the major source of foreign exchange.

Differences over nationalization intensified the ideological divisions within the two major Chilean centrist parties — the Radical and the Christian Democrat. Each party was divided into a left and right wing, with the right in control in the early 1960s and the left gaining increasing influence later in the decade. Finally in 1969, sparked by its youth organization, the left wing of the Radical party was able to move into an alliance with the Marxist parties, the Socialists and Communists, forming the *Unidad Popular* (Popular Unity). By the end of 1969, even before they had agreed on Salvador Allende as their candidate, the Popular Unity parties adopted a program that was committed to the nationalization of copper, iron, nitrate, coal, banking, foreign trade, electricity, transportation, communications, steel, cement, petrochemicals, cellulose, and paper. This was an ambitious nationalization program, although the authors of the Popular Unity program argued that the total number of enterprises to be nationalized would only number 150 (later reduced to 91) out of a total of over 30,000 industrial enterprises in the country.

The ideological currents in the ruling Christian Democratic party were more complex. In the 1964–70 period, during the presidential term of Eduardo Frei, the party was divided into the Frei supporters (*oficialistas*), the "rebel" (*rebelde*) group on the left, and the supporters of an intermediate third position (*terceristas*). The rebel group managed to gain control of the party machinery in mid-1967 and immediately began to pressure Frei to nationalize the banks. But six months later, the *oficialistas* were able to win a special party election aimed at ousting the left. In May 1969, most of the leaders of the left seceded from the party and formed MAPU, a small movement that later joined Allende's Popular Unity coalition.

Frei was forbidden by the Chilean constitution to run for reelection in 1970. Radomiro Tomic was the leading Christian Democratic candidate. Ideologically, Tomic was identified with the left of the party, and copper policy had been one of his areas of expertise when he served as a senator. Since 1964, there had been an informal agreement that he would be the 1970 Christian Democrat candidate. As a result, he did not follow the left wing out of the party, yet he made no secret of the fact that he was dissatisfied with the Chileanization agreements. His 1970 election program called for "immediate and integral nationalization of copper with equitable conditions of payment." It described the income from expanded copper production as a major source of a proposed Fund for National Independence and Development, which would be used to create a "New Economy." When questioned about how the nationalization would be carried out, Tomic indicated that the remaining shares would be bought from the companies with compensation paid out of future copper earnings.

As Chile tried to secure an increasingly large share of the benefits of its copper industry, "the ratchet effect," as some observers have called it, seemed to be driving Chile inexorably toward nationalization. Even on the right there were indications of support for nationalization. While this had been mainly a tactical maneuver to extract concessions from Frei which would weaken the agrarian reform bill adopted in 1967, at least one right-wing senator consistently and forcefully argued and voted for nationalization.

In contrast to the 1964 election, the September 1970 presidential race involved three candidates: Alessandri, the candidate of the right and a former well-known and popular president; Tomic, the Christian Democrat, whose rhetoric, although not his program, sounded radical; and Allende, who was already a three-time loser, the candidate of the leftist Popular Unity coalition. The Chilean constitution provided that if no candidate won an absolute majority (as Frei had done in 1964) the election was to be decided in the Congress — but a strong tradition called for the election of the front-runner. Thus, when Allende won 36.1 percent of the votes over Alessandri's 34.9 percent (Tomic was a poor third with 27.8 percent), the pressure was placed on the centrist Christian Democrats to vote for Allende.

UNITED STATES INVOLVEMENT—
THE MOVE TO STOP ALLENDE

After the popular election, the United States applied counterpressures to prevent Allende from being elected in the ensuing congressional runoff. Investigations, carried out by the United States Senate Intelligence Committee in 1975, have documented the fact that the CIA was directed by President Nixon in September 1970 to encourage a military coup. Documents leaked in 1972 to columnist Jack Anderson and 1973 hearings by a subcommittee of the Senate Foreign Relations Committee have also shown that the International Telephone and Telegraph Company (ITT) was deeply involved in the effort to prevent Allende from gaining the presidency. In addition, these papers have revealed that, during this period, there were close and continuing links between ITT and the CIA.

The ITT-CIA ties have been cited as proof of the inordinate influence of United States investors on American foreign policy. But the relationship between business interests and United States policy toward Chile is complex. According to the Senate Intelligence Committee report, an initial offer, in 1964, of $1.5 million by United States businesses in Chile to the CIA to be used to influence the Chilean presidential election was turned down, establishing the policy that the CIA would not accept funds from American businesses. The CIA itself gave covert support to the Christian Democrats, not because they were favorable to business — the rightist parties were much more sympathetic and the left wing of the Christian Democrats was strongly anticapitalist — but rather because they represented a reform force that offered an alternative to the Marxist parties domestically and to Cuba internationally.

In the late 1960s, after Edward Korry succeeded Ralph Dungan as United States ambassador to Chile, he adopted a "low profile" policy in Chilean politics, although he took an active behind-the-scenes role in 1969 in pressuring Anaconda to accept Chileanization. In April 1970, another approach by American businesses to the United States government for a joint effort in support of Alessandri in the September election was once more turned down, and United States assistance was restricted to an anti-Allende "spoiling" operation. Although the CIA and ITT maintained contact during the Chilean presidential elections, the Senate investigations have revealed that, when ITT approached the CIA with offers of collaboration on an anti-Allende program in June, it too was rejected, although the CIA provided ITT with Chilean contacts for its pro-Alessandri funding. In turn, in September, when the CIA approached ITT for assistance in applying economic pressure to Chile as part of Nixon's anti-Allende effort, ITT turned down the CIA plan when it could not get the cooperation of other United States businesses. (ITT had a special relationship with the CIA because John McCone, former CIA chief, was an ITT director, and at least one of ITT's Chilean representatives was a CIA agent.) According to the Senate report, the Nixon-Kissinger plan for a coup to forestall Allende's election was initiated as a result of a visit by a leading Chilean publisher and businessman who was introduced to Nixon by the president of Pepsi-Cola. However, the substantial documentary evidence from the period indicates that the principal reason for Nixon's anti-Allende effort was not the protection of United States investment, but rather the strategic threat of the spread of Communism to neighboring countries in Latin America if Allende were to take power.

After ITT's telephone holdings were taken over in 1971, it tried unsuccessfully to get the United States government to cut off pipeline aid and earthquake relief and to impose an embargo on trade with Chile. In a memo later published by columnist Jack Anderson, ITT lamented the State Department's continuing "soft-line low profile policy for Latin America."[6] The record seems to indicate that while business interests had ready access to the U.S. government, United States policy sometimes involved collaboration with business interests and sometimes it conflicted with those interests. Moreover, those interests themselves were defined differently by different companies.

THE ALLENDE NATIONALIZATIONS — COPPER AND EXCESS PROFITS

The United States efforts to prevent Allende from taking office were unsuccessful. When Allende agreed to add a Statute of Democratic Guarantees to the Chilean constitution, he was assured of Christian Democratic support in the congressional runoff which took place in late October. Upon taking office on November 3, 1970, Allende began almost immediately to implement the nationalization provisions of the Popular Unity program. For the nationalization of copper, he knew that he could get the support of the Christian Democrats and possibly even of some right-wing congressmen. In order to avoid any legal problems concerning the status of the earlier contract-laws authorizing the Chileanization agreements, Allende decided to resort to a constitutional amendment for the copper nationalizations. (An amendment required only an absolute majority of the Congress, and it had the added advantage of limiting the legal appeals of the companies on the question of compensation.) In other areas, where there was neither nationalist feeling nor potential Christian Democratic support, different means had to be used.

The copper nationalization amendment required lengthy negotiations with the Christian Democrats, but the Allende government had the upper hand in the negotiations since the Christian Democratic party had endorsed nationalization during the 1970 election campaign. Moreover, according to the constitution, Allende could call a plebiscite on the amendment if he were defeated by the Congress. A draft amendment was announced by Allende on December 21, 1970, exactly six years after Frei had announced the Chileanization agreements. As finally adopted by the full Congress, on July 16, 1971, the amendment provided for compensation over a maximum of thirty years at no less than 3 percent interest on the basis of book value, less "amortization, depreciation, fines, exhaustion of the mines, and reduced value due to obsolescence," as well as "all or part of the excess profits which those enterprises may have obtained." The so-called transitional provisions of the amendment provided that the controller general, a permanent civil servant responsible for the maintenance of proper administrative and legal procedure, was to determine compensation on the basis of the book value minus deductions as of December 31, 1970. He was also instructed to exclude any revaluations made after December 31, 1964 — a provision aimed at reversing the large increase in book value allowed to Kennecott at the time of the Chileanization of El Teniente. In determining the deductions, the controller general was directed to reduce the compensation for any installations found in "deficient" condition.

The most important and controversial provisions of the amendment were those dealing with the determination of excess profits. The Chilean Senate made this a nonreviewable presidential decision, authorizing Allende to deduct "all or part" of the excess profits at his discretion and leaving him considerable leeway for negotiation with the companies. He was instructed to begin his computation of those profits in 1955, the date that the Copper Department began to keep accurate records. In determining excess profits, he was instructed to take into account the average profits of the copper companies on a worldwide basis, the 1969 principle of higher taxation of profits derived from unusually high world market prices, and "the agreements made by the Chilean state concerning maximum profits of foreign enterprises" (a reference to Decision 24 of the Andean Pact agreed to by Chile in 1970 that prescribed a 14 percent ceiling on the remittance of profits by foreign companies). The companies were given the right to appeal the controller general's decision before a five-member Special Copper Tribunal, made up of members from the Supreme Court, the Santiago Court of Appeals, and the Constitutional Tribunal, as well as the president of the Central Bank and the director of Internal Revenue.[7] They could not, however, appeal the president's decision concerning excess profits.

During the congressional debates, the Christian Democrats did not ask for major changes in the draft amendment. They asked that the financial obligations incurred under the Chilcanization agreements be recognized as still binding — a concession opposed by some of the members of the Allende coalition but difficult to avoid since most of the loans had been made with the guarantee of the Chilean state, and Chile's international credit would be seriously jeopardized by default. The right-wing parties also went along with the amendment since they recognized that it had overwhelming public support. Whatever Chileans might think about the Allende government (and it never received the electoral support of a majority of the population), there was a clear national consensus in favor of the "recovery" of the copper mines, and on July 11, 1971, the constitutional amendment was adopted by a unanimous congressional vote.

On September 28, 1971, two weeks before the controller was to announce his figure on the value of the mines, Allende indicated the amount he intended to deduct as excess profits. Without giving the specifics on which his decision was based (he was reported to have deducted all profits over 12 percent in any given year, while ignoring years in which the companies received lower profits), he listed the excess profits for the three companies as $774 million — $364 million of which was being charged to Anaconda for the profits of Chuquicamata and El Salvador, and $410 million to Kennecott for El Teniente. When the controller general issued his report on the mines' book value minus deductions, Anaconda was left owing $78 million and Kennecott was presented with a bill for over $310 million (including a deduction of $198 million because of the disallowed revaluations of book value in 1966-67).

The Allende "doctrine" on retroactive excess profits was immediately attacked by the companies (Kennecott claimed that its deductions exceeded its total earnings since 1955) and by the United States government. In October, Secretary of State Rogers issued a statement in which he deplored the "unprecedented retroactive application of the excess profits concept," warning that "the decision could jeopardize flows of private funds and erode the base of support for foreign assistance." The Chilean copper nationalization led to the drafting of a formal presidential policy statement on expropriation by an interdepartmental group in the United States government. In January 1972, President Nixon announced that unless there were "major factors" to the contrary new United States bilateral aid would not be extended to countries expropriating American companies without taking "reasonable steps" toward compensation, and that United States repesentatives in international financial institutions would vote against international aid projects to such countries. In March 1972, when Congress voted on contributions to the international banks, it added the González Amendment, which enacted into law the mandatory negative vote by United States representatives to international financial institutions.

Neither the González Amendment nor the earlier Hickenlooper provisions, requiring a cutoff of foreign aid to expropriating countries, were ever formally invoked against Chile. In the case of the international banks, no such action was necessary because after January 1971 no new loans were proposed to the directors of the Inter-American Development Bank or to the World Bank. (After Allende's overthrow, the World Bank indicated that a small loan for Chile had been ready for presentation, but in both the Inter-American and World Banks knowledge of the likelihood of United States opposition slowed down the processing of aid projects, although there was no interruption of aid "in the pipeline.") It would not have been appropriate to invoke the Hickenlooper Amendment because the procedures for appeals to the Special Copper Tribunal had not been exhausted. Moreover, there was a legal question as to whether the nationalization of companies that were already 51 percent Chilean-owned fell under the provisions of the law. A further reason against the application of the amendment was that it would have required a cutoff in aid to the Chilean military—a group with whom United States policymakers wanted to remain in contact.

Existing AID programs continued to be implemented. There was even an increase in the amounts distributed in Chile under the Food for Peace program, part of which was used in 1971 to carry out an Allende campaign promise to distribute a daily liter of free milk to every schoolchild in Chile. No new bilateral AID programs were requested by the Chilean government from the United States, although throughout the Allende period several Chilean project requests were pending with the World Bank and the Inter-American Development Bank.

The most important use of United States economic pressure in the copper nationalization was the announcement, in August 1971, by the Export-Import Bank that credit guarantees for the purchase of three Boeing 707 jets for the Chilean airline were being "postponed," pending the resolution of the copper compensation question. This was the first public announcement of the use of economic pressure against Allende by the United States government. Subsequent investigations by the United States Senate revealed, however, that the termination of new bilateral and multilateral assistance and the discouragement of private investment became national policy immediately after Allende's election in November 1970. The investigation also showed that between the popular and congressional elections in Chile, the White House and the CIA had taken steps, as part of their effort to promote a military coup, to exacerbate the financial panic that followed the September 1970 election.

The 1970 decisions were not always implemented. The Export-Import Bank dropped Chile into its lowest loan category but continued to give loan guarantees until late 1971; the Inter-American Development Bank made a small loan to Chilean universities in January 1971 and reactivated an earlier loan to provide earthquake assistance in July of the same year.

After the copper nationalization, however, the banks' attitudes hardened. World Bank officials explained that new aid could not be extended because the bank's interpretation of its Articles of Agreement had always been, in the words of its Blue Book on bank policy, "to inform governments who are involved in [expropriation] disputes that the Bank . . . will not assist them unless and until they make appropriate efforts to reach a fair and equitable settlement." In the case of the Inter-American Development Bank, it was almost certainly the behind-the-scenes opposition of the United States that prevented further loans. Credit lines from private American banks were also sharply reduced in late 1971, but this seems more related to the increasingly serious financial problems of Chile (especially Chile's announcement of a moratorium on debt repayments) than to the copper expropriation.[8]

The copper companies themselves proceeded to do their best to make life difficult for the Allende government. In November 1971, facing a crisis in its balance of payments, Chile unilaterally declared a moratorium on the payment of most of its foreign indebtedness (except on military purchases and repayments to the multilateral banks). Thus, when the installments on its payments for the 51 percent of Kennecott and Anaconda's holdings, bought in 1967 and 1969, came due at the end of the year Chile refused to pay. Kennecott sued Chile in the District Court of the Southern District of New York (as provided in the Chileanization agreements) and obtained a court order blocking the bank accounts of nine Chilean government agencies, including the national airline.[9] The order was rescinded at the end of March, when Chile paid the installment less $8 million for money "not usefully invested." Anaconda had only secured guarantees from the Chilean Copper Corporation (Codelco) and the Chilean Development Corporation (Corfo). A court-ordered writ of attachment, issued in February 1972, blocking the United States accounts of those agencies had less effect since they were nearly empty, but it forced Codelco to carry out its purchases of United States goods in Canada and other parts of the world. A second payment was made to Kennecott in June 1972, but subsequently the Kennecott debt was included in the general Chile debt payments, which were renegotiated in 1972 and 1973. Because Anaconda had been less careful than Kennecott to secure guarantees and involve other financial institutions, Chile made no payments to it during the entire Allende period.

When Chile's Special Copper Tribunal finally ruled on the companies' appeals in August 1972, it managed to avoid a decision on the thorny "excess profits" issue by ruling that the constitutional amendment made the president sole judge as to the amount. The ruling led Kennecott to initiate legal proceedings in a number of European courts on the grounds that, because of a "denial of justice" in the nonreviewable retroactive excess profits deduction by the Chilean president, it was entitled under international law to payment for its expropriated mines with the income from the overseas sale of Chilean copper. A French court ruled in favor of Kennecott, compelling Chilean copper to be diverted to Rotterdam. In Germany an initial decision against Chile was reversed by an appeals court; suits were also initiated in Holland, Sweden, and Italy. No copper was actually seized, and court proceedings or appeals were still taking place at the time of the September 1973 coup. However, the suits must have had some effect in discouraging potential buyers of Chilean copper.[10]

In December 1972, OPIC worked out a compensation agreement with Kennecott on the remaining debt from the 1967 Chileanization agreement. It agreed to pay Kennecott $66 million for its Chilean notes, a price that was nearly $10 million below the outstanding debt. OPIC then resold the notes on the financial market, thus avoiding the payment of a large lump sum out of its financial reserves, which would have required it to go to the United States Congress for more money. In the case of Anaconda, OPIC paid for Anaconda's insured coverage of the new Exotica mine. But it denied a claim for compensation for the investments in the older mines, insured under the Frei regime, on the grounds that they had been effectively nationalized in 1969, at a time when Anaconda had only standby insurance with OPIC. Anaconda appealed and the OPIC decision was overturned by the courts, which ruled that Anaconda had maintained effective control between 1969 and 1971. A final settlement between OPIC and Anaconda was not worked out until March 1977, when Anaconda received partial payment from OPIC, and OPIC in turn guaranteed Chilean promissory notes pledged as compensation.

The Allende government could have avoided the international complications that followed the copper nationalization. For his 1975 testimony to the Senate Select Committee on Intelligence Activities, the former Chilean ambassador, Edward Korry, obtained declassification of his cable from Santiago to Washington, dated October 1, 1971, describing his negotiations with the Allende government on the issue of compensation for expropriated American companies. According to the cable, the embassy first helped to work out agreements for the purchase, on a long-term payment basis, of the Bethlehem Steel iron mines in Chile as well as a plant belonging to the Northern Indiana Brass Company. This was followed by negotiations on an agreement to compensate the Cerro Corporation for its new Rio Blanco copper mine, where production was just beginning. The Korry cable claimed that in May 1971 Allende had agreed to compensate Cerro and "the age of Aquarius seemed to be dawning," but that the agreement was vetoed by Allende's Socialist party (presumably through the Political Command of the Popular Unity coalition, whose approval Allende sought before all major decisions). In mid-August, after the copper nationalization amendment was adopted, Korry attempted, first with the Kennecott and Anaconda companies and then with the Allende government, to secure approval of an arrangement whereby OPIC would guarantee twenty-year bonds issued by the Chilean government to compensate the companies. The companies were agreeable to accepting a lower compensation because the United States government guarantee attached to them would permit the bonds to be sold at a relatively low discount and transformed into cash. The incentive for OPIC to issue the guarantee, of course, was to avoid having to pay the substantial amounts insured against expropriation by the two companies. After receiving a favorable response from the copper specialists in the Allende government, Korry was told on September 16 that Allende wished to have a "man-to-man" talk with him, on September 27, to discuss his proposals. At the meeting Allende turned down the proposal, citing opposition within the Popular Unity coalition as his reason, and suggested that the dispute be turned over to international arbitration. The next day, Allende made his excess profits announcement. Korry ended his report to the State Department by quoting Erasmus, "In great things it is good enough to have tried." He concluded by stating that the historical record could be revealed "without shame" even to "those editorialists at home . . . who know nothing of the commitments of the Socialist and Communist Parties here . . . and who revel in assuming guilt for their own land and government."[11]

It may be argued that since the Nixon administration was opposed to the Allende government from the start such an arrangement would not have made any difference to the policies of the United States or the copper companies. However, later investigations have revealed that there were deep divisions between the State Department, on the one hand, and the Treasury and the White House, on the other, concerning the possibilities of resolving the differences between Chile and the United States by diplomatic means. What Korry had hoped for was that the earlier, amicable arrangements with other United States firms would provide a precedent for a similar agreement on copper — but the left wing of the Allende coalition blocked such a settlement. There is no way to know what the attitudes of Washington and the companies would have been if Allende had accepted Korry's offer, but there were powerful incentives on the American side to avoid a crisis in OPIC's reserves and to maintain the principle of compensation in what had appeared to be a hopeless situation in Chile.

Allende's attempt to satisfy the left wing of his Popular Unity coalition, which had insisted that "not one cent" (*ni un centavo*) of compensation should be paid, resulted in the intensified opposition of the United States government, a drop in Chile's access to international credit, and international legal and supply difficulties that were not necessary, except for ideological reasons. The constitutional amendment gave the president complete freedom for negotiation on the question of excess profits. A stretched-out compensation settlement on the basis of book value paid out of future copper profits — possibly tied to a service contract with the companies that was linked to the expansion of production — could have achieved his objectives while avoiding external economic and diplomatic pressures at a time when he was beginning to face increased opposition to his effort to carry out a transition to socialism.

POSTNATIONALIZATION PROBLEMS

Allende's economic advisors saw the nationalized copper industry as a source of "surpluses" (*excedentes*) — the Marxist circumlocution for profits — which could fuel the expansion of the whole economy. Chile had been steadily increasing its share in the returns (*retornos*) from its copper industry. Yet each succeeding scheme for securing a larger Chilean share also seemed to produce a larger profit for the American companies. The size of the profit often depended on exogenous factors, such as the Vietnam War or strikes in African copper mines. Often, it was inflated as a percentage of book value because of accelerated depreciation allowances. But the nationalists only saw large amounts of scarce dollars leaving the country with little new investment coming in, while Chile's major mineral resource was being depleted. Now, with no compensation to pay and total ownership, it seemed that, at last, Chile could receive the full benefit of its most important natural resource.

Yet a series of factors—some avoidable and some not—combined to assure that the nationalization became a "game without winners." At the time of nationalization, the Allende government had estimated that the take-over of the copper mines would save Chile $92 million a year in repatriated profits and $33 million in depreciation, even if the world price of copper remained at 50 to 55 cents per pound. The government looked forward to a large increase in production because of the production from the new mines at Exotica and Rio Blanco, which had been financed by the Frei Chileanization agreements. However, the dislocations produced by the nationalizations produced a 9 percent decline in production at the three existing major mines. As a result, production from the new mines did little more than counterbalance the declines elsewhere. In 1971, when the new mines came on stream, total copper production only increased from 280,000 metric tons in the last half of 1970 to 281,900 tons in the first half of 1971, rising to 289,500 tons in the first half of 1972. During the last year of the Allende regime, when Chile was wracked by anti-Allende strikes and in a virtual state of undeclared civil war, copper production dropped by 7.5 percent.[12]

Explanations for the drop in production were usually ideologically conditioned. The defenders of Allende attributed it to sabotage by the companies and an "invisible blockade" by the United States government and foreign companies to prevent Chile from purchasing replacement parts. Thus, Allende government spokesmen claimed that in 1970 95 percent of the capital goods for the copper industry came from the United States, while in 1972 all such parts had to be purchased elsewhere. Opponents of Allende ascribed the production problems to the incompetence of the new management, which was appointed on political rather than technical grounds, and the politicization and lack of discipline of the workers after nationalization, citing such figures as a 41 percent increase in absenteeism in the six months following nationalization. Both sides are probably right, but since it was relatively easy to secure the replacement parts elsewhere, the management and labor problems at the mine appear to have had more to do with the drop in production than did the supply of replacement parts.

Probably the single most important factor was the rapid departure of the American and Chilean *tecnicos* from the mines. While politics clearly had something to do with those departures, the Allende government's decision to discontinue the payment of managerial salaries in dollars in foreign banks, the so-called gold roll, was also a significant determinant. In Chuquicamata, 138 of the 452 supervisors left between January and August 1971 — many of them Chileans who were offered jobs elsewhere by Anaconda. At the Kennecott mines there were fewer departures, but the number rose from 8 to 16 to 27 in the same period. Additional Chileans, in more junior positions, also quit over disagreements with the new government-appointed management. In addition, there were continual work stoppages at the mines. There was a total of 67 stoppages at Chuquicamata in 1972, as well as a lengthy strike for a wage hike at El Teniente from April to July of 1973 — shortly before Allende's overthrow. Many observers who were sympathetic to the Allende government complained of the "economism" of the copper workers (that is, selfish concern for wage increases at the expense of the nation). Yet this should not have come as a surprise since Chuquicamata had voted against Allende in the 1970 elections — probably because the miners feared the consequences of nationalization by a Marxist government that viewed them as members of the "labor aristocracy." By early 1973, the Christian Democrats had a majority in the Chuquicamata trade union elections, while the government parties only received 26 percent of the vote. In the national elections, the Popular Unity candidates *lost* votes in Chuquicamata between the 1970 presidential elections and the 1973 congressional vote, contrary to the pattern elsewhere in the country, with the anti-Allende opposition receiving 51.6 percent of the male votes and 62 percent of the female votes in 1973.[13]

The production problems were accompanied by a decline in the world price of copper, which dropped from an average of sixty cents per pound in 1970 to an average of forty-eight cents per pound in 1971. (In late 1972, it rose again to record heights.) Allende spokesmen estimated that a decline of one cent per pound meant a loss of $14 million in foreign exchange to the government. At the same time, costs increased because of absenteeism, managerial problems, and the hiring of additional personnel. (The number of employees at Chuquicamata went from 8,022 to 10,250 between 1970 and 1973. Among the employees was a resident sociologist, Francisco Zapata, whose work on the subject written in exile after the coup is a principal source of information about the effects of nationalization.) As a result, the projected bonanza from nationalization did not materialize. Indeed, when the world price dropped below fifty cents per pound, except at its most efficient mine at El Teniente, Chile lost money with each pound it produced.

On balance, it seems clear that the costs of the confrontational method of nationalization adopted by Allende far exceeded its benefits.[14] At least part of the production problems in the copper industry was caused by ideological sectarianism and an inability to transcend party rivalries, either in the management of the mines or the treatment of the workers. The mining nationalization began with a national consensus behind it. But for reasons related to the general strategy of the Allende coalition, which emphasized a divisive polarization along class lines rather than national unity, that consensus rapidly disappeared. Much of this was attributable to the dynamics of Chile's multiparty democracy. However, the evidence seems to indicate that the same goal — national control of, and benefit from Chile's principal natural resource — could have been achieved in a less disruptive and costly way by populist appeals to nationalism, rather than Marxist polarization politics, and by a compromise on compensation payments to the American companies.

OTHER NATIONALIZATIONS

The strategy of the Allende government was to expand the state-owned sector as rapidly as possible through a series of *faits accomplis* (*hechos consumados*). These would not only give the government the tools to accomplish its economic plans but would also undercut the financial base of the opposition's power. Because the opposition had a majority in the Chilean Congress, it was not possible to use new legislation or a constitutional amendment for other areas of the economy, and the Allende government had to find different means to establish what it called the Area of Social Property.

One simple method was to authorize Corfo to buy out existing owners. Since the foreign and domestic capitalists feared expropriation, it was not difficult to persuade many of them to sell out on a deferred compensation basis. The United States embassy encouraged this in the cases of the iron mines owned by Bethlehem Steel Corporation and the banks owned by First National and Bank of America, as well as the Guggenheim-owned minority share in the Anglo-Lautaro Nitrate Company. In the case of domestic banks, Allende announced in December that until the end of January 1971, shareholders could sell their shares to Corfo at the average price they had commanded on the Chilean stock market in the first half of 1970 (that is, before fears of the effects of the Allende election had driven their prices down). Compensation was to be paid in immediately negotiable certificates to the small stockholders, while larger stockholders were to receive payments over two to seven years, depending on the size of their holdings. By buying bank stocks in this way, the Chilean state acquired control of most of the Chilean banking system within a year of Allende's accession to power. (An exception was the Banco de Chile, the largest private bank, which resisted the purchase plan by offering to buy any shares that came on the market with the proceeds from a Fund for Liberty, collected from private contributions and, in all probability, the CIA. The Fund for Liberty was also used to prevent government purchase of shares in Chile's only privately owned paper company, a major source of newsprint for the opposition press.)

The Allende government also made use of more dubious procedures to carry out its nationalization program. It resurrected a number of little-known "legal loopholes" that enabled it to take over firms without getting congressional approval. In 1932, a short-lived Socialist government had adopted Decree-Law 520, authorizing either expropriation or "requisition" of enterprises that ceased production, failed to produce "articles of basic necessity . . . the sale of which is denied to the public," or "unjustifiably" produced deficiencies in supply. Expropriation required full payment in cash and approval by a board of legal advisors to the government (a majority of whom were holdovers from earlier governments). Shortly after Allende came to power, this procedure was used to take over a large textile mill in the south of Chile that had been idle since the elections; it was also used in six other cases. More commonly, however, the "requisition" provisions of Decree-Law 520 were used by the government to take "temporary" control without any payment requirements. Similar provisions for "intervention" of plants that were not functioning because of labor disputes had been included in earlier labor legislation, but, again, the take-over was supposed to be temporary. (Another tactic was to grant wage increases without allowing a corresponding price rise, thus bankrupting a targeted enterprise.) The intervened or requisitioned companies were then described as having joined the Area of Social Property, despite the fact that legally the extension of government control to the operation of the plant was a temporary measure. Many companies not on the list of ninety-one strategic enterprises slated for nationalization became part of the state sector during the two prolonged antigovernment strikes during October 1972 and July-September 1973. (The government press called them "employer lockouts," but they were supported by most of the middle class, professionals, shopkeepers, and part of the peasantry.) Estimates of the total number of enterprises taken over fluctuate because some—especially those seized by the workers during a one-day revolt of a tank regiment on June 29, 1973—were later returned to their owners; the total probably exceeded 500. In addition to copper, coal, electricity, telephones, nitrate, and iron and steel, the state sector included about 30 percent of distribution, nearly all the metal processing industry, soft drinks, textiles, beer, cement, and much of the construction industry. While there were cases in which companies were "intervened" as a result of labor difficulties instigated by the government, or "requisitioned" after the government issued a "production contingent" demand for a commodity of "prime necessity" with a deadline that was impossible to fulfill so that Decree-Law 520 could be invoked, many of the later take-overs resulted from spontaneous worker seizures or actions by militants of the left wing of the government coalition who were not under the government's control.[15] In October 1971, the government introduced a bill into Congress guaranteeing that smaller businesses would not be taken over, but the Congress replied with a constitutional amendment requiring that all nationalizations, interventions, and requisitions be carried out by specific congressional law. A constitutional deadlock ensued over whether a simple or two-thirds majority were needed to override the president's veto; neither proposal was adopted.

The growth of the state sector affected both domestic and foreign enterprises. In the foreign-owned sector the Allende government seems to have followed a conscious policy of distinguishing between American-owned enterprises from those owned by Europeans or Latin Americans. Thus, it did not take over a Brazilian-owned bank or a British tobacco company, and it returned Swedish-owned properties that had been seized. Since it was relying on European and Latin American credits to meet its mounting economic problems, this policy made sense—and in any event, the American-owned enterprises were larger and more controversial. After the purchase of the Bethlehem Steel subsidiary, the government intervened the food processing plant belonging to the Ralston Purina Company, the Ford and General Motors assembly plants, and, in September 1971, the Chilean Telephone Company, a subsidiary of ITT. Subsidiaries of other American companies that became part of the Area of Social Property included those belonging to the Northern Indiana Brass Company, RCA, the Coca-Cola Company, General Electric, Pfizer, Dupont, and six film distribution companies. The petrochemical plants of which Dow Chemical owned 70 percent of the stock, were requisitioned in October 1972, resulting in a strike *against* the government take-over by the engineers, supervisors, office staff, and some of the workers.[16]

During the first year of the Allende regime, the initial effect of the new economic policies appeared to be positive. Production increased in both the private and state-owned firms, the inflation rate dropped from 35 percent in 1970 to 22 percent in 1971, unemployment dropped to 3.5 percent by the end of the year, and the share of wages in national income rose dramatically because the government decreed large wage readjustments for low income groups and because, fearing nationalization, private employers yielded to the demands made by their workers or employees. In addition, worker participation in decisionmaking in the state sector led to considerable improvement in social welfare, including the creation of day care centers, clinics, libraries, and cafeterias.

Yet what appeared to be the beginning of a successful "transition to socialism" contained within it the seeds of its future destruction. After the government take-over, the structure of decisionmaking in the plants was altered to conform to the provisions of an agreement signed by the government and the Communist-controlled Central Workers Confederation (CUT) a month after Allende took office. The principal provisions of that agreement called for the creation of a Board of Directors (*Consejo de Administración*), consisting of three elected representatives of the workers, two representatives elected by the company administrators and technicians, five appointed members chosen by the government, and a manager who was also appointed by the government. The three workers were to be elected by and were responsible to a Worker Assembly, composed of all the workers in the factory. In addition, each "productive unit" was also to have a Production Committee, whose function was to improve productivity and "form the consciousness" of the workers. This structure was not supposed to replace the activities of the already existing trade union representatives; it was designed to supplement it. Predictably, however, it resulted in rivalries between the different political parties that dominated the various representative bodies involved in establishing plant policy. The scheme was not implemented in many of the state enterprises, although in areas like textiles and mining, which were taken over early, it was in full operation. New and inexperienced managers were appointed to run the plants. Divisions among the government parties and between those parties and the opposition Christian Democrats led to work stoppages. Conflicts developed among the unions, which were usually controlled by the Communists or Christian Democrats, the new managers appointed by the state, and young militants from the Socialist and left Catholic MAPU parties, who had the most influence in the local Production Committees.[17] Beginning in late 1971, serious shortages developed as a result of the increase in demand produced by rising wages, the exhaustion of unused capacity and inventories, the lack of imports because of balance-of-payments problems, the Allende government's arbitrary and unrealistic pricing policy and exchange rate, and extensive black market activity by all elements of Chilean society including employees, workers, and peasants in the state sector. As a result of price controls, it made more economic sense to buy a steel door produced by the state sector than a wooden door produced by a private company, and an empty sack of flour cost more than a full one. The exchange rate system became more and more irrational. By the end of the Allende regime, the price of one dollar ranged from thirty Chilean escudos for certain types of regulated transactions to three thousand escudos on the black market.

The economic policy of the Popular Unity government, especially in the state-controlled sectors of the economy, was increasingly irrational. The push for a rapid transformation of the property structure in the industrial sector was accompanied by similar upheavals in the countryside. After the first year (in 1970 harvests were bountiful), food production dropped catastrophically, and scarce foreign exchange or, more often, credits from foreign countries had to be used to pay the soaring bill for imported food. In the state-controlled areas of agriculture and industry, there was no effort to make economic use of resources, but an apparently limitless supply of credit was provided by the state to cover the increasingly large deficits. This occurred at the same time that tax collections dropped from 20 percent of the gross national product in 1970 to only 11 percent in 1973, owing to inflation and the black market. According to the Chilean Finance Ministry, transfers to the Area of Social Property to cover deficits amounted to nearly 7 billion escudos in 1971 (over half of it in the last quarter of the year), 31 billion escudos in 1972, and 91 billion escudos between January and August 1973. Since the regular government budget in 1973 had a 53 percent deficit, the only way the government could cover those credits was by printing money. The supply of money, therefore, increased by 1,750 percent between 1970 and 1973, fueling runaway inflation. According to government figures, which understated the real figure, annual inflation rates in Chile reached 163 percent by the end of 1972 and 303 percent for the twelve months preceding August 31, 1973.

Imports, especially of food, rose dramatically while exports declined. In 1972 there was a deficit of $500 million in Chile's balance of payments, which was covered by borrowing from Western Europe, the Soviet Union, and other Latin American countries, especially Argentina, Mexico, and Brazil. The deficit would have been much larger if the debtor countries had not agreed to a moratorium on repayment of Chile's debts, pending agreements on a rescheduling of payments. A rescheduling agreement, which covered the period from late 1971 to the end of 1972, was reached in April 1972, but no payments were made to the principal debtor country, the United States, because Chile would not agree that it was obligated to pay further compensation to the United States copper companies. Lacking a further rescheduling agreement, Chile made no payments at all on its foreign debts between January and September 1973. When the coup occurred on September 11, Chile had increased its international indebtedness by $800 million — or $800,000 for each day of the Allende government.

There is much that can be learned from the Allende experience — chiefly what *not* to do. The most important lesson is that nationalization is an expensive process, particularly if it is carried out rapidly and in a confrontational fashion. The government and people who undertake nationalization must be prepared, then, for a period of austerity and a reduction in living standards, at least in the upper and middle classes. No such effort was undertaken in Chile. Even before Allende came to power, the state was responsible for about 70 percent of capital formation in Chile. The Allende government vastly increased its role in the economy, squandering the economic reserves that had been built up by the Frei government and ignoring basic rules for the efficient use of a scarce resource, capital. The government assumed that the profits that had previously been taken out of the country would more than compensate for any economic inefficiencies. Yet as Markos Mamalakis concluded after reviewing the Allende policy,

> State ownership is neither a more necessary nor a more efficient condition for success than private ownership; what is needed are rules that reward efficiency and penalize incompetence by integrating and harmonizing production (effort), distribution (rewards), and capital formation on a regional, class, sectoral, international, and functional basis.[18]

These rules were never formulated by the Allende government, and the result was economic chaos.

The opposition of the companies and the international difficulties that Chile encountered were predictable, but no plans seem to have been made to deal with them. Since at least 1967 the Soviet Union had made it clear that it would not support another Latin American country economically as it had supported Cuba, and its assistance to Allende was minimal. (Actual Chilean indebtedness to the USSR, China, and Eastern Europe only increased by $26 million between 1970 and 1973.) United States government opposition was intensified by the uncompensated nationalizations, and the retroactive "excess profits" doctrine was strongly opposed as a threat to American investment everywhere.

At first glance, it seems that the striking improvement in the distribution of income to the lower classes, which occurred in the first part of the Allende administration, demonstrates that nationalization can be used to improve equity and welfare in a less developed country. This analysis, however, fails to consider the subsequent sharp reduction in living standards produced by runaway inflation, during the latter part of the Allende period and after the coup. The Allende government was incapable of enforcing price controls or preventing a burgeoning black market. After the coup, the policies undertaken to reactivate the economy resulted in more serious hardship to both the poor and the middle class. It was not until 1977 that the Chilean economy returned to the level reached in 1969. The Chilean experience seems to indicate that—in the absence of authoritarian economic controls, an explicit commitment to egalitarianism, and external financial support as in Cuba—nationalization may actually be counterproductive to the goal of creating social justice because it adversely affects productivity, investment, and prices. Tax policies, welfare programs, and changes in land tenure are likely to be more effective ways to redistribute income than is the transfer of ownership of industry and mining to the government.

In addition to creating international problems, confrontational nationalization also produced serious domestic costs. Allende began his nationalizations with almost unanimous support for the copper take-over, but the constitutional and political legitimacy of that act was undercut by the politically motivated rush to take over many other industries. In the final months of the regime, it was further exacerbated by worker seizures of plants that the government had not intended to nationalize. These two factors, combined with managerial inefficiency, absenteeism, and politically inspired strikes, had a drastically adverse economic effect on Chile. The lesson seems to be that if a nationalization is to maintain democratic legitimacy and economic efficiency, it must be carefully planned, and it must have the support of a broad national consensus, rather than a narrowly partisan constituency.

The democratic nature of the Allende nationalizations produced still another problem: the conflict between central planning and local participation. The new structures for worker participation, such as the Worker Assemblies, Production Committees, and the selection of worker representatives on the Board of Directors, did not replace but were added to the existing unions and management structure. Moreover, the politicization of relations in the factory and mine made it impossible to develop discipline or ask for sacrifices on the part of those involved. In a speech to workers in February 1973, Allende alluded to the selfishness of workers who resold on the black market the goods they received as part of their pay. The politicization of the workers also contributed to the copper strike at the El Teniente in 1973, in which the copper workers demanded special economic privileges at a time of national economic crisis. The Chilean approach is in marked contrast to the Cuban one, which only permitted worker involvement in decisionmaking fifteen years after the revolution and relied on Castro's charismatic appeal, rather than democratic legalism, to destroy American influence and socialize the economy. As other examples in this book will demonstrate, nationalization is particularly difficult for a democracy to carry out, although ironically it is rivalry among the parties competing for voter support that creates the political pressure for nationalization in the first place.

DENATIONALIZATION UNDER PINOCHET

Reacting against the Allende policies after the coup, the military junta, under General Augusto Pinochet, called on a group of conservative economists to direct the economic policies of the new government—the so-called Chicago boys at the Catholic University of Chile, many of whom had been trained by Milton Friedman and Arnold Harberger at the University of Chicago. A distinction was made between "legal" nationalizations, those carried out by purchase or by constitutional amendment, which were to be retained by the state or sold to private buyers, and those taken over on a supposedly temporary basis by intervention and requisition, which were to be returned to their former owners. The government decided to sell all but about thirty of the enterprises that were now legally the property of the state, retaining the large copper mines, the steel industry, and the state enterprises that had antedated the Allende nationalizations. Major beneficiaries of the sale were Chilean financial conglomerates, such as the Edwards, Matte, or Banco Hipotecario ("Piranhas") groups that could have access to foreign capital. Domestic interest rates were still prohibitive, and inflation rates for 1974 and 1975 were 375 percent and 340 percent. (In 1976 and 1977, the rates dropped to 175 percent and 63 percent, and in 1978, the rate was "only" 30 percent.) Initially, an effort was made to sell some state enterprises to worker cooperatives. However, that preference was ended in May 1974, although, before that time, the Inter-American Foundation and AID had assisted workers in buying the large textile factory in the south that had been the first expropriated by the Allende government.

The government strategy for the reactivation of the economy included the removal of restrictions on competition by lowering tariff rates, introducing realistic exchange rates, and combating monopoly. Prices for agricultural products were raised, illegally seized land was returned to former owners, and properties that had been taken over by the procedures prescribed in the 1967 Agrarian Reform Law were divided among the peasantry into family-sized plots. Agricultural production increased sharply: from a decline of 24 percent in the last year of the Allende regime, it rose by 14 percent in 1974. Nontraditional exports, especially wood, leather, cellulose, fish, and agricultural products, increased from $87 million in 1972 to $650 million in 1977. Copper production rose from 735,000 metric tons in 1973 to 1,005,000 metric tons in 1976, but low world prices reduced Chile's revenue from copper exports. (Because of its need for foreign exchange, Chile, like state-owned copper producers elsewhere, did not observe the recommendation of a 15 percent cutback made by the Copper Exporters Consortium, CIPEC.)

The government recognized that foreign investment could provide a source of capital that was not available domestically because of Chile's raging inflation. However, in order to attract foreign investors Chile would have to settle its dispute over compensation with the copper companies. This involved the 49 percent holdings of Kennecott and Anaconda, nationalized in 1971, and the defaulted payments on the 51 percent of those companies' properties Chileanized in the 1960s, although Kennecott had received compensation from OPIC for most of its investments in connection with the Chileanization agreement. After a total of 61 negotiating sessions, settlements (*contratos de transacción*) were arrived at in July and October 1974 with Anaconda, Kennecott, and the Cerro Corporation, whose compensation did not involve the same degree of complexity. The Chilean government agreed to pay Anaconda $65 million in cash. It also gave promissory notes for $188 million, to be paid over ten years as compensation, and agreed to pay interest for both the 51 percent Chileanization debt and the 49 percent nationalization. The compensation for the 1971 Anaconda nationalization was based on a December 1970 "book value" set at $49 million, far below the estimated book value of $195 million that it had used in its appeal to the Special Copper Tribunal. Kennecott's $65 million compensation for its 49 percent nationalized debt was based on a December 1970 "book value" figure of $45 million; again, this was a low figure, since Kennecott had estimated book value at $175 million in its appeals to the Copper Tribunal and had received $81.6 million for 51 percent of El Teniente at the time of the 1967 Chileanization. In both cases, however, interest payments substantially increased the compensation.[19]

The settlement was a complex one, but it seems that the companies received full compensation on the basis of book value for the Chileanized 51 percent of their original holdings but a good deal less for the 49 percent taken over by Allende. Going concern or replacement value does not seem to have been used, and no compensation was received for in-ground rights.

The Chilean government also settled with ITT, which had a claim of $155 million for its 70 percent interest in the Chilean Telephone Company. ITT was also insured for $108 million with OPIC, but OPIC did not make payments, claiming that ITT had provoked the nationalization by intervening in Chilean affairs during and after the 1970 election. In August 1974 a panel of arbitrators rejected OPIC's contention, arguing that the ITT seizure in 1971 could not have been provoked by information on ITT intervention that only became available in 1972. When the Chilean government settled with ITT for $125 million, OPIC participated in a financial guarantee of part of the settlement.[20]

In mid-1974, the junta issued a Decree-Law on Foreign Investment granting liberal tax, tariff, repatriation, and depreciation incentives to foreigners whose investment projects were approved by an interministerial Committee on Foreign Investments. A controversy ensued with the other members of the Andean Pact. It centered around whether the Decree-Law violated the provisions of Decision 24 of the pact members, which provided for a high common external tariff and limited the areas in which foreigners would be permitted to invest. After some negotiation, Chile agreed to restrict the application of the liberalized investment provisions to investors who would not be exporting goods to other Andean Pact countries. In return, it requested and, in April 1976, received exemption from Article 3 of Decision 24, which forbade the sale of nationally owned enterprises to foreign interests. Chile also asked the pact members to increase the limit on profit remittances above the 14 percent figure set in 1970. It announced that it intended to cut protective tariffs drastically. This action was designed to reorient Chile's economy so that its exports could, eventually, compete in world markets. The deep philosophical differences between Chile and most of the other members of the pact finally led to its departure from the Andean Common Market in late 1976. A more generous foreign invest- ment law, which eliminated all requirements to sell to Chilean nationals and offered a ten-year guarantee of "tax invariability," was adopted in March 1977.[21] By 1979, Chile's average tariff rate for imports other than automobiles had dropped to 10 percent.

After the coup, Chile received substantial loans at high interest rates from American and European banks, and foreign invest- ment began to flow to Chile, although not in the amounts hoped for. Almost 90 percent of the investment was in the mining sec- tor. American investors, in particular, were reluctant to make new commitments in Chile, especially since Chile was no longer covered by OPIC insurance. During the first four years after the coup, the only new major American investment was made by ITT as part of its compensation settlement. The settlement pro- vided that $25 million would be invested over a period of ten years in a nutrition research facility. In 1978, five years after the coup, an American oil company agreed to begin offshore oil and gas exploration, the Exxon Company bought a medium-sized Chilean copper mine, and Goodyear Tire & Rubber purchased the government-owned tire factory. Dutch, Japanese, and Ger- man investments were also almost exclusively in mining. Until late 1977, when there were the beginnings of a strong recovery and a sharp drop in the inflation rate, Chilean industry remained in a state of deep depression with high unemployment. Even af- ter the recovery, unemployment remained high (19 percent at the end of 1978) and foreign investment low, except in mining.

THE LESSONS OF CHILE

This study of the changing policies of Chile has indicated how difficult it is for a country to work out a viable strategy for the control and direction of foreign investment. Successively, Chile has tried an open door policy, increased taxation, the control of marketing, a tax concession to increase investment and production, state participation in ownership and sales, and complete nationalization. With the exception of the Chileanization arrangements of 1967 and 1969, none seems to have worked well. In each case including that of Chileanization, a combination of external factors, especially changes in the world market for copper, and internal pressures, such as the desire of the political opposition to capitalize on the mistakes of the government, caused Chileans to conclude that current policy was a "failure." The succession of partial failures led to the biggest failure of all — the way in which the nationalization of copper was carried out by the Allende government.

The mere fact of nationalization does not account for the Allende disaster. There have been, and will continue to be, successful nationalizations in terms of increasing, at minimum cost, national control of and benefit from economic activities that had previously been carried out by foreign interests. The Allende nationalizations, however, were designed and implemented in a way that made them unusually costly in terms of domestic strife, judicial and economic conflicts, and declining production.

Some of the problems stemmed from the openness of Chile's democratic political system. The freedom of expression and debate, the frequent elections, and the many competing parties representing a variety of orientations made it difficult to carry out a consistent policy toward economic development. This, in turn, discouraged domestic investment, and it compelled the state to rely more and more on public investment. However, even with the increased imposition and collection of taxes that took place under the Frei presidency, when government tax receipts rose by 50 percent in real terms, only limited resources were available for investment purposes because various pressure groups continually pressed for higher wages to combat Chile's chronic inflation. Before 1970, some of the investment gap was taken up by an increase in foreign investment, but before this could occur, the Chilean government had to grant considerable concessions. Yet once it did so, and the investment was made, the opposition accused the government of increasing the "dependency" of the country on foreign or multinational companies.

Reacting to this criticism and influenced by their own Marxist ideology, the economic policymakers of the Allende government decided that investment would be carried out more "rationally" if the state used the expropriated profits of the foreign imperialists and domestic monopolies. Unfortunately, once nationalization took place those profits disappeared, tax collections dropped catastrophically, and a politically motivated redistribution of income financed by foreign credits and the increased printing of money, took precedence over a rational investment policy. Allende's "socialist consumerism" followed a long tradition in Chilean politics. Income extracted from the export sector was spent on politically attractive welfare programs, food subsidies for the urban sector (where the votes were), or subsidies to importers, rather than on long-term investment and development.

The junta economists have recognized Chile's need for investment capital and have provided attractive investment incentives. However, the only area in which foreign investors have responded is the one in which Chile has a substantial comparative advantage — mining. Even there, they have insisted on stronger guarantees against changes in "the rules of the game," including judicial review of disputes outside of Chile. Recognizing the "exposed" enclave character of mining, some companies (such as Noranda and Falconbridge) have preferred a joint venture formula that gives the Chilean state a direct stake in ownership but leaves managerial control in the hands of the foreign investors.

It is easy enough to ascribe the favorable policies toward foreign investment to the triumph of domestic reaction and international imperialism, both of which had a demonstrable role in Allende's overthrow. However, this overlooks the basic need of a capital-short underdeveloped country for infusions of outside private capital under controlled but favorable conditions. How strict those conditions will be, as the case of Mexico demonstrates, depends on the overall bargaining position of the host country. The bargaining power of Chile is weak, as compared to that of, for example, Brazil and Mexico. Alternative sources of investment capital, from increased domestic taxation or from loans from international banks or financial institutions, are limited; in 1977, the servicing of Chile's foreign debt absorbed 54.2 percent of its export income.[22] Thus, *faute de mieux*, there emerges a resurgence of interest in foreign private investment. As elsewhere in Latin America, it has become evident to government policymakers that foreign investment provides capital, efficient management, technology, and export markets. Whether the investor will respond depends on the size of the internal or external market, the stability of the conditions under which he enters, and the profit potential. Chile offers the last but not the first two.

The Chilean experience also demonstrates the need for careful analysis of the ways in which a developing country employs its foreign exchange income — in particular the relation between investment and consumption. Although Marxism promises the Third World a program of rapid development and rational planning, the predominantly Marxist government in Chile went further in "decapitalization" and economic irrationality than any of its more capitalist-oriented predecessors.

Chile is also a useful case study of the relation between United States foreign policy and the defense of American investment. During World War II and the Korean War, United States government policy was chiefly concerned with maintaining a low price for copper during periods of domestic inflationary pressure. The arrangements it worked out with the American copper companies to accomplish this first led Chileans to consider the need for national control over the copper industry. During the cold war, the major preoccupation of the United States government was seeing that Communist influence did not increase in Latin America. The record, as documented by the United States Senate ITT and CIA investigations in 1973 and 1975, indicates that while the CIA's involvement in Chilean politics was aimed at fighting communism this often involved the active cooperation of American business representatives. After Chile became a showcase for the Alliance for Progress, and the AID Investment Guarantee program was extended to Chile, the United States government had an additional reason, besides normal diplomatic protection, to be concerned with the fate of American investments. In 1969, Ambassador Korry took an active role in pressuring Anaconda to accept Chileanization; this was clearly connected with the fact that AID Investment Guarantees had been signed with the copper companies in 1967. In 1971 the United

States embassy sought a compromise solution to the problems likely to be posed by the copper nationalization, and again embassy activity was increased because OPIC would otherwise have to pay a large compensation figure. Thus, although there was always an identifiable national security interest separable from, and occasionally opposed to (e.g., the pressure on Anaconda to Chileanize in 1969 and the resistance to the ITT economic blockade proposals in 1971) that of the United States investor, in practice they usually coincided. The revelations after the Chilean coup, linking American companies with the CIA, and the United States embassy's involvement in investment controversies as a result of the OPIC insurance program, led to pressure in the United States Congress for stronger controls on American-based multinationals, as well as arguments for the termination of the OPIC investment insurance program. The revelations also led to a more general questioning of past United States policy toward overseas business and to a number of proposals for policy changes which will be evaluated in the concluding chapter of this book.

The Chilean case also had an impact in the United Nations. As a result of President Allende's speech of December 1972, describing the activities of ITT in Chile, the UN formed a Commission and Centre on Transnational Enterprises and encouraged the preparation of a code of conduct for multinational enterprises. The Allende case also contributed to the radicalization in attitudes and policy of President Echeverria in Mexico during the last part of his administration.

The role of international law in the Chilean case seems to have been a standoff. Against American assertions of the duty to compensate, Chileans cited UN declarations on the control of natural resources and international law texts, which maintained that full compensation was not required in cases of large-scale changes in the economy, as distinct from individual expropriations. Against the companies' claims of "a denial of justice" in the appeals procedures, the Chileans spoke of the recognized right of governments to take action to recover "unjust enrichment." They cited American examples of retroactive deprivation of vested rights through the renegotiation of war contracts, through changes in tax laws applying to past income, and even through the abolition of slavery by constitutional amendment. The Chileans also supported the use of an arbitration treaty signed between the United States and Chile in 1914, but United States government negotiators dismissed this as a dilatory tactic.[23]

Finally, the fact that Chile received so little financial assistance from the Soviet Union will not go unnoticed by others contemplating a similar course of action. Although Ambassador Korry warned the Soviet ambassador, according to his 1971 cable, that the cost of "bailing Allende out" ($350 million a year in hard currency) would be high, it was already evident that the Soviet Union did not intend to support another Cuba, particularly one with little strategic value. The conclusion, therefore, must be that, short of a Maoist or Castroite centralized dictatorship which imposes a sharply reduced living standard on all except the poorest groups, confrontation-type nationalization is likely to be a bad policy for Third World countries. It is difficult and costly; it cuts the country off from outside sources of credit, investment, technology, and management; and it results in inefficiency, domestic polarization, economic chaos, and, quite likely, military intervention.

6

Peru—The Limits of Nationalization as a Weapon against Dependence

There is hardly a Peruvian participating in the money economy of the country who does not eat, wear, or use something processed, manufactured, or imported by Casa Grace.
— Grace Company Study 1954, in Charles Goodsell, *American Corporations and Peruvian Politics*

I never expropriated anything and yet I had to deal with the arrogance of the American oil companies and the unremitting hostility of the United States Embassy. My successors have nationalized American oil interests left and right, and Washington can't seem to do enough for them. How do you explain that?
— Fernando Belaúnde Terry, 1976

We knew we had you. The most sensitive point about American foreign policy is that you gringos want to be loved; if the Hickenlooper sanctions had been applied against Peru even that small amount of love you have here would be expelled by the wave of hate coming from the entire South American continent.
— Peruvian Foreign Ministry official

*The trends of increased host government antagonism to-
ward the foreign investor and decreased home support of
him mean that in the future we can expect international
business to face ever greater political difficulties in Latin
America. Increasingly overseas affiliates will be operating in
an antagonistic environment.*
> — Charles Goodsell, "The Politics of Direct
> Foreign Investment in Latin America," 1972

*I sense that the rising tide of nationalism and anti-foreign
capital attitudes could be approaching its high water mark.*
> — C. W. Robinson, President, Marcona Mining
> Company, 1972

*It is hard to make a loan to a country, if some of your old
customers in the United States feel that they have been
robbed by that country.*
> — New York banker during the Marcona
> negotiations, 1976

No More Expropriations
> — Headline in *La Cronica*, Lima, 1976

In the early 1960s, Peru was a classic case of an economy which
was dominated by foreign investors and a domestic oligarchy.
Most of its major commodities — cotton, sugar, fish products,
lead, zinc, silver, copper, and the bulk of its oil — were produced
and/or exported by American-owned companies. Peru's economic
policy was an open one. It provided for free convertibility of the
Peruvian sol into hard currencies. It encouraged foreign investment with provisions for rapid depreciation and, in the case of
the mining sector, a depletion allowance modeled on that of the
United States. The book value of United States investment
amounted to $600 million, of which two-thirds was in petroleum
and mining. The distribution of land was the most inequitable in
the world — 2 percent of the rural population owned 90 percent of
the arable land. Income distribution was not much better, with
the top 1 percent of the population controlling 25 percent of the

national income, while the bottom 20 percent had only 2.5 percent. Since the early 1950s, the rural population had been emigrating to the cities in search of a better life. But two-thirds of the population still lived in conditions of desperate poverty in the countryside and *sierra* highlands, and an Indian language was the mother tongue of about 40 percent. Nearly half the population was illiterate, and, because of a literacy requirement, they were denied the right to vote.

By 1975, the pattern described above had changed significantly. The mining and petroleum sectors, with the important exception of the Southern Peru Copper Company, were owned by the state; the structure of agricultural holdings had been transformed, with 300,000 families receiving land and the most productive areas operated by cooperatives; the W. R. Grace Company sugar plantations, manufacturing companies, food processors, and the fishmeal industry had been nationalized; there were strong controls on foreign investment, including a provision mandating a "fade-out" of foreign ownership over fifteen years and the gradual transfer of 50 percent of the ownership of industry to the workers; and an experiment in complete worker ownership ("Social Property") had been initiated by the state. Income distribution had improved in the modern sector (about one-third of those economically active), but except for an important educational reform, there had been little improvement in the life of the rural poor.

These changes had been carried out under the auspices of the nationalist regime that came to power in 1968 in a military coup, headed by General Juan Velasco Alvarado. Determined to eliminate Peru's *dependencia* on foreign companies and their domestic allies, the military regime took over the American-owned International Petroleum Company (IPC), the large agrarian landholdings, the International Telephone and Telegraph (ITT)-owned telephone company, the foreign-owned banks, all unused mining concessions, the fishmeal companies (some of them owned by American companies), the extensive properties of the Cerro mining corporation, and, finally and very suddenly, the American-owned Marcona iron mines. The badly timed and costly Marcona nationalization, which took place in July 1975, was directly related to the overthrow of General Velasco by General Francisco Morales Bermúdez in late August.

Velasco's military regime had attempted to use nationalization to establish a distinctive Peruvian "third way," aimed at creating a new model of development that was "neither capitalist nor Communist," neither individualist nor collectivist. Thus, the Peruvian experience, between 1968 and 1975, offers a useful study of the possibilities and limits of nationalization as an instrument to reduce or eliminate foreign economic influence. It also involved a number of innovative experiments in restructuring ownership in industry and agriculture.

The reorientation of Peruvian policy after Velasco's overthrow illustrates the problems that a nationalist reformer is likely to face in an effort to wrest control of the economy from foreign and domestic elites and pursue an independent nationalist course. Two of Velasco's nationalizations involved the possibility that the United States would implement legislative sanctions against expropriation. The Peruvian case reveals, however, that the most important limits on nationalization are more fundamental — the continuing need for new outside capital and for renegotiation of mounting debts to foreign banks and international financial institutions. Nationalization in Peru turned out to be more expensive than anticipated, and lack of credit, declining export revenues, and a weakened domestic economy finally forced its abandonment.

The Peruvian case is also interesting as it relates to the respective influences of concern for the protection of American overseas investment and national security interests in the formulation of United States foreign economic policy. Unlike Allende's Chile, the Peruvian military regime could not be accused of sympathy with Communism, however anti-American some of its statements were. It is true that Peru closed the United States military aid mission and accepted Soviet military equipment, but this was a reaction to the various conditions that the United States placed on its aid program. The Peruvian case, therefore, was different from those of Guatemala, Cuba, or Chile, where United States government opposition to the extension of Communist influence reinforced the claims of expropriated United States businesses for government support. The Peruvian military exhibited a quasi-neutralist, Third World orientation, but it was not sympathetic to Communism. As a result, United States policymakers were compelled to decide on the degree to which the interests of investors — as distinct from strategic interests — merited official support. When the identification of those interests with government policy as mandated in the Hickenlooper Amendment was tested, it was found too inflexible and was not applied; the amendment was subsequently amended to give the president freedom in deciding when it should be applied. On the other hand, the possibility of the application of a similar legislative sanction, the 1974 González Amendment requiring United States opposition to international loans to countries that expropriate without prompt, adequate, and effective compensation, was important to the resolution of expropriation disputes between Peru and the American companies in 1974 and 1976. Those disputes would probably not have been resolved without active United States government participation. That involvement suggests that, in the appropriate circumstances, the exercise by the United States of the role of "honest broker" between the contending parties in investment disputes may be effective in bringing about a solution.

The Peruvian case also illustrates two other developments, already noted in the examinations of Mexico and Chile. The Peruvian state was relatively weak in the early 1960s, but it was enormously strengthened and expanded as a result of the changes carried out under the Velasco regime. The Morales government, which succeeded Velasco, attempted to limit the cost of the burgeoning state apparatus and to reduce the preponderance of the government in the economy. Its approach was to promote private investment, which had been limited and even discouraged during the 1968–75 period. The reaction against statism and the effort to encourage private investment mean that it is likely that no further nationalizations will take place in Peru's immediate future. In any event, in the areas of mining, utilities, and finance, with the exception of the Southern Peru Copper Company which is engaged in an important expansion of copper output at Cuajone, there is almost nothing left to nationalize.

THE INTERNATIONAL PETROLEUM COMPANY AND THE RADICALIZATION OF THE PERUVIAN MILITARY

It is unclear whether, when the Peruvian military took power in 1968, it adopted as its goal complete state control of natural resources, communications, and banking, or whether that goal took shape more gradually in the years that followed. In 1974, the government published *Plan Inca* outlining its program for nationalization of many sectors of the economy, the establishment of worker participation in ownership in industry, and the creation of worker-controlled companies. Although the military claimed that the plans had been drawn up secretly in 1968, from the wording of the plan it appears that many sections were written long after the military leaders came to power. Moreover, the repeated insistence by military spokesmen in 1968 that the goals of the revolution in the area of nationalization were limited to the "recovery" of the oil properties of the International Petroleum Company and the intensification of agrarian reform seems to support the latter interpretation.[1] There is no disagreement, however, that from the outset the long-standing dispute over the status of the International Petroleum Company's holdings at La Brea y Pariñas in northern Peru was a major concern of the Peruvian military.

The International Petroleum Company produced and refined about two-thirds of Peru's oil in 1968. Its major wells at La Brea y Pariñas had been the object of public controversy for over fifty years. The actual subsoil title to a tar pit on the site of the present fields had been granted to a Peruvian aristocrat by the Peruvian government in 1826, in payment of a debt incurred during the independence movement. Its text seemed to assign to the owner absolute subsoil property rights — in a grant that some Peruvian lawyers were later to insist was in violation of the principles of Peruvian constitutional law. In 1888, the Peruvian government issued a decree recognizing the ownership of both surface and subsoil, but it also imposed a special tax regime equivalent to the tax for ten, ten-acre mining claims (*pertenencias*), although the area, in fact, comprised over 400,000 acres.[2]

In 1913 a Canadian subsidiary of Standard Oil of New Jersey

leased La Brea y Pariñas and, a year later, another Canadian company, the International Petroleum Company (IPC), was created to operate the Peruvian oil holdings. Shortly thereafter, the highly irregular tax status of the property became a matter of public controversy. In the meantime, production of petroleum had risen from 8,000 barrels a year, in 1890, to 1,800,000 barrels in 1915. Because of the special tax regime, taxes paid by the company amounted to only $150 a year. In 1914 the Peruvian government ordered a survey of the property and imposed a tax bill of $6 million. Standard Oil of New Jersey reacted by securing the intervention of the American and British embassies against the "confiscatory" tax. While the matter was being debated in the Peruvian Congress, both the company and the Canadian government exercised some not-too-subtle pressures on the Peruvians. IPC, having already discontinued oil exploration in Peru, let it be known that it was contemplating the cessation of all oil extraction at its fields, and the Canadian government requisitioned for war purposes one of the two Canadian tankers that transported oil from the fields to Lima, announcing that the other tanker would soon be withdrawn unless a settlement was reached. Standard Oil then withdrew the second tanker, and in December 1918, under pressure of a cutoff of Lima's oil supply, the Peruvian Congress agreed to submit the dispute to international arbitration.

Six months later, dictator Augusto B. Leguía seized power, commencing an eleven-year rule during which he followed a policy that strongly favored British and American investors. Leguía agreed to an arbitration agreement with the British government which provided that a decision on the tax status of La Brea fields would be made by a tribunal comprised of a Briton, a Peruvian, and a neutral third party.

In March 1922, a British representative and the Peruvian foreign minister signed an agreement in Lima, which was incorporated in the Tribunal's Award (*Laudo*) issued in Paris a month later. It established a special tax regime for a period of fifty years that was favorable to the company. In addition, the company was to pay the Peruvian government $1 million in settlement of all back claims.

After the overthrow of Leguía in 1931, the Peruvian Congress attacked the 1922 settlement on the grounds that it had not received congressional approval, and it attempted to submit the matter to the Permanent Court of International Justice. IPC successfully blocked the moves to revoke the agreement through its financial and political influence with the new government. Thus, it was not until the late 1950s that the issue again became salient in Peruvian politics. In 1957, the company, recognizing that its anomalous tax situation left it open to nationalist attack and desperate for an increase in the government-regulated price of domestic gasoline which now consumed 75 percent of its production, applied to have its status changed to conform to that of a concession under the 1952 Petroleum Law.

On July 25, 1959, the government finally authorized a large increase in the price of gasoline, which at this time was priced at the equivalent of less than ten cents a gallon. It also announced that negotiations were to begin for the transformation of IPC's holdings to concession status. At once, the price increases were attacked in the Peruvian press and by Congress, and they soon became the basis for a more generalized attack on the validity of the 1922 award. The attack against the oil company combined the members of future president Fernando Belaúnde Terry's centrist Acción Popular party with various left-wing parties and with the conservative newspaper, *El Comercio.* A significant addition to this unlikely anti-IPC coalition took place during the following year. A commission of army chiefs issued a document declaring that the 1922 award was null and void because it exceeded the congressional instructions of 1918 and because it violated the constitution in yielding Peruvian subsoil, a view that was reasserted by the joint chiefs of staff a month later. The officers' conclusion was that IPC should pay all back taxes due for a regular concession from January 1, 1915 until the present.[3]

In 1962, the Peruvian armed forces seized power to prevent the possible election to the presidency of their old enemy, the antimilitarist, populist leader, Víctor Raúl Haya de la Torre. The Kennedy administration, pursuing the goals of the Alliance for Progress, extracted a promise from the Peruvian military that they would permit an early return to civilian rule. In 1963, in a rerun of the presidential election, Fernando Belaúnde Terry was elected, running on a platform that included a promise of the "progressive nationalization" of IPC. Anxious to avoid a direct confrontation with IPC, he promised in his inaugural address to resolve the controversial issue through negotiations within ninety days. The Peruvian negotiators offered IPC a twenty-five-year operating contract if the oil fields were turned over to Peru, but IPC insisted on retaining full control. After the ninety days had expired, Belaúnde submitted legislation to the Congress providing for the establishment of a new legal and tax status for the company and threatening nationalization in the event it was not accepted by the company. The opposition-dominated Congress responded by passing its own bill, unilaterally annulling the 1918 legislative authorization of arbitration and declaring the 1922 award null and void — and there the matter rested.

It was at this point that the United States government began to be actively involved in the controversy. In early 1964, after President Johnson appointed Thomas C. Mann as assistant secretary of state for Latin America, the flow of aid to Peru, which had been stepped up (Peru, like Chile, was to be a "showcase" of United States aid to democratic regimes) under Kennedy's Alliance for Progress, was slowed down and a new economic assistance package was permanently sidetracked, pending a settlement with the company. When Lincoln Gordon took over the position of assistant secretary in early 1966, the slowdown was reversed, following informal assurances by Belaúnde that he would not expropriate IPC. However, in the meantime, aid commitments had been reduced from $30 million for fiscal 1964 to $2 million for fiscal 1966. (Food for Peace, the Peace Corps, and technical assistance were unaffected.)

The quasi embargo on new aid seems to have had no real effect in producing a resolution of the IPC problem. The embargo is explicable chiefly in terms of Assistant Secretary Mann's pro-business attitudes and frequent hostility to the more extravagant promises embodied in the Alliance for Progress. Like later "non-overt" slowdowns, it was never publicly linked to the settlement of the IPC dispute; instead, the Peruvians were supposed to "get the message."[4]

The message that the Peruvian military leaders got was that the

United States government was engaging in strong-arm methods to pressure the Peruvians to take actions that they viewed as harmful to the national interest. Besides the Hickenlooper Amendment, threatening a cutoff of aid to nationalizing countries, the United States Congress had amended the Sugar Act to withdraw the sugar import quota from any country that nationalized American property without taking steps within six months that were "determined by the president to be appropriate and adequate . . . including the prompt payment [of compensation] to the owner." To make matters worse, shortly after the reopening of aid flows to Peru in 1966, Congress passed additional legislation aimed directly at Peru: (1) it mandated the termination or reduction of aid to any country engaged in excessive military expenditures, especially on "sophisticated weapons systems" (the Peruvians wanted to purchase supersonic jet fighters); and (2) it reduced aid by amounts equivalent to any fines imposed on United States fishing vessels (the Peruvians had been attempting to establish a 200-mile fishing zone under their exclusive jurisdiction, levying fines on United States fishing boats within that area).[5]

In July 1967, the Peruvian Congress again took action on the IPC dispute, adopting a law that declared IPC's title null and void and declaring its oil fields a national reserve to be developed in accordance with the 1952 Petroleum Law. A Peruvian tax court declared that IPC owed $144 million for "illegal" profits received over the last fifteen years (the period of the statute of limitations), which, in view of the retroactive nullification of the 1922 award, were to be returned to the state as "unjust enrichment." Again, beyond an attachment order of company assets in the amount of $650,000, nothing was done to collect the debt, but the principle that it enunciated was later extended back to 1924 by the military, during the postexpropriation negotiations over compensation in 1969.[6]

The annual State of the Nation address given by the Peruvian president on July 28, had been the occasion each year for a renewed effort, on one side or the other, to settle the continuing IPC problem. After years of intransigence, IPC decided just before the 1968 address to announce its willingness to turn over voluntarily its holdings at La Brea y Pariñas to the small Peruvian state oil company in return for refining and marketing contracts on a concession basis and the allocation of new exploration acreage elsewhere. After an all-night negotiating session, which included a postmidnight intervention by the United States ambassador to persuade the IPC general manager to return to the Presidential Palace and accept the government's terms, Belaúnde formally took possession of the IPC oil fields on August 13, 1968.

Following the publication of the hastily concluded agreements between the government and the company and the announcement of the take-over of the disputed oil fields, a dramatic reversal of Belaúnde's political position took place. The Peruvian economy was suffering from rampant inflation (30 percent), and the sol had been devalued after nearly a decade of stable prices and exchange rates. Even though a new presidential election was not due until mid-1969, the political parties were already maneuvering to gain maximum advantage for their candidates. Within a month of the Act of Talara, by which Belaúnde had taken possession of the IPC properties, all the political parties were attacking the agreement's provisions as a sellout to IPC. The attack was led by the head of the state oil company, who made a dramatic television appearance on September 10, announcing his resignation and claiming that a missing page of IPC's oil purchase contract with the state company had guaranteed that it would pay the Peruvians a favorable price in dollars. IPC denied that the "missing page" ever existed, but the announcement provoked a public uproar, and a group of thirty-six army generals held a meeting, led by the Army chief of staff, General Juan Velasco Alvarado, at which they denounced the recent actions of the government. When Belaúnde's party split into two factions on September 21 making it almost certain that Haya de la Torre, the old enemy of the military, would be elected in the 1969 elections, the military decided to move.

As a result of nine years of incessant nationalist agitation by left, right, and center, the IPC position had become untenable, and by the time it decided to yield to nationalist pressure, it was almost too late. Other factors, notably the state of the economy and the impending election of Haya de la Torre, were influential in persuading the military to intervene, but the IPC issue offered both an excuse and a justification. As later developments would demonstrate, it also set the new regime on an anti-*dependencia* course that led to continuing friction with the United States, a drop in foreign investment, and a fundamental restructuring of the Peruvian economy. From an economic point of view, there was no particular need to nationalize IPC. From the political and ideological standpoint, it gave legitimacy to the Velasco regime and a reformist orientation that differed strikingly from that of most contemporary Latin American military regimes.

IPC EXPROPRIATION
AND THE EYEBALL-TO-EYEBALL CONFRONTATION

On October 3, 1968, Belaúnde was ousted from the presidency. A day later, the military junta, headed by General Velasco, denounced the recent IPC agreements as null and void, and on October 9 both the oil fields at La Brea y Pariñas and the IPC refinery at Talara were occupied and expropriation procedures were initiated. The take-over of the refinery was justified as partial payment of the "debt" that IPC owed the nation. The expropriation decree carefully pointed out, however, that "the exercise of the power to expropriate does not militate against foreign investment, much less against private property in general."[7]

In January and February 1969, the government took over the rest of IPC's properties in Peru, including its Lima office and the network of Esso stations throughout the country. It indicated that it was willing to pay full compensation once the company had made restitution to Peru for the value of all the petroleum "illegally" extracted since 1924 — which it fixed at $690 million.[8] The Peruvian government evaluated IPC properties at $71 million, while IPC estimated that its holdings were worth over $200 million, including $35 million for subsoil reserves that were not recognized by Peru as belonging to the company.

The take-over of IPC was relatively simple since most of its technicians were Peruvian. It was now primarily concerned with supplying Peru's domestic market because in the early 1960s Peru had become a net importer of oil. Thus, Peru was not faced with the kinds of dependence on the multinational companies for technology, marketing, and transportation that hampered other nationalizing countries. It already possessed a small state oil company with some expertise, and Esso International had "Peruvianized" the personnel and much of the management of its IPC operation. The only serious problems that faced Peru then, arose from the sanctions mandated by the United States Congress, especially the Hickenlooper and Sugar Act cutoff provisions.

Both those provisions provided a deadline of six months for the imposition of sanctions. That clock started to tick on October 9, 1968. During that same period, in January 1969, a new Republican administration under Richard Nixon took office in Washington. The Peruvian expropriation provided the first instance of possible implementation of the Hickenlooper and Sugar Act sanctions in Latin America. In early March, President Nixon warned that they would be invoked if compensation were not forthcoming from the Peruvians. A few days later, he sent a special emissary to Peru, John N. Irwin, who held a series of meetings between March 17 and April 3 with President Velasco to discuss outstanding issues between the two countries, chiefly the IPC dispute. According to Irwin's dispatches to the State Department, the Peruvians told him that IPC could appeal the $690 million debt through administrative channels, submitting proof of the validity of their titles and their good faith possession. Irwin suggested international arbitration or conciliation. The Peruvians immediately rejected his proposal, stating that it violated the Calvo principles contained in the Peruvian constitution. At later meetings, Irwin suggested that token compensation be given to the company, which would involve Peru's acceptance of the $200 million evaluation set by the company, followed by deduction of a figure near the $144 million tax bill that had been presented to the company by the Belaúnde government. (Irwin mentioned $75–150 million.) Velasco, however, insisted that the maximum compensation that the Peruvians would recognize was $71 million and asserted that the lowest possible figure on the petroleum products "illegally" extracted since 1924 was $490 million. Irwin also alluded to the possibility of "indirect ways" of financing the compensation – through a large Export-Import Bank loan for the mining sector – but the Peruvians continued to adhere to what the embassy dispatch called their "theological and intricate web of logic." There was a brief flurry of embassy interest in a scheme proposed by Occidental Petroleum to provide indirect compensation to IPC from the proceeds of a possible Occidental service contract to operate IPC's nationalized Lima holdings, but it soon became apparent that Peru would not accept such an arrangement. On April 3, Irwin returned for conversations in Washington and indicated that he was pessimistic about the outcome.[9]

The bargaining position of the United States in these negotiations was particularly weak. An embargo on oil sales would be ineffective. Peru did not need external markets or shipping for the oil it had nationalized, and it had the technical capacity to keep its domestic oil flowing. Because of earlier aid reductions, the threatened cutoff of United States assistance involved relatively small amounts – about $36 million in undistributed development loans, $11 million in technical assistance and commodity grants, and an estimated $20–45 million (depending on the world sugar price) resulting from the cutoff of access to the higher United States sugar price under the quota system. More serious, however, was the possible denial of access to future loans, foreign investment flows, and credit from the Export-Import Bank and the multilateral and private banks. For their part, the Peruvians could have declared a moratorium on repayments for past loans, about $50 million a year, but this would have certainly involved the end of access to international credit. Peru could also have threatened a freeze on profit repatriation and amortization by other United States investors, estimated at between $70 million and $90 million a year.[10]

However, the Velasco government was not interested in a confrontation with all foreign investors and the international financial community. Besides asserting the unique character of the IPC case in the very act of expropriation, Velasco stated in an otherwise highly inflammatory speech on February 9, "The revolutionary government declares to the world that any other foreign investing company does not have to worry at all." Irwin had referred in his March conversations with Velasco to a possible

Export-Import Bank loan because Peru was currently attempting to secure nearly $500 million in external financing from many sources for the development of a huge new copper mine at Cuajone. On the side of the foreign investors, the other companies had no love for IPC, which they considered to have behaved badly in the past. They were reluctant to see the rest of the American business community suffer for IPC's transgressions. Esso itself was divided on the wisdom of applying the Hickenlooper Amendment, and there were pressures on American policymakers from other business interests arguing against the application of the amendment.[11] Thus, the differences among the foreign investors in Peru and Peru's emphasis on the special character of the IPC case argued against the implementation of sanctions.

In what the press called the "eyeball-to-eyeball" confrontation between Presidents Nixon and Velasco, it was Nixon who blinked. On April 6, Irwin returned to Peru to report that the company had agreed to pursue the administrative appeal against the alleged $690 million debt. A day later the secretary of state declared at a press conference that the administrative appeal together with the continuing negotiations in Peru would be taken by the United States government as fulfillment of the legislative requirement of "appropriate steps" toward compensation in order to satisfy the requirements of the Hickenlooper Amendment and the Sugar Act.

Over the next six months, IPC continued to file appeals with various administrative bodies, the governing junta, and the cabinet. On August 6, 1969, the government declared that the process of administrative appeal had been terminated, and two weeks later it expropriated all of IPC's remaining assets in Peru. Success in further appeals appeared unlikely, especially after December 1969 when the government carried out a purge of the judiciary replacing all but two of the members of the Supreme Court and creating a National Council of the Judiciary with the power to suspend or remove any judge. The process of transfer of the company's assets was not completed until May 1972, at which time all appeals had been definitively rejected.

On April 9, Ambassador Irwin returned to the United States and announced that a Peruvian negotiating team would come to Washington at the end of April. No progress was made, although lengthy discussions took place in April and May. Irwin returned to Peru in late August, remaining in Lima until September 9. However, neither the United States Congress, the business community, nor the new ambassador to Peru, Taylor Belcher, was in favor of invoking Hickenlooper at this point, and it was decided in September to continue to defer its application.[12]

Instead, a policy of nonovert economic sanctions by the United States was adopted (Velasco complained to Irwin about the credit squeeze that Peru was already encountering), and it was continued until 1974. The sanctions applied were the indefinite deferral of bilateral aid projects and behind-the-scenes pressures to prevent loans from the multilateral banks, the World Bank, and the Inter-American Development Bank. It was hoped that combined with the decline in foreign investment, these sanctions would persuade Peru to come to some kind of settlement with IPC. The policy had mixed results, as will be described later in this chapter. It did not produce a compromise agreement between IPC and Peru, but it probably contributed to Velasco's willingness, in 1974, to agree to an overall settlement of all outstanding expropriation disputes, including the payment by Peru to the United States government of a lump sum to be distributed at its discretion. One of the beneficiaries of that sum — over the objections of the Peruvian government — was IPC. For its $200 million claim it received the relatively small amount of $23.1 million, out of a total lump-sum payment by Peru of $76 million.

OTHER EXPROPRIATIONS

The other United States companies in Peru had hoped to avoid a fate similar to that of IPC. Yet the IPC nationalization set a pattern that led to a similar outcome for many of them. The next American properties to be taken over were the coastal sugar estates owned by the giant W. R. Grace Company. They had been exempted from the Belaúnde Agrarian Reform Law of 1964 because they were efficient and productive, but the military was determined that a much stronger law was necessary. Their determination to engage in more radical land reform seems to have been influenced by their experiences combating rural unrest and guerrilla movements in the mid-1960s. In addition, attendance at the new social science program at the School of Advanced Military Studies (CAEM) in the early 1960s is usually cited as a radicalizing influence on the military, but another writer has claimed that the driving force for reform came from a group of officers associated with Military Intelligence.[13] On June 24, 1969, the government promulgated an agrarian reform decree-law that was much stronger than the law adopted in 1964, both in its scope and in its specific provisions. An indication of the developmentalist orientation of the Velasco government was the decree-law's provision that compensation bonds issued to the expropriated landowners could be used to finance up to 50 percent of new industrial investments in Peru if the bondholders drew on other resources to provide the other 50 percent. The provision that affected the W. R. Grace Company forbade companies or corporations from holding rural property, with a deadline of six months for the transfer of these properties to rural cooperatives.[14]

The Grace investments in Peru dated back over a century to the founding of the company by William Russell Grace, who had emigrated to Peru from Ireland at the age of nineteen. (Grace later moved to New York.) By the 1960s, the company owned an airline (sold to Braniff in the mid-1960s); a shipping company; four textile mills; two large sugar plantations; chemical, paper box, and paint plants; as well as fishmeal and mining enterprises. When its two sugar estates were expropriated, Grace rejected the government appraisal of their value at $10 million, asserting that they were worth several times that amount, and described the bonds in which most of the compensation was paid as nearly worthless. The Grace company proceeded to lobby the United States House Agriculture Committee for the insertion of a financial penalty in the Sugar Act that would be used to compensate the owners of expropriated properties. The provision, adopted in the House of Representatives, was made even harsher in the Senate, thereby eliciting the threat of a presidential veto. It was finally watered down by the addition of a proviso that such sanctions were to be invoked at the pleasure of the president. The measure was opposed by the State Department, and the president never implemented its financial sanctions. The American business community in Lima was also opposed to the Grace maneuver. Shortly thereafter and not coincidentally, the Peruvian government arrived at a general agreement with Grace on the transfer of all its Peruvian properties. The actual amounts of compensation to be paid to Grace were not worked out until three years later, when they formed part of the general United States-Peruvian settlement of all outstanding expropriation claims.[15]

The next American holding to be nationalized was ITT's 69-percent interest in the Peruvian Telephone Company. Since the early 1960s, the company had been unable to get rate increases in order to finance expansion and improvement of its service. The resulting deterioration of the telephone service created a vicious circle, since it increased public resistance to any rate increase. By 1967, the Peruvian Congress had passed a law providing for the gradual nationalization of the company, but the new military government decided that the process should be carried out immediately. In speedy negotiations, an amicable arrangement for compensation was worked out: ITT would receive $17.3 million for its telephone holdings (80 percent of book value) but would reinvest this amount and additional funds of its own in the construction of a Sheraton hotel (an ITT subsidiary) and a telephone equipment factory. The arrangement was satisfactory to ITT since it removed itself from the politically sensitive communications area and received contracts to supply the state company with telephone equipment and technical assistance. The government, on the other hand, acquired control over communications and new ITT investments, which would promote tourism and increase Peru's technological capacity. The Peruvians cited the ITT settlement as a demonstration of their willingness "to work constructively with foreign private companies and investors."[16]

The Peruvians were anxious to reassure foreign investors because international financing still had not been obtained for the new Southern Peru copper mine at Cuajone. In 1969, the foreign mining corporations with undeveloped concessions in Peru were told that they must file development schedules or lose the concessions. Although the programs were filed, most were rejected by the government, and the concessions were cancelled without compensation. The concessions that reverted to the Peruvian state became the nucleus of a new state enterprise, Mineroperu, which was given a monopoly in foreign mineral trading and most domestic refining. However, the concession at Cuajone continued to be developed by the Southern Peru Copper Company (SPCC). Since the 1950s, SPCC (a consortium of American mining companies in which a majority of the stock was owned by American Smelting and Refining-ASARCO) had developed a large and successful copper mine at Toquepala, near Cuajone, and it was able to use profits from that mine to pay preliminary development costs for Cuajone. However, it needed substantial outside financing to bring Cuajone into production. Given the uncertainties of the investment climate for mining and the continuing investment disputes, the outside financing was not secured for a number of years. Indeed, it was not until the settlement of these disputes in February 1974 that the way was paved for an Export-Import Bank loan, which, in turn, signaled the private banks that the project was politically as well as economically secure. (The Export-Import Bank had also made the original development at Toquepala possible by granting a $100 million credit in 1954, the largest single loan made by the bank up to that time.)[17] Southern Peru's special position, both as a source of investment and because of its access to outside financing, enabled it to survive the expansion of nationalization of mining in the first half of the 1970s. Because of the size of the project and the number of agencies involved in its financing in several countries, SPCC continued to operate in a cooperative relationship with Mineroperu without feeling the continual threat of expropriation that hung over the other foreign mining companies during the period.

THE INDUSTRIAL COMMUNITY
AND FADEOUT REQUIREMENTS

Many observers had expected the Peruvian Revolution to slow down after the expropriation of IPC and the implementation of a more vigorous agrarian reform. Yet, in retrospect, it seems that

1970 marked the beginning of a more radical course, intended to demonstrate that Peru was pursuing an independent "third position" in its approach to economic development. In keeping with his promise to develop a mixed economy, one that was "neither capitalist nor communist," General Velasco promulgated an Industrial Law in July 1970 that divided Peruvian industry into a sector reserved for the state, a mixed sector, a private sector, and a private reformed sector. The last category, comprising the bulk of Peruvian industry, was to be characterized by the establishment of Industrial Communities in all enterprises with more than five employees and a $25,000 gross annual income. The Community was to distribute to its workers 10 percent of its annual profits and contribute an additional 15 percent in shares to be held in the name of the workers. The gradual expansion of worker ownership was to continue until it had reached 50 percent, or parity with management. This process could be delayed, however, by additional investment by the owners, but its ultimate goal was joint worker-management ownership of the Industrial Community. The law also required all foreign firms to sell majority control of their holdings to national investors over a "fadeout" period of fifteen years.

The new Industrial Law meant that Peru was setting severe limits on foreign investment. Only certain kinds of investment for specific purposes and for limited periods of time would be permitted, and existing investment was to be subject to the opposite procedure, that is, divestment. The reluctance of outside investors was increased by a new Mining Law, issued in 1970, that gave the government a monopoly on mineral sales and replaced the general depreciation allowance of the 1950 legislation with a much stricter tax deduction for reinvestment.

Next the government moved into banking. In July 1970, the government imposed exchange controls, requiring that foreign currency holdings by Peruvians be declared and changed into Peruvian currency. It also used the state-owned Banco de la Nacion to buy out the Banco Popular, owned by the Peruvian oligarchical Prado family; the Banco Continental, owned by Chase Manhattan; and the Banco Internacional, in which there was minority American participation. The compensation terms paid to Chase

Manhattan were so generous (three times book value and nearly six times the current depressed market value) that one writer described the valuation estimates on which they were based as "travesties of proper accounting practice. Crucial numbers were plucked from thin air; valuations based on past cost and future profitability were added together."[18] The reason for this was not difficult to determine. Peru wanted to maintain good relations with the New York bankers because it needed to borrow abroad. As the same observer noted, "In the future Peru would have a friend at Chase Manhattan."

Good relations with the international banks were essential to Peru since it had to rely on international loans as a source of investment capital. The transformation of the enterprise into an Industrial Community with ultimate 50 percent worker ownership and the transfer of majority control of foreign-owned firms to Peruvian nationals discouraged both foreign and Peruvian private investment. Beginning in 1970, foreign investment figures turned sharply negative. Domestic private investment had already dropped to half the rate achieved in the early 1960s.[19] The only new American investment was the construction of the Lima Sheraton, agreed upon as part of the ITT settlement.

The only remaining sources of investment capital were increased taxation, or—more feasible politically—borrowing from abroad, especially from private banks. Because of the IPC dispute, Agency for International Development (AID) and World Bank loans were difficult to secure. The World Bank made only one loan between 1968 and 1973, and only a few small loans and grants were made by AID. The United States also spoke against some Peruvian loans made by the Inter-American Development Bank, and when it ultimately voted for them emphasized the importance of a settlement of outstanding investment disputes. However, private banks, both American and European, were willing to lend to Peru, especially after the OPEC price rise gave them Petrodollars to recycle. (The private bank loans were more costly than official loans since interest rates were set at a premium over the variable London Interbank Borrowing Rate, LIBOR, and maturities were much shorter and without a grace period before beginning repayments.) Because the Cuajone loan was so large, it required Export-Import Bank participation in any consortium of private bank loans. Although the government and SPCC had agreed in principle on the project in 1969, financing problems continued to delay it, basically because the IPC dispute was still unsettled.

THE NEED FOR FOREIGN CAPITAL

In addition to Cuajone, Peru was interested in raising money for the undeveloped mining concessions that were reverting to the state for development by Mineroperu. The most attractive concession was Anaconda's Cerro Verde mine. Because it was located near the city of Arequipa, it required less investment in infrastructure. Looking for a joint venture relationship, the government held a series of negotiations with Anaconda, but these broke down over Mineroperu's insistence on majority ownership. As a result, a contract was signed with British Smelter Constructions Limited to finance and build the new mine. Funding came from export credits of the British and Canadian governments, as well as from the first of many Eurodollar loans. After the promulgation of a law in 1971 requiring a minimum of 25 percent state participation and strict time limits for developing any concessions, no new capital was secured for additional mining ventures, except for the Cerro Verde development. Lack of capital also accounted for the inability of Mineroperu to take over full control of marketing, as authorized by the Mining Law.

Petroperu also needed capital for oil exploration. In 1971, it signed a 50/50 oil exploration contract with Occidental Petroleum which was ingeniously designed to place all the risk on the foreign contracting company at no expense to the state oil company. The risk-contract provided that the company should carry out exploration in an assigned area at its own expense, but if it struck oil the proceeds would be divided between Petroperu and the company. Petroperu's 50 percent share of production would be considered a payment in lieu of taxes (thus partly deductible from United States taxes), and the company's 50 percent was compensation for exploration costs. The contract provided for the initiation of exploration within six months and drilling within thirty months. Within a little over two years, Occidental had struck oil on all five of its drillings. Combined with three successful strikes by Petroperu, this led to a rush by other companies to secure similar contracts. In those contracts, Petroperu increased its take at the wellhead to 55 percent, and later to 60 percent. Ironically, none of the explorations by the other companies proved successful, and by mid-1976, they had all ceased exploration.

This was particularly unfortunate for Peru since in anticipation of new finds it had begun to borrow heavily on the international money market. One of the most important projects that it sought to finance was the construction of a 500-mile pipeline over the Andes to the jungle oil exploration area. In May 1974, Peru secured a loan to finance the pipeline from the Japanese Petroleum Development Corporation. The Japanese agreed to provide $400 million for the pipeline, repayable out of crude and refined oil sales at 6.5 percent interest over ten years, after a four-year grace period. The attraction for the Japanese, in the period immediately following the OPEC price increase, was that the loan gave them first option on a substantial portion of the pipeline oil. Peru's urgent need to finance the pipeline is underscored by a feature in that contract. In the event of dispute over matters not specifically covered in the contract, *English* law was to be applied by a board of arbitrators of three, one Peruvian, one Japanese, and the third probably British. This provision marked a significant departure from the Calvo principle incorporated as Article 17 of the Peruvian constitution – that investment disputes were to be settled in domestic courts. When the agreement was publicized in the English-language *Peruvian Times* on September 6, 1974, the government suppressed that publication. (The government later argued that the constitutional prohibition did not apply to a contract with an agency of a foreign government.) The pipeline, completed in 1977, has a capacity of 320,000 barrels a day, but unless further finds are made, it will be operating well below capacity for the foreseeable future.[20] However by 1978 increased production permitted Peru to become a net exporter of oil.

THE FISHMEAL DEFENSIVE NATIONALIZATION

Peru's balance of payments problems during the early 1970s were further aggravated by an export crisis in the fishmeal industry — a leading source of foreign exchange for Peru. The vagaries of the Niño current in the Pacific, which led the anchovies away from the normal fishing areas off Peru's coast, were compounded by an overexpansion of the fishmeal industry. By 1973, fishmeal export revenues dropped to one-sixth of their 1970 totals. Although the government had already taken control of fishmeal marketing, it was clear that many of the fifty-five companies in the fishmeal industry were going bankrupt. Only the American-owned companies, representing about 12 percent of the production, were likely to survive. In May 1973, the government suddenly announced that all the fishing companies were to be nationalized and integrated into a single state enterprise, Pescaperu. Compensation was provided at book value with 10 percent paid in cash; the rest was to be paid in 6 percent bonds over ten years. The American companies involved included General Mills, Heinz, Cargill, and International Proteins Corporation.

In normal times, fishmeal exports were an important source of Peru's foreign exchange. According to the Five Year Plan, 1971–76, fishmeal was to remain in private hands. But in 1973, the government claimed that nationalization was necessary in order to prevent a take-over of the industry by the foreign companies. However, the sudden new nationalization eroded even further the confidence of the private sector since it seemed to demonstrate that government assurances against nationalization could not be relied upon.

Although expropriation was intended both to rationalize the fishmeal structure and place it under national control, it could not solve the industry's problems. When the government announced plans to reduce the number of workers in the industry, it met strong union resistance to mass firings. The fishmeal nationalization increased the number of investment disputes between American companies and the Peruvian government, because the proposed compensation was considered by the companies involved as unacceptable.[21]

THE CERRO EXPROPRIATION,
THE GREENE MISSION,
AND IPC INDIRECT COMPENSATION

In 1973 one of the oldest investors in Peru, the Cerro Corporation, seemed likely to be added to the list of expropriated American companies. Cerro was founded in 1902 by an American mining engineer who formed a syndicate with J. P. Morgan and others to build a railroad to the old silver mining district of Cerro de Pasco in order to extract and smelt copper. By the 1960s, the Cerro Corporation owned six mines, four hydroelectric power plants, shares in mining supplier firms and metal manufacturing plants, as well as oil and gas concessions in the jungle. As a result of the favorable provisions of the 1950 mining law, which it had had a considerable influence in writing, Cerro had increased its investments in Peru and expanded the production of lead and zinc. By the mid-1960s, it was the country's largest employer (17,000 people), and the book value of its investments was the highest of any foreign company ($253 million). It also owned 22 percent of the other major foreign mining company, SPCC.

Since the adoption of the Mining Law and the establishment of state control of minerals marketing in 1970, the company had been considering the sale of its wholly owned Peruvian copper mines to Mineroperu. Cerro was concerned that the uncertain future of its mines was depressing the value of its stock in New York. In December 1971, it proposed to the Peruvian government that they discuss nationalization by purchase or the establishment of a joint venture combined with Cerro-backed external financing. When these negotiations began in July 1973, the atmosphere for negotiation seemed to be propitious since the American-instigated credit slowdown toward Peru seemed to be softening. In April and May, the Inter-American Development Bank had approved two loans to Peru, and the Wells Fargo Bank had arranged a $100 million loan from sixty-three United States, Canadian, Japanese, and European banks. However, it was not long before the negotiators discovered that the two sides were far apart on the central issues of compensation. At the end of August, General Velasco was quoted as saying that the government was determined to take over Cerro's holdings "by force if necessary," a statement that Cerro spokesmen interpreted as a maneuver to pressure the company to come to an agreement.

In the meantime, the senior vice-president of Manufacturers Hanover Bank, James Greene, had arrived in Peru as a special representative sent by President Nixon to negotiate an overall settlement of the outstanding expropriation disputes. On September 24, perhaps because Cerro hoped to be included in that overall settlement, Cerro's president accused Peru of "legalistic harassment" and "public vilification" of the company. He then announced that Cerro was withdrawing its offer to sell, citing as the cause the wide divergences that existed on the issue of compensation, including Peru's insistence that it did not intend to pay more than $12 million (Cerro evaluated its holdings at $175 million book value and $250 million appraised value). He cited additional Peruvian demands: that the price be determined only after nationalization and that all contracts made after December 31, 1971, be subject to renegotiation. The Peruvian government replied that Cerro "perfidiously and in bad faith" was trying to damage its "well-earned prestige in the international financial world." It went on to accuse the company of violating Peru's housing laws and maintaining its workers in inhuman conditions.[22]

Negotiations were resumed in November. The two sides agreed that the question of compensation would be left unresolved and included in the Greene negotiations for the overall settlement of outstanding expropriation disputes. The date for the expropriation was set at December 31, 1973, so that Cerro could use its losses for a tax write-off during the current year. At the time, the Peruvian compensation offer was said to have been $20 million and Cerro's book value estimate, after taxes and other deductions, $145 million.[23]

The nationalization decree cited a long list of justifications for the take-over, including housing violations, pollution, failure to reinvest, and bad faith in the negotiations. It established yet another state enterprise, Centromin-Peru, to run the mines and made it clear that all personnel, both foreign and Peruvian, would be retained. The mines, which produced lead, zinc, and copper, had been operating at peak capacity in 1973, and an agreement was reached between the Peruvians and Cerro that Cerro's technical cooperation would continue in the transition. Cerro was still represented in Peru in two other mining companies. It retained a 22 percent interest in SPCC, which still was seeking financing of the Cuajone expansion, and it was a part owner in several industrial companies. The compensation issue was delaying the conclusion of the Cuajone package, and therefore, it was to Peru's interest to arrive at a sufficiently favorable settlement with Cerro so that the Cuajone loans would be forthcoming.[24]

Like Cerro, the Grace Company also wished to be included in the Greene settlement. Its sugar estates, taken over in 1969, were already included in the negotiations since a $14 million difference remained between the government and the company's valuation. However, no compensation agreement had been reached for its expropriated paper, chemical, and cardboard box factories, although an agreement to sell had been concluded in late 1971. In mid-February, just in time to be included in the Greene agreement, Grace announced that it was turning over its holdings to the Peruvian government.

The Greene agreement, as announced on February 19, 1974, was complex. It settled all outstanding disputes, including, in an indirect way, the longstanding IPC problem. It involved two types of payments. First, it provided for the release of $74 million of blocked funds in Peru that were owed to Cerro ($67 million), to Grace, and to three American fishmeal companies. (Cerro, in turn, was obliged to remit to Peru $38.5 million in payments owed to Peru that *it* had blocked in the United States.) The main part of the agreement, however, involved a lump-sum payment by Peru of $76 million, the distribution of which was in the words of the agreement, "within the exclusive competence of the government of the United States without any responsibility arising therefrom on the part of the Government of Peru." The reason for this wording was, of course, the thorny problem of compensation to IPC.

In August, when the negotiations began, the two governments had issued a joint statement declaring that, "It has been clearly established by the Government of Peru that the IPC case will not for any reason be a subject of said conversations inasmuch as this is a matter which has been definitively resolved. The Government of the United States recognizes that this is the position of the Revolutionary Government." The February agreement also contained two annexes. In one annex, the Peruvian government listed the companies — Cerro, four Grace subsidiaries, five fishmeal companies, a small Chevron refinery, and three highway construction companies — covered by the agreement, omitting any mention of IPC. In the other, the United States again recognized the position of the Peruvians but noted that, "this position is stated without modifying by interpretation or otherwise the terms of this Agreement," meaning, in this case, its exclusive competence to decide who was to receive compensation. In the final distribution of the $76 million by the State Department, IPC received $23.1 million and Cerro received $10 million. Cerro, thus, received a total of $77.7 million, if the blocked funds are included. According to one estimate made before the agreement was reached, this figure was slightly more than the $70–75 million needed by Cerro in order to break even, if its tax deductions are included in the computation.[25] (All the companies involved had worked out with the State Department the minimum amounts they would accept in final settlement of their claims.)

After signing the agreement, Greene was quoted by the *Andean Times* as saying, "It is fair to assume that Southern Peru Copper Company will immediately apply to the Export-Import Bank to complete the financing of Cuajone and that the Bank will give the required loans." In fact, two months later, the bank announced a $55 million loan for equipment purchases. The conclusion of the Export-Import Bank loan was a signal for the signing of additional loans and credits totaling $400 million for the project, involving fifty-four lending institutions in fifteen countries (thus spreading risk more widely than ever before). Combined with loans from the parent companies of SPCC, the project now had assurances of a total of $550 million in financing. Because of the expropriation disputes and especially of the United States credit freeze, it had taken five years to secure these loans, during which time costs had increased an estimated $150 million. A consortium headed by Morgan Guaranty Trust also extended an $80 million loan, which was not specifically earmarked for the Cuajone project. By design, the loan approximated the amount needed to provide the foreign exchange for the Greene lump-sum payment. It was no coincidence either that, immediately after the Greene agreement, the World Bank began to approve a long list of Peruvian projects that had been held up pending resolution of the IPC dispute.

The settlement of the expropriation disputes seems to have been rather advantageous to the Peruvians. In the end, they were obliged to pay only about one-third of the claims made by the companies, estimated at between $250 million and $300 million. *Business Latin America* took pains to reassure its readers that the package settlement was not considered by Washington as a precedent since it involved a "special situation existing in Peru." An article in its issue of February 27, 1974 quoted State Department sources as saying that they hoped, "any future disputes will be settled without government intervention." President Nixon also commented on the accord, noting that it demonstrated the need for the Interamerican Investment Tribunal, which had recently been proposed by Secretary of State Kissinger. In fact, the settlement had demonstrated something quite different—that the requirement of "prompt, adequate, and effective compensation" would not be insisted upon by the United States government if a compromise settlement could be worked out, permitting the removal of a major irritant to relations with the country involved. On the Peruvian side, it showed that the need for continuing access to international sources of credit may induce expropriating countries to make a settlement recognizing the general principle that some compensation is to be paid for nationalized American property. The particular arrangement whereby the IPC issue was settled was a triumph of subtle diplomacy. The agreement achieved the goal of payment without compromising what seemed to be an intractable position on the part of the Peruvian military.

SOCIAL PROPERTY

Although the Peruvian military had promised a genuine alternative to capitalism and communism, apart from some land redistribution and very modest beginnings of a scheme to enable workers to share in profits and management, the principal accomplishment of the regime up to 1974 had been to expand the state sector of the economy—through nationalization of minerals, banking, and communication. However, civilian advisors to the government from a variety of political backgrounds had been working for several years on a genuine set of alternative economic institutions. The outlines of those institutions were revealed in May 1974, when the Velasco government finally announced the Social Property Law authorizing the establishment of worker-owned and worker-managed enterprises.

The new law, prepared in consultation with foreign advisors from Yugoslavia and the United States who were experts on the economic aspects of self-managed enterprises, provided for the gradual establishment of Social Property Enterprises, run by a general manager and a board of directors, elected by an assembly made up of all the workers in the enterprise. Each year, in addition to wages, the workers would receive a share in the "surplus" (profit) of the firm proportional to the number of days they had worked. The law also provided for the allocation of funds for housing, health, and other worker benefits. Revenue for these programs was to come from a National Social Property Fund managed by three representatives from the government and four members, including the Fund Chairman, elected by an annual assembly of representatives from all social property firms. Projects were to be submitted to the fund by a National Social Property Council, made up of twelve government representatives and six representatives of the self-managed enterprises. After fund loans were repaid by the firms, they would continue to make "capital rental" payments, which could be used to finance the expansion of the social property sector. The firms could also raise additional capital through the issuance of "stockbonds" (*acciobonos*), the income from which would be tax exempt.

One of the more difficult problems associated with the new experiment was the relationship of wealthy industries to poorer ones. The problem could be clearly seen in the former Grace Company sugar enterprises. Because sugar production was very profitable, substantial economic benefits accrued to the members of the cooperative – far more than those in other industries. There were also problems with the degree of control exercised by the central government in its role as source of the initial financing, and the competitive advantage that the tax regime of the new enterprises and other governmental preferential arrangements might give over the private sector. The social property experiment moved very slowly. This was due, in part, to a lack of enthusiasm in some government sectors, but the main cause was a lack of state funds since the experiment was initiated at a time when Peru was entering a period of extreme economic stringency. Two years after the law was announced, only three Social Property Enterprises were in full operation, forty-eight were "in formation," and 500 were "under study."[26] When President Velasco announced that social property was to be the "predominant" sector in Peru's mixed economy, a new element of uncertainty was introduced. The announcement only served to heighten the already negative effects on investment of the earlier requirements that shares in profits and ownership be distributed to workers and that foreign investors sell out a percentage of their holdings on a fixed schedule. It was followed by the publication of Plan Inca, which slated additional areas such as cement and insurance for nationalization. In June 1974, Velasco also nationalized Gulf Oil's Peruvian subsidiary because of "moral offenses," following revelation of bribery payments by Gulf to a number of foreign governments. (Agreement on a $1,540,000 compensation payment to Gulf was arrived at only in late 1977.)

The social property firms were generally small and either involved the initiation of a new enterprise or the acquisition of an inefficient or bankrupt private firm. The government attempted to discourage worker take-overs of the Chilean type by requiring a two-thirds vote of owners, partners, and shareholders, as well as an elaborate bureaucratic process of approvals before the firm could be constituted. It also imposed a 10 percent tax on profits to finance new enterprises, and attempted to tap the considerable profits of the sugar cooperatives for the benefit of poorer enterprises. However, it appeared that it would be many years before social property would become the dominant economic form in Peru, as Velasco had promised. The state-owned sector did not participate in the new program, probably because the government feared the adverse effect of worker participation on mineral and petroleum production. Once again, economic constraints limited the "revolutionary" character of Velasco's revolution.

MARCONA — THE LAST NATIONALIZATION

Despite new foreign financing after 1973, Peru faced increasing economic difficulties. By 1975 it was clear that, because of low international prices for copper and fishmeal, there was a serious imbalance between export income and a growing import bill, in part owing to substantial increases in the price of imported oil and agricultural imports. While it would seem that such economic difficulties might discourage a government from taking any bold new action, General Velasco took a step in July 1975 that proved to be his undoing a month later — he nationalized the Marcona iron mining company.

Marcona had been organized by two United States parent companies, Utah Construction Company (now Utah International) and Cyprus Mines, for the purpose of developing the Marcona iron deposits in Peru. The deposits had been known to exist since 1905, but it was not until 1932 that the Peruvian government adopted a law authorizing their development and only in 1945 was a serious effort made to develop them. The semiautonomous state corporation charged with this purpose invested $2 million in infrastructure, but it lacked additional capital to develop the mine. In 1952, it entered into a twenty-year lease agreement for iron ore extraction with the Marcona Company. The agreement provided for payment of a 7 percent royalty and a special reduced price for iron ore supplied to the state steel mill at Chimbote. That agreement was subsequently revised five times in connection with further investments by Marcona amounting to $110 million. The new investments included the development of refining facilities, a pelletization plant, a power generator, and other plants. In 1966, the royalty was raised to 25 percent and the contract extended to 1982, with a provision for the formation of a 50/50 joint venture with the state corporation thereafter. The expansions were financed by the large tax-free depletion allowance provided by the 1950 Mining Code and, after 1970, the new Mining Law's reinvestment allowance that replaced it.[27]

Marcona also owned a shipping company, registered in Liberia, to carry the ore, and Marcona Sales, registered in Panama, to sell all production not used by Chimbote. Before the nationalization, 70 percent of its sales were to Japan. Although its executive offices were in San Francisco, it was a true multinational corporation.

During the early 1970s, there had been sporadic negotiations between the Peruvian government and the company concerning its future operations. In 1970, the government suggested replacing the concession with a joint venture operation—a proposal to which Marcona later agreed. However, President Velasco vetoed the joint venture proposal. He also turned down a 1974 proposal by Marcona which provided that the mine be taken over by the government with compensation paid out of future production, that Marcona would receive a management and technical assistance contract, and that it would cooperate in marketing, transportation, and securing foreign (mainly Japanese) financing for a proposed expansion. The reason for Velasco's negative attitude became clear with the publication of Plan Inca in 1974, which indicated that the government intended to "put the state in charge of exploitation of the large (mineral) deposits, refining, and marketing," under the auspices of "a strong state company responsible for all the mining activities of the State."[28]

By 1974, at the time the plan was published, SPCC's complex, including the expensive expansion project at Cuajone and the Marcona iron mines, was the only large mining operation not under state ownership. As early as 1964, a Peruvian congressional committee had claimed that, under the provisions of the 1950 Mining Law, Marcona had averaged 81 percent a year in profits if depreciation and the depletion allowance were included. (The trick here, of course, was to use book value under the accelerated depreciation permitted by the law as the basis for the percentage calculation.) In addition, it was widely known that the Marcona shipping operation was an efficient and profitable one, and those profits did not appear on Peruvian books except as charges to the mining company. A hypothetical reconstruction of those additional profits by a Swedish writer in 1969 (which conveniently ignored additional Marcona investments financed by Export-Import Bank loans) raised the average profits, for the years up to 1962, to 132 percent.[29]

Marcona, in turn, replied that it had reinvested most of its earnings and had developed new technologies for Peru's ore, including a special flotation process to get rid of sulphur, a liquid slurry process (Marconaflo) for transportation of the iron, and a method of processing the iron using seawater. In addition, it pointed out that its discount on sales to the state steel corporation, Siderperu, saved the company $10.6 million between 1952 and 1974.

In late 1974, the Peruvian minister of mines alluded to the negotiations concerning the transfer of Marcona to the government, noting that it was only a matter of "how and when" the company would be nationalized. That question was resolved suddenly on July 25, 1975, when General Velasco announced that Marcona was to be nationalized for "grave non-compliance with its contract obligations." The nationalizing decree listed a series of offenses, including failure to maintain reserves and to replace and maintain equipment, nonpayment of taxes and royalties, and profiteering on sales and shipping while showing a loss on the mines in order to avoid Peruvian taxes.[30] The decree created a new state enterprise, Hierro-Peru, which took over Marcona's Peruvian assets, rescinded all contracts between Marcona and Peru, and froze its bank accounts in the country. In his speech following the nationalization, the minister of mines also mentioned fictitious fines levied by Marcona Sales on Marcona Mining, unjustified sales commissions, illegal depletion allowances, and violations of the 1966 contract.

The timing of the nationalization could not have been worse. In 1975, Peru was running up a balance-of-payments deficit that would eventually total over $1 billion. It would need to renegotiate both its past debt and new foreign loans in order to pay for increasingly expensive food and oil imports at a time when copper prices were down, fishmeal exports were only beginning to recover, and the oil from the jungle fields had not yet begun to flow. In addition, the Velasco regime, which had not been particularly repressive in its control of dissidence (it had nationalized Peru's newspapers in 1974 and had deported some intellectuals and writers, but there had been, by Latin American standards, few political prisoners or cases of torture and political violence), put down a police strike for higher wages in February 1975 with considerable bloodshed. Moreover, various efforts to develop mass support for the regime, including the *Sinamos* system of mobilization of interest groups supported (and controlled) by the regime, had, by then, proved to be notably unsuccessful. General Velasco, himself, suffered from serious health problems, including a tumor that required the amputation of his leg in 1973, and word circulated in Lima that he had become increasingly subject to fits of temper and irrational actions. Only a month before the nationalization, Velasco had heard that discussions of his possible removal had taken place among some of his closest confidants in the military. Following a stormy cabinet session, however, those involved apologized, and he accepted their apologies.

The Marcona step, then, seems to have been an attempt to gain popular support, through another nationalization, in the face of waning popularity. As in the past, the expropriation was timed for the national independence day celebrations on July 28. The decision was made without consulting the minister of mines, General Jorge Fernandez Maldonado, who, despite his leftist sympathies, was known to be opposed to the move. (He was out of the country at the time the decision was made.)

The reasons for the minister's opposition were evident in the aftermath of the action. Peru exports 95 percent of its iron production, and it did not possess the capacity to replace the Marcona ships. In addition, the Marcona ships were designed specifically for the transportation of liquid slurry (the Marconaflo process), while other ships were not. Most important, the nationalization took place at a time when the world market for iron was weak owing to the worldwide recession, and Marcona's Japanese customers were not interested in signing new contracts with Peru, especially since Japanese courts are very strict in imposing judicial sanctions on uncompensated expropriations.

The result was that Peru's iron exports dropped from

5,000,000 tons (to Japan, the United States, and West Germany) in the period from January to July 1975 and to 33,000 tons (to Rumania) in the period from July to December 1975.[31] Marcona had designed a shipping and marketing arrangement that made forced nationalization very costly, and Velasco had not taken this into account. On an annual basis, Peru was losing $100 million in export earnings at a time of increasingly grave financial crisis.

Yet for a month after the nationalizations, no negotiations took place. At the end of August, however, President Velasco was overthrown by his prime minister, General Francisco Morales Bermúdez, with the support of most of the other leaders of the Peruvian armed forces. While the nationalization was not the direct cause of the overthrow, it clearly was a contributory factor. Morales pledged to continue with the revolutionary dynamic of the regime, but subsequent events showed that Velasco's ouster initiated a significant slowdown, if not reversal, of the post-1968 reforms.

Initial discussions between Marcona and Peru took place in September, but it was evident that the company and Peru were far apart on their valuation of the expropriated assets. The Peruvians made deductions wherever they could find any possible pretext for doing so and came up with an initial proposal of $9 million as a compensation figure. Marcona, on the other hand, valued its properties at $166,691,000 and assumed that an agreement would soon be reached because Peru needed to get the ships moving again. In October, when no progress had been made, both sides agreed to ask the United States government to negotiate a settlement directly, following the precedent of the Greene mission two years earlier. As in the Greene case, the prospect of additional United States loans to bail out Peru's ailing economy was also seen as an additional inducement. Unlike the Greene case, however, the negotiators this time were State and Treasury Department officials rather than a New York banker acting as personal representative of the president.

The negotiations proceeded in four stages. The first problem needing resolution was to get the Marcona ships moving again. In December, an interim agreement was signed between Peru and the United States government (not Marcona). It provided that Marcona ships would begin to transport the iron in anticipation of an agreement, to be concluded within 90 days, that would include in the final compensation figure a premium on shipping payments of one dollar a ton.[32] The second stage of the negotiations involved an estimate as to the value of the nationalized assets. To bring the widely divergent positions closer together, both the Peruvians and the Americans made use of outside consultants; Peru employed a French consulting firm and the United States used the Stanford Research Institute. It was at this stage, when the seriousness of Peru's economic problems became evident, that the threat of denial of foreign bank loans and multilateral (the World Bank and the Inter-American Development Bank) aid became an important contributory factor in solving the dispute. By March 1976, a preliminary overall figure had been arrived at, but the compensation package had not yet been put together. This was done in a third stage. A negotiator appointed by the State Department, Carlyle Maw, a New York lawyer, worked out with the Peruvian Mining Ministry a three-part package that involved a $37 million promissory note to be financed by loans from a United States banking group; $22.4 million from discounts to Marcona by Peru to be paid from the sale of 3.74 million tons of iron ore pellets over the next four years at a fixed price set at $6 a ton below the estimated future world market prices; and $2 million from the $1 a ton payments under the December shipping contract.[33] The total compensation figure announced in September 1976, was $61.4 million, far in excess of Peru's initial offer but well below the company's original estimate of its value. Since it was financed by foreign loans, the compensation would not initially create any drain on Peru's balance of payments. The sales contract would also guarantee Peruvian access to the United States iron market, and there would be an inflow of dollars over the next four years in excess of the outflow involved in repaying the promissory note.

The Peruvians claimed the compensation agreement was a victory since their experts had valued the Marcona assets at nearly $70 million, even after the deduction of $31 million in unpaid taxes and penalties (other estimates placed net asset value at $78–

$80 million). Peru had also acquired processing installations worth $28.5 million without compensation because of alleged contract violations. (Marcona's White Paper, while evaluating fixed assets and inventories at $189 million, described the company's "unrecovered investment," after deduction of earnings and depreciation, at $31 million.)

The agreement gave both sides the impression that they had the better bargain — Peru because it paid compensation below both book and replacement value and received guaranteed access to the United States market, and Marcona because the compensation was much higher than Peru's first offer and was supplemented by indirect compensation in the shipping and sales contracts.

THE "SECOND PHASE" OF THE PERUVIAN REVOLUTION

As a result of the settlement of the Marcona dispute, the threat of the use of the González Amendment to oppose aid from the multilateral banks was removed; the logjam on private bank loans was broken; and Peru was assured of a package of $240 million in loans (at 2.25 percent over LIBOR repayable over five years) from American banks, as well as a likely $100 million from the Europeans and Japanese. The money came none too soon. Despite a severe cut in government spending in 1976, the government was said to owe $500 million in foreign currency at the time that President Morales announced a devaluation of the Peruvian currency in July 1976. Morales's "Second Phase" of the Peruvian Revolution also involved the implementation of a number of drastic measures designed to deal with the balance-of-payments crisis. These measures, needed to persuade the foreign bankers (and later the International Monetary Fund) of Peru's creditworthiness, included ending subsidies on food; a cutback on imports; several large increases in the price of gasoline (which had not changed from 1960 to 1975, despite the fact that Peru paid OPEC prices for the one-third of its supply); and termination of the nationalization policy of the past several years. In May 1976, the minister of industry, General Gaston Ibañez O'Brien, announced there would be "no more expropriations." In mid-1976 the fish-meal industry was denationalized, and the boats were sold to small private owners (a maximum of three boats per owner). It was hoped that the private sector would make the politically un-palatable cuts in the industry's swollen employment that the state could not make. In agriculture, productivity rather than land re-distribution was emphasized, and the government took over many of the rural cooperatives. A committee was appointed to "evaluate" the Social Property experiment, the director of the So-cial Property Commission was removed, and President Morales announced that the Social Property System would be utilized mainly in labor-intensive enterprises, each of which was to be fi-nancially self-sufficient. (By 1977, only six Social Property enter-prises were in full operation and 34 were described as "in forma-tion.") Others who were forced out of office included General Fernandez, from the Mining Ministry, and the foreign minister, Miguel Angel de la Flor, who had frightened the international banking community in December 1975 with a call for a debt mor-atorium for the developing countries. Even the sacred Industrial Community, which had been a central feature of the Velasco re-forms, was modified. A new Small Enterprise Law exempted en-terprises with up to 25 employees from the requirement of a share in profits and ownership, and in November 1976 President Mo-rales undercut the basic goal of the entire complicated system by announcing to a businessmen's group that the maximum work-ers' share would be lowered from 50 percent to 33.33 percent. In addition, he announced that shares would be distributed individ-ually to the workers rather than held by the community, and that they could be sold by the individual workers. While proclaiming its continued fidelity to the principles of the Peruvian Revolu-tion, the regime clearly altered its attitude to private and foreign investment. The government took a tough line against labor un-rest, and in May 1977 it declared that the foreign companies that had entered Peru before 1974 could apply for annulment of the previously obligatory "fadeout" to 49 percent ownership by 1986. As a result of his austerity program, Morales was able to secure standby credits from the International Monetary Fund and renegotiate international bank loans that were coming due. Besides raising prices and eliminating Velasco's more costly reforms, General Morales's government had to submit to the monitoring of public expenditures, first by foreign banks and then by the International Monetary Fund, an indication of how far the regime had moved away from its initial anti-*dependencia* position. At the end of 1977 Morales took another step to impress the international financial community. He scheduled elections to a constituent assembly for June 1978 and promised a return to civilian rule in 1980. In 1978, when it appeared that Peru would have to pay 60 percent of its export earnings in debt amortization and interest, agreements were reached with its creditors to "roll over," that is, postpone, 90 percent of the payments due. All the agreements, except those with the Eastern European and Latin American countries, were contingent upon observance of a strict International Monetary Fund austerity program.

Short of a dramatic turnaround in policy, such as that carried out by General Pinochet in Chile, it was difficult to reverse the movement toward statism that had gone on for so many years. From 12 state-owned enterprises in 1968 the parastatal sector had grown to between 170 and 180 in 1976, employing 120,000 people. Moreover, the state was now responsible for over 50 percent of the nation's capital formation. Between 1967 and 1973, the overall number of public employees had grown from 270,000 to 401,000. The public debt grew from slightly over $1 billion in 1969 to nearly $5 billion by the end of 1977. Domestic savings dropped from 16 percent of GNP in 1970 to 7.6 percent in 1976 and the percentage of investment financed by foreign borrowing rose from 2 percent in 1970 to 53 percent in 1975. Inflation skyrocketed to 70 percent in 1978, as successive devaluations raised the exchange rate from 45 sols to the dollar in 1976 to nearly 200 sols to the dollar two years later. In 1977 industrial production dropped by 6 percent, and the purchasing power of Lima wages and salaries declined by 16 to 20 percent. Except for the absence of political repression, the Peruvian "Revolution" seemed to have ended as dismally as did Allende's revolutionary changes in neighboring Chile.[34]

THE LESSONS OF PERU

Some of Peru's economic problems can be attributed to accidents of nature (the Niño current's effect on the anchovy catch) or world prices beyond its control (copper fluctuations and the OPEC oil increase). At least some of the difficulties, however, are attributable to the statist domestic course pursued by the government, including the nationalization of mining and other industries. As a result of huge price subsidies for food and fuel, the expansion of state employment and bureaucracy, a decrease in efficiency,[35] large credits from the government to public enterprises, and public investment financed by foreign borrowing rather than by domestic savings or taxes, Peru experienced a massive increase in indebtedness. In turn, this contributed to a new kind of "debt dependency." Rather than being dependent on foreign investors and governments, Peruvians now depended on national banks and multilateral lending agencies. Moreover, the need for foreign lending compelled Peru to provide relatively generous compensation for its expropriations and to pursue a rigidly orthodox economic policy because of its financial difficulty.

In its opposition to dependence on foreign investment, Peru had sharply reduced the foreign presence in its economy. Besides SPCC and the Homestake Mining Company, some foreign investment by manufacturers remained, such as Dodge automobiles, Goodyear and Dunlop tires, and Sears, Roebuck. However, the overpowering influence of the foreigner that existed in 1968 had been sharply reduced. New petroleum exploration is based on an innovative risk-contract policy that assures a minimum 50 percent share for the government of any petroleum discovered by foreign companies. In addition, a massive redistribution of agrarian land has taken place, and there has been a modification of industrial ownership, involving a modest but growing workers' share in profits and ownership. Given the weakness of the Peruvian private sector, the only way that these changes would have taken place was through state action.

The question that remains is, Who benefits from the nationalization? Even before the shift in government policy, it was argued that the Velasco reforms really had not improved the conditions of those most in need. As Richard Webb has demonstrated, the traditional rural sector gained little from the reforms.[36] The real beneficiaries of the Velasco reforms were the upper to middle sectors (still in the top 25 percent of the income distribution pattern of Peru), including urban bureaucrats, members of the agrarian cooperatives, and, especially, unionized workers. Even the gains for these groups have been substantially eroded or nullified by the post-1975 policies of economic stringency.

The Velasco reforms were expensive. If there is a lesson to be learned from the Peruvian experience, it is that in order to carry out internal reforms without a violent revolution a government must be in a strong economic position to bargain successfully with foreign interests. Without such a position, attempts to control or take over foreign corporations are seriously limited by the continuing need for foreign technology, markets, and, above all, external financing. (In the case of petroleum those limits are less stringent than in other minerals or manufacturing.) When commodity prices and production were high in the early 1970s, Peru was able to make major reforms. When they dropped, Velasco's revolution ran into trouble.

One can construct an alternative scenario for the Peruvian military that would have involved following the main outlines of the reforms of 1968 and 1969: a takeover of IPC (with perhaps a token compensation such as that urged by the Irwin mission) and an intensified agrarian reform combined with measures to increase the productivity of Peruvian agriculture. Tax measures could also have been incorporated into the plan to induce increased investments and/or "Peruvianization" of the mining sector on a joint venture basis. This might not have satisfied the ideologues or given Peru the "neither capitalist nor Communist" third position that President Velasco desired, but it would have kept the foreign and domestic capital flowing. In addition, it would have established national control over natural resources without the costs in risk, increased inefficiency, massive foreign indebtedness, and the sharp decline in popular support that the regime, in fact, incurred.[37]

On the other side, it can be argued that most of Peru's indebtedness was owed to variables beyond the government's control, especially shortfalls in fishmeal and petroleum production and violent swings in commodity prices. Furthermore, positive "externalities" did result from Velasco's nationalist policy: the reforms in industrial structures; the development of national pride, expertise, and technical competence; savings on repatriated profits; and the development of a refining and marketing capacity in the minerals sector. But the evidence can also lead to the conclusion that statism and radical, or even not so radical, reforms cost money that, lacking the ability or willingness to mobilize what are limited domestic sources, leads to deepened foreign indebtedness and negative domestic economic repercussions, such as inflation and devaluation.

For the foreign investor the Peruvian experience, once again, demonstrates the pitfalls of investing in nonrenewable natural resources, even when, as in the Marcona case, the terms of those investments are periodically renegotiated. It also shows that foreign investors react negatively to frequent changes in the rules of the game. Despite the fact that the foreign manufacturing sector, except for the Grace holdings, has not been touched, foreign investors have been reluctant to go into Peru, even on a joint venture basis. The fadeout and industrial community requirements have also acted as deterrents, even after they were modified. As one foreign investor told an interviewer after a visit to Peru, "From what I saw I think you can really do business and make money. But I wouldn't want to invest there."[38]

The role of the American government in the Peruvian case was limited to facilitating the settlement of investment disputes. In pursuing that objective, official policy progressed from counterproductive (the credit squeeze on Belaúnde that exacerbated his economic difficulties) to ineffective (the "nonovert" sanctions between 1969 and 1973) to highly successful (the Greene and Marcona negotiations). They moved from close cooperation with the companies to independent initiatives as an honest broker. The legislative provisions mandating an aid cutoff were not applied, but they were useful in the negotiations (especially the influence of the González Amendment on inducing a settlement of the Marcona dispute). Much more important than the formal legislation, however, was the relationship between the settlement of expropriation disputes, often financed by additional loans, and the willingness, or lack of willingness, of the Export-Import Bank to extend credits or guarantees, and of the multilateral, American, and European banks to engage in lending for balance-of-payments or investment purposes. While Allende was able to arrange for credit from countries other than the United States, the Cuajone loan and others indicate that banks and investment companies have now learned to spread risk widely as insurance against default or expropriation. The United States and American-influenced lending agencies occupy a central position in deciding whether that risk will be assumed.

United States policy toward Peru underwent major changes in the period under discussion, but the general pattern is one of increasing sophistication, flexibility, and willingness to deal with Third World nationalism. In order to force Peru to conform to United States demands, the Kennedy and Johnson administrations engaged in public pressure — Kennedy in support of democracy and free elections and Johnson on behalf of the International Petroleum Company. Richard Nixon, in contrast to his Chilean policy, pursued a more "low-profile" approach. Instead of invoking the Hickenlooper Amendment, he engaged in more subtle, behind-the-scenes pressure and negotiation and ultimately made use of a lump-sum settlement, maintaining the principle of compensation but ignoring the requirements of "prompt" and "adequate" payment. The Marcona negotiation, carried out under the Ford administration, exemplified a new pattern in the settlement of investment disputes. It involved the use of personal representatives as intermediaries, outside consultants on evaluation, and continuing marketing and transportation links between the multinational corporation and the nationalizing country as a method of indirect compensation and access to international sales.

Security interests were relatively marginal in the Peruvian case since its exports were not vital to the United States, and it was never likely to swing toward Communism — although it did break the United States monopoly on weapons supply, first by buying supersonic jets from France and later by purchasing tanks from the Soviet Union. The overall lesson concerning United States relations with radical nationalism seems to be that, in the long run, an accommodation can be arrived at if there is a mutual interest in economic relations – above all, because Third World countries need to finance – and refinance – their increasingly large international loans.

The Peruvian case also seems to demonstrate that it is easier now than it has been in the past for a Third World government to nationalize foreign-owned holdings, especially in the area of mineral extraction, although the resulting expansion of state ownership creates new economic problems. Nationalization does not solve the basic scarcity of investment capital – indeed, it may exacerbate it because it increases costs of production and diminishes access to international sources of capital.

The Peruvian case shows that a shortage of capital is likely to inhibit efforts to develop an alternative economic model for the Third World. Because of the economic costs involved, especially the adverse effect on private investment, Peru finally was compelled to give up even the fairly modest steps it had taken toward the development of a worker-owned and worker-managed economy. The fact that such experiments were not introduced in the nationalized petroleum industry and were only implemented to a limited degree in the state-owned mining industry (through bonds in the state development bank rather than shares in the enterprise) is an indication that the government was dubious about their effects on efficiency and productivity. The Chilean experience under Allende seemed to demonstrate that those doubts were justified.

The basic problem still remains, How can the government promote a productive and just economy that can create new jobs and can bring a better life to Peru's poor? The elimination of the large foreign holdings has given Peruvian policymakers much more power to attempt to resolve this problem. However, it is still unclear whether the resulting shift to state ownership and the experiments in worker participation have contributed significantly to this end. The recent move toward a more favorable foreign investment policy may be explained better in terms of Peru's continuing need for external resources and the high costs of its earlier reforms than through interpretations that attribute it to imperialism and oligarchic control. The permanent significance of the Velasco reforms will be tested in the coming years as Peru cautiously returns to constitutional democracy.

7

Venezuela —
A New Pattern of Nationalization?

The conciliatory attitude of the more moderate (and author-itarian) governments towards the companies unintention-ally made possible, or at least viable, the more aggressive thrusts of succeeding reformist regimes. Thus Gomez's "open arms" policy before 1935 allowed a rapid growth which followed him; the 1944–45 concessions "round" set the companies up for the radical measures of the AD re-formers; and the 1956–57 round allowed an expansion of the industry upon which the interim junta and the Betancourt administration could draw.
> —Franklin Tugwell, *The Politics of Oil in Venezuela*, 1975

We have nationalized the iron mines, but we have not been able to nationalize the iron workers.
> —President Carlos Andrés Pérez, 1975

Nationalizing the petroleum industry without interrupting production is like painting the inside of your house without moving out of any of the rooms.
> —Attributed to Valentín Hernandez, minister of mines, 1975

We proved it was not necessary to do what Chile did or what Cuba did, in order to regain control over the management of our economy, and sovereignty over our natural resources. What we did was a triumph of democracy.
—Carlos Andrés Pérez, 1977

On January 1, 1976, the president of Venezuela, Carlos Andrés Pérez, raised the flag over the country's oldest producing oil well, first drilled in 1914, as Venezuela took over its foreign-owned oil industry. In striking contrast to most of the other cases examined in this book, the Venezuelan nationalization was peaceful and relatively free of conflict. It was the climax of many years of increasing state regulation and control of Venezuela's principal natural resource and was carried out in complete accord with the principles of Venezuelan constitutional democracy.

Why was the Venezuelan nationalization so free of conflict? And why did the United States government stay out of the negotiations preceding the nationalization? What happened in Venezuela, and in world politics, that made it possible for the multinational oil companies to face nationalization with equanimity —indeed, with optimism—as it related to their future relationship with Venezuela?

As nationalizations increased in the early 1970s, it began to become clear that the United States government was no longer so likely to engage in reprisals against take-overs of United States property. One reason for this shift was the decreasing credibility of national security arguments for doing so, when anti-Communist governments, such as that of Eduardo Frei in Chile, took over United States holdings. It now appeared that American foreign policy interests might not always entail the defense of the American investor. When the OPEC countries increased oil prices and began to take over foreign oil companies, United States policymakers, aware of both United States dependence on imported oil and the OPEC producers' need for markets for their petroleum production, found it possible to adjust to the OPEC nationalizations. It was now possible to conceive of a new relationship with the raw material producers of the Third World:

national ownership of basic mineral resources was not automatically seen as a threat to the United States national interest.

Instead of panicking and calling for government assistance, the companies began to realize that alternative relationships with the oil-producing countries were possible, involving contracts for marketing, technology, and other services. Furthermore, if production was under the control of the Third World governments, historic labor and political conflicts would no longer be factors with which to contend. In some cases, too, the companies could shift to more secure sources elsewhere, keeping the Third World production in reserve. (Thus, for example, copper could be supplied from Canada, Australia, and marginal areas of the United States, rather than from "unstable" countries, such as Chile, Peru, Zaire, and Zambia.)

In petroleum, some shifting to the Alaskan and North Sea oil fields took place, but the dependence on Third World oil remained. Thus, boycotts and economic sanctions were not effective instruments of pressure against Third World oil producers. Once they had been ruled out for petroleum, it became difficult to propose such tactics when other resources were nationalized. Provided that the nationalizations did not pose a direct threat to United States security interests and that at least some concessions were made to the principle of compensation, Third World policymakers could now consider nationalization without worrying about strong countersanctions by the United States government.

The Venezuelan case made this strikingly clear. There, an impeccably democratic government carried out a carefully thought out nationalization policy that respected United States security interests, offered the oil companies partial compensation and the advantages of continued contractual relationships, and maintained internal economic and political stability throughout the difficult period of transition from foreign to national ownership. Venezuela was able to do this because of the strength of its democratic institutions (developed since the overthrow of its last military ruler in 1958) and because of the gradual tightening of national controls over the foreign companies that made the final step of state ownership relatively easy. Linked to these internal factors were the external ones—the lessening of United States predominance in East-West relations, the precedents of the Middle Eastern nationalizations, and the intensification of nationalism throughout the Third World.

The Venezuelan oil nationalizations, then, marked a new stage in the relationship between the United States and the Third World. It became a model for a more realistic appreciation of the possibilities and limitations in the respective positions of raw-material-consuming and raw-material-producing nations. Venezuela demonstrated that a shift in property relations can take place in other than a violent and conflictual fashion, and that continuing mutual interests can make it possible to move from a relationship of almost total dependence to one of increasing interdependence. The analysis that follows will examine how this model emerged.

THE DEVELOPMENT
OF THE VENEZUELAN OIL INDUSTRY

The initial foreign investments in the development of Venezuela's oil had taken place while the country was under the iron fist of a ruthless dictator, Juan Vicente Gómez, who ruled Venezuela as a private fiefdom from 1908 until 1935. Oil seepages had been noted in parts of Venezuela since the early sixteenth century, and the first oil concession had been granted to an American in 1865. However, the beginning of the modern petroleum industry in Venezuela dates from 1914 when Zumaque-1, the well over which President Pérez later raised the Venezuelan flag, was drilled by a subsidiary of Royal Dutch Shell, initiating production in the rich Mene Grande oil field. Many other companies came into Venezuela in the early 1920s, attracted by the fabulous "blowout" of Los Barrosos in 1922, which produced 1 million barrels of oil per day for nine days. That same year, legislation that was to regulate petroleum concessions for twenty years was adopted. It provided for a royalty payment of between 8 percent and 15 percent of market value and limited concessions to forty years. By 1927, oil was the country's principal export, and by 1929, Venezuela was the largest oil exporter in the world.[1]

In December 1935, Gómez died of natural causes and was succeeded by his minister of war, General Eleazar López Contreras. Civil liberties were restored, a labor code was published permitting the organization of trade unions, and royalties and other payments by the oil companies were increased. Following the pattern established in other countries, the companies responded to the tax increases and other demands by threatening to stop oil exploration and development. Venezuela's bargaining position was not strong since one-third of the government's revenues came from oil taxes. The companies, on the other hand, did not want to repeat the problems that they had recently encountered in Mexico. Under General Isaías Medina Angarita, who was elected president in 1941 by a complaisant Congress, a new concessionary arrangement was worked out. In 1942, as part of Venezuela's first income tax law, a progressive tax on profits was applied to the companies. In the new petroleum law, written with the aid of United States oil company advisors and adopted in 1943, the royalty rate was raised to 16.66 percent, and surface taxes were increased in exchange for the establishment of a new concession arrangement that was to run for forty years. Between 1943 and 1945, Medina offered further forty-year concessions involving oil territories larger than all those granted previously by the Venezuelan government.

THE 50/50 FORMULA

In 1945, a group of dissatisfied military officers backed by the left-of-center Acción Democrática (AD) party removed Medina from office. The AD provided four members of the seven-man interim junta that presided over the writing of a new constitution and the holding of the first genuinely free elections in Venezuelan history. The junta decreed an extraordinary tax of $27 million on the oil companies that, according to computations, would bring the government share of oil profits to 50 percent. The 50/50 formula, requiring that all petroleum companies holding concessions in Venezuela pay 50 percent of profits and income to the government, was enacted into Venezuelan law in 1948; it was later imitated by the Middle Eastern oil-exporting nations.

Fearing nationalization, the companies were willing to comply with the demands of the new government. The interim junta and the AD government subsequently elected named Juan Pablo Pérez Alfonzo as minister of development, charging him with development of a new petroleum policy. Pérez Alfonzo announced a policy of no further oil concessions and began collecting taxes in crude oil and offering the oil on a petroleum-short international market in order to raise the international price set by the companies. He also initiated steps to establish an oil-financed reserve fund, both to compensate for cycles of demand and to improve the nation's bargaining power. In 1948, a commission was appointed to study the possible establishment of a Venezuelan state oil company, but before it could report, the AD government had been overthrown by a military coup.

Why did the AD, which had earlier advocated nationalization, not take over the oil industry when it was in power? At least part of the reason that Venezuela was reluctant to nationalize must have been the problems experienced by the Mexican nationalization. Unlike Mexico, Venezuela was exporting 98 percent of its production, and by 1947, oil exports accounted for 94.7 percent of Venezuelan export income. To face a boycott, as Mexico had done, would have been far more costly to Venezuela. In addition, it seemed that squeezing the companies could produce more benefits for the government at less cost. The government "take" for the oil industry doubled in real terms between 1946 and 1947. Therefore, there did not seem to be any incentive to incur the disruptions likely to result from nationalization. Finally, the companies were using new techniques to maintain oil pressure and were expanding production, which increased to 1 million barrels a day in 1946 because of the opening of new wells.[2] The classic deterrents to nationalization—technology, marketing, and the advantages of cooperation—thus operated to override the ideological preference for state ownership.

During the ten-year period of military rule that followed the overthrow of the AD government in 1948, labor unions and political parties were repressed, many of the democratic political leaders fled into exile, and corruption was widespread. The dictator, Marcos Pérez Jiménez, amassed a huge personal fortune, much of it based on oil revenues. In 1956–57, he opened another round of forty-year oil concessions, receiving $675 million for the award of over 800,000 hectares. By the end of the Pérez Jiménez period, government oil production in Venezuela had doubled and government income from oil had tripled, accounting for two-thirds of the government budget. In Romulo Betancourt's words, Venezuela had become a "petroleum factory."[3]

PÉREZ ALFONZO AND OPEC

In January 1958, Pérez Jiménez was overthrown by a military-civilian coalition and a spontaneous uprising by the people of Caracas. Elections were held in December 1958, and Romulo Betancourt won with 49.2 percent of the vote. His Acción Democrática party won control of both houses of Congress. Once again, as minister of mines and hydrocarbons, Juan Pablo Pérez Alfonzo was put in charge of oil policy. He came into office after an interim junta had already increased taxes on the oil companies with the government now receiving 65 percent of profits. Pérez Alfonzo made no change in the tax. Instead, he reaffirmed the principle of opposition to new concessions and moved to create a state oil company, the Corporación Venezolana del Petroleo (CVP), which was established in 1960. It was intended that CVP would open up new oil lands by entering into service contracts with foreign companies. The foreign companies were not responsive to this suggestion, and CVP only produced a small percentage of Venezuela's oil production up to the time of the oil nationalization at midnight, December 31, 1975. The company was also supposed to provide a training ground for Venezuelan administrators who could take over the industry when the concessions ran out, but almost immediately it became bogged down in bureaucracy and inefficiency, supporting the position of those who argued that the Venezuelans were incapable of operating a nationalized industry.

Pérez Alfonzo is known as "the father of OPEC," and the story behind his initiative is well known. In 1959, in order to assure stability of prices and markets for domestic producers, the Eisenhower administration established a system of import quotas on foreign oil. The quota system exempted Canada and Mexico, but when Venezuelan requests for a similar exemption, on grounds of hemispheric security, were rejected, Pérez Alfonzo concluded that it was necessary to defend oil producers from the unilateral actions of consuming countries. In addition, he was concerned with the need to conserve Venezuela's limited oil reserves and to develop an alternative economic base in Venezuela before oil reserves were exhausted. In exile during the dictatorship, he had been impressed with the way the Texas Railroad Commission controlled Texas oil production, and in 1959 he set up a Coordinating Commission for the Conservation and Marketing of Hydrocarbons within the Ministry of Mines. The commission was designed to exercise controls over production levels, exports, and prices of Venezuelan oil, but this could happen only if Venezuela acted in concert with the Middle Eastern oil producers, who had much larger reserves and lower production costs. After an initial meeting in 1959 and following two price cuts by the oil companies, the Middle Eastern countries and Venezuela met, in September 1960, to form the Organization of Petroleum Exporting Countries (OPEC), with one of its goals "[to] study and formulate a system to insure the stabilization of prices by, among other means, the regulation of production."[4] During the 1960s, OPEC never succeeded in achieving this objective, owing to differences among its members. It was not until the next decade that it would achieve that goal—with far-reaching effects.

TAX REFERENCE VALUES

In the early 1960s, the Kennedy administration actively supported President Betancourt, who was being threatened by Castroite guerrillas. However, Betancourt was unable to get the United States to accept a proposal for a government-to-government agreement on oil imports on a hemispheric basis. Nor could he prevent the American oil companies from decreasing their exploration and new investment in Venezuela in favor of the more profitable Middle Eastern oil fields. Production leveled off during the 1960s, and prices declined to the point that a barrel of oil, which had brought $2.50 in 1958, was selling at $1.87 ten years later. As a result, although the government now received two-thirds of company profits, total government income did not increase proportionately. In 1966, as part of a general solution to a tax reform crisis, the government and the concessionaires agreed on a five-year system of fixed "reference values" for tax purposes. In an informal agreement, the companies agreed to increase production in exchange for new incentives for reinvestment and exploration. Pérez Alfonzo, out of government since 1963, denounced the agreement and claimed that the companies were making from 30 percent to 50 percent profit on their investments.[5] In 1968, further tax incentives were granted to the companies in exchange for the installation of desulphurization equipment; desulphurization was necessary to meet environmental standards on the United States East Coast, Venezuela's principal market for heating oil.

In 1968, Rafael Caldera Rodríguez of the Social Christian (Christian Democratic) party was elected president by a narrow margin, with only 29 percent of the vote. The unquestioned acceptance of the legitimacy of his assumption of office demonstrated how quickly constitutional democracy had become a part of Venezuelan life. It was the third consecutive set of free elections held in a country in which, before 1958, no elected president had ever finished his term in office. The AD handed over control of the presidency to its Social Christian opponents, but it retained its strong position in Congress. In December 1970, the AD and its congressional allies pushed through another tax increase on the companies, combining it with a provision that the government could unilaterally change tax reference values for export purposes at any time. With the new taxes, the government's share of oil profits rose to 78 percent. (The question of whether the tax increases, adopted in December 1970 and implemented in March 1971, applied retroactively to the companies' income for 1970 and the first quarter of 1971 was still being argued in the Venezuelan courts in 1979.) Congress also finally approved the guidelines for service contracts between the state oil company and the foreign oil companies — a concept that had been under discussion since the establishment of the CVP ten years earlier. (In the bidding for service contracts to open up new oil fields, Occidental Petroleum, which had no concessions in Venezuela, took the lead. In late 1975, Occidental was accused of having distributed $5 million in bribes in 1971 to Venezuelan politicians in order to secure its service contract; for this reason, it was denied compensation at the time of nationalization.)

THE REVERSION LAW

Over the years, Venezuela's income from oil had increased to the point that it was receiving nearly four times as much as the companies that were actually extracting the oil. It had also established controls over pricing and, to a limited degree, over production. Yet it was not able to compel the companies to make new investments in the development of Venezuelan oil because the oil fields in the Middle East were so much more profitable. In addition, because the majority of the concessions were scheduled to revert to the state without compensation in a little over a decade, the companies had little or no incentive to invest. This produced a movement in the Venezuelan Congress for stricter regulation of the oil companies, especially in the area of investment, during the period before the concessions ran out. A new law, known as the Hydrocarbons Reversion Law, initiated the process that ultimately led to the nationalization of the entire industry.

Introduced by a member of the Movimiento Electoral del Pueblo (MEP), which had split from the AD in 1968, the bill received the support of the two major parties, the AD and the Social Christians, and, after some delay, of President Caldera. The law specified that all company properties within Venezuela related to the concessions would revert to the state when the current forty-year concessions ran out beginning in 1983. It also contained a new requirement: the companies were directed to deposit an annual amount equal to 10 percent of the value of their installations with the Venezuelan government as a guarantee that the installations would be handed over in good condition. Finally, in order to ensure that the companies did not cut back in anticipation of the impending reversion, the law established extensive government controls over drilling and exploration, investment, and production. When the companies reduced production in 1971 and 1972 from the 1970 all-time high of 3.7 million barrels a day, the government raised the tax reference price and instituted a system of penalties for production deficiencies. The maintenance of production was important since the government relied on oil income to finance a large part of its budget. But some, like Pérez Alfonzo, argued against maintaining production, claiming that it would result in the rapid depletion of Venezuelan proven oil reserves, which were now estimated to run out in a little over 10 years. The complicated system of controls and bargaining with the companies was one of several factors that began to persuade more and more Venezuelans that full nationalization of the industry should not wait until the concessions ran out.

A proposal by President Caldera to nationalize gas production in Venezuela furthered the debate. Legislation enacted in 1971 established a state monopoly over all gas produced in the country —both that which came as a by-product of oil production and that from natural gas fields. The Caldera government originally intended to seek joint ventures with foreign companies, but Congress did not want foreign involvement. The debate revealed the increasing hostility of the legislators toward the foreign oil companies.

A further element in the nationalization debate was the question of the future development of the Orinoco Tar Belt, estimated to contain reserves of 700 billion barrels of oil. (Later estimates went as high as 2.8 trillion barrels.) During this period, discussions were carried on with United States government representatives concerning possible American investment in the development of these resources in return for guaranteed United States market access and fixed prices. However, the only result of these discussions was a public outcry over a possible "sellout" to the foreign companies.

THE OPEC PRICE INCREASE

Venezuelans were still hesitant, however, to move to nationalization for the same reasons that deterred them in the past—their heavy dependence on oil income and their lack of confidence in

Venezuelan abilities to manage a state-owned industry efficiently. (The state petroleum company, which produced 2 percent of Venezuela's oil, employed 20 percent of the oil industry's labor force, and the state petrochemical industry was continuously involved in scandals and bottlenecks.) The final "push" toward nationalization came as a result of the OPEC increase in the price of oil during 1973.

Beginning at the Caracas meeting of OPEC in December 1970 and continuing at the Teheran meeting in 1971, the members began to impose a series of tax and price increases on the companies. In 1972, they adopted plans for acquisition of oil company assets through increasing national participation in ownership. Then, in late 1973 and early 1974, the price of Persian Gulf oil was sharply increased, and an embargo was imposed by the Arab and North African oil-producing countries. Venezuela did not participate in the embargo, but it raised its tax reference price from $3.10 in January 1973 to $14.08 a barrel in December. The resulting oil bonanza increased government oil income from $2 billion in 1972 to $3 billion in 1973 to $9.7 billion in 1974. Most important, it gave the country both an additional incentive to take over the industry completely and a cushion to insulate it from drops in income. Production, too, could be cut back as part of OPEC's general restrictions, and oil could be conserved for the future without forcing anyone, least of all the government, to make any sacrifices in income.

In contrast to the handling of the nationalization issue in the multiparty politics of Chile, the two large centrist parties dominating Venezuelan politics took a moderate approach on the oil question. Despite the fact that the December 1973 election for the presidency and legislature was too close to call, the AD and the Social Christians, by mutual agreement, kept the oil question out of the partisan debate. Both parties recognized that major policy moves in the area were necessary, but neither wanted to be committed to a specific policy beforehand. As a result of his own brilliant electoral campaign and the lackluster performance of his principal opponent, Carlos Andrés Pérez, the AD candidate, won a sweeping victory with 48.6 percent of the vote.[6] His party also achieved a working majority in both houses, electing a total of 28 out of 49 senators and 102 out of 200 deputies.

THE REVERSION COMMISSION

When Pérez took office on March 12, 1974, he announced his intention to move immediately to "accelerate the process of reversion" by "a new nationalist and national policy." Despite his large electoral majority, he indicated that the transition to state ownership would be carried out on the basis of a "great national consensus." To develop this consensus, he announced the establishment of a Presidential Advisory Commission to Study the Alternatives for the Acceleration of Reversion. It was composed of four ministers; the head of the state oil company; the chairmen of the Petroleum Committees of the two houses of Congress; a representative of the armed forces; one representative from each of Venezuela's eight political parties; three labor representatives (including one from the petroleum workers union); three business and banking representatives; five representatives from the universities; representatives from organizations of engineers, lawyers, economists, and scientists; and five petroleum experts named by the president. The commission was divided into subcommittees concerned with operations, structure, finances, marketing, and labor.

At its first meeting in May 1974, Pérez indicated that the principal goals of the commission would be the development of an administrative formula for the transition to state ownership, the resolution of the problems involved in maintaining the oil workers' welfare benefits, and, especially, the elaboration of a compensation formula. The companies would receive a just compensation in accordance with the Venezuelan constitution, Pérez said, based on "real value minus amortization," and they would be paid in bonds "on terms convenient to the national interest." Relying on the suggestions of the Venezuelan Association of Petroleum Engineers, he also recommended that the subsidiaries of Exxon (Creole Petroleum), Shell, and Gulf (Mene Grande) retain their organizational identities after nationalization. In addition, at least one other operating company should be maintained for the other, smaller foreign concession holders. Finally, he suggested that the operating companies be placed under the overall direction of a "National Petroleum Enterprise," which would carry out the supervisory functions formerly exercised by the overseas company headquarters.[7] The commission was given until December to produce a report and recommend a draft law. Pérez promised to present his final bill to the Congress three months later, taking into account the recommendations of the advisory commission.

NATIONALIZATION OF IRON

While the commission proceeded with its work, President Pérez began the nationalization of the iron ore concessions, granted in 1950 for fifty years to U.S. Steel and Bethlehem Steel. Venezuela already had a state mining company and a small state-owned steel industry producing 1 million tons a year, about half the country's current needs. The nationalization of the iron mines was seen as important in the development of an expanded steel capacity over the next decade. Following Pérez's accession to office, the AD-controlled Congress adopted an "organic law," giving the president extraordinary decree powers for one year in economic and financial matters, as permitted by Article 190 of the Constitution. Besides authorizing the president to impose a stiff excess profits tax on the oil companies, it gave him the power to take measures to "reserve for the state the exploitation of the iron industry and to establish mechanisms for the recovery of concessions which have been granted." On June 11, 1974, Pérez began to negotiate with the companies concerning the nationalization of the two concessions. On November 26, 1974, he issued another decree "extinguishing" the concessions and providing for the payment of promissory notes in compensation at 7 percent interest over a period of ten years in an amount based on book value of all installations less depreciation. In December, an agreement was signed with the two steel companies providing nearly $84 million to U.S. Steel and in excess of $17 million to Bethlehem Steel. Establishing an important precedent for the oil nationalization, the agreement also provided for one-year management service contracts and three-year technical assistance contracts with the two companies under the supervision of the state steel company. Bethlehem Steel also signed a contract to purchase 3.3 million metric tons of iron a year, for three years, with a renewal option for two years, while U.S. Steel agreed to purchase 11 million metric tons a year over the next seven years.[8]

Congress approved the agreements on December 27, 1974, with the votes of the AD and a small right-wing party. The other parties objected to the fact that the nationalization had been carried out without congressional participation, and they criticized the policy of continuing the relationship with the multinationals. For the Pérez government, however, the agreements meant that the nationalization process would involve no interruptions in production, and the nationalized mines would be assured of a market for part of their production during the time that domestic steel capacity was being expanded.

The iron nationalization provided a useful model for the subsequent and much more important oil nationalization. In both cases, the companies' reluctance to accept compensation at book value minus depreciation was diminished by payments for technical and other assistance, and it was understood that Venezuelan production would continue to find a large market in the United States. Legally, however, the two processes were quite different. In the iron nationalization, no attempt was made to develop a multiparty consensus, and lengthy secret negotiations were carried out between the executive and the steel companies, over a period of six months, before the agreements were made public.

Some Venezuelans argued that the same process should have been utilized for petroleum, and the substantial returns that Venezuela received in the first year of national ownership of iron — 700 million bolivars in 1975 as compared to 300 million bolivars in 1974 — seemed to support the idea of a more rapid nationalization. However, according to one government estimate, the excess profits tax on petroleum meant that even without nationalization Venezuela was already receiving 95 percent ($8.75 per barrel) in 1974 and 94 percent ($9.45 per barrel) in 1975 of the profits of the oil companies.[9] In retrospect, it is clear that there would have been problems in marketing the oil on an independent basis in 1974, for world demand had fallen sharply as a result of recession and price increases. In addition, as the iron nationalization illustrated, a nationalization based on a national consensus would have been impossible to achieve.

The Reversion Commission maintained a remarkable degree

of harmony throughout its deliberations, but the consensus did not survive the congressional debate. The commission's report and draft law, published in December, recommended that the petroleum workers be guaranteed their jobs and social benefits. It accepted the recommendation of President Pérez that the larger operating companies retain their individual identities and that along with the state oil company, CVP, their activities should be coordinated by a state holding company. It also established general principles for compensation, including payment in bonds for net book value (cost minus depreciation and amortization) after deductions for taxes, worker benefits, property in deteriorated condition, and "drainage" from outside concession areas (a provision that was the basis for a suit by the Venezuela Society of Accountants). Finally, the commission called for the establishment of a Guarantee Fund equal to 10 percent of the gross accumulated investment of the companies and recommended that the compensation amounts be reviewed and approved by the Supreme Court.

The Communist party objected to any compensation for the companies, but the independent leftist Movement to Socialism (MAS) stated that, although morally Venezuela owed nothing to the companies, it was willing to support compensation. The business representative favored leaving open the possibility of private participation in some aspects of the industry, but the final report recommended a complete state monopoly at all stages including exploration, refining, transportation, and marketing. It was on this issue that the consensus broke down during the congressional debate on the nationalization law.

THE DEBATE OVER ARTICLE 5

Article 5 of the commission's draft bill provided that all the industry's activities were to be carried out by "state entities" created by the government with the approval of the Senate. Those entities could sign contractual agreements with other companies for specific operations but could not give up ownership rights. The Pérez administration, however, did not want the government's flexibility limited to this degree, particularly in exploration for oil in the Orinoco Tar Belt and off the shore. When the government's draft bill was presented to the Congress in March 1975, it sharply departed from the commission's version of Article 5. In the government version, the state was authorized "in special cases and when it suits the public interest" to "enter into agreements of association with private entities of a limited duration and in terms which will guarantee the full control of the state. Such agreements will require the prior authorization of Congress meeting in joint session."

It was around this clause that the congresssional debate centered. Led by the COPEI-Social Christian party, the opposition attacked the provision, claiming that such joint ventures would lead to the reestablishment of the power of the multinational companies over Venezuela's principal mineral resource. In vain, the government pointed to the necessity of congressional approval and the need for flexibility in the future development of the industry. The government bill, when it came out of the Petroleum Committee of the Chamber of Deputies, contained still another version of Article 5. It provided considerable flexibility for joint ventures outside of the territorial limits of Venezuela but restricted such relationships within Venezuela to minority participation over fifteen years of "nonconventional" production and refining. The executive, however, insisted that the original text be retained, and the AD congressional majority restored the government's language in the bill.[10]

The debate in the two houses of the legislature lasted for most of the summer of 1975. It continued to center around Article 5 with the Social Christians leading the attack and proposing, in the name of a national consensus, that a compromise be adopted that would provide for a special law on "agreements of association." COPEI also wanted to exclude foreign companies from the Orinoco Tar Belt, but the government adamantly opposed this proposal.

Why was there such a deep difference of opinion on Article 5? Part of the answer lay simply in the game of democratic politics. Cynics have noted that Pérez may have permitted the difference between the commission and the executive to arise in order to deflect criticism from other parts of the bill. More likely, however, the government was not aware of the extent of the statist and antimultinational feelings on the commission, which was presided over by the head of the state oil company. Once the difference had emerged, the COPEI saw an issue that it could use to stake out a left-nationalist position in the hope of gaining popular support. The public, however, was confused by what appeared to be relatively minor differences between the "operating agreements" in the commission's bill and the "agreements of association" in the government's bill. In any event, as the government spokesmen pointed out, Congress would have ample opportunity to defend the national interest since it had to approve such agreements before they could go into effect. Except for the speeches of former Presidents Betancourt and Caldera (the Venezuelan constitution provides that all former presidents serve as senators for life), the congressional debate was described by *Resumen*, a Venezuelan newsweekly, as "one which will go down in history for its mediocrity."

The government text, including its version of Article 5, was adopted by the AD-controlled Congress, and on August 29, 1975, President Pérez signed the Petroleum Industry Nationalization Law providing for the reservation to the state of all petroleum industry activity in Venezuela. He announced the creation of Petróleos de Venezuela (Petroven) as the state petroleum agency and pledged that it would be kept out of politics.

Following the signing of the law, Pérez named the board of directors of Petroven. None of its nine members was a politician, and most possessed technical backgrounds in petroleum or related industries. The chairman was General Rafael Alfonso Ravard, a graduate of the Massachusetts Institute of Technology with a long and successful career in state administration who most recently had served as chairman of the state-owned Guayana Corporation, which had successfully developed iron, steel, aluminum, and electric power complexes in central Venezuela.[11]

THE COMPENSATION QUESTION

The oil companies did not like the use of net book value for compensation since that amount, already computed for company tax purposes at about $1.1 billion, was only about 20 percent of their actual investment and about 10 percent of its replacement value. However, it was difficult for them to contest a valuation based on their own books, particularly in the face of the overwhelming national consensus and the impeccable constitutional legitimacy of the nationalization process. In addition, they would receive indirect compensation if they maintained a working relationship after an amicable settlement through payments for technical assistance and rights to purchase crude petroleum for company refineries.

In October, all the oil companies but one (El Paso Oil, which had a larger tax bill than the proposed compensation) accepted the government offer of compensation. For the record, the companies objected that the terms did not constitute "prompt, adequate, and effective" compensation and expressed concern over the possible effects of assessments for "drainage" from state-owned oil properties. However, "in an effort to cooperate in a tranquil implementation of the process of nationalization in accordance with law," they did not enter appeals to the Supreme Court. The total compensation to be paid came to $1,012,571,901.67. Exxon received $512 million, $73 million in cash and the remainder in bonds to be paid out over five years with 6 percent interest; Shell agreed to $250 million, $10 million of it in cash; and the other companies agreed to lesser amounts.[12] (As noted above, because of bribery charges, Occidental did not receive compensation for its 1971 service contract. The charges were subsequently thrown out in court, and as of 1979, Occidental was suing for compensation for the oil it had discovered.) In 1978, the companies were billed $134 million for deficiencies in equipment and other assets, thus reducing the actual compensation to about $900 million. Other claims, especially the 1970 tax dispute, continue to impede full implementation of the compensation agreements.

THE ROLE OF THE UNITED STATES GOVERNMENT

The United States government played a minor role throughout the negotiations. Before they began, a former ambassador to

Venezuela publicly urged that the government become involved. However, the oil holdings were not insured by the Overseas Private Investment Corporation (OPIC), and the companies did not request government intervention or assistance. There seemed to be no reason for official involvement since, as the iron nationalization indicated, the principle of compensation was to be observed and economic relations with the United States were likely to continue.

There was one problem, however, in connection with the compensation. From the time of the Mexican nationalizations, payment on the basis of book value had usually not been considered "adequate" by United States policymakers. The use of book value in the Venezuelan case led to a formal statement on compensation by the State Department. On December 30, 1975, two days before the Venezuelan take-over, the department reaffirmed its adherence to the principle that compensation should be based on "going concern" value. It added that acceptance of net book value by a United States company did not mean that the United States government accepted that basis for compensation. The statement received no attention from the American or Venezuelan press. Because there was no obvious violation of international law, and given the interest of the companies in continuing to do business with Petroven and of the United States government in a continuing reliable source of oil, the general perception was that a stronger response was neither desirable nor necessary.

THE TECHNICAL ASSISTANCE AGREEMENTS

Once the issue of compensation had been resolved, the next step was to reach agreement on technical assistance. This was made contingent upon the conclusion of agreements on the purchase of crude oil that finally were signed only as the Venezuelans took possession of the oil fields in January. The companies stalled for time, hoping that Venezuela would be forced to cut prices as a result of a world oil surplus. The maneuver did not succeed, but the agreement only provided that the former concessionaires would buy 1.75 million barrels a day out of the 2.2 billion that Venezuela had hoped to sell. (By mid-1976, Venezuela was selling 2.4 million barrels a day so that the temporary shortfall, in the early part of the year, was later made up.)

The details of the technical assistance agreements were not revealed by the government. In February the minister of mines announced that Venezuela would pay an average of 19 cents per barrel to the companies (36 cents minus 17 cents tax). Later government announcements, however, indicated that payments had been much less because different payments were made to various companies for crude and refined petroleum. According to the government, payments ranged from 8 cents a barrel of "feedstock" (prerefined) petroleum for small companies, to 15 cents per barrel of crude plus 15 cents per barrel of refined petroleum for large companies such as Shell and Exxon, averaging out to 13.4 cents per barrel. (Atlantic Richfield refused to sign an agreement, claiming that its payments were too small.) The technical assistance agreements include the loan of technicians, training, direct access to new technology, computer programs, and assistance in the establishment of research capability. (In the case of Exxon, for example, the agreement provided for 80,000 hours of technical assistance.) The contracts were for up to four years, that is, until 1980. The sales agreements were signed for two years, but the amount and price were to be renegotiated every three months. In early 1978, Exxon was purchasing 50 percent of Petroven's exports but was said to be considering letting its contract expire. The technical assistance payments of 8 cents to 30 cents per barrel compare with an estimated average company income of 25 cents a barrel (plus depreciation and amortization) received in 1975. With average production around 2.2 million barrels a day, the initial technical assistance payments after taxes probably amounted to about $100 million a year.[13]

Observers on the left argue that the arrangement puts the oil companies in a better position than before: they no longer are required to operate the oil wells but can make as much or more profit from the technical assistance and marketing contracts. The left also sees foreign investors and domestic entrepreneurs in other areas as benefiting because the Venezuelan government now offers them new investment opportunities with the revenues from the nationalized petroleum industry. The two large companies have increased their profits over 1975, when almost all their earnings were paid out in taxes to Venezuela, but most of the companies have not. Moreover, in 1978, the technical service contracts with Texaco, Mobil, and Standard Oil of California were not renewed, and when those with Exxon, Shell, and Gulf were renegotiated in 1980, payments were calculated on the basis of technology-man-hours rather than per-barrel-produced or -refined, thus sharply reducing technological assistance fees. New marketing agreements also reduced the percentage marketed by the foreign companies to 50 percent of total oil exports, down from 85 percent in 1976. Other economic opportunities in Venezuela are being offered, on a preferential basis, to domestic investors, and at least initially strict regulations have been placed on the foreign investor. State power has been vastly strengthened in both negotiating with foreign companies and determining the future of domestic investment. Thus, the assertion that "the foreign oil firms, on the other hand, are guaranteed higher net profits than they would have enjoyed had they retained their installations and concessions" is inaccurate and misleading.[14]

PETROVEN IN OPERATION

The 1976 transition to national ownership was remarkably smooth. Nearly all of an estimated 525 foreign employees (out of a labor force of 23,000) remained with the operating companies. The companies were reimbursed for their salaries by the Venezuelans, but they were employed by service company subsidiaries of the oil companies and retained their tenure rights with their international employers. The twenty-two concessionary companies were reduced to fourteen under the overall direction of Petroven. On January 1, 1976, Petroven became the eleventh largest non-American company in the world, inheriting 12 refineries, 14 tankers, 6,000 miles of pipeline, and a production capacity of over 3 million barrels a day. Money was appropriated for an enlarged petroleum technical research institute (Intevep); over $500 million was pledged for investment and exploration in 1976 and $700 million in 1977, with higher amounts planned for the future; and contracts with other governments for the sale of oil were initiated. (In mid-1976, sales agreements were signed with Spain and Colombia, but about two-thirds of Venezuelan production continued to go directly, or indirectly through Caribbean refineries, to the United States.) Particular efforts were made to improve and to expand relationships with other Latin American states. (Special sales agreements had been made earlier with the Central American countries, Jamaica, and Peru involving loans from the Venezuelan Investment Fund of surplus oil revenues to finance their oil purchases.) But the most significant demonstration of the new marketing capacity of Venezuela was a barter agreement worked out with the Soviet Union in late 1976 and implemented several years later. This agreement involved Venezuela shipping its oil to Cuba, Russia's customer, and the Soviet Union shipping its oil to Venezuela's customers in Europe. It was estimated that the arrangement would save $1.20 a barrel in shipping costs on each side.

In the first two years of operation, the nationalized oil industry of Venezuela seemed to have avoided most of the pitfalls that have become associated with nationalization of foreign mineral investments. While there had been strikes and labor problems in the iron mines, the petroleum workers were remarkably quiescent, despite an initial threat of a strike aimed at securing part of their company welfare benefits in a lump sum and persuading the government to turn over the company-owned housing gratis.[15] The foreign technicians remained, and the operating companies, although legally completely new corporations, initially operated as before. (In 1977 and 1978, steps were taken to reduce the number of companies from fourteen to four, but for reasons of continuity and efficiency, Petroven intends to retain a quasi-competitive structure.) The Venezuelans who worked for the industry continued to be paid the high salaries that they had received from the companies — much higher than those of Venezuelan civil servants. Petroven did not suffer from politicization, and after some initial difficulty, the marketing situation straightened itself out after the world recovery in 1976. The Venezuelan nationalization seemed to be a model of how to transfer ownership from the foreign investor to the state at minimal cost.

PROBLEMS AFTER NATIONALIZATION

There were problems, of course. The number of employees increased from 23,000 to 27,500 in the three years following nationalization. The dispute over the 1970 retroactive tax claims continued to drag on in the courts. The imposition on the new operating companies of a 10 percent assessment for Petroven, added to an already heavy tax burden, meant that the industry was likely to end up in the red. Thus, six months after nationalization, the tax rate on the operating companies was lowered from 71.4 percent to 65.5 percent. (It was raised to 67.7 percent in 1977.) An artificially low exchange rate that had amounted to another tax on the companies was eliminated. The subsidized price of domestic gas (14 cents to 32 cents per gallon) was increased by 11 percent in 1976. There was also uncertainty as to the proper relationship between Petroven as a supervisory holding company and the Ministry of Mines and Hydrocarbons, whose previous functions were similar to those now carried out by Petroven. Above all, there was continuing concern about what would happen to a country so totally dependent on income from oil exports when the proven reserves ran out.

This concern was manifested in an increased emphasis on conservation of oil reserves, now estimated at about twenty years at the reduced consumption rate, and in new exploration and investment, which had declined in recent years until they were required by the Reversions Law. The problem, of course, could be ameliorated if an effective and relatively cheap way was found to extract oil from the Orinoco Tar Belt. With this in mind, in 1976, a technical cooperation agreement was signed with Canada, which was trying to develop a similar process for its Alberta tar sands.

As outlined in its five-year plan published in 1976, the government's solution to the potential exhaustion of its oil reserves was a massive investment program that would create a domestic industrial base and modernize its inefficient agricultural system. It outlined a program for the fifteenfold expansion of the steel industry by 1986 (one Venezuelan politician called it "pharaonic"), the creation of an enlarged petrochemical industry (until now a disaster among Venezuelan state enterprises), large increases in electric power and aluminum production, and the establishment of three shipyards under state sponsorship.

These basic industries were to be state-owned (often using management contracts with foreign companies) or joint ventures, and the financing for the expansion was to come principally from oil revenues. However, because of increased consumption and imports, those revenues were not sufficient for the country's capital investment needs. In 1977, the country went into deficit financing, and Venezuela, like so many other countries in Latin America, began to borrow from American and European banks. Unlike the other countries, it still had large foreign exchange reserves ($6 billion in 1978, down from $9 billion two years earlier), much of it in the Venezuelan Investment Fund. By the end of Carlos Andrés Pérez's term in March 1979, Venezuela's public debt was $11.7 billion.

Critics of the new program doubt that Venezuela is capable of efficiently operating the enlarged state sector. The controller general has only 1,600 employees and must check on the operation of 200 state enterprises comprising 60 percent of the gross domestic product. In 1974, a Public Administration Reform Committee recommended the creation of a National System of State Enterprises under a special minister of state, and in January 1977 a minister of basic industries was appointed to oversee the development of the state sector in areas other than petroleum. A central budget office was also created in the secretariat to the presidency. But state enterprises, such as the petrochemical institute (IVP), the housing institute (INAVI), and Nitroven, the state nitrogen corporation, incurred hundreds of millions of dollars in losses owing to inefficiency and corruption.[16]

Despite the government's announced commitment to a mixed economy, with a major role for private investment, the increased state role in the economy raised doubts in the private sector. Yet the government tried to stimulate domestic private investment. It made low interest loans available to small- and medium-sized industries and took measures to improve housing. Foreign private investors had more reason to be worried about the orientation of the Pérez government than did their Venezuelan counterparts. The "fadeout" provisions and rigid restrictions on foreign investment in the Andean Pact were more vigorously applied by Venezuela than by any other members of the pact. A Superintendency of Foreign Investment (SIEX) was established to monitor and to enforce the regulations. Foreign investors were required to register the value of their investments, and banks, insurance companies, and companies in the fields of communications, advertising, and marketing were told to reduce foreign ownership to 20 percent. Chiefly because of the stringent investment requirements and profit repatriation limits, as well as a five-year limit of patent protection for new technology, new foreign investment dropped off sharply. The Venezuelans believed that they could be tougher on the foreign investor because they are less dependent than other countries on foreign exchange and on foreign investment since capital for both is provided by the oil industry. In February 1978, however, the divestment requirements were eased, exempting from the 80 percent domestic ownership requirement various services and companies marketing durable goods. SIEX was also given authority to extend the patent fadeout period to fifteen years and to waive the Andean Pact's 20 percent limit on profit remittances. The more favorable attitude to foreign investment paralleled similar steps in other Latin American countries. It demonstrated that even an oil-rich country like Venezuela could not afford to cut itself off from the capital, technology, and export markets offered by foreign investors.

THE OWENS-ILLINOIS EXPROPRIATION

In April 1976, foreign private investors were further disturbed when the government suddenly announced that it intended to expropriate the Venezuelan subsidiary of the Owens-Illinois Glass

Company. The announcement was a reaction to the publication by Owens-Illinois, in three foreign newspapers, of a communiqué from a Venezuelan guerrilla group attacking the Venezuelan government. Publication of the communiqué was a condition set by the guerrillas for the release of Owens's general manager for Venezuela, William Niehous, who had been kidnapped in February. Declaring that the company had "violated the constitutional and legal norms of Venezuela" by publishing a communiqué that "supported subversion and offended and defamed members of the government," the minister of the interior announced on April 6 that the government would acquire the stock of the Venezuelan subsidiary, "granting just compensation." The State Department expressed "its concern about the use of expropriation as a criminal sanction"; the opposition leader and former president, Rafael Caldera, observed that while "no foreign or transnational entity can ignore our domestic norms . . . I frankly do not understand the nature and purpose of the action"; and Gonzalo Barrios, the AD president of the Congress, admitted that "while the measure is clear from a political point of view, there are problems with its legal and juridical implementation." Those problems could have been resolved if the company had been willing to sell, but when the Venezuelans made an offer 25 percent above book value, it was refused. There were sporadic government-company negotiations thereafter, but the company continued to operate in Venezuela assuming (as it turned out, correctly) that the government would drop its nationalization plans when Pérez went out of office in March 1979. The threat of expropriation, however, delayed a planned expansion by the company, involving a special glass process that promised considerable savings in foreign exchange. In addition, the company possessed technical patents that it refused to share with the government on a service contract basis, insisting on full equity ownership. The case provided a sharp contrast to the petroleum nationalization in the precipitate way that it was carried out and in the weak bargaining position of the Venezuelan government vis-à-vis the company.[17] (Niehous was freed on June 30, 1979, after being held captive for more than three years.)

AGRICULTURAL AND SOCIAL PROBLEMS

Critics of Venezuela's dependence on oil are quick to point out that agricultural problems continue to persist. They claim that Venezuela urbanized too quickly and that insufficient attention was paid to the maintenance of a productive capacity in agriculture. In the early 1970s, the agricultural sector employed 19 percent of the labor force (down from 46 percent in 1950) but produced only 4 percent of the gross domestic product.[18] The government spent large amounts of foreign currency ($340 million in 1975) for imported food, which constituted nearly one-quarter of total consumption, and it subsidized domestic producers to keep the price of food down for urban consumers. In an effort to expand agricultural production, President Pérez established an Agricultural Credit Fund that provided low interest loans, gave special tax exemptions to agricultural investments, and required Venezuelan banks to make 20 percent of their loan funds available to agriculture. By 1979, there were signs that these measures by the government were beginning to produce results.

In addition, there are continuing problems of social justice that, for all its populist commitment, the Pérez government did not succeed in remedying. Income distribution remains highly skewed, with the bottom 20 percent of the population receiving only 3 percent of the total income. Sewage disposal facilities are lacking in 50 percent of Venezuelan homes and 70 percent of the Venezuelan population is undernourished. Taxes are among the lowest in the world. Only 400,000 Venezuelans pay taxes, accounting for 14 percent of the national budget.[19] When he took office, President Pérez decreed a minimum wage and mandated large wage increases for low-income groups, as well as other measures designed to increase employment (for example, compulsory restroom attendants, elevator operators for automatic elevators, and a 5 percent increase in hiring by companies with over ten employees). Price controls were imposed on many basic consumer items—and on some that were not so basic, such as certain types of automobiles. Budget expenditures for housing, health, and education increased, and a tax reform was adopted. In December 1978 the candidate of the opposition Social Christian party, Luis Herrera Campins, was elected with a program that promised greater social justice for the low-income groups.

THE LESSONS OF VENEZUELA

The first lesson to be learned from the Venezuelan experience is that highly favorable policies to induce foreign investment followed by increasingly tough demands once the investment has been made can extract maximum benefit for the country. In Venezuela, this happened not once but several times, and it meant that the country benefited earlier and to a greater degree from its foreign mineral resources than other countries studied in this book. By pursuing a flexible and pragmatic policy, the Venezuelans were able to extract more and more of what the Chileans call *retornos* from the foreign companies, leading up to and culminating in the smooth and efficient nationalization of 1976. The transition was made particularly easy by the fact that the companies had trained a whole generation of Venezuelans to operate the petroleum industry.

In addition, the process of nationalization was facilitated by the election in 1973 of a president with a working majority in both houses of the Congress. This enabled the delicate procedure of nationalization to be carried out on a consistent basis and with undisputed democratic legitimacy.

As in other cases studied earlier, there was also an almost irresistible combination of factors leading to a "nationalization situation" in the 1960s. Two factors in particular should be singled out: the approach of the expiration of the majority of the concessions, which created problems in the maintenance of investment and exploration, and the action of OPEC in raising prices and limiting production, which insulated Venezuela from potentially serious problems of maintaining government income and foreign exchange had there been a decline in oil revenues resulting from a reduction in exports or prices after nationalization.

The structure devised for the nationalized industry can serve as an example for state-owned industries in other countries since it retains an element of competition among the operating companies that can be used as a measure of comparative efficiency. Fears of a decline in efficiency had been a major deterrent to earlier nationalization since it was known that, in response to the increasingly large tax bite of the Venezuelan state, the companies had made continuing and successful efforts to improve the economic efficiency of the industry. The Venezuelan state sector, on the other hand, had some notable examples of inefficiency in its petrochemical plants and the state oil company, although the Guayana complex was better organized and managed. The problem for the future is to make certain that the oil revenues are not consumed by the expansion of the bureaucracy and subsidies to inefficiency in the state sector, but are invested in productive activity.

While featherbedding, bureaucratization, and politicization have so far been avoided in the nationalized oil industry, delicate policy questions remain concerning the future use of the oil revenues. How much of the oil bonanza should go to consumption (Venezuela has the highest per capita import rate in Latin America) and how much to investment? What should be the relation of welfare expenditures (investment in human capital) to investment in capital-intensive technology? Should the oil revenues go mainly to the public or private sectors, to agriculture or industry, to Caracas or elsewhere in the country? With the state as the recycler of oil revenue, these questions are part of the policymaking process of, government—and in a constitutional democracy, the object of continuing public debate and criticism. How Venezuela handles them will demonstrate whether a democratic welfare state can be the master of its mineral resources.

The continuing relationship with the companies in technology and marketing will be closely watched by the domestic opposition. As the debate on Article 5 demonstrated, it may be difficult to keep the question of relations with the foreign oil companies from becoming a political issue.

As discussed above, the companies received two types of compensation—a direct payment, mainly in bonds based on net book value, and an indirect payment, through technical and marketing agreements. Except for the State Department statement on the eve of nationalization opposing the use of book value, the

United States government did not become involved in the compensation negotiations. Unlike the Chilean and Cuban cases, East-West questions were not involved. Both the United States and Venezuela recognized that there was a mutual interest in continuing good relations: Venezuela needed a continuing market for its products, and the United States government needed to maintain a secure source of oil in the Western Hemisphere. The companies did not ask for assistance and preferred to make individual arrangements with the Venezuelans. As a result, the large companies received much more than the small companies in real compensation because of the variable payments for technical assistance, and the net book value compensation formula was reinforced as a precedent for future nationalizations.

Similar arrangements for nationalization and continuing technical and marketing assistance were negotiated with other OPEC states. In those cases, too, the companies agreed to minimal compensation, and the United States government did not become involved. While oil has certain characteristics that encourage such nationalizations, the ease with which the major changes in ownership were carried out indicates that the international environment has been altered. These and other aspects of the emerging new pattern of the politics of international investment and expropriation will be discussed in succeeding chapters.

8

Nationalization and Its Alternatives: The Latin American Experience

The myth of nationalization and the transfer of ownership to the state should be revised to incorporate the concrete . . . class interests that the state apparatus manifests and serves.
> — Luis Pasara, "The Reforms of Copper Mining," 1975

Expropriation and nationalization have been alleged to be crude and unsophisticated forms of host government intervention soon to pass into complete oblivion, replaced by more elegant forms of wealth deprivation.
> — J. Frederick Truitt, "Expropriation of Foreign Investment," 1970

From the corporate perspective, the attractions of equity investment in, and managerial control of, foreign facilities are waning. A growing number of U.S. firms have decided that the risks associated with overseas capital investments have become too high for realized rates of return. . . . In these changing circumstances U.S. firms are finding new opportunities to earn returns on their managerial and technological assets.
> — Jack Baranson, *Technology and the Multinationals: Corporate Strategies in a Changing World Economy,* 1978

There is good news coming out of Latin America for the hundreds of U.S. and other foreign companies with a stake in this vast region: In a startling turnabout, major countries are opening their doors wider to private enterprise.

— "Latin America Opens the Door to Foreign Investment Again," *Business Week*, 1976

Foreign investment is welcome and necessary. It signifies access to markets we do not have, technology we do not have, and financing that is useful to us. But we want partners, not bosses.

— José Lopez Portillo, "The Next President of Mexico Views the Issues," *Business Week*, 1976

In the preceding chapters, the nationalizations of American enterprises in five Latin American countries have been reviewed and analyzed. This chapter will attempt to evaluate those experiences and to draw some general conclusions, particularly as they may affect the policy choices of Third World governments. (The implications of the case studies for United States government policy will be examined in chapter 9.) While each of the five cases is distinctive, it is possible to draw certain general conclusions about the positive and negative aspects of nationalization.

THE POLITICAL APPEAL OF NATIONALIZATION

The case studies demonstrate that Third World countries today can resort to nationalization more easily and successfully than in the past. Since 1960 the number of nationalizations has increased dramatically. Prior to that date most Third World governments lacked both the will and the expertise to take over foreign enterprises. The cold war also worked against nationalization. American-owned companies could appeal to national security in securing United States government support against nationalization because the government viewed such actions as the result of Soviet influence and ideology. Castro's rapid take-over of foreign property in 1959 and 1960 provoked countermeasures by the United States, such as the Hickenlooper Amendment. The obvious economic dependence of Cuba on the Soviet Union as well as the use of Marxist-Leninist theory to justify the internal changes imposed by Castro reinforced the association of nationalization with the radical left. From the end of World War II until the 1960s, nationalization was identified with Communist ideology and the defense of private investment with the defense of "the free world."

In the mid- and late-1960s, however, such take-overs were no longer so closely associated with either Marxism or the Soviet Union. When the anti-Communist government of Eduardo Frei in Chile moved to secure majority control of the American-owned copper mines, the American government pressured the reluctant Anaconda Copper Company to sell the large and profitable mines that it had initially refused to include in the Chileanization scheme. When the Peruvian military seized a controversial Esso subsidiary and introduced a series of dramatic measures to reduce American influence in mining, agriculture, and other sectors, the United States decided not to invoke the Hickenlooper Amendment against a government which was not seen as likely to threaten United States security interests.

Changes in attitude and approach to the problems involved in nationalizations were not made only by the United States. The nationalizing countries, too, learned to recognize that confrontational nationalizations were not in their best interest. If they were to secure continuing loans from private banks, from international financial agencies, and, increasingly, from international banking consortia, nationalizing governments were obliged at least to recognize the principle of compensation when they took over foreign property. In addition, the multinationals also maintained monopoly or oligopoly control of technology and marketing networks that were needed after nationalization. The agreements made by Peru in 1976 with the Marcona Company for marketing and shipping the ore produced in its nationalized iron mines, and those signed by Venezuela at the time of the nationalization of its petroleum industry for technological assistance from the multinational oil companies showed that it was now possible to nationalize major mineral holdings and still maintain vital continuing links with the former companies.

There are now numerous cases of "successful" nationalizations by impeccably anti-Communist governments (for example, in Venezuela and the Middle East) that have been carried out with the cooperation of the companies involved and without undermining the growth of foreign investment or the economic development of the countries involved. It seems, then, that if some recognition is given to the principle of compensation, even if, as in the cases cited, actual payments are well below the market or "going concern" standard endorsed by the United States government, nationalizing governments have less to fear from retaliatory action than in the past. The decline of the cold war; the increasing recognition that the interests of the multinational corporation are separable from, and may even be opposed to, the United States national interest; and the weakening of United States legislative provisions like the Hickenlooper Amendment against expropriation and the executive branch's unwillingness to use them mean that the threat of United States government action against the nationalization of American companies is no longer the powerful deterrent it was in the past.

International politics has also played a role in changing the atmosphere so that nationalizations are more readily accepted. The formation of organizations of producers of primary products on the OPEC model has encouraged government ownership of the commodities involved, and a vocal majority in the United Nations argues for the sovereign right of every nation, under international law, to nationalize with whatever compensation it feels is appropriate. Internationally, there are fewer deterrents to and more support for nationalization than ever before.

There are also internal reasons why it is easier to nationalize than in the past. Particularly in Latin America, the capacity of the government to regulate and direct economic life has substantially increased over the last four decades. Administrators and planners with a sophisticated understanding of international economic relations have been developed both in and out of government. In addition, the existing pool of native managerial personnel, trained by the multinationals, has facilitated the transition to state ownership. While the learning process was painful for Mexico and Cuba, the more recent take-overs in Peru and Venezuela have been managed smoothly. Even if there is a lack of domestic expertise, the required managerial or administrative talent can be hired internationally, foreign consultants can be employed, and training programs can be established, although this may sometimes be a costly alternative to foreign ownership.

Domestic political pressures for nationalization are also greater today. When exposed enclaves of extractive industries appear to be making large profits and are important sources of foreign exchange, political leaders and national public opinion automatically think of nationalization as a way of assuring that the policy and profits of vital industries are brought under national control. National leaders, especially military leaders aware of the strategic importance of certain industries to the economy, find it galling to be dependent on foreign decisionmakers. Hence, they seek to control vital economic resources such as mining, transportation (e.g. Perón and the British-owned railroads or the Mexican nationalization of their rail network), and banking (although in this area the need for access to foreign credit would argue for keeping some branches of foreign banks open). When an oppressive government is overthrown, as in Iran and Nicaragua in 1979, there are also strong political pressures for the nationalization of the properties and investments of the former ruler and those associated with him.

In the area of raw material extraction, some writers on foreign investment have described the shifting relation of host country and investor as an "obsolescing bargain" leading to demands for national ownership. According to this theory, the governments of developing countries are initially willing to grant generous concessions to foreign investors in order for capital, technology, and managerial expertise to be brought into the countries. The companies are able to drive a hard bargain at this time because the situation is strongly in their favor. However, after the investment has been made and the companies have committed substantial resources in the countries concerned, they often begin to reap high profits from their investments. Recognizing the loss of potential revenues, the host government and nationalist politicians and writers begin to press for renegotiation of what appear, in retrospect, to have been overly generous concessions. Once the investment is made, the companies are vulnerable because they cannot easily withdraw. For example, in Chile and Venezuela, the nationalist ante was continually being raised until it finally became clear that the solution to the obsolescence of the bargain was a complete government take-over. In petroleum, high profits and the general availability of technology have made nationalization the rule rather than the exception in the Third World.

Nationalization is always politically popular. Pressures for the extension of national control escalate as competing parties and leaders try to outbid one another in displaying opposition to foreign domination. Dramatic take-overs, such as those by Cárdenas in 1938, Castro in 1960, or the Peruvian military in 1968, can produce a wave of nationalist feeling that makes national heroes out of those who carry out the nationalization. The Chilean copper nationalization of 1971 demonstrated that, even in a period of intense political polarization, no politician could afford to oppose the nationalization of foreign-owned mining enclaves. While domestic business groups may be hesitant to support the extension of state control, if they see that it is economically to their advantage they, too, will support government action to limit or expropriate foreign corporations.

THE ECONOMIC COSTS AND BENEFITS
OF NATIONALIZATION

Given the diminished deterrents to, and increased support for nationalization of foreign enterprises, why have there not been more nationalizations in recent years? Part of the answer lies in the fact that many of the governments that have come to power in Latin America are conservative in orientation. Yet there also appears to be another factor—a growing recognition that nationalization may not be the simple remedy for underdeveloped nations that some have claimed it to be—that, particularly when nationalization takes a confrontational form, its economic costs may considerably outweigh its potential benefits.

Examples of the potential economic problems resulting from

expropriation disputes are readily available: Peru could not secure financing for the expansion of its copper production while it had unsettled nationalization disputes; after it had nationalized the United States-owned copper mines, Chile under Allende was forced to look elsewhere for loans to finance vital imports, it had to fight company legal action in many countries, and it was compelled to find spare parts outside the United States in order to circumvent a company blockade; Cuba could only make a go of its nationalization programs by being assured of Soviet economic support and aligning itself politically with the USSR. The only examples reviewed in this book of take-overs that did not involve serious costs to the nationalizing government were the agreements negotiated by Mexico after 1960 with United States-owned mining and utility companies, by Peru in 1970 with International Telephone and Telegraph, and by Venezuela with the iron ore and petroleum companies in 1974 and 1976.

Further negative costs can result from nationalization. First, marketing the nationalized commodity often becomes a serious problem, as Peru's difficulties in marketing its nationalized iron ore bear out. The multinational corporation has established customers and marketing channels that are lost by the nationalizing government unless special arrangements are worked out, as they were in Venezuela. When there is a worldwide surplus of the export commodity, the state agency may end up as a supplier of last resort. In the petroleum industry, a producers' cartel has attempted to prevent this from happening, but in the copper industry the multinational companies rely on their own, more politically secure sources, while the Third World copper producers (Chile, Peru, and Zambia) are so desperate for foreign exchange that when the world market price declines they continue to produce even at a loss.[1]

State-owned marketing agencies, on the other hand, have more flexibility in finding markets in the Communist countries, where the multinational companies have not ventured. Peru and Chile both actively developed such markets after nationalization. In addition, state ownership of raw materials makes it more likely that what is marketed will be processed or refined within the country, thus providing employment, encouragement to industrial development, and higher profits. (State agencies in Latin America are also attempting to develop a shipping capacity on a national or regional basis.)

A second negative effect of nationalization is the reduced availability of investment capital: where nationalization has occurred, private and international financial institutions are often less willing to lend capital. In addition, nationalization means sacrificing the special access that the multinational corporation may have to international credit or to the profits produced by its operations in other countries. Critics of the multinationals have argued that in fact much of the capital of the multinationals is borrowed locally; however, in many countries limits have now been placed on domestic borrowing by international companies. (One reason that such borrowing took place is that government regulation of interest rates made borrowing on the domestic market, sometimes at a negative interest rate because of inflation, highly advantageous.)

In addition to capital and market problems, nationalization also may mean the loss of technological innovation because access to advances made by the research and development branches of the multinational corporation is relinquished. Venezuela has been particularly concerned with this problem, and it has been willing to pay for that access after nationalization while it develops technological capacities of its own. The potential loss of access to needed technology has also prevented Venezuela from carrying out the announced expropriation of the Owens-Illinois Glass Company's subsidiary. The record on technological innovation by state-owned enterprises is not encouraging, despite the fact that the inappropriate capital-intensive technology utilized by the multinationals has long been a major argument of the critics of foreign investment. The state enterprises seem just as concerned to economize on labor costs as were the multinational corporations. State enterprises acquire their technology chiefly on the international market, and where confrontational nationalization has cut off or reduced access to that market, as in Cuba, the economy suffers.

An alternative way to secure skilled management, market access, capital, and technology after nationalization is to purchase each element separately — what some writers have called "unbundling" the foreign investment package. Foreign enterprises can be hired for specific purposes for limited periods of time through service contracts that are paid for by borrowing on the international money market at a rate that is considerably lower than is necessary to attract and hold the foreign investor.[2]

Unbundling is a controversial issue. Grant Reuber has argued that the differential cost, in the late 1960s, between obtaining investment capital from the multinational investor and direct borrowing on the European money market was about 4 percent (12 percent compared with 8 percent). However, other factors have altered this rate. On the supply side, it has been affected by the availability of Petrodollars for recycling and on the demand side by the increased borrowing in the 1970s by less developed countries to finance imports of oil and food. Critics of foreign investment, such as Constantine Vaitsos, would also insist that real profit rates are much higher than the multinationals report owing to overpricing of inputs from other subsidiaries; defenders of foreign investment, such as Raymond Vernon, maintain that if all costs are taken into account there is little or no difference between the two forms of capital transfer. Vernon argues that loan capital actually costs around 15 to 20 percent to which 3 to 4 percent should be added for service contract fees, while equity costs about 15 percent for profit, 1 percent for royalties, and a possible additional 4 percent for overpricing in purchases. It seems likely that Vernon's figure for the cost of loan capital is excessive, suggesting that there is a real difference of about 5 percent between the costs of the two alternative approaches.[3]

Such a cost differential seems to argue that Third World governments should simply nationalize and purchase any missing inputs on the international market. Yet experience has shown that this is not that easy. Marketing may or may not be a problem. The Chileans were able to sell their copper after nationalization through the same agents that the multinational copper companies had used in Europe, at a time when copper was in short supply and prices were rising, although, as noted, Peru could not sell its iron ore because there was a worldwide oversupply. Certain technologies cannot be purchased because of company policy.

Many companies — IBM being the best known — will not sell their trade secrets. As the Allende government discovered in the copper industry, management teams may not be able to come into a highly technical industry and maintain productivity and efficiency, and even with outside help host governments may lack the expertise to oversee such projects. There is also another advantage to investments by multinationals or foreign corporations. When projects or industries are developed through foreign investment, the risk is borne by the investor rather than the government, but if the investment turns out to be particularly profitable or the world market price for an export product increases significantly (such as the situation that led to the imposition of the copper "overprice" in Chile in 1969), it can provide a source of increased tax revenues for the host country.

Governments in the Third World also face borrowing problems because they are already deeply in debt. The shift toward state ownership by the Echeverria government in Mexico, the Velasco government in Peru, and the Allende government in Chile all led to large increases in the international debts of those countries. Since 1974, the rising costs of food and energy have necessitated further international borrowing, resulting in a heavy debt-service burden and a balance-of-payments deficit that in some cases has been as high as 50 percent of annual export revenues. In these instances, the expansion of the state sector is not likely to be supported by enthusiastic lenders in international financial markets. It is true that the prospect of greatly increased oil revenues in the early 1980s has enabled Mexico to secure loans for its state-owned steel and petroleum sectors. In the mid-1970s, Peru was also able to increase its international indebtedness in anticipation of oil finds in the jungle. However, when these did not prove to be substantial, a serious financial crisis ensued.

Finally, any economic calculation concerning nationalization must include the cost of compensation. While there has been no example, in the cases studied, of full compensation, the principle that *some* compensation must be paid has been upheld, and it has been recognized even by those states where the official ideology is opposed to private ownership of the means of production. In the cases examined, compensation at book value was the norm, although its real cost was often reduced by the payment of compensation out of future production or in the form of bonds at relatively low interest.

The other method for resolving compensation disputes is the lump-sum settlement. The lump-sum method has been used mainly to settle long-standing disputes involving Communist governments, but it was also employed by the Greene mission to Peru in 1974 to resolve a large number of outstanding expropriation controversies. The lump-sum method involves substantially lower payments than book value, but it usually comes at the end of a lengthy period of strained relations in which other costs have been incurred, for example, the loans and investments foregone by Peru during the Velasco period. An additional problem with such settlements, as the case of Czechoslovakia demonstrates, is that they may incur opposition in the United States Congress.[4]

EFFICIENCY COSTS OF STATE OWNERSHIP

Probably the strongest argument against nationalizing existing foreign investment and carrying out development primarily through government-financed public or private (usually the former) domestic firms is the resulting decline in efficiency. Even if foreign loans can be obtained at a lower rate of interest to finance such development, the real cost involved may be higher than that of foreign investment. As one observer put it:

> It would be preferable for a country's resources to be developed by local effort if the means to do so exist and if it can be done without economic penalty in relation to alternative opportunities. Where the means do not exist . . . it seems to be desirable (and clearly socially and politically necessary in the light of growing populations) that they should be developed by foreign capital rather than not developed at all. . . . Foreign private risk capital has a cost, though whether its real cost is ultimately greater than other forms of financing is a matter that demands greater analysis than has yet been given to it, particularly if effective economic contribution is taken into account. Put crudely, loans at, say 6% to 8% used

with 50% efficiency may need to be compared with equity at, say 10% to 15% used with 80% efficiency.[5]

There is now fairly convincing evidence that there is a qualitative difference in efficiency between state-run operations and competitive private enterprises. In Mexico, Chile, and Peru after nationalization, costs rose while prices were kept down for political reasons. As a result, the nationalized enterprises both lacked investment capital and became serious drains on the public treasury. Without strong government control over the unions in nationalized industries, wages and "featherbedding" increase and efficiency declines. Administrative reforms in Peru and Mexico have attempted to deal with these problems, demanding self-sufficiency for the state enterprises and/or a clearly defined and accurately measured public purpose for state subsidies. But without an incentive equivalent to the profit motive, public enterprise seems to have a built-in tendency to bureaucratization and spiraling costs. When the industry produces for export, the world market price or competition will act as a limiting constraint, but when production is for a limited and protected internal market or, as in the case of petroleum, the world price is high, there is considerable leeway for inefficiency or for political considerations to creep into decisionmaking.

Each of the countries studied has struggled with this problem; none has found a solution. Stricter auditing by the controller general or his equivalent may reduce waste. A strong budget office may establish alternative priorities, and an interministerial council can make decisions as to their relative importance. However, the lack of the external discipline of the market (except in some export industries), the wage pressures of organized groups, especially unions, declining productivity, and the use of subsidies to avoid price increases that may be politically unpalatable seem to constitute structural elements that make inefficiency endemic to the state or parastatal sector. Because of the access of the public enterprise to government funds, costs are not kept down; because of the political power of unions, wages skyrocket. In addition, in particularly profitable areas such as the sugar cooperatives in Peru under President Velasco, a "labor aristocracy" is formed. Rational investment and pricing policies are made difficult because of political pressures. The initial economic benefits of the take-over of foreign property (availability of profits formerly sent out of the country, national control of investment decisions) are dissipated over the longer term. Through the expansion of employment and the improvement of salaries and labor conditions in the state sector, bureaucrats and organized labor became the principal beneficiaries of nationalization since, unlike the private employer, the government cannot use the possibility of bankruptcy as a credible threat in resisting labor and employee demands.[6]

A by-product of state ownership that contributes to inefficiency is the increased opportunity for corruption. Corruption is by no means absent in private enterprise systems especially when they are dependent, as they are in many less developed countries, on government permits and legislation to operate successfully. However, without the surveillance of an ideological — usually Marxist — party, or an unusually vigilant and free press, and neither of these are characteristic of most Latin American states today, the combination of economic and political power in a large state sector seems to provide almost irresistible opportunities for graft and corruption.

In the area of public enterprise, the consensus seems to be that the closer such enterprises approach the economic conduct of a comparable competitive private enterprise the more efficient they are likely to be. Thus, studies in Brazil reveal that the management and operation of the most successful state enterprises look remarkably similar to those of Brazilian private enterprise in terms of encouraging independent management, setting realistic prices, and even floating issues on the stock market.[7] In Peru, the nationalized industries have become as adept as private industries at evading the relevant job security requirements of labor legislation through the practice of hiring and firing temporary workers.

Proponents of nationalization respond to the charge of inefficiency in several ways. First, they argue that government ownership will enable development to be carried out on a more rationally planned basis than the anarchic and crisis-ridden course of development of international capitalism – in other words, they use the classic argument for socialism. However, if the economy of the country is based on exports, it will still be linked to, and partly dependent upon, the international capitalist system. This does not hold true, of course, if the government makes a deliberate decision to align itself with the Communist world, as Cuba did, or to pursue a course of autonomous development that is independent of outside influences, as Burma has. Neither country seems to be an appropriate model for the more developed nations of Latin America because of their considerable needs for foreign exchange to pay for imports of food, fuel, and capital goods.

The second argument frequently heard in Latin America is that nationalization will enable the government to capture the large exploitative profits that have been sent abroad by the foreign corporation. To evaluate this argument, any economic gains such as increased income or alternative markets resulting from a government take-over must be weighed against the potential losses discussed above. In the area of petroleum, where superprofits were made even before the OPEC price rise, and possibly in other extractive industries, it seems evident that the balance lies on the side of nationalization. In other areas, however, it is not clear that the potential gains will not be outweighed by the losses resulting from the cost of compensation, diminished access to capital, lack of investment, reduced marketing, antiquated technological capacity, increased risk, and reductions in efficiency.

THE SOCIAL BENEFITS OF NATIONALIZATION

The case for nationalization includes a further argument – an appeal to the noneconomic benefits that are likely to result – especially the increased control over economic decisions affecting the nation and the social benefits of government ownership. The nationalizing government can use its enhanced economic power to pursue socially beneficial goals, such as the development of labor-intensive technology, increased employment, investment in less favored regions, production of goods needed by the mass of the population, and a more equalitarian distribution of income. While some of these measures may have an economic cost, others, such as a distribution of income that promotes greater domestic demand, may benefit the economy as a whole.

Our case studies illustrate some of the difficulties encountered in trying to achieve social goals through nationalization. Thus, while Cuba socialized its economy and made remarkable advances toward the establishment of a more equalitarian society, it paid a double price for this achievement in the sacrifice of individual liberty and economic efficiency. In other cases where similar efforts were made, either the redistribution of income was minimal and produced a sharp drop in private and foreign investment, as in Peru, or it released explosive inflationary forces that were an important element in persuading the armed forces to overthrow the government, as in Chile. In both cases, too, the workers in the state sector opposed the extension of benefits to other groups in the society. The question of who benefits from state ownership is usually resolved in favor of those who already have access to political power—the organized workers and the economic elites. Nationalization can only be a part—and it often is a counterproductive part—of a more general program to promote social justice; other measures, such as land reform and labor-intensive industrialization, are more effective in improving the lot of low-income groups.

In the case of state-owned petroleum, the government revenues of oil-producing countries have increased substantially since the OPEC price increase, and these can be used to benefit the poor and underprivileged. For example, the Venezuelan government has made an effort to "recycle" oil revenues to improve housing, health care, and education. It has also placed a high priority on investment aimed at developing an industrial base in anticipation of the time when its petroleum reserves are depleted. While these policies could have been pursued even without nationalization, that step dramatized the need for a rational development policy for the use of oil revenues.

The social effects of nationalization depend on who is doing the nationalizing. State ownership does not automatically produce social equity—there must also be a commitment to measures to promote social justice. In addition, it may be necessary, as in Cuba, for the government to possess coercive power and authoritarian control in order to change the pattern of income distribution. But even a regime fully committed to socialism must recognize that state-owned enterprises are not established for welfare purposes but to make a productive contribution to the economy. Thus, choices must be made, and tradeoffs between efficiency and equity must be acknowledged.

NATIONALIZATION AND SOCIAL COST-BENEFIT ANALYSIS

How can such decisions be made rationally? One method of public sector decisionmaking that has received considerable attention is social cost-benefit analysis. This technique takes into account the distinctive characteristics of the economies of the developing nations in two ways. It uses a system of "shadow prices" to compensate for departures from market allocation and pricing that typically exist in such economies because of tariff protection, surplus labor, and a noncompetitive market. In addition, it tries to quantify the "external" social benefits that a given project or undertaking will produce. Planners for the public sector can then presumably make decisions concerning alternative allocations of resources on the basis of an estimate of both their real impact on the economy and the contribution of any given investment to social goals, such as employment, exports, and income distribution.

One important "social" or "external" goal of nationalization is national autonomy in decisionmaking in vital sectors of the economy. Sometimes this may take the form of a decreased reliance on imports or greater self-sufficiency in certain types of production, such as food. More often, however, the goal is more elusive — a reduction in dependence or, more rhetorically, "the struggle against imperialism." It is most difficult to carry out a cost-benefit analysis involving such a goal, although it has long been recognized that nationalists are often willing to give up some direct economic benefits in return for the "psychic income" of freedom from foreign control.[8]

Techniques of social cost-benefit analysis applicable to investment decisions have been developed by the United Nations Industrial Development Organization (UNIDO) and advocated by development economists.[9] However, their application has been restricted to investment decisions by public enterprises or projects proposed by foreign investors. It would seem that a decision whether or not to nationalize an existing foreign-owned firm could also undergo the same type of analysis. Using economic or quasi-economic methods, one might attempt a quantitative estimate of the benefits of nationalization of a foreign-owned firm in terms of remittances of profits and depreciation returned to the government; the lower cost of international loan capital rather than equity; the increased income generated (if it is generated) by altered income distribution; and the social goals achieved, such as the development of an integrated industry, expansion of employment, training of national management and technical personnel, and improved economic planning and national autonomy.

The list of negative factors that should be taken into account is a lengthy one. Besides remittances abroad for compensation (or the costs to the economy of international retaliation if remittances are not made or are considered inadequate), an estimate must include the following: (1) possible declines in productivity owing to inexperienced management or declining labor discipline; (2) reduced access to international markets and technology when it is not possible to purchase these on the international market, or when they are more expensive or less efficient in "unbundled" service contract form; (3) lost income from both the nationalized industry itself and declining or lost investment elsewhere because of fear of nationalization; (4) the increased cost of investment capital needed by the nationalized industry and the drain on other areas of the national budget; (5) distortions of pricing, management, or investment policy owing to political pressures; and (6) losses from corruption. Based on techniques of economic analysis, it should be possible to provide a rough quantitative estimate for such a calculation.[10]

The case studies have provided examples of ways to reduce the negative effects of nationalization. Compensation can be stretched out over a number of years. Management can be insulated from political pressures and given autonomy to set prices so that all costs are reflected, including those of capital and profit for reinvestment. Taxation, interest, and depreciation policies can be similar to those for the private sector, and service contracts can cover missing inputs. The maintenance of competition between state-owned operations and private enterprises, as in the Mexican steel industry, is another way to promote and measure efficiency.

Yet even if these measures are taken, it is virtually impossible to reproduce the discipline of the market where it does not exist. Bureaucrats will not become entrepreneurs overnight, and when the rewards for risk taking are minimal and the penalties severe, caution and an aversion to experimentation are the rational response. When the public enterprise attempts to simulate the conduct of the private firm, through profit incentives, competition, and autonomy in decisionmaking, some of the negative aspects of the private sector reappear—large disparities of income, the creation of independent centers of power, and the cooptation of the public enterprise by the domestic or foreign private sector. Yet when political control is exercised, costs rise as administrators build bureaucratic empires, labor unions exert political power to increase wages, prices are determined politically, and production is directed toward quantitative goals rather than toward market demand.

While nationalization may eliminate or reduce foreign influence, it substantially increases the influence of the state in the economy. Thus, in any cost-benefit analysis, the benefits of increased autonomy and other social goals resulting from nationalization (such as worker participation, income redistribution, planned allocation of investment) must also be measured against the possible adverse effects of the overexpansion of the state. The European states, with many years of experience in public administration, are concerned about the "system overload" induced by the expansion of state activity in the areas of economics and welfare. The problem is much more serious in countries with less developed political and administrative structures and a more limited economic base. In most Latin American states a major portion of investment already comes from the state, and the nationalization of other sectors can accelerate this development. In addition to the problems of administration and efficiency discussed above, the effect of nationalization is to produce a centralization of government power and politicization of economic life that make the development of a pluralist society and the exercise of democratic participation much more difficult.

It may be argued that most Third World governments are not democratic and that the choice is really between private monopoly power, exercised by foreign corporations and their domestic allies, and government ownership of the basic sectors of the national economy. In reply, it might be suggested that government can be more effective at regulating private economic power than at replacing it, and that the struggle for control of government will become much more intense if all or most of economic life depends upon government decisions. As the Chilean case shows, the combination of economic incompetence and heightened politicization may produce instability and repressive government rather than social justice. Conversely, while economic freedom is not a sufficient condition for political liberty, it seems historically to have been closely associated with the development of democracy.[11]

In the cases examined here, the decision to nationalize was not preceded by anything like the process just described. With the possible exception of petroleum, most nationalizations resulted from political factors or the personal ideology of a particular leadership rather than a calculation of costs and benefits. Even when, as in the case of petroleum, the costs of national ownership were sharply reduced and the benefits heightened, there was a certain reluctance to nationalize on the part of those who were not accustomed to seeing the government in such a role and aware that their governments were notably lacking in the administrative skills to carry out such an action successfully. On the other hand, as the Peruvian case shows, when the government has already successfully taken over one sector such as petroleum, it is no longer unthinkable for it to extend state control to others, and a prostatist ideology develops which encourages similar actions elsewhere.

THE NEW ATTITUDE TOWARD FOREIGN INVESTMENT

In Latin America and elsewhere in the Third World, it appears that a less ideological and more economic or cost-benefit approach to the treatment of foreign investment is now beginning to emerge. Ironically, while nationalization is now perceived as easier to carry out, Latin American governments are increasingly aware that alternative approaches can achieve the goals of nationalization without its costs.

As recently as 1971, following the Peruvian and Chilean nationalizations, the secretary of the treasury, John Connally, advocated strong United States government sanctions against Latin American governments that were taking American property, replying to arguments that such sanctions were likely to be counterproductive with the statement, "We don't have any friends down there anyway." Yet only a few years later, those supposedly unfriendly governments were making special efforts to attract foreign investment. After the 1973 coup, the Chileans began to encourage foreign investment, and, in 1976 it withdrew from the Andean Pact because its foreign investment regulations were considered to be too rigid and adopted, instead, a favorable foreign investment law. Months before he took office, the president-elect of Mexico, José Lopez Portillo, gave an interview to *Business Week* in which he let it be known that his administration would take a more favorable attitude toward American investment. In the late 1970s, Bolivia and Peru adopted more liberal investment statutes. Even Cuba has begun to explore the possible development of its nickel mines by American companies once diplomatic relations are reestablished with the United States. As Latin American governments have begun to reopen their economies to foreign investment with emphasis on export promotion rather than import substitution, the contribution of the foreign investor has been viewed more favorably than it was in the past.

Yet the new attitude toward foreign investment does not include the belief that the interests of the investor and the host country will automatically coincide. *Dependencia* theorists and those who argue that the interests of foreign capital and Latin

American development are fundamentally opposed have had an impact on policymakers, who are now increasingly sensitive to the possible adverse effects of foreign investment. However the contemporary Latin American economic nationalist is also willing to acknowledge that the national interest in development and the investor's interest in profit may coincide in several areas. The policymaker, then, must carefully evaluate each case in an effort to distinguish between the positive and negative effects of foreign investment, both actual and projected.

The most serious adverse effects of foreign investment have already been alluded to — the lack of national control over economic decisionmaking and the loss to the national economy of high profits and other payments to the foreigner — in rhetorical terms, imperialism and exploitation. There is no lack of evidence on either score. When one learns that the Cerro Corporation wrote the Mining Code in Peru in 1950, that the ITT subsidiary in Cuba gave Fulgencio Batista a golden telephone because he granted a rate increase in 1957, that the tin companies in prenationalization Bolivia hired all the best law students in each graduating class at the San Andrés University Law School, and that ITT and the CIA plotted to prevent Allende's election in Chile and to overthrow him after his election, it is difficult to argue that foreign investors have not wielded excessive political and economic power in Latin America. In addition to these instances of excessive influence, decisions as to whether Chilean or Peruvian copper would be refined in Peru, Chile, or Perth Amboy, as to how much sugar would be produced in Cuba, and whether Mexican oil production would decline because cheaper sources became available in Venezuela or the Middle East were made by corporate headquarters in New York, not by governments that were critically dependent on these exports for foreign exchange. These decisions were made by foreign corporations interested in maximizing profits on a global scale, not in the economic development of the host country. As for profits, the record shows that in the past multinational corporations, such as the foreign oil companies in Latin America, United Fruit in Guatemala, ITT in Chile and Cuba, and the International Petroleum Company in Peru, have made large profits and paid low taxes because of special tax concessions, political influence, and in some cases the manipulation of transfer prices among subsidiaries or outright bribery of public officials.

Other criticisms of foreign investment have less validity. The widening gap in income between rich and poor that it is accused of creating, the effects of investment-induced development on domestic cultural patterns, and the use of inappropriate capital-intensive technology are all more properly attributed to the impact of industrialization on traditional and largely agricultural economies. The frequent comparison of current outflows, based on past investment, with current inflows from foreign investors, based on new investment opportunities, to prove Latin America is being "underdeveloped" by the foreign investor is a patently fallacious comparison of two distinctly different, and indeed unrelated, phenomena. The amount repatriated for profit and amortization may be excessive, but this must be determined on the basis of total past investment, which in some areas of Latin America has been quite substantial. If investment has been going on for many years and remains foreign-owned, the profits to be repatriated will be considerable, even if, as a percentage of invested capital, they are low. New investment capital, on the other hand, depends on the investor's assessment of the present investment climate and the possibilities of future productive and profitable economic activity. Partly because of the wave of nationalizations, the investment climate is now regarded as less favorable in Latin America than in other parts of the world, such as Europe, Canada, and Asia, where most new American overseas investment is being directed. What must be measured is not unrelated capital flows but the extent to which the investment creates net new wealth in the country—that is, whether the growth and other benefits it produces in the economy exceed the costs of the inputs involved. While it may be true that Latin America is being exploited by foreign investors, it cannot be proved by the mere recitation of inflows and outflows of capital.

Other negative aspects of foreign investment may be the result of the policies of the Latin American countries themselves, including artificially low interest rates that have encouraged domestic borrowing, tax exemptions for the import of capital goods that promote production that is capital-intensive rather than labor-intensive, tax holidays and high tariff walls that produce higher profits for efficient foreign producers, and military take-overs and repression which in all probability would have occur-red whether or not there was substantial foreign investment in the economy. The basic attack, however, on the foreign investor should center not on these peripheral issues but on the two cen-tral problems — the division of economic rents and the direction of economic policy ("exploitation" and "imperialism").

The positive effects of foreign investment have already been discussed — capital, technology, management and organizational skills, and a worldwide distribution and marketing system. The objective of the host government is to secure these advantages at the lowest possible cost to the domestic economy. The bargaining is carried on between the potential investor — who can grant or withhold access to special processes, knowledge, capital, and skills — and the host government, which can permit or refuse ac-cess to resources and advantages that the investor cannot secure as easily elsewhere such as oil, copper, sugar, bananas, cheap labor, low taxes, and a protected domestic or regional market. Thus, the investor and the host government are in the position of two oligopolists possessing the ability to limit access to those scarce resources from which the other seeks to derive maximum benefit, and also possessing alternatives that may be available at greater cost elsewhere. It is the recognition of both the advan-tages to be secured from the foreign investor and the increased possibilities of securing a better bargain in terms of policy con-trol and benefits for the host nation that account for the renewed interest in such investment in Latin America.

The apparent decline in the pressure for nationalization in Latin America cannot be explained, therefore, simply in terms of the emergence of rightist regimes in recent years. While national-ization has become easier, Latin American policymakers realize that it is only one alternative in dealing with foreign investment, and its usefulness is limited to certain areas and circumstances. More recently, in Mexico, Peru, and to a lesser extent, Venezu-ela, renewed emphasis has been placed on development of the domestic private sector and encouragement of the *selective* entrance of foreign capital. This change stems from the realization that a mixed economy is a more efficient and productive way to national development than either issuing a blank check to foreign capital or establishing total domination and operation of the economy by the state. It also indicates that Latin American policymakers have recognized that neither the automatic harmony of interests assumed by the advocates of free enterprise nor the inevitable conflict of interests espoused by the Marxists is an accurate description of the relation of the less developed country to foreign capital—that the most accurate paradigm for that relationship is one of bargaining.

THE SHIFT IN BARGAINING POWER

Third World countries are engaging in bargaining because their starting position is stronger now than before. While the foreign companies still possess major bargaining chips, they are much less impressive than in the past, and for all the talk of the increasing power of the multinationals, the inequalities in bargaining power between investor and host country have been considerably reduced in recent years.

What has changed? First, Third World governments have access to the information needed to strike a bargain; they are no longer exclusively dependent on the companies for knowledge. They have developed their own technical staffs through public development corporations, such as Corporacion de Fomento de la Produccíon (Corfo) in Chile, COFIDE in Peru, *Nacional Financiera* in Mexico, and the Venezuelan Development Corporation (CVF). International consultants are available to assist in evaluating investment proposals. Permanent research staffs of the United Nations Conference on Trade and Development, the United Nations Centre on Transnational Corporations, the Andean Pact, and universities and private research groups in the United States and Latin America, as well as international consultants can now provide government negotiators with information about alternatives, with examples of other successful negotiations, and with documentation from public sources in the developed countries. Negotiators of mineral resource agreements from Third World countries even have a "do-it-yourself" handbook written by two Harvard University professors on how to extract maximum concessions from the multinational corporations.[12]

Second, the bargaining no longer consists of a monopolistic position on the investor side against competing nations on the host country side. The percentage of foreign investment in Latin America from European countries and Japan rose from about 22 percent in the 1950s, to 40 percent in 1970. In Brazil, the largest recipient of American investments, the United States share of foreign investment has dropped from 48 percent in 1969, to 31.5 percent in 1975 — a diversification that was the result of a conscious policy decision made by the Brazilian government. Similarly in Venezuela, the share of new foreign investment that came from France, Germany, Spain, and Italy increased in 1975 and 1976, while the United States share declined.[13] The Japanese and the Europeans are often willing to invest or lend capital on terms that would be rejected by American companies or banks. This is particularly true of the Japanese investments in natural resources where, as in the case of Peruvian oil and copper, Japanese capital is advanced for the extraction of minerals or petroleum in return for advance contracts on sales to Japan of the production that results. On the host country side, the success of the OPEC cartel and the increasing militance of the less developed countries on the question of North-South economic relations have also resulted in a greater degree of cooperation aimed at the development of a common policy and sharing of information.

Third, host countries, especially in Latin America, have now developed the institutional capacity to engage in such bargaining. The wave of nationalizations from 1960 to 1975 was part of a broader phenomenon — the expansion of the Latin American state. Another part of this expansion was the development of investment screening and registration mechanisms. These mechanisms provide a broad range of policy choices other than nationalization in the treatment of foreign investment. The new, more sympathetic attitude toward foreign investment results from increased confidence on the part of Latin American governments that through other means they can achieve the goals of nationalization without the adverse consequences that some nationalizations have produced in the past.

In the new situation, the companies have some bargaining counters of their own. They have developed defense strategies aimed at spreading the equity risk, as was done in the Cuajone investment of Southern Peru Copper Company and in Kennecott's new investments in Chile in the late 1960s, so that expropriation will provoke opposition from many countries and financial institutions. Techniques such as "offset-sourcing" are used, that is, purchases are made from the host country for use by the multinational elsewhere — which would be cut off in case of nationalization. The production process is distributed over several countries to discourage expropriation of a part of what is an internationally integrated operation. In some cases (for example, Texas Gulf in the development of copper in Panama), companies have arranged joint ventures, with most of their profit coming from service fees and most of the equity exposure undertaken by the host country or by banks rather than by the company itself. They have maintained control of important distribution, technology, and marketing networks. They direct new investment in mineral resources toward politically secure areas, including the United States, even when the mineral deposits are more expensive to extract. They can play one country off against another in order to secure better terms. Even when less developed countries adopt a common set of rules on foreign investment, as the Andean Pact members did, rules will be differentially applied according to the varying interests of each country. After the 1973 OPEC price increase the balance-of-payments difficulties faced by the non-oil-producing countries of Latin America have also made foreign investment capital look more attractive. Finally, rising unemployment, resulting from high birthrates and migration to the cities, increases the appeal of investments that create jobs and that offer an easy road to development and make use of domestic inputs that might otherwise go unutilized.

Besides the continuing bargaining capabilities of the multinationals, there are also structural constraints that limit the possibilities of Third World governments. They include the availability of substitutes elsewhere, the competition among the less developed countries to attract investment capital, and their own internal class and interest group structures. Indeed, the very definition of the national interest in such bargaining is conditioned by the perceptions of those engaged in making the bargains and of the domestic and international groups to which they respond. Likewise, if the countries involved lack natural or human resources of interest to the foreign investor, they will have difficulty making any kind of bargain. The Third World is not a monolith, and not all its members have the capabilities, knowledge, or favorable situation of the countries examined in the case studies. The reforms called for in the New International Economic Order are aimed at improving the context in which the bargaining takes place so as to make it more favorable to the less developed countries, but those involved must still be able to offer and conclude a bargain that is perceived as advantageous to both sides.

THE RANGE OF POLICY CHOICES

There is a continuum of government control of foreign investment that begins with prohibition of entry or nationalization without compensation (confiscation) and ends with the universally acknowledged right of the state to tax property within its territorial limits for national purposes. The degree to which the action of the government approaches confiscation will depend on the amount and nature of the compensation that is paid, and the extent of any continuing (and compensated) relationship that is maintained directly or indirectly with the former owners of the nationalized property. Moving in the other direction on the continuum, some moderate forms of nationalization, with full or nearly full compensation and continuation of an important role for the former owners through service contracts or licensing agreements, may not look very different from a joint venture between the government and the foreign investor.

For purposes of analysis, it is possible to locate nationalization in the range of policy choices on the treatment of foreign investment through the use of a left-right scale (see figure l).

The two variables, policy control and share of benefits, are

Government		Policy control/Share of benefits			Foreign investor	
Confiscation or prohibition of entry	Nationalization, with full, partial, or lump sum compensation, with or without continuing links (service contracts)	Joint venture with government	Required joint venture with, or divestment to, domestic private sector	Investment screening; special requirements (employment, sourcing, gradual divestment, etc.)	Special taxation for foreign investment	Normal taxation, domestic treatment

Figure 1. Range of government control of foreign investment

analytically separable but are usually linked. It is possible for the host government to adopt regulatory legislation with no concern for its impact on government revenues or, conversely, to levy taxes for revenue purposes only, without any interest in the effects on company policy that those taxes induce. In actual experience, however, the two are linked in varying degrees — legislative regulations do result in increasing costs to the company and taxes do modify behavior. The two are considered together because they both influence government policies toward foreign investment.

For some, the conflict of interest between the foreign investor and the host country is so basic and pervasive that the relationship will always be exploitative and imperialistic, and nationalization — with little or no compensation — seems to be the only solution. This was the view of the Allende government (although it did not, in fact, nationalize European investments) and of Castro (but only after a decline in United States-Cuban relations further radicalized his world view, leading him to embrace a doctrinaire Marxism rather than the eclectic Marxist-influenced populism with which he came to power). In the other cases examined, however, non-Marxist nationalists have been more selective in the use of nationalization.

In the table listing Latin American nationalizations in chapter 2, it appeared that the take-overs of foreign property by Latin American governments have mainly taken place in certain areas and tend to share certain common characteristics. Nearly all the larger nationalizations have occurred in the extractive industries. They have involved a standardized product located in an exposed enclave containing "depleting" natural resources that were often an important source of foreign exchange. Frequently, they had required a substantial initial capital investment that had taken place many years before and had not been followed by much new investment. As the host country developed an increasing sense of its own capabilities, production and marketing became standardized and profits increased as in the case of petroleum. The costs of nationalization decreased, and its benefits seemed considerable. The experiences of Cuba and of Chile under Allende, however, argue that confrontational take-overs in the extractive industries may involve the loss of managerial expertise and of access to international capital, technology, and markets. Others, notably the cases of Venezuela, of Chile under Frei, and of petroleum nationalizations elsewhere, seem to demonstrate that the nationalization of mineral resources can be carried out through a process of bargaining and negotiation that minimizes its costs.

Countries that are attempting to develop new extractive industries still usually find that direct foreign investment is the easiest and most efficient way to carry out that development. The case of the Cuajone copper mines in Peru is an instructive example in this regard: the Velasco government, strongly committed to the nationalization of basic industry, especially in the extractive sector, continued to encourage substantial foreign investment in Cuajone despite the opposition of the Peruvian left.

It seems, therefore, that despite the lengthy record of nationalization of extractive industries in Latin America, there continues to be a role for foreign investment — although often in a different relationship — as provider of services, as a minority owner with specified managerial rights, or as the recipient of exploration contracts that guarantee a certain percentage of the findings to the government. Company interest in the new relationships will depend on the profit possibilities and the extent to which they can continue to exercise managerial control.

There are two other areas in which there have been numerous nationalizations — public utilities and transportation. As early as 1962, after electric and telephone companies had been taken over in several Brazilian states, the Kennedy administration decided that foreign investment should not be located in such politically exposed natural monopolies, where every rate increase automatically becomes the occasion for an attack on the exploitative character of foreign investment. (This has been recognized by ITT, which has now divested itself of all its telephone companies in foreign countries.) Similarly, railroads are under public ownership in most countries because of their strategic character, their frequent need for subsidy, and their lack of attractiveness to private investors, whether domestic or foreign.

Latin American countries have also taken on an increasingly important role in the area of banking. While representatives of foreign banks are needed to facilitate access to foreign capital markets and sources of investment, state fiscal and monetary policy, especially the control of interest rates and the allocation of credit, requires such substantial government intervention that many governments have attempted to minimize the role of foreign banks, arguing that in capital-scarce economies the policy decisions made by the banking sector should be under government control. In implementing government control of banking, however, Latin American governments, including both the Allende government in Chile and the Velasco government in Peru, negotiated favorable compensation agreements with the foreign banks because they needed continuing access to international financial markets.

Beginning in 1976, over half of American investment in Latin America was located in the areas of manufacturing and trade. Except for the ideologically inspired nationalizations carried out by Castro and Allende, there have been remarkably few government take-overs in these areas. When they have occurred, they have often been "defensive" in character and have been designed to prevent important manufacturing industries from going bankrupt. One reason for the increase in foreign investment in these areas is that Latin American governments have pursued a policy of import substitution, that is, establishing high tariffs and non-tariff barriers in order to encourage domestic manufacturing of previously imported goods. Thus, foreign companies desiring access to the domestic market had to invest behind the tariff wall. Enticed by the prospect of tapping a protected market in Latin America, American investment in manufacturing and processing rapidly increased in the 1950s and 1960s. To date, there has been little pressure to nationalize American manufacturing subsidiaries. Unlike miners, bankers, and utility companies, manufacturers can make a convincing case that they benefit the national economy on a continuing basis: there are frequent innovations in manufacturing; technology is closely held on a proprietary basis; and secondary effects through the creation of employment and suppliers are more evident. (Sears, Roebuck boasts that most of the products sold in its Latin American outlets are locally produced.) In addition, when the manufactured goods are produced for export, the host country's exports also benefit from access to the multinational corporation's distribution, marketing, and sales networks. Foreign investors may also provide a stimulus to the efficiency of domestic producers, and in the area of agriculture, they can revolutionize production, distribution, and sales, especially food exports abroad.

On the government side it is recognized that in these areas policy control can be secured by methods other than nationalization. Latin American governments regularly utilize joint ventures, import licensing, differential taxation, export subsidies, and promotion schemes to impose performance requirements upon foreign investors. More recently, the development of investment screening has provided many governments with an important bargaining tool in their relations with the multinational corporation.

SCREENING FOREIGN INVESTMENT

The new sophistication in attempting to attract and to control foreign investment in manufacturing is clearly illustrated by three recent examples of legislative attempts made by Latin America to screen and regulate the entry of foreign investment: the laws regulating foreign investment adopted by Mexico in late 1972 and early 1973, the Andean Pact's investment regulation decisions, and the increasing control of foreign investment by Brazil.

In the Mexican case, there had long been legislation limiting the employment of foreigners and requiring government permission for foreign investment. In early 1973, Mexico adopted a comprehensive Law to Promote Mexican Investment and to Regulate Foreign Investment. It lists basic areas reserved to the state (petroleum, nuclear energy, electricity, railroads, and telephone and telegraph communications) and to exclusively Mexican ownership (radio and television, domestic air, road, and sea transport, forestry, and gas distribution), and empowers a National Commission on Foreign Investment to decide on the percentages and conditions of new foreign investment (normally, it is to be limited to 49 percent of equity). Exemptions from the 49 percent limit are based on listed criteria including job creation, expansion of exports, foreign capital contribution, and the importation of new technology. The investment law is complemented by a Technology Transfer and Patent and Trademark Law that reviews the cost and content of technology and royalty agreements and mandates the Mexicanization of trademarks. (The implementation of the last requirement has been repeatedly postponed since 1973.)

The Mexican laws were adopted in response to the criticisms that foreign investors were using inappropriate and overpriced technology, charging excessive royalties, and making use of domestic capital for the purpose of expansion. While the laws allow considerable flexibility in application, they attempt to assure that the claimed benefits of outside investment are, in fact, present when each new investment is made.

In the early 1970s, particular attention was focused on what radical critics called the "denationalization" of the Mexican economy because of the expansion of the multinationals in the most dynamic areas of the economy. Most of the increase in foreign investment in Mexico was generated from reinvested profits and was made in areas related to the original investment, but some resulted from buying out existing Mexican firms with local credit. Studies published in Mexico and the United States indicated that between 1960 and 1972 about 16 percent of the expansion of United States investment in Mexican manufacturing took place through the acquisition of Mexican-owned firms, and that borrowing from Mexican sources increased, accounting for 20.8 percent of the multinational's Mexican liabilities in 1963, and 25.7 percent in 1970.[14] The new legislation was designed to prevent such foreign acquisitons; its objective was to direct foreign investment into areas where it would supplement rather than replace domestic investors.

In Mexico, as in many Latin American countries, the government was faced with a dilemma regarding the profits of foreign investors. Either the investors were to be permitted to repatriate profits, creating a drain on the balance of payments, or the profits were to be reinvested in Mexico, resulting in the expansion of foreign firms in the most profitable and productive areas of the economy. The new laws attempted to encourage reinvestment in ways that would promote development without increasing Mexico's *dependencia* on the multinationals.

At the time the laws were being debated, the United States ambassador warned that they would have a serious negative effect on United States investment. In fact, the pattern of United States investment in Mexico in the mid-1970s is mixed. Department of Commerce figures indicate that new American investment in Mexico declined in 1975, dropped off substantially in 1976 — probably in response to the uncertainties concerning the impending devaluation of the peso — and recovered in 1977 and 1978. With the favorable economic prospects produced by the new oil discoveries, it is unlikely that United States investment in Mexico will decline in the future, especially since the regulatory laws have been applied flexibly and exceptions have been made when investors have demonstrated that the law's criteria are met.

Decision 24 of the Andean Pact approached the same problem somewhat differently. Like the Mexican legislation, it limited foreign access to domestic credit and provided for review of contracts for licenses, patents, trademarks, and technology. It went considerably further, however, prohibiting, except in special circumstances, all foreign purchase of existing local companies and forbidding majority ownership by foreigners of banks, communications, the media, and public utilities. It also differed from the Mexican legislation in that it established a fixed limit of 14 percent of invested capital on the repatriation of profits (which was later raised to 20 percent) and 5 percent on reinvestment (later raised to 7 percent). Most important, it compelled the forced divestment of all new investments to a minority position on a strict schedule over fifteen years (twenty-two years for Bolivia and Ecuador). Established firms that did not intend to take advantage of the trade liberalization among the pact countries were exempted as were certain areas, such as mining, petroleum, and forestry, which operated under concession agreements.[15]

It seems clear that the Andean Pact remedy was too rigid. One member country, Ecuador, has applied only a few of its provisions, and others have used loopholes in the legislation to escape its provisions. As previously noted, Chile has left the pact entirely, despite modification of some of its provisions in 1976. Critics of the "fadeout" formula have observed that perhaps no domestic buyers may be found for the stock that the foreign firms would be forced to sell, and, in any event, such a purchase might not be the best alternative use for domestic investment capital. More significant, however, the fadeout formula seemed to discourage certain types of investors who might control useful technology, trade secrets, or internationally integrated operations.[16] Others, seeking a relatively large protected market or diversification of their operations, might still be lost as potential investors because the benefits gained would not be worth the cost of increased national control of investment decisions. The more flexible Mexican method seems a preferable way to control and direct foreign investment, but the Andean Pact formula apparently was felt to be necessary in order to hold the divergent interests and bargaining positions of the pact members to a single common standard. In some of the member countries, such as Venezuela and Colombia, it has provided an effective set of standards to assure that foreign investment benefits the host country, but at least some new investment has been discouraged, and there is little evidence that existing foreign firms are preparing to divest themselves of their holdings.[17]

Investment screening and bargaining with foreign investors are also being conducted successfully by another Latin American country, not included in this study because it has not resorted to nationalization—Brazil. Permission to invest in certain fields (such as electronics) may be granted only when investment takes the form of joint ventures with Brazilian private or state-owned firms. Royalty payments are permitted only if the foreign investor does not have majority control. Strict regulations govern the repatriation of profits, and there has been no hesitancy to use differential taxation to influence the direction of foreign investment. Local content requirements are imposed, and import of capital goods is permitted only if it can be justified by a resulting increase in exports. In Brazil, nationalization of existing foreign investment is unlikely because of its presumed adverse effect on new investment and foreign lending. However, Brazil has shown that considerable control over foreign investment can be achieved with tax and regulatory legislation. Because Brazil is aware that its large market, natural resources, and low labor costs make it attractive to the foreign investor, it can drive a hard bargain with the multinational corporation without diminishing the flow of new investment. The result has been an astonishingly high growth rate, beginning in 1967 and lasting until 1974. More recently, the effects of worldwide recession and the oil price increases have taken their toll on the largely export-oriented growth that Brazil had experienced, and price controls and import restrictions have led to a reduction in new United States investment, but reinvestment remains high ($445 million in 1977).[18]

Investment screening programs usually involve considerations, like those listed in the Mexican law, that are exceedingly difficult to estimate. One writer on foreign investment Grant Reuber, summarizes the appropriate calculation on a projected foreign investment as follows: the value added to production less the opportunity cost of local factors used in production and the after-tax profits and dividends paid to the foreign investor plus the "external benefits" of the investment minus its "external costs." This sounds simple enough, but when the author describes the elements involved in the calculation of "externalities," they become annoyingly imprecise. The external benefits of increased tax receipts, increased employment, new technology, increased productivity, promotion of exports, and replacement of imports are difficult enough to calculate, but when Reuber surveys the external costs of direct foreign investment mentioned in the literature, he finds no less than eighteen factors — some of them, such as bringing in too much or too little external capital or participating too little or too much in community development, clearly contradictory. He concludes, "There undoubtedly are grains of truth in many of these allegations. What is uncertain is whether they add up to a mountain or a molehill."[19] Unfortunately, the distinction between a mountain and a molehill is often in the eye of the beholder. The political benefits of national control of basic resources or the protection of domestic entrepreneurs may override the more strictly economic advantages of foreign investment. Conversely, new investments may be permitted because of a general policy that welcomes foreign investment or encourages import substitution (for example, the automobile industry in Chile or Peru), regardless of the economic arguments against a given project.

The costs and benefits must also be compared with alternative possibilities. Public ownership and its costs and benefits, have already been discussed. A second alternative, which has received renewed attention as the real costs of foreign investment have become more evident, is simply to import the goods produced abroad. That decision would be likely to be made if the computation described above indicated that the value added was negative —even after considering the drain in foreign exchange and the loss of taxes, jobs, and external linkages because the investment was not made.

THE JOINT VENTURE ALTERNATIVE

The bargaining model between joint oligopolists described above suggests that the most appropriate ownership structure should be some form of joint venture. In recent years, this method has been used by the governments of Zambia, Jamaica, Mexico, and Chile under Frei. It maintains access to the skills of the foreign enterprise—its marketing, managerial, and technological expertise—and avoids the traumas of nationalization, while it simultaneously assures the government of ultimate control of decisions affecting the national economy. It has been used both to modify existing ownership structures and for new investments. Companies, such as Dow Chemical in Chile, share joint ownership with the host countries. Petroleum explorations have been carried on in Peru, Ecuador, and Argentina based on production-sharing agreements that guarantee government oil companies 50 percent or more of any resulting production, and joint ventures are contemplated in Venezuela for the development of the Orinoco Tar Belt. The Mexicans have had the most experience with this arrangement since "Mexicanization," through shared ownership with a government agency or with private Mexican investors or through floating shares on the Mexican stock market, has been encouraged or legislated for many years. Another group with which has participated in joint ventures is the Atlantic Community Development Group for Latin America (ADELA); the group is made up of European and American capital interests that invest on a joint basis in many Latin American countries.

On the government side, the capital for a joint venture can come from several possible sources. It can be financed by government-guaranteed loans from foreign financial institutions, as in the case of the Chileanization program of the 1960s. When the inputs are domestic, the government can provide credits to cover the costs involved, or private investors can be offered shares. Another possibility, which has been used in the areas of natural resources and petroleum, involves payments in the form of bonds financed out of the income from future production. In Zambia in 1969, in the Arab oil take-overs, or in joint ventures with Communist countries the producing companies accepted this method of payment because they wished to acquire or retain access to raw materials, markets, or other advantages that the host government could provide.[20]

The joint venture form promises a reduction in the risk of expropriation because the government or national investors are joint — usually majority — owners. Yet experiences in Chile and Zambia indicate that in the area of natural resources the joint venture may only be a way station toward full control, itself becoming an obsolescent bargain subject to revision when the government feels that it is in a stronger position.

The question of management control is central. Foreign investors may be willing to give in on the question of majority ownership, provided they can be assured through a management contract or other arrangement, that they will not be involved in an enterprise that is likely to go bankrupt because of mismanagement. (In the Jamaican joint ventures with foreign aluminum companies, for example, the government owns 51 percent of the company, but the foreign investors retain control for a period of seven years. When the Anaconda Company was forced to negotiate the "agreed-upon nationalization" with the Frei government in Chile in 1969, it, too, insisted on managerial control.) Yet the main reason that host governments assume majority ownership is that they perceive that there is a basic conflict of interest between the worldwide goals of the foreign corporation and national economic objectives. Thus, the joint venture route seems to be fraught with potential tension and disagreement between the partners because of their conflicting interests. It also involves costs in efficiency since what is most efficient from the point of view of the multinational firm may be different from what appears most desirable to a host government or domestic investor.

The problem with joint ventures may be partially resolved by distinguishing between the policies on which there is likely to be conflict and those on which there is a community of interest. Thus, if management is defined as control of personnel, production, and inputs, the common interest of both partners in maximizing profits, maintaining efficiency, and financing compensation would seem to argue that the foreign corporation should be given maximum freedom. However, on broader questions of financial and investment policy, marketing, refining or processing, and overall objectives the government will want to make the final decision, and the company may be willing to sacrifice some flexibility and profit in exchange for the reduced risk of the joint venture arrangement. A distinction, then, can be made between majority control of the board of directors and managerial control of daily activities. (The distinction can be maintained more clearly in the case of joint ventures with government than with private investors.)

Because questions of overall policy are either uncertain or decided by government, joint ventures are less likely to secure the latest technology or "company secrets" from the foreign participant. Joint ventures also may be used to give workers or national investors a share of ownership, and if those shares are bought from the government, and only in specific industries or when encouraged by special tax provisions, they do not have the same negative effect on new investment as do compulsory divestment provisions, such as those of the Peruvian Industrial Community. Three-way joint ventures are also possible among government, the multinational corporation, and domestic private investors. In addition, the government can promote majority national ownership by awarding government contracts only to companies that are 51 percent nationally owned—a policy currently followed in some sectors by Brazil. The joint venture with private investors in the host country is particularly appropriate in industries where they bring a particular contribution, such as retailing, hotels and tourism, transportation, and construction. When the multinational corporation is involved in an integrated worldwide operation, the joint venture is less appropriate.

Because joint ventures reduce the likelihood of investment disputes and benefit both the foreign corporation and the host country, it has been suggested that the United States use incentives such as tax benefits or the Overseas Private Investment Corporation to encourage shared ownership. However, it is not clear that the considerations favoring joint ventures are so compelling that the United States taxpayer should be asked to subsidize them. Indeed, the recent experience of seeming collusion between the multinational petroleum companies and the OPEC countries had led other observers to argue that, from the point of view of the United States national interest, joint ventures in raw material production are antithetical to the United States national interest and should not be promoted by official policy.[21] From the point of view of the host country and the foreign investor, however, the joint venture formula is attractive, and it remains attractive as long as each can contribute elements that the other does not possess. Particularly in the area of manufacturing, foreign investors in joint ventures are able to produce a continuing stream of inputs over which they have monopoly or oligopoly control, a situation that seems less true of investments in natural resources. The number of joint ventures is increasing, and earlier resistance by American companies has eroded as European and Japanese competitors have indicated their willingness to enter into them.[22]

Another approach to joint ownership is to combine the service contract and the joint venture by a "fade-in" process. According to this arrangement, the foreign company would provide services, such as management, marketing, or technology, on a fee basis with the option to buy equity stock in the enterprise at a certain rate up to a maximum of 49 percent. This would give the company added incentive to provide the most efficient and modern inputs. It would also lessen the drain on the nation's balance of payments while avoiding the development of foreign-dominated industries or enclaves. Moreover, the foreigner would have an opportunity to assess the degree of risk and the potential profitability of a new enterprise without being obliged to put in his own capital unless he wished to do so.[23]

Another version of the joint venture was proposed by the People's Republic of China in 1979. It calls for the multinational corporation to build the factory and provide the plant, machinery, initial training, and export marketing in return for payment in kind from the resulting production. Profit remittances and patents would be guaranteed, but the Chinese would be able to buy out the foreign share after a specified period.

NATIONALIZATION AND THE FUTURE OF FOREIGN INVESTMENT IN LATIN AMERICA

In 1951, a survey of 107 American businesses, representing 54 percent of direct United States foreign investment, revealed that only 8 percent even mentioned "nationalization or expropriation" as a possible deterrent to investment abroad. In August 1977, *Fortune* published an article entitled, "Why the Multinational Tide is Ebbing." It was illustrated by a multicolored reproduction of the playing board of a dice game entitled "The Multinational Game." Square one read "Welcome!! Stay as Long as You Like." Each move described increasing demands for control by the host country until the final square was reached; it was labeled "Congratulations!! You've Been Nationalized."[24] The difference in attitude, over a quarter of a century, was symptomatic of the heightened sensitivity of United States investors to the threat of nationalization.

Because United States investors are convinced that investment in less developed countries is increasingly risky, a number of multinational corporations now prefer to derive their overseas profits from sources other than equity investment, especially in the Third World. The sale of technology, marketing, or service contracts does not carry with it the risks of devaluation, expropriation, increasing regulation, and periodic renegotiation that accompany overseas investment. One writer even recommends "giving up control to increase profits" as a possible solution for "multinationals in a hostile world."[25]

In Latin America, the earlier assurance of high profits no longer acts as a counterbalance to the uncertainties, instability, and the perceived possibility of expropriation or at least of a change in the rules of the game for foreign investments. Except for Brazil and Mexico, Latin American domestic markets are not large, and they lack the skilled labor force and infrastructure that Europe, Japan, Canada, and Australia possess. Investors have reacted accordingly. Most new United States investment has been directed to the developed world. In 1976, Latin America actually suffered a net loss of new investment, although reinvested earnings led to a favorable net balance of capital flow. Between 1969 and 1974, foreign investment in the developing world as a whole, if tax haven countries are excluded and dollar figures are deflated for price increases, only grew by less than 1 percent per year. In 1978, only 8 percent of United States foreign investment in extractive industries was located in Latin America — compared to 60 percent in 1950. Foreign investment now comprises only 16 percent of the external capital flow to Latin America, compared to 40 percent in the 1960s. The Latin American countries may be getting a larger share in the division of economic rents with the foreign companies, but on a worldwide scale, it is a much smaller share of a much larger pie.[26]

The decline in new investment in Latin America may be symptomatic of corporate overreaction to recent nationalizations that is as exaggerated as was the belief of a few years ago that the multinationals would soon rule the world. Latin America possesses certain advantages that will continue to be attractive to the investor. In a situation of worldwide shortage of minerals, it offers unexplored possibilities in the development of raw materials and energy extraction. If there is a large potential market in a given country (for example, Brazil with 100 million people; Mexico with 65 million; or Argentina with a population of 26 million but a much higher per capita income) the multinational should be interested in investing, especially if it can minimize its financial exposure through government guarantees or international bank loans. Manufacturing for export is particularly attractive because there is less likelihood of expropriation of industries integrated with international production processes and markets.

Nationalization of the exposed enclaves of extractive industries and utilities has already occurred in most Latin American countries, removing the most obvious targets of economic nationalism. If the foreign manufacturing sector can demonstrate that it brings with it increased exports, labor-intensive methods or other "ripple" effects, or technology that will benefit the economy, its future prospects would seem to be favorable. In the extractive industries, new relationships with host countries are being developed. In the bargaining process between the foreign investor and potential host countries, the possibilities for non-zero-sum games that benefit both players are still considerable in Latin America. Perhaps a new stage in the relationship between Latin America and foreign capital has been reached, characterized by greater pragmatism and selectivity in the negotiation and operation of investment from abroad, and dominated by state investment boards and the large multinationals rather than the freewheeling investors and their local accomplices of the past. If the recent wave of nationalizations, the rise of state regulation, and the establishment of relatively stable rules of the game have cleared the air, it may be premature to predict the demise of United States investment in Latin America. The United Nations study, *The Future of the World Economy*, prepared under the direction of Wassily Leontief, projects a continuing capital inflow into Latin America for the rest of the century with an altered composition dominated by loan and portfolio lending rather than reliance on direct investment. The Leontief study sees neither nationalization, state enterprise financed by foreign borrowing, nor private foreign investment as "waves of the future"; instead, the new structure will be a somewhat altered mix of the two, with greater emphasis on loan capital. Nationalizations may still take place if high profits from a particular industry make the expected benefits to the nation appear to outweigh likely costs, or if abuses by the foreign investor provoke a nationalist reaction. Increased state control is likely in the more developed Third World countries, but it will probably follow the Mexican pattern

—a mixture of state ownership in some basic industries, public-private enterprises with both domestic and foreign partners, and careful screening of new foreign investment. Foreign investment in manufacturing will continue, especially where labor costs are low. However, the profits of the multinational corporation will come increasingly from the sale of technology, marketing, and service contracts. For the future, Arthur Lewis's comment will be increasingly apt, "The importance of direct private investment in the international flow is greatly exaggerated, both by those who oppose it and by those who believe it should be the principal channel of foreign transfers. . . . The developing countries will depend on foreign borrowing long after they have ceased to depend on foreign enterprise."[27]

While much writing and research have been devoted to the multinationals and, more recently, to nationalization, insufficient attention has been given to the importance of mobilizing domestic investment capital through taxes, internal borrowing, and the development of domestic entrepreneurship and savings. (It is estimated that about $23 billion of Latin American savings were on deposit in European banks in 1975.) Some domestic sources of investment capital are alternatives to the multinationals and the foreign banks and governments, and other forms of enterprise exist besides the state corporation and the affiliate of the multinational corporation. For all the talk about penetration of Latin America by the foreign corporations, only 5 percent of gross domestic investment and 7 to 11 percent of capital flows are accounted for by foreign investment.[28] In countries other than Brazil, Mexico, and perhaps, Argentina and Venezuela, development capital must come principally from the domestic private sector, the state, or foreign borrowing.

Now that the major natural resource enclaves have been taken over, Is the likelihood of nationalization in Latin America diminished, or will the pressures for nationalization that took place in the extractive industries, banks, and utilities be repeated in the manufacturing sector? It seems that a combination of strict investment controls and joint ventures is more likely to be the future pattern for the regulation of the new forms of foreign investment, resulting in "a benign and productive combination between the advantages of the MNC, with its global scan of markets and technology, and the growing domestic expertise based on the specificity and particularities of the local resource endowment and institutional factors."[29] Assuming that the present pattern of alternation of military and constitutional regimes in Latin America continues, one can expect strong state influence in the economy and regulation of foreign investment with a degree of severity that is inversely proportional to the felt need for greater infusions of outside capital, technology, and other special advantages of foreign investment. Taxation, contract renegotiations, and performance requirements offer an easier way to secure control of economic policy and of profit sharing than the confrontational nationalizations of the past. In the new stage of Latin American nationalism, the foreigner may be squeezed, taxed, and regulated, but it is less likely that he will be expropriated.

The context and form of foreign investment in Latin America have changed, but foreign investment will still play an important role there. In the areas of mining and petroleum, there is little left to nationalize. However, foreign companies will continue to operate under either production-sharing or service contracts, as in Venezuela or Peru, or through joint ventures, as in some of the new copper mines in Chile and the minerals area in Mexico. Other investment will be subject to more or less stringent screening procedures, depending on the relative bargaining position of the negotiators and the attractiveness of the investment. Efforts may be made to secure a common investment regime on a continental basis, possibly under the auspices of the new Latin American Economic System (SELA), a cooperative Latin American economic program aimed at promoting regional economic development. However, the divergent interests and development strategies of the various members are likely to limit its effectiveness, as the Andean Pact has proven.

The development of investment controls, of legislation, and the extension of state ownership and participation in many areas of Latin American economic life have meant that economic decisions, especially those involving foreigners, have become increasingly politicized and complex. The old relationship between a relatively weak and unstable government and powerful and knowledgeable investing companies has been replaced by multiple negotiations involving large corporations with varying degrees of economic and political support from home governments, international banks and financial institutions, and host countries with their own domestic and international support systems.

In this new international situation, the old rules governing the relations of the United States government, American-based multinationals, and host governments in the Third World may no longer be appropriate. Should American policy on foreign investment and nationalization be altered to meet the new relationships? What are the lessons for government policy that can be drawn from the experience of nationalization in Latin America? These issues are discussed in the final chapter.

9

Nationalization, Foreign Investment, and United States Policy

The inherent contradiction of capitalism is that it develops rather than that it exploits the world. A capitalist international economy plants the seeds of its own destruction in that it diffuses economic growth, industry, and technology, and thereby undermines the distribution of power upon which that liberal interdependent economy has rested.
— Robert Gilpin, *U.S. Power and the Multinational Corporation,* 1975

We can not justify on trade or employment grounds measures that subsidize outward investment . . . [but] we should not adopt restrictive measures to keep American companies at home. Rather our goal should be neutrality in the treatment of outward investment and domestic investment; that is, insofar as possible we should maintain policies that do not bias the corporate decisionmaking process one way or another. . . . We all have a stake in insuring that international flows of capital, goods, services and technology continue to move competitively according to fundamental liberal principles.
— Richard N. Cooper, undersecretary of state for economic affairs, 1977

The U.S. government can not ignore the rights of its citizens under international law, but neither can it assume that U.S. corporate interests are homogeneous nor that the national interest automatically coincides with the perceived interest of an individual firm. Coercive sanctions which escalate individual disputes into nationalistic confrontations between governments should be avoided.
>   — Commission on United States-Latin
>   American Relations, *The Americas in a*
>   *Changing World,* 1975

Most Latin American countries hold to the absolute submission of foreign capital to national sovereignty . . . the United States bases its right of intervention upon international law. . . . There is a considerable gulf between principle and reality on both sides. . . . Latin America needs foreign investment and knows it all too well. . . . On its part, the United States sanctifies international law, but enforces it inconsistently. Realism dominates and compensation arrangements that deviate from market value are accepted when they appear to be the best that can be obtained.
>   — Albert Fishlow, "The Mature Neighbor
>   Policy," 1978

For an international investment code to receive LDC [less developed country] ratification, it would have to be so radical that it would offer MNC's only the security of the condemned prisoner.
>   — Nathaniel Leff, "Multinationals in a Hostile
>   World," 1978

It may not be time for a complete reorganization of the structure of international economic relations, as the advocates of the New International Economic Order maintain, but it is clear from the developments described earlier that significant changes in the area of international investment have occurred in recent years. Third World nationalizations during the 1960s and 1970s have produced shifts in ownership, especially of natural resources.

Significant changes in decisionmaking power over international investment flows have resulted from the increasing efforts of host governments to influence the direction and type of those flows, from the growing interest of the multinational corporation in alternatives to fully owned equity investment, and from the increasing proportion of foreign investment going to the developed world or to a restricted number of countries in the Third World with favorable investment climates.

In the past, United States policy has encouraged the flow of American investment abroad and taken diplomatic and legislative measures to protect that investment once it is located in the host country. This policy has been justified on the basis of the benefits it brings both to those countries and to the United States. It promotes the transfer of skills, the mobilization of resources, and the utilization of underemployed or unemployed labor in the host country; at the same time, it increases international trade and expands exports, jobs, and markets for the United States. This policy helped Europe and Japan to recover from the devastation of World War II and to become America's leading trade partners and competitors. However, from the outset, the assumption that foreign investment is always beneficial to the host country was seriously challenged in Latin America. More recently, the corresponding American belief that overseas investment by American-based firms is in the United States national interest has also been questioned — and demands have been made, particularly by American labor, for changes in the government's policies encouraging and protecting United States investment abroad.

The evaluation of the effect of investment abroad on American national interest must include both its domestic and foreign political consequences and its short-and long-term economic costs and benefits. From the cases studied in this book, it is clear that the political impact of the presence of the United States investor in an undeveloped country can be both positive and negative. As the dependency theorists have emphasized, when a weak country's policies are "conditioned" economically by those of United States investors, American political and economic influence is likely to be substantial. On the other hand, American influence is also likely to be quite controversial — particularly when the foreign presence is concentrated in one industry that is the principal source of export income. As the capabilities and self-image of the less developed countries improve, the presence of the United States corporation becomes a constant irritant, and pressures increase to expand the role of the host country in decisionmaking. As Robert Gilpin has argued, this condition is inherent in international capitalism; as national economic capabilities grow, desires for economic self-determination increase, and these, in turn, eventually stimulate a challenge to the economic hegemony of the corporation. While the process of assertion of national control can be impeded, and United States corporations — sometimes assisted by the United States government — have often attempted to do so, in the long run these forces cannot be prevented from manifesting themselves in a variety of ways, including the demand for national ownership.

A distinction must be made, however, between the general interest of the United States government and the specific interest of the corporation. The two coincide to the degree that the government has a duty to extend diplomatic protection to its citizens, including its corporate citizens, by acting through diplomatic channels to see that they are not subjected to gross denials of justice in cases involving disputes with foreign governments. In addition, it is in the government's interest to promote the international rule of law and to work toward peaceful resolution of disputes. The national and corporate interests may diverge, however, as they did in the petroleum nationalizations in Mexico and in the Anaconda Copper Company case in Chile in 1969. The government's broader political interests — good relations with other countries and the maintenance of American power and influence abroad — may override the interest of individual companies or even the more general interest in investment protection.

The argument has been made that it is in the national interest to maintain the worldwide influence of United States companies since they can implement governmental policy decisions, and because the benefits they derive from foreign investments also benefit the United States economy. There certainly are cases in which American companies have done the bidding of the United States government even at some economic sacrifice, as in the economic boycotts of China and Cuba. However, there are other cases — for example, currency manipulations that adversely affect the dollar — where they act for reasons of their own, contrary to national policy. It is not clear that the control of the United States government over their activities is so great as to demand that the government give them unconditional support. In fact, American companies prefer to keep government influence and control to a minimum. In addition, from the point of view of the government, political interference in economic activity is in conflict with a generally held belief in encouraging free trade and an open international economy. Both sides wish to maintain freedom of action. It is for this reason that the State Department consistently opposes measures like the Hickenlooper Amendment, which automatically commits the government to support the United States investor with strong and sometimes counterproductive actions, without giving the government the ability to influence or to restrain actions by the investor. A general policy of indiscriminate support for American corporate investment abroad, thus, presents both theoretical and practical difficulties.

The question of the gains to the American economy from investment abroad raises an entire spectrum of questions. Does United States foreign investment export jobs to countries that have lower wage scales, or does it promote world economic expansion in ways that ultimately benefit the United States economy? Does investment abroad reduce the capital available for domestic investment in the United States, or does it come principally from foreign sources, such as Eurodollars, Petrodollars, or local banks in the country concerned? Do profits and other payments from investment abroad constitute a significant or a marginal contribution to American prosperity?

A considerable controversial literature exists for each of these questions, but there is no clear and compelling answer to any of them. Certainly, there is no answer on the negative side which would warrant United States government intervention in order to discourage the flow of foreign investment.[1] In the late 1960s, short-term measures were taken to protect an overvalued dollar against balance-of-payments difficulties, but the dollar's more recent difficulties are not due to investment outflows. There are cases of American companies establishing "export platforms" to take advantage of cheap labor in countries like Taiwan, Korea, or Hong Kong to export textiles and electronic goods to the United States and Europe, but not to the degree that stronger countermeasures than tariff and quota protection are justified. At least in the early stages of American investment in less developed countries, there seems to be considerable evidence that the American economy benefits in terms of increased exports, jobs, and profits. On the other hand, it is not clear that those benefits are sufficiently great to warrant special legislative action to encourage such investment as a matter of government policy, particularly since there is some evidence that in the longer run the effects on the balance of payments, on employment, and on the development of foreign competition may be negative.

One area of foreign investment, however, that seems directly related to the United States national interest is mineral resources. Because of possible worldwide shortages in the future and American dependence on these imported commodities, especially petroleum, government action may be warranted to promote secure and cheap sources of raw materials and energy. In these areas, the less developed countries have already increased their control through measures up to and including nationalization. They have also attempted to raise prices by forming cartels and to stabilize earnings through international action. The United States interest in assured secure access to raw materials may justify special measures to encourage American investors to expand mineral resource exploration and development in ways that are less likely to be subject to manipulation or control by economic nationalists in other countries.

Development of the extremely poor countries—the so-called Fourth World—may also require special legislation. In these countries, ordinary inducements to investment are so weak, as compared with more developed countries, that investment will not flow to them without government inducements. The need for such inducements has been recognized by international financial institutions, which have established "soft-loan" windows and special funds for development, as well as by the Carter administration, which has supported aid aimed at the least developed countries. The benefits to the United States economy through the increase in trade and exports that result from aid to the very poor are much easier to argue for than is the promotion of investment in the more developed countries of the Third World, where most investment flows to less developed countries now go.

The conclusion can be drawn, then, that while there is a general diplomatic interest in the peaceful settlement of disputes and the protection of United States citizens abroad, only in the areas of strategic raw materials and of the development of the poorest countries are there compelling arguments for legislative action to encourage American investment abroad.

How does current and proposed United States policy relate to this analysis? Although the Carter administration has announced a policy of neutrality toward United States foreign investment, current policy encourages such investment through three instruments — the tax code, the Export-Import Bank, and the Overseas Private Investment Corporation. Proposals have been made by recent administrations to increase investment in natural resources in the Third World and in the poorest countries. International measures have been taken, with United States support, to promote the peaceful settlement of investment disputes. The United States government has consistently adhered to the position that international law requires the payment of "prompt, adequate, and effective compensation" for nationalization, and the United States Congress has enacted legislative sanctions in support of this position. Each of these policies will be evaluated in terms of the experiences examined in preceding chapters and the changing character of international economic relations.

TAXATION, EXPROPRIATION, AND FOREIGN INVESTMENT

Tax policy is relevant to both nationalization and foreign investment. With respect to nationalization, United States firms are permitted to write off, for tax purposes, the book value of losses that they have incurred through uncompensated or under-compensated take-overs by foreign governments. The book value basis for computing tax losses is often low, particularly if it has been reduced by depreciation allowances or inflation. In Cuba, for example, the effect of this policy on an older investment meant that only a small proportion of the current value of the investment could be used as a tax loss. There is an inconsistency between the position of the United States government as it relates to tax deductions based on book value and the government's support for the much more generous "going concern" or market value standard with regard to payment of compensation by foreign governments. One way to resolve the discrepancy between the two approaches is to use book value for compensation purposes, but this seems unfair in cases of fully-depreciated investments and land values which have not been readjusted for inflation. Even if companies have received tax benefits from depreciation allowances, some compensation for the current value of their investment and an adjustment for inflation seems equitable.

There are also specific proposals for change in the current tax policy as it affects foreign investment by American-based companies. The provisions of the United States tax laws that favor foreign investment and that have been challenged include the deferral of taxes on many types of overseas income until it is repatriated and the tax credit (up to the United States tax rate) against United States taxes for those paid to foreign countries. A few corporations engaged entirely in export or investment in Canada or Latin America, the so-called Western Hemisphere Trading Corporation, have also benefited from a special tax reduction of 14 percent. However, in 1976 the United States Congress voted to phase out this provision by 1980.

The credit for foreign taxes has been attacked by those who argue that overseas taxes should be treated as a deduction like any other business expense, thus considerably increasing the tax burden of United States companies having substantial overseas investment. In keeping with its overall policy of discouraging foreign investment by United States business, which it views as likely to lead to a loss of jobs for Americans, organized labor supports the replacement of the tax credit with a deduction. The proponents of the present policy argue that a change would result in a massive alteration of the pattern of American investment abroad since United States companies would be forced to "spin off" foreign subsidiaries. They also argue that such "double taxation" would put American investors at a serious competitive disadvantage with investors from all other developed countries, who are permitted such credits, often with more generous provisions than those presently allowed by United States law. In effect, it is argued that the change would replace a bias favoring overseas investment with one that operates strongly against it — by one estimate, raising the effective tax rate on overseas profits by 5 percent.

Largely on the basis of the double taxation argument, a general abolition of the credit for foreign taxes has not secured congressional backing. In 1974, however, the Senate Subcommittee on Multinational Corporations held hearings that criticized an Internal Revenue Service policy in effect since 1950 permitting oil companies to treat royalties paid on oil concessions from foreign governments as a fully creditable tax against United States taxes, rather than as a business expense deductible from taxable income. (The ruling was designed to enable Saudi Arabia to raise its oil take from 12 percent to 50 percent without reducing oil company profits.) The hearings showed that in 1972 such credits had enabled Gulf, Texaco, and Mobil to pay only between 1.2 percent and 1.7 percent of their income in United States taxes and, in 1970, had permitted one company to reduce its tax liability from $231 million to $18 million. Today in many oil-producing countries, the royalty issue is passé since oil extraction has been taken over by the host governments, and the oil companies are receiving their income from service contracts, marketing, and refining. In 1978, the Internal Revenue Service issued guidelines for United States companies engaged in extractive industries abroad, which sharpened the distinction between royalties and foreign taxes eligible for a tax credit. In 1979, further limitations on tax credits for foreign operations of American oil companies were proposed by the Carter administration, and liberal members of Congress unsuccessfully attempted to eliminate them altogether, arguing that this would encourage domestic oil exploration.[2]

Because of the existence of the credit for foreign taxes and the possibilities it opens for bookkeeping manipulations, the Internal Revenue Service and members of Congress have been compelled to tighten the rules for allocating domestic and foreign expenses for tax purposes. They have also required that pricing within the firm be based on an "arm's-length" standard, that is, intracompany prices must be the same as those for sales to an outside buyer. However, as Third World countries and critics of the multinational corporations have noted, enforcement of these rules is difficult without some international accounting and reporting requirements. In 1977, a UN Group of Experts proposed a set of standards for such accounting, but most of the UN work in this area has been devoted to the development of guidelines for bilateral tax treaties between developed and developing nations. The whole area of international taxation and reporting of income by multinational companies needs further international attention.

The deferral provisions of the tax law have received more serious congressional criticism than has the credit for foreign taxes (except in the oil industry). Here, the argument is that the exemption from the United States tax of most unrepatriated profits (royalty payments and profits of sales companies and holding companies are taxable) amounts to an interest-free loan for the American-based multinational corporation. The exemption skews the corporation's financial policy by encouraging it to keep its overseas profits abroad, as well as to allocate expenses in ways that reduce United States taxes. Thus, the ending of deferral is supported for economic reasons (efficiency and world welfare), as well as on the policy grounds (discouragement of overseas investment) that underlie American labor's opposition to foreign investment. In 1975, the Senate voted to end deferral, but the provision was eliminated from the tax law in the conference committee with the House. In 1978, as part of its tax reform program, the Carter administration also proposed that deferral be eliminated, but it received little support. Among other arguments, the prodeferral forces maintained that some overseas profits are never repatriated and therefore should not be subject to United States taxes.

Counterbalancing the two provisions favoring foreign investment is the fact that the United States investment tax credit, which is now 10 percent, does not apply to investment outside the United States. Tax reformers argue that if there is no strong national interest in either encouraging or discouraging foreign investment, the two provisions favoring it (credits for foreign taxes and deferral of taxation on foreign earnings) should be eliminated, and that the investment credit should be extended to include foreign investment, thus making domestic and international investment decisions subject to the same rules.[3] It has also been proposed that the United States impose countervailing taxes to offset foreign tax incentives similar to the countervailing duties imposed against imports that receive special foreign subsidies.[4]

Proponents of the status quo reply that earlier investment decisions were made in the expectation that there would not be such substantial alterations in the tax structure as to make overseas investment much less profitable and competitive. In addition, tax treaties concluded with other countries may require substantial revision if major changes are made. A further argument supporting the present policy is that world welfare, and especially the welfare of the capital-short, less developed countries, is improved by promoting United States investment.

As we have seen, the question of the benefits of foreign investment to both host and home countries is controversial and difficult. If there is no clear answer as to whether the United States national economic interest is helped or hurt by foreign investment, there is an argument—although a weak one—for abandoning the present tax provisions that encourage it. On the other hand, if such action results in disruption of the patterns of trade and investment built up for many years, the economic impact of such consistency in policy may be negative. Tax policy as it affects investment needs a comprehensive review that should concentrate, in particular, on the likely impact of the two most controversial current practices—credits for foreign taxes and deferral of taxation on unrepatriated foreign earnings.

THE EXPORT-IMPORT BANK

The United States government has also encouraged foreign investment and taken action against expropriation through the

Export-Import Bank. Established in 1934 to give government loans and loan guarantees to promote United States exports, the bank facilitates access to credit for the purchase of American goods by foreign buyers. In effect, it provides lower rates of interest and greater security than would have been the case in the absence of a lender or guarantor enjoying the full faith and credit of the United States Treasury. While the Bank is supposed to encourage exports of American-produced goods, it also promotes United States investment overseas by making it easier and cheaper to buy the capital goods and machinery in the United States necessary to establish overseas subsidiaries. It is often involved in the financing of the purchase of American transport aircraft, and it has used its financial power to further United States policy. For example, in the case of Allende's Chile, the purchase of several Boeing planes by the Chilean airline was "postponed," in August 1971, pending the announcement of the form and amount of the compensation for the recently nationalized American-owned copper mines.

This action by the Export-Import Bank was related to a United States government policy decision being debated at the time, to punish expropriating countries by denying them access to subsidized credit. In January 1972, that decision became public policy when President Nixon announced that "new bilateral economic benefits" would not be extended to countries that expropriated United States property "without making reasonable provision for compensation." The 1978 amendments to the Export-Import Bank Act limited the "non-financial and non-commercial" (that is, political) considerations that could be used to deny applications for insurance, loans, or credit guarantees to cases when "the President determines that such action would be in the national interest and where such action would clearly and importantly advance U.S. policy in such areas as international terrorism, nuclear proliferation, environmental protection, and human rights."[5] However, the Bank directors have interpreted uncompensated nationalization as an indication that a country does not demonstrate the "reasonable assurance of repayment" required by law. It is unlikely, therefore, that the amendments will deter the Bank's directors from denying loans to countries involved in nationalization disputes. The United States legislative sanctions (for example, the Hickenlooper Amendment) against uncompensated expropriation do not apply to the Bank, but the Bank consults with the Inter-Agency Group on Expropriation concerning the status of such disputes. Since Export-Import Bank credit guarantees are often required by major investment banking consortia — for example, the Cuajone project in Peru — the likelihood of its being unwilling to do so provides a deterrent to uncompensated nationalization and an incentive to settle such disputes that is more powerful than the threat of denial of aid embodied in the Hickenlooper and González Amendments. Since the negative decision is made on the basis of economic criteria, it is also less subject to criticism than the invocation of the two amendments.

Another amendment adopted in 1978 directed the United States International Trade Commission to prepare a study of the impact of present and past Bank loans and guarantees upon American industries and employment. This was a further indication of the growing concern in Congress about the possible adverse effects on the United States economy of the encouragement through government policy of American investment abroad. The Bank's primary role is the promotion of United States exports, but when those exports include support for the establishment of subsidiaries that may later harm the economy, Congress may wish to prevent the Bank from doing so. Whether or not the International Trade Commission is able to establish that this is the case, a consistent policy of neutrality toward United States investment abroad would argue against loans and credit guarantees by the Bank for foreign investment projects, except in the areas identified earlier as in the national interest.

THE OVERSEAS PRIVATE INVESTMENT CORPORATION: PROS AND CONS

For thirty years, the United States government has been promoting foreign investment by insuring investors abroad against "political" risks that private insurers were unwilling to cover. Beginning with the Investment Guarantee Program of the Marshall

Plan in 1948, the United States has maintained a program to encourage investment abroad by insuring American investors against war, currency conversion problems, and expropriation, with expropriation becoming more important as the program became concentrated on the developing countries. Beginning in 1969, the Investment Guarantee Program was removed from the aegis of the Agency for International Development (AID) and established as the Overseas Private Investment Corporation (OPIC), an autonomous government corporation "under the policy guidance of the Secretary of State" with majority private sector representation on its board of directors. When OPIC was established, it was given authority to insure a maximum of $7.5 billion of investments backed by "the full faith and credit" of the United States Treasury. OPIC took over the reserves of the Investment Guarantee Program, and an initial appropriation of $40 million was made by Congress. However, it was intended that the corporation should charge insurance fees that would be sufficient to make it self-supporting financially. The corporation began formal operations in 1971 — just in time to be hit by large claims for reimbursements for the nationalizations by the government of Salvador Allende in Chile. As described in chapter 5, OPIC was able to survive the initial onslaught of claims. In the case of the three largest companies involved in the Chilean nationalizations, it issued notes to cover the Kennecott claim and, initially, denied those of Anaconda and International Telegraph and Telephone (ITT). After the 1973 coup, it recovered some of what it had paid in claims from the Chilean government, and despite arbitration decisions against it in the Anaconda and ITT cases, the continued inflow of insurance fees and the scheduled repayments by Chile and other countries have now insured that it is financially sound and self-sustaining. In 1978, its insurance and financing reserves were over $380 million, and it is also authorized to borrow up to $100 million from the United States Treasury. Over the last ten years, OPIC has paid out $112 million in claims for inconvertibility, expropriation, and war damage, nearly half of which will be paid back as a result of compensation agreements under which it will receive delayed reimbursement from foreign governments.

OPIC is not as secure politically as it is financially. At the time that the Investment Guarantee Program and OPIC were established, the assumption that government support for overseas investment was in the national interest went almost unchallenged.[6] In the 1970s, that assumption has been repeatedly questioned — particularly in the congressional hearings and debates in 1973 and 1977 concerning renewal of its authorization. In 1973, it was strongly criticized by the Subcommittee on Multinational Corporations of the Senate Foreign Relations Committee. The subcommittee argued that it was not clear that United States overseas investment was a positive influence for development ("at best only a marginal contributor"). It challenged the justification for a special government program to encourage such investment, claiming that OPIC insurance could involve the United States government in political conflicts with other governments. (The specific examples cited were the efforts of the United States ambassador during the 1972 Jamaican elections to get assurances from the candidates that the aluminum companies insured by OPIC would not be nationalized, and the pressure on behalf of ITT by former CIA Director John McCone, seeking United States intervention against the election of Allende in Chile in 1970.) The subcommittee's report recommended that OPIC be phased out as a direct insurer by 1980 and that before that date the various parts of its insurance program be transferred or shared with private insurers on a specific schedule.

The report by the Subcommittee on Foreign Economic Policy of the House Foreign Affairs Committee was more favorable to OPIC. Noting the Senate subcommittee's objections, it observed that there was an inherent conflict of goals in the existing mandate to OPIC, which was supposed to be self-supporting and to observe sound principles of risk management, yet was also intended to promote investment in what were, by definition, risky areas that private insurers would not cover. In response to the Senate subcommittee's point about political involvement, the House subcommittee replied that the existence of OPIC *reduced* the possibility of government-to-government confrontations since it could influence the form of the initial investments (encouraging, for instance, joint ventures and nonequity investments in raw materials) and act as an intermediary to assist in arriving at an equitable settlement of disputes before they escalated to the governmental level.[7]

The final result of the differing approaches of the two houses of Congress was a renewal of OPIC's authorization but the adoption of the Senate timetable for privatization. However, it soon became apparent that private insurers would not cover war risks and were dubious about the other risks unless the United States government was involved in some capacity as a reinsurer. Thus, when it came up again for authorization in 1977, OPIC requested that the phaseout requirement be removed.

In the 1977 congressional debates, the roles of the two houses were reversed. The Senate Subcommittee on Multinational Corporations had been abolished, and OPIC was discussed by the Subcommittee on Foreign Assistance, chaired by Senator Humphrey, who favored renewal of authorization. The subcommittee heard only one critical witness, and his testimony was cut short by a closure vote. He attacked the concentration of OPIC insurance on middle-level developing countries with bad human rights records, such as Brazil, South Korea, and the Philippines, and its support of investments by large multinational corporations, such as Dow Chemical, Getty Oil, and ITT. More fundamentally, the witness argued that investments insured by OPIC were having adverse social and economic effects in many developing countries.[8]

OPIC ran into more serious trouble on the floor of the House of Representatives. The committee hearings in the House had focused principally on the usefulness of OPIC in encouraging investments in natural resources and energy, but in the floor debate in early November, OPIC was subjected to bitter attack by the late congressman Leo Ryan, who began his speech as follows: "Thanksgiving comes in about three weeks. I want to present the Members personally with their own turkey because that is what this bill is." He then accused OPIC of supporting tourist facilities for the rich (including a $150-a-day hotel in Haiti) and of exporting United States jobs by insuring "runaway" textile and steel plants in low-wage countries that had led to the closing of plants and loss of employment in the United States.

The Ryan attack came just after several American steel plants had closed. Backed by AFL-CIO lobbyists, Ryan appeared to be receiving considerable support. The House leadership felt obliged to postpone consideration of the bill, and it was adopted only in February 1978 with a series of amendments that prohibited OPIC from insuring the overseas production of copper, palm oil, sugar, and citrus. The final bill, as adopted by both houses, removed the phaseout requirements and authorized OPIC to continue to operate until September 30, 1981. It required OPIC to give preferential assistance to insuring and financially assisting United States small businesses, increasing their proportion of projects to 30 percent. It also directed OPIC to give priority to countries with annual per capita incomes of $520 or less, and except in special cases, such as mineral development, not to insure projects in countries with a per capita income of over $1,000 a year. Furthermore, the bill required a development impact statement for each insured project and forbade loans to any project that would result in a significant reduction in United States employment.[9] Besides the changes mandated by Congress, the corporation's directors also authorized it to insure projects in the area of minerals and petroleum exploration in countries that are not members of OPEC. The changed emphasis of the OPIC program demonstrates the difficulties encountered by its critics. They are directing their fire at a moving target. Every time they criticize its program, OPIC agrees to modify it to meet their criticism. Thus, it has gone through a period of "fine-tuning" in recent years to assure that government-backed support goes to those areas identified earlier as in the national interest—the promotion of the development of the neediest countries and the expansion of mineral and energy resources. In response to arguments that foreign investment does not contribute to development or the United States national economy, it has established screening mechanisms to assure that investment projects make a positive contribution to both goals. In practice, OPIC goes even further. It examines proposed projects for their effects on United States financial flows, displacement of exports, development of new sources of raw materials, and promotion of new exports and employment. Between 1974 and 1977, it rejected forty-five projects because of their potential adverse effects, and for the same years, OPIC has claimed that its insured projects produced a net favorable financial flow to the United States of $73 million, created direct and indirect trade benefits of over $3 billion, and benefited United States employment by 90,000 work-years, while saving host countries nearly $4 billion in foreign exchange and creating 169,000 jobs.[10]

How does the experience reviewed in earlier chapters relate specifically to United States policy toward OPIC? An important part of its activities is insurance against expropriation, a major deterrent to new American investment in the Third World. OPIC was involved in only one of the five countries studied — Chile — and its exposure at the time of the Allende nationalizations was substantial. The existence of OPIC insurance programs motivated the United States ambassador to be particularly active in attempting to secure a compromise settlement on the copper nationalizations, in part because of their potential impact on the OPIC reserves. After the coup, OPIC engaged in direct negotiations with the Pinochet government in order to recover some of its payments to nationalized American firms. However, at the present time it is not insuring new investment in Chile, Brazil and Mexico now have per capita incomes that make them ineligible for OPIC coverage except in special circumstances, and only the Dominican Republic and Jamaica are substantial recipients of OPIC insurance in Latin America. The emphasis on encouraging investments in the neediest countries means that OPIC probably will not be active in Latin America in the future. Even before the change in policy, some larger companies were exploring self-insurance in the belief that it might be cheaper than the relatively high premiums that OPIC charges for its insurance.

Although OPIC should continue to assist the United States government in achieving certain specifically pinpointed objectives, such as energy and raw materials development or the promotion of investment in very poor countries, it is not now, nor is it likely to be, a major policy instrument in protecting United States overseas investors against the risk of expropriation. Only a small percentage of American overseas investment is covered by OPIC insurance, and that percentage is dropping as more investment goes to the developed world or to the more advanced Third

World countries that are no longer eligible for most OPIC programs. The history of the corporation and the controversies surrounding the renewal of its authorization demonstrate that government support for foreign investment is difficult to achieve when there is no consensus as to its contribution to the national interest, especially when one major interest group, labor, is clearly opposed to its continuation. It has survived because there is no cost to the taxpayer, it is dependent on the government only for its use of the "full faith and credit" of the Treasury to back up its guarantees, and it has been able to respond to specific and demonstrable public purposes in recent years.

Giving OPIC a larger role, such as the recent proposal to make its head Special Representative of the President for Foreign Direct Investment Policy, would drastically change the character of the corporation.[11] Similarly, the efforts of OPIC in minerals and energy exploration should be expanded, but as presently constituted, the corporation does not have the financial capacity to make a major commitment in this area.

RESOURCE EXPLORATION WITHOUT EXPROPRIATION

There is a clear national interest in encouraging minerals and energy exploration in less developed countries. However, American companies are increasingly hesitant to engage in such exploration in localities they view as politically risky. Large amounts of investment capital, such as the multinational corporation has been able to mobilize, are required for resource development, but as the case of the Cuajone copper deposits in Peru demonstrates, it is now much more difficult to put together the capital for large, long-term minerals projects in the Third World. Neither individual companies nor banks are willing to risk individual exposure in politically unstable countries. Increasingly, investors attempt to expand their involvement by forming multicompany consortia and borrowing the capital from many banks in different countries that assure themselves against risk by cross-default clauses. This is a lengthy and time-consuming procedure, and it could be accelerated by internationalizing the process of capital formation and risk avoidance.

Proponents of international action on natural resource exploration argue that 80 percent of all mineral exploration in the early 1970s took place in the United States, Canada, Australia, and South Africa. High-grade ore in countries like Zaire is left undeveloped, while mineral deposits of much lower quality are developed in the United States. They cite World Bank studies of petroleum exploration that show that, on a statistical basis, there are likely to be substantial oil deposits in the Third World, and that exploratory drilling in the developing countries has declined by 20 percent since the early 1970's compared with a 33 percent increase in drilling in the United States.

In 1976, the United States responded to this problem with a proposal for the creation of an International Resources Bank, presented by Secretary of State Kissinger at the Nairobi meeting of the United Nations Conference on Trade and Development (UNCTAD). Secretary Kissinger's proposal involved a special lending facility associated with the World Bank group that would raise money for resource development both from member countries and by selling bonds secured by future commodity production. It would participate in the projects along with host governments and investing companies and would act as a co-guarantor of performance by both the companies involved and the host countries. Agreements could include provisions for production sharing by both the investor and the host country and arrangements to help develop the managerial, technological, and marketing capabilities of the host country.[12]

After a hasty presentation and inadequate lobbying, the proposal was defeated by 33 votes to 31, with 44 nations abstaining. While the adverse votes came from a coalition of the more radical Third World countries and the Communist representatives, the large number of abstentions by developing countries may indicate that the proposal or a variant of it still has possibilities for the future. The resistance by the radicals was based on the belief that it amounted to an international subsidy to multinational corporations and that it might bring down the price of raw materials by increasing the supply. The latter charge could become true if the countries in which new discoveries were made refused to participate in the various commodity stabilization plans now emerging, or in the case of oil, if they undercut the OPEC price. However, both Third World solidarity and economic self-interest make this unlikely. The reply of the proposal's defenders to the charge that it would benefit the multinationals was to note that the agreements supported by the Bank could take a variety of forms other than direct equity investment, including bank-guaranteed loans to state corporations, joint ventures, service contracts, provisions for the development of refining or processing, as well as fadeout arrangements that would turn over ownership to the host country after a given period of years. The multinationals themselves also expressed some reservation about the original proposal because it might limit their flexibility in discontinuing exploration and development when it became clear that a given investment would not be profitable.

After the defeat of the Kissinger proposal at Nairobi, the World Bank and the Inter-American Development Bank (IDB) began to work on similar projects. The World Bank plans to increase lending for energy purposes from 1 percent to 10 percent of its program and the IDB has proposed an Inter-American Energy and Minerals Fund that would provide international financing and insurance for the exploration and development of new sources of minerals and petroleum in Latin America. At the time of this writing, United States officials had expressed interest in the proposal but indicated concern about the size of the expected United States contribution for loan guarantees—$550 million (although with congressional agreement such guarantee authority could be transferred from OPIC)—and uncertainty about the voting procedures within the fund. As the recent Mexican petroleum discoveries have demonstrated, large areas of Latin America have not been explored for minerals and energy; by one estimate, there has been less oil exploration in all of Latin America than in Texas and Oklahoma. Given the United States interest in increasing access to raw materials under stable conditions, the IDB proposal merits support.

INTERNATIONAL PROTECTION OF INVESTMENT

Two other areas relevant to United States international investment policy remain to be studied — the development of international institutions for the settlement of investment disputes and the use of diplomacy and unilateral economic pressure by the United States government on behalf of investors.

One way to give greater security to the flow of international investment is through the establishment of international machinery for the arbitration of investment disputes. The World Bank has taken the lead in this area by establishing an associated institution, the International Centre for the Settlement of Investment Disputes (ICSID). In 1965, the directors of the bank proposed an International Convention for the Settlement of Investment Disputes between States and Nationals of Other States, and in October 1966, after twenty countries had ratified it, the document went into effect. It provides that governments interested in making use of the center sign and ratify the convention by which they consent to submit such disputes to conciliation commissions or arbitration tribunals established by the center. As of 1978, seventy-one countries had ratified the convention. Notable by their absence, however, are all the countries of Latin America. They objected to the convention from the outset on the grounds that it violates the Calvo principle that such disputes should be decided by national tribunals. The center now has a long list of arbitrators named by its member countries, but in twelve years of existence, up to the end of 1978, it has dealt with a surprisingly small number of cases. Between 1966 and 1978, it handled cases involving only six countries and made a decision in only one case. Its first dispute, involving Holiday Inns and Morocco, was submitted in 1972 and was finally settled by the parties involved without a formal arbitral decision in October 1978. Its second case, involving an Italian firm and the Ivory Coast, began in 1974 and was only decided by the Arbitral Tribunal in August 1977. Its decision has not been published, but both parties pronounced themselves satisfied with it. The most important cases submitted to ICSID involved three American aluminum companies, Alcoa,

Kaiser, and Reynolds Aluminum. The companies objected to a large tax increase imposed by Jamaica through its 1974 Bauxite Levy, claiming that it violated earlier contracts guaranteeing them against further tax increases without their consent. Shortly before imposing the levy, Jamaica notified the center that it was now exempting natural resources from the areas it had agreed to submit to ICSID's jurisdiction when it ratified the convention in 1966. The ICSID Arbitration Tribunal decided that Jamaica was still bound by its earlier agreement, but in late 1976 and early 1977, the cases became moot when the companies settled their disputes with Jamaica. A dispute in Gabon was also settled bilaterally in 1977. As of 1978, three new disputes involving the Congo and Nigeria have been submitted to the center. If past experience is any indication, progress on their resolution will be slow.[13]

Given the limited use of the center and the length of time it takes to get a decision, one may question whether it contributes significantly to the promotion of international economic relations. Yet the existence of ICSID clauses in investment laws and agreements around the world does act as a reassurance to the investor that he may have recourse to an impartial tribunal and to the host country that diplomatic channels and other instruments of the investor's home country will not be used against it. The one great gap in ICSID's coverage is Latin America, and it is possible, but not likely, that because of recent policies favoring foreign investment in countries such as Chile ratification might be considered. (According to ICSID, Brazil has recognized ICSID arbitration principles in one of its loan agreements.)

Further evidence that the development of such a framework may be viewed favorably is a Sri Lankan resolution, adopted by the 1977 UN General Assembly, calling on the Secretary General to convene a group of experts to prepare a report for the 1978 General Assembly on "the feasibility and desirability of establishing a multilateral investment insurance and reinsurance agency, as well as the possible enlargement of the guarantee powers of international financial institutions to improve the access of less-developed countries to international loans." Under the title, the International Investment Insurance Agency (IIIA), multilateral investment insurance has long been advocated by the United

States and other members of the Organization for Economic Cooperation and Development (OECD) as a useful way to promote
coordination and expansion of investment protection. From 1962
until 1968, the World Bank worked on the drafting of a convention establishing the IIIA. However, when the text was sent to the
member countries, it became apparent that there was opposition
both on the part of developed and developing countries. The developed countries, other than the United States, were skeptical
about the advisability of making individual investment disputes
into international issues. They were also reluctant to protect the
many American-based multinational corporations when they had
no control over their activities. The developing countries, led by
Latin America, objected because the proposed insurance convention would bypass national tribunals and because, under its subrogation provision, the agency would be obliged to continue to
attempt to secure compensation after an insurance payment had
been made.

The report of the UN experts, when it was published in November 1978, saw much more merit in the expansion of loan guarantees than in multilateral investment insurance. While the encouragement of cooperative ventures among investors from different
countries was viewed as an advantage of an international insurance agency, and while present bilateral investment insurance
programs were described as restrictive and limited, the report
warned that there were many technical problems connected with
the establishment of such an agency, including financing, voting
rights, and the resolution of disputes, and it expressed doubt
whether a new facility would appreciably increase investment
flows to the developing countries when there were already bilateral programs in the major capital-exporting countries. Once
again, it seems that the possibilities for international action in the
investment field are limited by the divergent national interests between and among developed and developing nations.[14]

The OECD is also currently working on the coordination of
the investment insurance programs of its members, which should
be easier to secure than in either the UN or the World Bank. One
area of coordinated action that has recently been proposed
against both debt default and confiscatory expropriation is a so-

called Hot Products Convention. According to this proposal, the signatories of the convention would agree that foreign creditors and investors who had not been paid or compensated would be permitted to bring suit in the signatory countries in order to attach the output, properties, or financial accounts of the nationalized enterprises.[15] However, the Kennecott Corporation employed this technique against the Allende regime in the year before its overthrow, and one of the reasons that the Peruvians agreed to settle the Marcona nationalization dispute was that they could not sell the iron ore from their nationalized mines, except in small quantities to Eastern Europe. Since corporations already are able to use the courts, as Kennecott did, it seems unlikely that government intervention to formalize the process is necessary, especially since it would elicit fierce opposition from Third World countries.

If arbitration under ICSID makes only a marginal contribution, and if internationalizing insurance or other institutional structures face considerable opposition, are there other ways to promote a stable framework for international investment? One suggestion that has received considerable attention in the current decade, partly because of publicity given to abuses by multinationals such as ITT in Chile, is the development of codes of conduct for multinational corporations. In 1976, the OECD issued a set of voluntary guidelines for multinationals. A year later, the International Labor Organization adopted a Declaration of Principles concerning Multinational Corporations and Social Policy. A Latin American group in the Organization of American States has prepared draft guidelines for a code (which include the Calvo Doctrine, denying diplomatic protection to foreign investors), UNCTAD is working on a code for the transfer of technology, and the UN Commission on Transnational Corporations has convened a series of meetings of an Intergovernmental Working Group on a Code of Conduct. However, the primary focus of the codes under discussion has been upon ways to limit the operation of multinational corporations, and little discussion has been given to establishing standards of fair treatment for foreign investors. Although at the first meeting of the UN Commission on

Transnational Corporations in 1975, the governments of the United States, France, Italy, the Federal Republic of Germany, and the United Kingdom submitted a list of "areas of concern," which included "the extent to which expropriation of properties undertaken for public purposes related to the internal requirements of the countries concerned, are non-discriminatory in application, and accompanied by prompt, adequate, and effective compensation," as well as a reference to the desirability of using international arbitration, "including that provided by the International Centre for the Settlement of Investment Disputes" in order to settle disagreements involving corporations. It became apparent during the meetings of the Commission's Working Group that the question of nationalization and compensation sharply divided the representatives of the so-called Group of 77 — the less developed countries — from the capital-exporting nations, most of them members of the OECD. In late 1978, the Swedish chairman of the Intergovernmental Working Group, in an effort to develop a draft formulation embodying the views of both sides, was compelled to add a special appendix which stated that on the issue of "fair and equitable compensation, according to one view . . . international law has no relevant rules or it provides that national law is the only law applicable. According to another view, international law also includes certain independent standards that override or supplement national law in order to protect the aliens affected." It does not seem likely that a consensus will be produced on the question of compensation — although the "fair and equitable" formulation used by the Intergovernmental Working Group chairman is more likely to receive general support than the "prompt, adequate, and effective" wording proposed by the developed countries led by the United States.[16]

These negotiations seem to demonstrate, once again, that all efforts at international action are limited by the basic conflict between the belief of the capital-exporters that their property is entitled to protection under international law, and the belief of the capital-importers that foreign investment should be subject to national law and to any changes in the economic or political system in the host country that may take place. As long as there is no consensus on the international rules, promotion of a favorable climate for investment must remain with the nation-state and the multinational corporation itself.

UNITED STATES DIPLOMATIC PROTECTION

The conclusion that can be drawn from the efforts to develop international institutions to promote a stable environment for investment flows is that no major instrument for the promotion and protection of international investment is likely to be developed on the international level in the near future. However, the unilateral efforts of the United States government to use diplomatic, and occasionally economic, pressures on behalf of its investors remain to be considered.

The State Department has always held that its duty to extend diplomatic protection to its citizens includes the defense of the property of American-based corporations against arbitrary or confiscatory actions by foreign governments if local remedies are exhausted. Nationalization without "prompt, adequate, and effective" compensation as well as "creeping nationalization" through confiscatory taxes or major unilateral alterations of contracts have also been considered as arbitrary deprivations of property. Diplomatic efforts by the executive branch (protests, negotiations, or withdrawal of economic benefits such as foreign aid) as well as congressionally mandated sanctions have been utilized or threatened in order to secure compensation. However, international law recognizes that the extension of diplomatic protection is carried out at the option of the home government. Moreover, as we have seen, other considerations, especially United States security and the maintenance of good political and economic relations with the governments involved, have sometimes overridden the *prima facie* obligation to help American investors. In all cases in Latin America except that of Cuba, some type of compensation was paid, and in every case it was less than the theoretical standard advocated by the United States government. In addition, the State Department has not been able to protest every contract modification or large and sudden tax increase; too many have occurred. If "the obsolescing bargain" view of natural resource investments is valid, such modifications are inevitable in the relations of multinational investors and countries that depend on minerals or petroleum for a large part of their export revenues.

The usefulness of the "prompt, adequate, and effective" standard has been questioned earlier in this book. Some reformulation of the principle seems necessary — or, at least, a more flexible wording is needed. Most settlements have been made on the basis of book value, and the continued insistence on market value by the State Department seems to involve an unrealistic gap between theory and practice. It can also exacerbate tensions, as in the case of the State Department's 1959 protests over the Cuban agrarian reform law. It may be argued that insistence on the market value standard is necessary as a starting point for bargaining purposes, but then the question is whether the United States government has any particular obligation to assist American companies in securing as generous a settlement as possible. The encouragement of a stable framework for international economic relations, including foreign investment, can be achieved by a less demanding standard than that of prompt, adequate, and effective compensation at full market value. For example, the "fair and equitable compensation" formula used by the Intergovernmental Working Group would seem to be a more workable and generally acceptable formulation. It has also been argued that since investors often benefit from the book value standard when paying taxes, the same standard should be used for compensation. However, book value often fails to take into account inflation, and governments sometimes fail to update book value tax assessments for land values, as in Guatemala before 1959 and in some of the Cuban cases. Book value is one possible basis for determining fair compensation, but as a single standard, it seems excessively rigid. However, intervention by the United States government on behalf of the unrealistic standard of prompt, adequate, and effective compensation is neither a necessary nor a useful way to promote its general interest in discouraging arbitrary and confiscatory deprivation of the property of its citizens.

Yet even if a less specific standard like "fair and equitable" is adopted, there will inevitably be conflicts over the evaluation of the nationalized assets. Here, the Peruvian case suggests a number of useful ways to aid in the settlement of compensation disputes, including the employment of outside evaluators, indirect compensation through transportation and marketing contracts, the involvement of special negotiators, and a lump-sum settlement to settle the most difficult cases. The good offices of the embassy should also be used, both to mediate and conciliate investment disputes and to anticipate possible future disagreements and problems. The experiences reviewed in this book argue for a behind-the-scenes role by the United States embassy well before disputes escalate. Although the line between anticipatory action and intervention in domestic politics is a difficult one to draw, it seems that the early involvement of the embassy in Chile in 1971 in developing a compromise solution to the impending copper nationalizations through a United States government-backed compensation arrangement would be an example of this type of anticipatory action.

THE ROLE OF CONGRESSIONAL LEGISLATION

The legislation adopted by the United States Congress in order to deter or punish uncompensated expropriations both limits and aids the State Department in negotiations. It limits it because the legislation utilizes the "prompt, adequate, and effective" formula; this is the case with the González Amendment, which prohibits United States support for loans from the multilateral financial institutions, as well as with the Hickenlooper Amendment, which until 1973 (when a presidential waiver in "the national interest of the United States" was added), also gave the executive branch no discretionary power as to whether or not to invoke its sanctions. On the other hand, the legislative sanctions provide an additional incentive for the nationalizing country to arrive at a settlement since loans by private banks to developng countries are often linked to, or at least influenced by, the United States government attitude. As the case studies have shown, the decision of the Export-Import Bank on a possible loan package is sometimes crucial in determining whether a loan will be supported by private banks. Furthermore, tariff benefits under the 1974 Trade Act must also be withdrawn from governments that engage in uncompensated expropriations, unless the President certifies that it would not be in the United States economic interest to do so. (Before the Sugar Act was allowed to expire in 1974, it also mandated the withdrawal of sugar quotas from countries failing to pay "prompt, adequate, and effective" compensation for expropriated American properties.)

In practice, the Hickenlooper Amendment has only been invoked once, against Sri Lanka in the early 1960s, although it was threatened (and probably should have been invoked if the language of the law means anything at all) in the International Petroleum Company (IPC) case in Peru and, more recently, in cases involving the nationalization of two American oil companies' properties in the Congo. Similarly, the González Amendment has only been applied to Iraq in 1975 and to the Congo in 1976. Initial steps were taken to apply the 1974 Trade Act sanctions to the Congo, and similar action was threatened in a dispute between Exxon and Sri Lanka, but in both cases, the required compensation negotiations were initiated.

The problem with making expropriation policy by congressional amendment is that while the legal *threat* is useful the actual *use* of the legislative sanctions may worsen relations between the United States and the other nation. In the interest of defending one company, it may provoke a nationalistic reaction that could harm other American investors and United States interests in general. Such reasoning led to the insertion of the 1973 presidential waiver in Hickenlooper and argues for similar action in the case of the González Amendment and the Trade Act sanctions. It is doubtful that they can be formally repealed, but at least the waiver gives the president desirable flexibility for negotiations.

As long as the legislation is on the books, the Interagency Group on Expropriations, chaired by a State Department representative, will continue to examine investment disputes involving expropriation or unilateral impairment of contracts and will decide and coordinate the expropriation policies of the Depart-

ments of State, Treasury, and Commerce, as well as the Overseas
Private Investment Corporation.[17] The group's activities could
be broadened to include discussions of overall policy, rather than
simply restricting itself to examining individual cases as it presently does and its jurisdiction might be extended to borderline
cases of "creeping nationalization" through escalating requirements of local sourcing, exports etc. Some input from the State
Department's Public Advisory Group on Transnational Corporations might also be sought. However, overall policy on overseas investment would have to be developed at a more general
level, such as the National Advisory Council on International
Monetary and Financial Policies.

SELF-DEFENSE BY THE MULTINATIONALS

Many multinational corporations do not want strong government involvement in their affairs, even if its purpose is to protect
their investment. In its pre-1973 version, the Hickenlooper
Amendment was opposed by the Council of the Americas, the
"umbrella organization" for United States investors in Latin
America. Some companies have said that OPIC insurance is bu-
reaucratized and expensive and is taken out only because of an
obligation to stockholders to safeguard the company's investment. Both investors and host countries are increasingly aware
that the most important sanction against uncompensated expropriation is its adverse effect on new investment in the country
concerned and on the loans that oil-importing countries in the
Third World now find essential to their economic survival.

The international system has much stronger sanctions against
default on international loans than it does on international investment. Default on loans is now seen as a direct threat to the
whole international economic system, and both creditors and
debtors take extraordinary measures to avoid it, including the establishment of international lending consortia ("The Paris
Club") and repeated "rollovers" of debts. The result has been
that the debt defaults of the pre–World War II period, for which
Latin American countries were notorious, no longer take place.

Uncompensated expropriation in the investment field, which is the equivalent of default in international lending, does not produce the same kind of adverse pressure from the international community, although the two are becoming more closely linked. As noted earlier, the World Bank will not lend to countries that do not make "genuine efforts at a reasonable settlement" of investment disputes. It defends this position by asserting that it would have difficulties raising funds in the international money markets if it continued to lend to countries that engaged in confiscatory expropriations. International Monetary Fund standby loans and multilateral international bank loans also are not undertaken unless investment disputes have been resolved. As Chile discovered in 1971–72, renegotiations of international debts can also be delayed or impeded by investment disputes. In recent years, international investors have taken measures to minimize and spread risk, including the creation of international consortia to invest in resource development and borrowing from banks in many countries and sometimes from the World Bank itself, buttressed by a variety of cross-default clauses. These measures are the new defenses against nationalization, replacing the old ones that have crumbled. Nationalizing countries also still want access to the capital, markets, and technology that the multinationals can provide. Even such radical countries as Libya and Iraq have paid compensation, and the new Cuban constitution, adopted in 1976, specifically guarantees "due compensation" for expropriated property. Thus, the need for extraordinary intervention by the United States government is not as great as was felt following the Cuban and Chilean nationalizations. In the area of expropriation, the maintenance of a watchful "low profile" by the United States government seems to make sense on grounds both of principle and pragmatism. It is true that there are special problems and sensitivities in the areas of utilities, finance, petroleum, and mineral resources. However, the United States does not have a special interest in maintaining American ownership of utilities or finance, and in the areas of petroleum and natural resources there are other ways to maintain access to vital raw materials, such as service contracts, joint ventures, international guarantee mechanisms, and the development of alternative sources —

although without the degree of control that direct equity ownership provided in the past.

POLICY CONCLUSIONS

The policy conclusions that have emerged in this chapter are
the following:
1. The costs and benefits of U.S. investment abroad to the
American economy and polity should be evaluated in a more
sophisticated and critical way than has been done in the past.
This means that some of the measures that have been adopted
to encourage American investment abroad, and to protect it
once it is located there, should be reconsidered in light of the
changing views of the national interest.
2. In the area of taxation, several modifications of present policy
should be considered: in particular, the end of deferral of taxation of overseas earnings, and close scrutiny of the tax status
of payments to foreign governments for oil and mineral concessions.
3. The impact of Export-Import Bank loans on United States
employment and future exports should be considered in decisions on its foreign loans and guarantees. Overseas investment projects should be supported only in cases where a clear
national interest in doing so can be identified.
4. The Overseas Private Investment Corporation (OPIC) should
continue to play a role in encouraging investment in low-
income countries, and it should expand its activities in the
field of energy and raw materials exploration.
5. New ways should be found to provide international capital,
including equity investment, to expand the production of raw
materials in the less developed countries. Among the more
promising is the proposed Energy and Minerals Fund of the
Inter-American Development Bank.
6. The International Centre for the Settlement of Investment
Disputes is a useful, but limited, way to deal with investment
disputes. However, it is unlikely that the Latin American countries will participate in its programs in the foreseeable future.

7. If a UN-sponsored code of conduct for transnational corporations is adopted it should include, in addition to prohibitions of misconduct by international corporations, guarantees of fair treatment of foreign investors by host governments and accounting standards for international reporting on taxation.
8. The United States legislative sanctions against uncompensated expropriations are not a particularly effective way to deter such actions. More important deterrents are the adverse effects of expropriation on access to international loans, Export-Import Bank guarantees, and the renegotiation of international debts.
9. The State Department's insistence on the "prompt, adequate, and effective" compensation standard is unrealistic and impractical. "Fair and equitable" compensation is more in keeping with actual international practice and with the moral and economic requirements of international law. The use of outside evaluation teams may help to bridge the gap between the estimates of the foreign investor and of the host country on the value of the assets involved.
10. Multinational corporations have developed their own defense strategies against expropriation, and beyond the basic requirements of diplomatic protection, they do not need special, coercive government-imposed sanctions. The United States embassy can play a useful role, however, as mediator in investment disputes, and should attempt to anticipate problems before they arise.

NATIONALIZATION AND THE NEW INTERNATIONAL ECONOMIC ORDER

Except for the Marxist left, the appeal of nationalization has diminished as an easy solution for the transformation of the economies and societies of less developed nations. Social justice does not necessarily improve after nationalization although some groups, such as bureaucrats and organized labor in the nationalized industry may be better off. Indeed, where nationalization is not accompanied by other changes in society, the classes and groups that were dominant before the expropriation are even stronger thereafter. If expropriation with little or no compensation is seen as one of the ways to achieve a massive transfer of resources from the rich to the poor, the cases examined here have shown that it is not an effective way to do so, and that it may even be counterproductive.

If the benefits of nationalization are not great, the cost of nationalization is less than in the past. Compensation can be paid from international loans, and there are alternative, although usually more expensive, ways of achieving access to technology, marketing, and managerial skills. In particular cases involving international cartels making large profits such as petroleum, nationalization, at a certain point, becomes almost a political necessity.

Since 1973, the structure of international economic relations has been substantially modified. The non-oil-producing countries of the Third World have increased their international indebtedness, and there has been a perceptible reduction in the rate of expansion of international investment.[18] Nationalization of natural resources and increased domestic controls on foreign investment in manufacturing have contributed to this process. Apologists for the multinational corporation may yearn for the freedom and security guaranteed by the Pax Americana for the 25 years following World War II. But that era has ended, and a new period of intensified bargaining involving the multinational corporation, the host and home governments, and various international forums and institutions has begun. Solutions can be achieved but not by appeals to principles that are not shared by the participants in the process. Rather, the common benefits of relatively stable economic relations, in which foreign investment plays an important, although relatively smaller part, should prevent a breakdown of the system into warring economic nationalisms. Differences between the North and the South on the virtues of the free market and the role of the multinational corporation are not likely to disappear. But the skills that the international corporation can mobilize and move across the globe will still be attractive even to radical developing countries, as has been demonstrated by the opening of China to joint ventures with foreign investors. As in the case of earlier predictions of the triumph of the multinational corporation over national sovereignty, the reports of the imminent demise of the multinational corporation, through mass expropriation, are greatly exaggerated.

Reference Matter

Notes

Chapter 1

1   On the 1962 resolution, see Stephen M. Schwebel, "The Story of the U.N.'s Declaration on Permanent Sovereignty over Natural Resources," *ABA Journal* 49 (1963): 463–69. For the United States position, see Frank G. Dawson and Burns Weston, "Prompt, Adequate, and Effective: A Universal Standard of Compensation?" *Fordham Law Review* 30 (1962): 727–58. The 1962 resolution was considerably weaker than a similar resolution adopted ten years earlier, which recommended to all member states "in the exercise of their right freely to use and exploit their natural wealth and resources . . . to have due regard, consistently with their sovereignty, to the need for maintaining the flow of capital in conditions of security, mutual confidence, and economic cooperation among nations."

2   Some writers distinguish between "expropriation," defined as a government take-over of one or more individual firms, and "nationalization," which involves the establishment of public control over an entire area of economic activity. In practice, however, the terms are used interchangeably although the word expropriation stresses the taking of private (*propius*) property, while nationalization emphasizes the transfer to national ownership. See J. Frederick Truitt, *Expropriation of Private Foreign Investments* (Bloomington: University of Indiana Press, 1974), pp. 5–6.

3   Fair market or going concern value is defined as "the price a willing buyer would pay a willing seller at the time of the loss, uninfluenced by the circumstances of state interference." It may or may not include intangibles, such as goodwill or company reputation. Book value is "the owner's equity in the enterprise," that is, "the amount that remains after deducting the liabilities from the assets of a com-

341

pany in the amounts that these items appear on the company's books of account." Assets are usually recorded at the price originally paid for them, and liabilities include discounted long-term obligations and amortization. It is obvious that depreciation, inflation, and general market conditions will usually make fair market value much higher than book value. Hence, nationalizing governments typically base compensation offers on book value. Other methods for evaluating properties include replacement cost minus depreciation, capitalization of average production, or of past or future profits over a given period of years, and declared or assessed tax value (usually the same as book value for industry but often a very low figure for land). See the essays in Richard B. Lillich, ed., *The Valuation of Nationalized Property in International Law* (Charlottesville: University of Virginia Press, 1972).

4   Bernard Nossiter, "The New Economic Order—A Dialogue of the Deaf," *Washington Post*, 17 October 1975, p. A24; Karl Brunner, "The New International Economic Order," *Orbis* 20 (1976): pp. 106-7.

5   American response to the proposals for a New International Economic Order was not uniformly hostile. The Overseas Development Council called for "new modes of beneficial cooperation" rather than "attempts to win points in a debate about the inequities of the world"; see *The United States and World Development* (Washington, D.C.: Overseas Development Council, 1976), p. x. Also see Jack N. Behrman, *Toward a New International Economic Order* (Paris: Atlantic Institute, 1974). This monograph, written for the Atlantic Institute, described current United States foreign economic policy toward the Third World as "irrelevant" because it was solely concerned with "fairness . . . defined as playing by the rules, and not designing the game so that it is a contest among relatively equal participants."

6   For a discussion of the status of nationalization in international law, see Eduardo Novoa, *Nacionalización y Recuperación de Recursos Naturales ante la Ley Internacional* (México City: Fondo de Cultura Economica, 1974), pp. 80 ff.; Samy Friedman, *Expropriation in International Law* (London: Stevens, 1953), pp. 207, 253; Konstantin Katsarov, *The Theory of Nationalisation* (The Hague: Martin Nijhoff, 1964), p. 339. Both Katsarov and Novoa attempt to distinguish between expropriation, as a specific and limited taking, and nationalization, as a general economic measure that by its broader character does not require full compensation. For similar

views by other writers, see Dawson and Weston, "Prompt, Adequate, and Effective," pp. 735–36.

7   The best known discussion of the adverse effects of foreign private investment is Richard J. Barnet and Ronald Müller, *Global Reach: The Power of the Multinational Corporations* (New York: Simon and Schuster, 1974). It is strongly influenced by Latin American writers, and much of the evidence it cites is drawn from Latin American sources. For a positive view of the benefits of foreign investment, see Raymond Vernon, *Sovereignty at Bay* (New York: Basic Books, 1971), and his *Storm Over the Multinationals* (Cambridge: Harvard University Press, 1977). The UN Report by the Group of Eminent Persons, *The Impact of Multinational Corporations on Development and on International Relations* (New York: United Nations, 1974), and the debate it produced are probably the best single summary of the criticisms of direct foreign investment and the replies by its defenders. For an influential earlier criticism, see Hans Singer, "The Distribution of Gains between Investing and Borrowing Countries," *American Economic Review* (1950): 474–85.

Chapter 2

1   Emmerich de Vattel, *The Law of Nations*, book 2, (London: G. G. Robinson, 1797), chap. 6.

2   On the history of the Calvo Doctrine and the Calvo Clause, see Donald R. Shea, *The Calvo Clause* (Minneapolis: University of Minnesota Press, 1955). For its role in inter-American meetings, see Gordon Connell-Smith, *The United States and Latin America* (New York: John Wiley, 1974).

3   Shea, *Calvo Clause*, p. 20; L. Oppenheim, *International Law*, 8th ed. (London: Longmans, 1955), p. 309.

4   See John Locke, *Second Treatise of Civil Government* 3rd ed. (Oxford: Blackwell, 1966), chap. 5.

5   There is a large literature dealing with the influence of the Spanish colonial legacy on contemporary Latin American politics and economics. For a good, short discussion, see William Glade, *The Latin American Economies* (New York: Krieger, 1969), chap. 2. In many books and articles Louis Hartz and Richard Morse have discussed the respective influence of John Locke and Spanish scholasticism on North and South America. See, for example, their respective chapters in Louis Hartz, ed., *The Founding of New States* (New

York: Harcourt, Brace, 1964). In addition, Alfred Stepan, *State and Society, Peru in Comparative Perspective* (Princeton, N.J.: Princeton University Press, 1978), traces the influence of "organic statism" from Aristotle and St. Thomas to contemporary Latin America. For related discussions of Latin American "corporatism" emphasizing the role of the state in organizing society and the economy in Latin America, see Frederick Pike and Thomas Stritch, eds., *The New Corporatism* (South Bend, Ind.: Notre Dame University Press, 1974), and James Malloy, ed., *Authoritarianism and Corporatism in Latin America* (Pittsburgh, Pa.: University of Pittsburgh Press, 1977).

6   On Latin American ideologies, see Miguel Jorrin and John Martz, *Latin American Political Thought and Ideology* (Chapel Hill: University of North Carolina Press, 1970); Harold C. Davis, *Latin American Thought* (Baton Rouge: Louisiana State University Press, 1972); and Paul E. Sigmund, ed., *The Ideologies of the Developing Nations*, 2nd rev. ed. (New York: Praeger, 1972).

7   For discussions on the extent to which compensation provisions of Latin American agrarian reform laws can be described as confiscatory, see Kenneth L. Karst, "Latin American Land Reform: The Uses of Confiscation," *Michigan Law Review*, 63 (1964): 327ff. Karst concludes that "one way or another, every agrarian reform is confiscatory" but that "the myth of compensation" serves a positive social and economic function (pp. 369–71). This same point is discussed in Kenneth L. Karst and Keith S. Rosen, *Law and Development in Latin America* (Berkeley, Calif.: University of California Press, 1975), chap. 3.

8   On ECLA structuralism, see Albert O. Hirschman, *Latin American Issues, Essays and Comments* (New York: Twentieth Century Fund, 1961), pp. 69–123.

9   For an early (1928), influential Marxist statement, see José Carlos Mariátegui, *Seven Interpretive Essays on Peruvian Reality* (Austin: University of Texas Press, 1971). Recent evaluations of the theory include Benjamin Cohen, *The Question of Imperialism* (New York: Basic Books, 1973), and Steven J. Rosen and James R. Kurth, eds., *Testing Theories of Imperialism* (Lexington, Mass.: Lexington Books, 1974).

10   Victor Raúl Haya de la Torre, "A Donde Va Indoamerica?," in *The Ideologies of the Developing Nations*, rev. ed., ed. and trans., Paul E. Sigmund (New York: Praeger, 1967), p. 344.

11   There is an enormous literature on *dependencia*. The most influential

Latin American writers of the radical wing of the dependency school are Teotonio dos Santos, "The Structure of Dependence," *American Economic Review*, May 1970, pp. 231–36; André Gunder Frank, *Capitalism and Underdevelopment in Latin America* (New York: Monthly Review Press, 1967) — Frank was a Canadian writing in Chile; and Anibal Quijano, "Imperialism and International Relations in Latin America," in *Latin America and the United States: The Changing Political Realities*, ed. Julio Cotler and Richard Fagen, (Stanford, Calif.: Stanford University Press, 1974). The best-known reformist *dependentistas* are Osvaldo Sunkel, "National Development Policy and External Dependence in Latin America," *The Journal of Development Studies*, October 1969, and "Big Business and Dependencia, a Latin American View," *Foreign Affairs*, April 1972; Celso Furtado, "Dependencia Externa y Teoria Economica," *Trimestre Economico*, April-June, 1971; and Helio Jaguaribe, *La Dependencia Politico-Economico de America Latina* (Mexico: 1970). Fernando Enrique Cardoso seems to have moved from the radical position in *Dependencia y Desarrollo en America Latina* (Mexico City: Siglo Veintiuno Editores, 1969) to a reformist position in "Associated Dependent Development," in *Authoritarian Brazil*, ed. Alfred Stepan (New Haven, Conn.: Yale University Press, 1973), pp. 142–76, especially because of his acceptance of a positive effect of foreign investment on economic growth. For reviews of the dependency writers, see Ronald Chilcote, "A Critical Synthesis of the Dependency Literature," *Latin American Perspectives*, Spring 1974; C. Richard Bath and Dilmus D. James, "Dependency Analysis of Latin America," *Latin American Research Review*, II (1976): 3–58; and Ronald Chilcote, "A Question of Dependencia," *Latin American Research Review*, 12 (1978): 55–68. The most persuasive criticisms of dependency theory (that dependency characterizes communist as well as capitalist international economic relations, that foreign investment is not always and everywhere detrimental to development, and that any underdeveloped country, whether capitalist or socialist, will be involved in economic relationships with more developed economies in which it will have varying degrees of bargaining power) are developed in David Ray, "The Dependency Model of Latin American Development: Three Basic Fallacies," *Journal of Inter-American Studies*, February 1973, pp. 4–20. Dependency theory is criticized from a Marxist point of view (for paying too much attention to international economic relations and not enough to internal class structures) in *Latin American Perspectives*, Fall 1976.

12 Quoted in Edward Weisband, *The Ideology of American Foreign Policy* (Beverly Hills: Sage Publications, 1973), p. 39.

13 The prevailing American hostility toward state intervention in international economic relations was summed up in an enumeration by Jacob Viner, of its undesirable consequences: ". . . the conversion of international trade from a predominantly competitive to a predominantly monopolistic basis; a marked increase in the potentiality of business disputes to generate international friction; the transfer of trade transactions from a status under which settlement of disputes by routine judicial process is readily feasible . . . to a status where . . . by inherent necessity the possibility of resort to force in case of an unsatisfactory outcome of the diplomatic negotiations will be a trump card in the hands of the powerful countries. . . ." Jacob Viner, *International Economics* (Glencoe, Ill.: Free Press, 1952) p. 221. On the shared assumption of American policymakers and social scientists between 1947 and 1965 that economic, social, and political development were mutually reinforcing ("All Good Things Go Together"), see Robert Packenham, *Liberal America and the Third World* (Princeton, N.J.: Princeton University Press, 1973), chap. 7.

14 The emergence of public interest lobbies in Washington concerned with Latin America and generally critical of the role of the multinationals there was particularly evident in the United States reaction to the 1973 Chilean coup. Congressional cutoffs of aid to a number of Latin American military regimes were partially attributable to lobbying by these groups and antedated, by at least two years, the Carter administration's emphasis on human rights.

15 Four different approaches have been taken in the literature on nationalization. The economists have studied its economic effects in terms of international or domestic redistribution of income, see Harry G. Johnson, ed., *Economic Nationalism in Old and New States* (Chicago: University of Chicago Press, 1967), and Martin Bronfenbrenner, "The Appeal of Confiscation in Economic Development," *Economic Development and Cultural Change*, April 1955, pp. 201-18. International lawyers have discussed appropriate standards of compensation, see Richard S. Mill and Roland J. Stanger, eds., *Essays on Expropriation* (Columbus: Ohio State University Press, 1967); Richard A. Falk and Cyril E. Black, eds., *The Future of the International Legal Order,* vol. 2, *Wealth and Resources* (Princeton, N.J.: Princeton University Press, 1970); as well as the many volumes edited by Richard S. Lillich on the topic.

Political economists have analyzed the relations between host countries and foreign investors using a game theory approach, see the writings of Charles Kindleberger, Raymond Vernon, and Raymond Mikesell, as well as the application of their theories in two useful case studies, Theodore Moran, *Multinational Corporations and the Politics of Dependence: Copper in Chile* (Princeton, N.J.: Princeton University Press, 1974), and Franklin Tugwell, *The Politics of Oil in Venezuela* (Stanford, Calif.: Stanford University Press, 1975). United States government policy aimed at the protection of American investment has been evaluated in Robert H. Swansbrough, *The Embattled Colossus* (Gainesville: University of Florida Press, 1976), and Cole Blasier, *The Hovering Giant: U.S. Responses to Revolutionary Change in Latin America* (Pittsburgh, Pa.: University of Pittsburgh Press, 1976).

Chapter 3

1 Harry K. Wright, *Foreign Enterprise in Mexico* (Chapel Hill: University of North Carolina Press, 1971), pp. 55, 57, 59. The most detailed discussion of the legal background in Spanish law of mining legislation appears in Merrill Rippy, *Oil and the Mexican Revolution* (Leiden: E. J. Brill, 1972), chap. 2.

2 For figures on Mexican petroleum production, see Wendell C. Gordon, *The Expropriation of Foreign-Owned Property in Mexico* (1941; reprint ed., Westport, Conn.: Greenwood Press, 1975); pp. 53-54, and Lorenzo Meyer, *Mexico and the United States in the Oil Controversy, 1917-1942* (Austin: University of Texas Press, 1977), pp. 8-9. The Pearson and Doheny holdings were later sold to Royal Dutch Shell and Standard Oil of Indiana. (The latter properties were later acquired by Standard of New Jersey.)

3 E. V. Niemeyer, Jr., *The Revolution at Queretaro: The Mexican Constitutional Convention of 1916-17* (Austin: University of Texas Press, 1974), p. 145. See chaps. 4 and 5 for accounts of the evolution of Article 27. For a dissenting Mexican view that considers Article 27 as a legitimation of "the systematic despoliation" of the owners of property, see Alfredo B. Cuellar, *Expropiacion y Crisis en Mexico* (Mexico: Universidad Autonoma, 1940), chap. 9.

4 Clifford Trow, "Woodrow Wilson and the Mexican Interventionist Movement of 1919," *Journal of American History*, 1 (June 1971), 46-72; Meyer, *Mexico and the United States in the Oil Controversy*, pp. 69-70. Shortly after taking office, in 1913, Wilson had

denounced the domination by "foreign capitalists" of the domestic affairs of Latin American countries, and he was sympathetic to agrarian reform and national self-determination in such areas as the development of natural resources, but he does not seem to have seen the contradiction between these views and the continuing United States pressure in defense of American property rights.

5   See Meyer, *Mexico and the United States in the Oil Controversy*, pp. 86–89.

6   The text of the law is printed in Leopoldo Gonzalez Aguayo, *La Nacionalización de Bienes Extranjeros en América Latina*, 2 vols. (Mexico City: Universidad National Autónoma, 1969), pp. 222–27.

7   The text of the decree is reproduced in Jesús Silva Herzog, *Historia de la Expropiación Petrolera* (México: Cuadernos Americanos, 1963), pp. 92–95. Silva Herzog was a member of the committee of experts.

8   J. Richard Powell, *The Mexican Petroleum Industry, 1938–1950* (Berkeley, Calif.: University of California Press, 1956), p. 26.

9   Meyer, *Mexico and the United States in the Oil Controversy*, pp. 180–81. John Morton Blum, *From the Morgenthau Diaries, Years of Crisis, 1928–1938* (Boston: Houghton Mifflin, 1959), pp. 493–97.

10   Josephus Daniels, *Shirt-Sleeve Diplomat* (Chapel Hill: University of North Carolina Press, 1947), pp. 230–34.

11   U.S., Department of State, *Foreign Relations of the United States, 1938,* vol. 5, (Washington, D.C.: Government Printing Office, 1938), pp. 676–78. For an account of the differences between Hull, on the one side, and Morgenthau and Daniels, on the other, see E. David Cronon, *Josephus Daniels in Mexico* (Madison: University of Wisconsin Press, 1960), chaps. 8–9. For United States silver purchases from Mexico, see U.S., Department of Commerce, Bureau of Foreign and Domestic Commerce, *Commerce and Navigation of the United States for the Calendar Year 1937* (Washington, D.C.: Government Printing Office, 1938), p. 748; U.S., Department of Commerce, Bureau of Foreign and Domestic Commerce, *Commerce and Navigation of the United States for the Calendar Year 1938* (Washington, D.C.: Government Printing Office, 1940), p. 923.

12   See Cronon, *Josephus Daniels*, pp. 190–91. According to the memoirs of Eduardo Suarez, Mexico's finance minister at the time, President Cárdenas feared possible United States armed intervention on behalf of the companies and planned to resign as president if it took place, *Comentarios y Recuerdos* (Mexico City: Porrua, 1977), p. 201.

13 Powell, *The Mexican Petroleum Industry*, pp. 112-15; Meyer, *Mexico and the United States in the Oil Controversy*, p. 325; Rippy, *Oil and the Mexican Revolution*, pp. 254-57; Suarez, *Comentarios*, pp. 211-15.

14 For details on the compensation negotiations, see Juan Barona Lobato, *La Expropiación Petrolera*, 2 vols. (Tlatelolco: Secretaría de Relaciones Exteriores, 1974), and Suarez, *Comentarios*, chaps. 15-16. The texts of the agreements settling the compensation issue appear in Leopoldo Gonzalez Aguayo, *La Nacionalización*, pp. 262-74. The conflicting evaluations appear in Samuel Flagg Bemis, *The Latin American Policy of the United States* (New York: Harcourt, Brace, 1943), p. 347.

15 Powell, *The Mexican Petroleum Industry*, pp. 39, 79; Rippy, *Oil and the Mexican Revolution*, p. 264.

16 Meyer, *Mexico and the United States in the Oil Controversy*, p. 178-79; Rippy, *Oil and the Mexican Revolution*, p. 269; Powell, *The Mexican Petroleum Industry*, p. 130.

17 See Antonio Bermúdez, *The Mexican National Petroleum Industry* (Stanford, Calif.: Hispanic American Institute, 1963).

18 Powell, *The Mexican Petroleum Industry*, pp. 166-67.

19 Powell, *The Mexican Petroleum Industry*, pp. 48-49; Bermúdez, *Mexican National Petroleum*, pp. 33-34, 180; B. Sepulveda, Olga Pellicer, and Lorenzo Meyer, *Las Empresas Transnacionales en Mexico* (Mexico City: Colegio de Mexico, 1974), chap. 3.

20 Bermúdez, *Mexican National Petroleum*, p. 257.

21 On the problems of union domination, featherbedding and corruption in Pemex, see Antonio Bermúdez, *La Política Petrolera Mexicana* (Mexico City, Mexico: Joaquin Ortiz, 1976), chap. 11.

22 See Wright, *Foreign Enterprise in Mexico*, pp. 133-40, 172-74. and *Mexican Newsletter*, 58 (1975): 4-5. According to Wright, beginning in 1962 a different type of "Mexicanization" was applied to the automobile industry — 60 percent of production costs were to be incurred in Mexico. On the take-over of the sulphur industry, see Miguel Wionczek, "A Foreign-Owned Export-Oriented Enclave in a Rapidly Industrializing Economy: Sulphur Mining in Mexico," in *Foreign Investment in the Petroleum and Mineral Industries*, ed. Raymond F. Mikesell (Baltimore: Johns Hopkins, 1971), pp. 264-311.

23 *Mexican Newsletter*, 30 (1975): 7. In early 1978, after it was discovered that the Las Truchas steel complex had incurred over $1 billion in losses, President Lopez Portillo reorganized the state steel holdings.

24 For defenses of the foreign investor, see Jose Antonio Fernandez and Herbert May, *The Effects of Foreign Investment on Mexico* (New York: Council of the Americas, 1971), and Harry Robinson and Timothy Smith, *The Impact of Foreign Investment on the Mexican Economy* (Stanford, Calif.: Stanford Research Institute, 1976). For criticisms, see Richard S. Newfarmer and Willard F. Mueller, *Multinational Corporations in Brazil and Mexico*, Report to the Subcommittee on Multinational Corporations of the Senate Foreign Relations Committee (Washington, D.C.: Government Printing Office, 1975); John M. Connor and Willard F. Mueller, *Market Power and Profitability of Multinational Corporations in Brazil and Mexico*, Report to the Subcommittee on Foreign Economic Policy of the Senate Foreign Relations Committee (Washington, D.C.: Government Printing Office, 1977); and Fernando Fajnzylber and Trinidad Martínez, *Las Empresas Transnacionales* (Mexico City: Fondo de Cultura Economica, 1976). Foreign investment accounts for only about 5 percent of gross fixed investment in Mexico, but in 1970 foreign companies were responsible for about one-quarter of Mexican manufacturing and for much higher percentages in industries such as chemicals.

25 The legislation on technology, patents, and trademark payments lists fourteen reasons why the government may refuse to approve such contracts. In his last report to the Mexican Congress, in September 1976, President Echeverria claimed that the new registration procedures had saved Mexico 4–8 billion pesos in foreign payments between 1973 and 1976. (The estimate seems to have included all payments for the life of the contracts.) Because of business protests, the implementation of a 1976 law requiring the Mexicanization of foreign trademarks has been postponed.

26 On the effects of the 1973 laws, see Richard D. Robinson, *National Control of Foreign Business Entry* (New York: Praeger, 1976), chap. 6. Robinson states that in 1974, 74 out of 103 requests for exemptions from the percentage requirements were approved. The United States Chamber of Commerce in Mexico reported a continuing decline in United States investment in Mexico in 1977, see *Latin American Economic Report*, 7 (May 1978).

27 *El Mercado de Valores*, 24 January 1977. Further steps taken in April 1978 are described in *Mercado de Valores*, 24 April 1978.

28 See testimony by Redvers Opie in U.S., Congress, Joint Economic Committee, Subcommittee on Inter-American Relations, *Recent Developments in Mexico and their Economic Implications for the*

U.S. (Washington, D.C.: Government Printing Office, 1977), p. 30.

29 For critical views of Pemex, see Powell, *The Mexican Petroleum Industry*, and Eric N. Baklanoff, *Expropriation of U.S. Investments in Cuba, Mexico and Chile* (New York: Praeger, 1975). Favorable views appear in Clark Reynolds, *The Mexican Economy* (New Haven, Conn.: Yale University Press, 1970); Leopoldo Solis, *La Realidad Económica Mexicana* (Mexico City: Siglo Ventiuno, 1970); and Antonio Bermúdez, *La Política Petrolera Mexicana*, (Mexico City: Joaquín Ortiz, 1976).

30 A Mexican economist has calculated that the price subsidies in the public sector, especially the low price of petroleum products, in 1977 amounted to 123 billion pesos, substantially more than the budget deficit, exclusive of debt amortization. (See *Visión*, January 13, 1978, p. 35).

Chapter 4

1 For testimony and documentation on United States policy toward Iran in the early 1950s, see U.S., Congress, Senate, Committee on Foreign Relations, Subcommittee on Multinational Corporations, *Multinational Corporations and U.S. Foreign Policy*, 93rd Cong. 2nd sess., February-March 1974, parts 7, 8.

2 The 1952 arms shipment is described in Herbert Matthews, *A World in Revolution* (New York: Charles Scribner's, 1972), pp. 262–64. Matthews's source was Edward G. Miller, assistant secretary of state for Latin America in 1953. The State Department memorandum is in the Dulles Papers at Princeton. The estimates on the date of the decision to attempt to overthrow Arbenz were made by E. Howard Hunt and Richard Bissell in personal interviews with Richard Immerman in 1977. See Richard Immerman, "Guatemala and the United States, 1954: A Cold War Strategy for Americans," (Ph.D. diss. Boston College, 1978), pp. 243–52, 257, 305. Immerman argues that cold war considerations were dominant in the decision, and that the United Fruit expropriations were viewed as simply further evidence of the Communist orientation of the Arbenz government. On the politics of Guatemala at the time, see Ronald Schneider, *Communism in Guatemala* (New York: Frederick A. Praeger, 1958). For new documentation on the United States role based on Freedom of Information files, see Stephen Schlesinger, "How Dulles Worked the Coup d'Etat," *The Nation*, 227 (1978): 426, 439–44. Guatemala had not readjusted its tax assess-

ments since 1935, despite the company's submission of much higher appraisals in 1948 and 1951. See U.S., Department of State, *Bulletin*, September 14, 1953, pp. 357–60.

3 The most influential book published in Latin America by a member of the Arbenz government was Guillermo Toriello, *La Batalla de Guatemala* (Mexico: Cuadernos Americanos, 1955). See also Juan José Arevalo, *Guatemala: La democracia y el imperio* (Buenos Aires: Renacimiento, 1955), and Juan José Arevalo, *La fabula del tiburón y las sardinas* (Buenos Aires: Meridión, 1956), available in English as *The Shark and the Sardines* (New York: Lyle Stuart, 1960).

4 See Andrew Sinclair, *Che Guevara* (New York: Viking, 1970); Ricardo Rojo, *My Friend Che* (New York: Dial Press, 1968); Hugo Gambini, *El Che Guevara* (Buenos Aires: Paidos, 1968); John Gerassi, ed., *Venceremos, The Speeches and Writings of Che Guevara* (New York: Simon and Schuster, 1969).

5 The picture is reproduced in Jules Dubois, *Fidel Castro* (New York: Bobbs Merrill, 1959). For Cuban views of the rule of United States business interests in the 1950s based on company files, which indicate that at least two major American-owned companies — Esso and the Cuban Electric Company — were losing money in 1958 see Julio le Reverend, ed., *Los Monopolios Norteamericanos en Cuba* (Havana: Instituto Cubano del Libro, 1973), pp. 72, 150. Barbara Walters reported in her television interview with Castro on June 9, 1977, that "Castro insists he has been a Communist since his university days," but this goes counter to contemporary evidence.

6 Earle E. T. Smith, *The Fourth Floor* (New York: Random House, 1962). The title of the book refers to the location of the Latin American policymakers in the State Department who, Smith claims, ignored his repeated warnings of Castro's Communist sympathies.

7 Hugh Thomas, *Cuba, the Pursuit of Freedom* (New York: Harper and Row, 1971), p. 1090.

8 The literature on United States-Cuban relations between 1959 and 1961 is extensive. Besides Ambassador Smith's book and Edward Boorstein, *The Economic Transformation of Cuba* (New York: Monthly Review Press, 1968), quoted in the chapter epigraph, who represent the polar positions noted above, evaluations of United States and Cuban policies between 1959 and 1961 appear in James O'Connor, *The Origins of Socialism in Cuba* (Ithaca: Cornell University Press, 1970), p. 5. "Cuban socialism was inevitable in the sense that it was necessary if the island was to be rescued from per-

manent economic stagnation, social backwardness and degradation, and political do-nothingism and corruption." Maurice Zeitlin and Robert Scheer, *Cuba, Tragedy in Our Hemisphere* (New York: Grove Press, 1963), p. 207. ". . . the United States has undertaken to achieve three policy goals simultaneously: to defend United States private investment abroad, to further its position in the cold war, and to extend our forms of freedom. . . . The attempt to achieve all three goals simultaneously is an important reason for the ineffectiveness of U.S. policy in achieving any of them." Theodore Draper, *Castro's Revolution, Myths and Realities* (New York: Frederick A. Praeger, 1962), p. 15. "Was the Cuban revolution betrayed? The answer obviously depends on what revolution one has in mind – the revolution that Castro promised before taking power or the one he has made since taking power." Andrés Suárez, *Cuba: Castroism and Communism, 1959–1966* (Cambridge, Mass.: MIT Press, 1967), p. 156. "[Castro was] a consummate opportunist, gifted, it is true, with the audacity and courage to act with the most exaggerated radicalism if this serves his purposes." Philip Bonsal, *Cuba, Castro, and the United States* (Pittsburgh, Pa.: University of Pittsburgh Press, 1971), p. 156. ". . . the reluctant and cautious Russians [were] forced into the Revolution's own warmly welcoming arms by the drastic actions of the Americans."

9   Welles three times asked the Roosevelt administration to intervene militarily in order to maintain order, but in keeping with the new administration's altered attitude toward intervention he was refused. He did, however, persuade the United States government to withhold recognition from the Grau government on the grounds that it did not enjoy general support and could not maintain order. Hugh Thomas comments on his hostility to Grau: "He was clearly less concerned about U.S. property or his physical security, than to back his friends (the moderate Cespedes government which had succeeded that of Machado), and he seems to have genuinely confused their interest with the will of the people." Thomas, *Cuba: The Pursuit of Freedom*, p. 672.

10 *Washington Post,* 6 March 1977.

11 This account is based principally on Thomas, *Cuba: The Pursuit of Freedom*, pp. 1203–14, and Rufo López-Fresquet, *My Fourteen Months with Castro* (Cleveland: World Publishing, 1966), chap. 17. Nixon's account of his meeting with Castro appears in *Six Crises* (New York: Pyramid, 1968), pp. 351–52. Jorge Dominguez, *Cuba: Order and Revolution* (Cambridge, Mass.: Harvard University

Press, 1978), chap. 7, believes that Castro's instructions to his economic advisors not to accept United States aid if offered indicated that he decided at this time against a policy of cooperation with the United States.

12 The Castro speech appears in Paul E. Sigmund, ed., *The Ideologies of the Developing Nations*, rev. ed. (New York: Praeger, 1967), pp. 314–18.

13 See Bonsal, *Castro, Cuba, and the United States*, pp. 74–75, 95. The State Department note appears in U.S., Department of State, *Bulletin*, June 29, 1959, p. 958; see also p. 959 for a government note declining a Castro offer to sell 8 million tons of Cuban sugar to the United States at four cents a pound. After the 1960 nationalizations, the United States representative to the United Nations stated that the State Department insistence on prompt, adequate, and effective compensation had not been a demand for payment in cash, but only "government negotiation of the question of compensation in accordance with accepted principles of international law," *New York Times*, 15 October 1960.

14 See the *New York Times*, 10 January 1960, for a summary of the notes exchanged from June 1959 until January 1960. For the State Department press release concerning the exchanges see U.S., Department of State, *Bulletin*, February 1960, p. 158.

15 Telegram, U.S. Embassy, Havana, to Secretary of State, No. 2025, February 15, 1960 (declassified under Freedom of Information Act), p. 2.

16 *New York Times*, 10 March 1960.

17 U.S., Congress, Senate, Select Committee on Intelligence Activities, 94th Cong., 1st sess., *Alleged Assassination Plots Involving Foreign Leaders* (Washington, D.C.: Government Printing Office, 1975), pp. 93, 114. The report indicates that Eisenhower was not merely approving a contingency plan but a broader decision to attempt Castro's overthrow. For evidence by a participant in the operation that "the Guatemala scenario" was used as a model, and that planning for an invasion in November or early December of 1960 began immediately after Eisenhower's decision, see David Atlee Phillips, *The Night Watch* (New York: Atheneum, 1977), p. 86. According to Gordon Gray, Eisenhower's national security assistant at the time, the decision was precipitated by a request in February from Allen Dulles for permission to carry out a program of sabotage of Cuban sugar mills (personal conversation, May 25, 1978). The Senate Select Committee does not seem to have found any in-

dication that money and material were provided to anti-Castro exiles before January 1960. In March the CIA began to work on operations designed to discredit Castro (e.g., hallucinatory chemicals, depilatories in his shoes) and beginning in July 1960, the agency initiated the first of a number of attempts on Castro's life.

18 The Guatemalan example was cited again by Richard Nixon in the pre-election debates with John Kennedy in October 1960. Replying to Kennedy's charge that the administration should arm the Cuban freedom fighters (as they were, in fact, doing) Nixon said, "What can we do? We can do what we did in Guatemala. There was a Communist dictatorship that we inherited from the previous administration. We quarantined Mr. Arbenz. The result was that the Guatemalan people themselves eventually rose up and they threw him out." On the initial Soviet reluctance to become too closely identified with Castro, see Edward Gonzalez, "Castro's Revolution, Cuban Communist Appeals, and the Soviet Response", *World Politics*, October 1968, pp. 39–68.

19 Nikita Khrushchev, *Khrushchev Remembers*, vol. 1 (Boston: Little, Brown, 1970), p. 490.

20 See Suárez, *Cuba: Castroism and Communism*, pp. 107–12.

21 Archibald Ritter, *The Economic Development of Revolutionary Cuba* (New York: Praeger, 1974), p. 101. In 1962, Cuba also nationalized all private clothing and hardware stores. In 1968, all remaining private businesses were nationalized.

22 Castro called the revolution socialist on April 16, 1961, at the funeral of those killed in the pre–Bay of Pigs air raids, but the official proclamation on the subject took place on May 1. See Suárez, *Cuba: Castroism and Communism*, pp. 124–30. See also, Draper, *Castro's Revolution*, p. 59.

23 "If the United Fruit matter were settled, if they gave a gold piece for every banana, the problem would remain just as it is today as far as the presence of Communist infiltration in Guatemala is concerned." John Foster Dulles, *American Foreign Policy, 1950–1955, Basic Documents*, vol. 1 (Washington, D.C.: Government Printing Office, 1957) p. 1310.

24 Those who argue that Castro always intended to radicalize his revolution can point to his approach to Betancourt in February 1959 and to statements he has made concerning his need to conceal his true intentions in order to get support. However, his public and private attitudes and statements in the first six to nine months in power seem to argue against this—unless he is a person of extraordinary duplicity.

25 For details on the economic adjustments, see Boorstein, *Economic Transformation of Cuba.*

26 Carmelo Mesa-Lago, ed., *Revolutionary Change in Cuba* (Pittsburgh, Pa.: University of Pittsburgh Press, 1971), p. 214.

27 For figures on the Cuban balance of trade see Eric Baklanoff, "International Economic Relations," in *Revolutionary Change in Cuba,* ed. Carmelo Mesa-Lago (Pittsburgh, Pa.: University of Pittsburgh Press, 1971), pp. 266-67.

28 In the speech Castro said, "We understand the need to go to the aid — even with troops — of a fraternal country to confront the schemes of the imperialists," in *Granma* (English weekly edition) August 25, 1968. For evidence of the Soviet petroleum slowdown, see Castro's discussion of Cuba's petroleum shortage and the introduction of gasoline rationing because the Soviet Union's "present possibilities of providing us fuel . . . are limited," in *Granma* (English weekly edition) January 7, 1968, pp. 3-4. For the 1967 polemic between Castro and the Latin American Communist parties and criticism of him in *Pravda,* see Paul E. Sigmund, ed., *Models of Political Change in Latin America* (New York: Praeger, 1970), pp. 101-15, 250-54. The split is analyzed in D. Bruce Jackson, *Castro, The Kremlin, and Communism in Latin America* (Baltimore: Johns Hopkins, 1969). The critics of Castro's policy included René Dumont, *Cuba, Est-Il Socialiste?* (Paris: Editions du Seuil, 1970); K. S. Karol, *Guerrillas in Power* (New York: Hill and Wang, 1970); Maurice Zeitlin, "Inside Cuba: Workers and the Revolution," *Ramparts* 8 (1970): 10-11, 14, 18-20, 66-78; and Leo Huberman and Paul Sweezy, *Socialism in Cuba* (New York: Monthly Review Press, 1969).

29 The July 26, 1970 speech is printed in full in *The New York Review of Books,* 24 September 1970. For an illuminating instance of the centralization of decisionmaking see the amusing eyewitness account of the rise and fall of a Castro-sponsored new method of cattle feeding in Maurice Halpern, "Looking Back at Fidel," *Worldview,* 19 (1976): 20-22.

30 *Granma* (Havana edition), November 17, 1973; Carmelo Mesa-Lago, *Cuba in the 1970's* (Albuquerque: University of New Mexico Press, 1974), pp. 72-85; Marifeli Perez-Stable, "Institutionalization and Workers' Response," *Cuban Studies* 6 (1976): 31-54.

31 The sources for the statistical data in the last two paragraphs are the following papers delivered at "The Role of Cuba in World Affairs," University of Pittsburgh, November 15-17, 1976; Jorge

Perez-Lopez, "Cuban-Soviet Terms of Trade: Sugar and Petroleum"; Carmelo Mesa-Lago, "Present and Future of Cuba's Economy and International Economic Relations"; Cole Blasier, "The USSR in the Cuban-American Conflict"; and Jorge Dominguez, "The Cuban Armed Forces and International Order." Revised versions of these papers are published in Cole Blasier and Carmelo Mesa-Lago, eds., *Cuba in the World* (Pittsburgh, Pa.: University of Pittsburgh Press, 1979). The $12 billion figure is my own estimate. For the details of the December 1972 trade agreement with the USSR see Ritter, *Economic Development of Revolutionary Cuba*, pp. 334–37, and *Granma*, January 4, 1973.

32 U.S., Department of Commerce, Bureau of East-West Trade, *United States Commercial Relations with Cuba, A Survey*, August 1975 (Washington, D.C.: Government Printing Office, 1975).

33 See Rogers's testimony, September 23, 1975 in U.S., Congress, House, Committee on International Relations, Subcommittees on International Trade and Commerce and International Organizations, 94th Cong., 1st sess., *U.S. Trade Embargo of Cuba*, (Washington, D.C.: Government Printing Office, 1976), pp. 360–64. The October 1974 Linowitz Report has been published in *The Americas in a Changing World* (New York: Quadrangle Press, 1975), pp. 11–61, along with supporting papers including Jorge Dominguez, "U.S. Policy Towards Cuba: A Discussion of Options," pp. 112–31. For the argument that the Cuban approach to the United States was the result of Soviet pressure, see Roger Fontaine, *On Negotiating with Cuba* (Washington, D.C.: American Enterprise Institute for Public Policy Research, 1975), chap. 4.

34 See U.S., Congress, Code of Congressional and Administrative News, Laws of 93rd Cong., 2nd sess., P.L. 93-618, pp. 2290ff. The relevant Trade Act prohibitions are contained in sections 401, 402, 404, 405, 407, 409, and 502 of the law. The tariff advantages for Most Favored Nations relating to products exported by Cuba are 1.2 cents a pound for sugar, $3.25 a gallon for rum, $3.55 a pound for cigars, and twenty percent *ad valorem* for nickel. See U.S., Department of Commerce, *Commercial Relations with Cuba*, p. 61.

35 *New York Times*, 30 September 1967. In 1967 Cuba concluded compensation agreements with France and Switzerland and it is negotiating larger claims with Spain and Canada. The Swiss agreement ties compensation to the purchase of Cuban agricultural products. For the text of the two agreements see Richard B. Lillich and Burns H. Weston, *International Claims: Their Settlement by*

Lump Sum Agreements, 2 vols. (Charlottesville: University of Virginia Press, 1975), pp. 339–45. See also Michael W. Gordon, *The Cuban Nationalizations: The Demise of Foreign Private Property* (Buffalo: William S. Hein, 1976), chap 5. The final determinations on the Cuban claims are published in the Foreign Claims Settlement Commission, *1972 Annual Report* (Washington, D.C.: Government Printing Office, 1973), pp. 67–416. For a compensation scheme based on a Cuban agreement to pay a lump sum of $315 million or about one-sixth of the FCSC evaluation out of a fund made up of 20 percent of the income from Cuban sugar sales to the United States over a lengthy period, see U.S., Congress, House, 1975 Hearings, *U.S. Trade Embargo of Cuba*, p. 102 (testimony of Jorge Dominiguez).

36 See *Business Latin America*, 30 June 1976, for Cuban estimates of the desirable future division of Cuban trade as 40 percent with the Socialist countries, 30 percent with the United States, and 30 percent with other market economies. On the potential for, and obstacles to, United States trade with Cuba see mimeographed *Statement* of Arthur T. Downey, Deputy Assistant Secretary of Commerce for East-West Trade to the Subcommittee on International Trade and Commerce, House International Relations Committee, July 22, 1976. See U.S., Department of Commerce, *U.S. Trade Embargo with Cuba*, pp. 384–92 for statements by the representatives of Lone Star Industries, that its tax write-off on an investment valued at nearly $25 million by the Claims Settlement Commission was only $800,000 — owing to depreciation and nonrepatriation of reinvested profits since 1915. The Joint Corporate Committee on Cuban Claims surveyed its membership on their tax write-offs to arrive at the 1970 figure. See its pamphlet, *Questions and Answers about U.S. Claims against Cuba*, p. 5.

Chapter 5

1 See especially U.S., Congress, Senate, Select Committee on Intelligence Activities, *Covert Action in Chile, 1963–1973* (Washington, D.C.: Government Printing Office, 1975); U.S., Congress, Senate, Foreign Relations Committee, Subcommittee on Multinational Corporations, *Hearings on ITT and Chile, 1970–71*, 2 vols. (Washington, D.C.: Government Printing Office, 1973); U.S., Congress, House, Foreign Affairs Committee, Subcommittee on Interamerican Affairs, *Chile and the Allende Years* (Washington, D.C.: Gov-

ernment Printing Office, 1975). For an evaluation of the relationship of the external United States pressures to domestic economic and political factors in Chile, see Paul E. Sigmund, *The Overthrow of Allende and the Politics of Chile, 1964-1976,* (Pittsburgh, Pa.: University of Pittsburgh Press, 1977).

2 For accounts of the evolution of the Chilean copper industry, see Markos Mamalakis and Clark Reynolds, *Essays on the Chilean Economy,* (Homewood, Ill.: Irwin, 1965), pp. 205 ff.; Norman Girvan, *Corporate Imperialism: Conflict and Expropriation* (White Plains, N.Y.: M. E. Sharpe, 1976), chap. 2; and Markos Mamalakis, *The Growth and Structure of the Chilean Economy* (New Haven, Conn.: Yale University Press, 1976), pp. 40 ff. The best discussion of the effects of the *Nuevo Trato* appears in Theodore Moran, *Multinational Corporations and the Politics of Dependence* (Princeton, N.J.: Princeton University Press, 1974), pp. 94-118.

3 Moran, *Multinational Corporations,* pp. 132-36 and Theodore Moran, "Transnational Strategies of Protection and Defense by Multinational Corporations," *International Organization,* 27 (Spring 1973), pp. 273-87. For the curious argument that "none of Kennecott's own money" was involved in the new investments, see Barbara Stallings, *Class Conflict and Economic Development in Chile, 1958-1973* (Stanford, Calif.: Stanford University Press, 1979), p. 107.

4 Keith Griffin, *Underdevelopment in Spanish America* (London: Allen and Unwin, 1969), chap. 4.

5 Theodore Moran, "Después des las Nacionalizaciones," *Panorama Económico,* August 1972, pp. 27-32.

6 U.S., Senate, *Hearings on ITT and Chile, 1970-71,* pt. 2, pp. 950-79. The Nixon-initiated CIA effort to provoke a coup is described in U.S., Congress, Senate, *Covert Action in Chile,* pp. 25-26, 36-37, and in U.S., Congress, Senate, Select Committee on Intelligence Activities, *Alleged Assassination Plots Involving Foreign Leaders* (Washington, D.C.: Government Printing Office, 1975), pp. 225-54. See also Thomas Powers, *The Man Who Kept Secrets: Richard Helms and the CIA* (New York: Alfred A. Knopf, 1979), chap. 13.

7 The text of the amendment and the background of its adoption appear in Eduardo Nóvoa Monreal, *La Batalla por el Cobre* (Santiago, Chile: Quimantu, 1972). The idea for a constitutional amendment, like the alternative strategy of using "legal loopholes," came from Nóvoa, the chief legal advisor to Allende (he used the term,

"legal recourses," *recursos legales*). See "Vías Legales para Avanzar hacia el Socialismo,"*Revista de Derecho Económico*, 33-34 (October 1971), pp. 27-38. Related documents and speeches are published in Gonzalo Martner, ed., *El Pensamiento Económico del Gobierno de Allende* (Santiago, Chile: Editorial Universitaria, 1971).

8 The literature on the economic relations between the United States and Chile during the Allende years is considerable. For representative discussions, see Paul E. Sigmund, "The 'Invisible Blockade' and the Overthrow of Allende," *Foreign Affairs*, 52 (January 1974): 322-40, and the debate between Elizabeth Farnsworth and Paul E. Sigmund in *Foreign Policy* 16 (Fall 1974): 126-56. For a Marxist view, see James Petras and Morris Morley, *The United States and Chile* (New York: Monthly Review Press, 1975); see the review by Paul E. Sigmund in *Latin American Research Review* 11 (Fall 1976): 121-27, and Petras and Morley's reply and Sigmund's rejoinder in *Latin American Research Review*, 13 (Spring 1978); 205-24. On the bureaucratic infighting that preceded the January 1972 statement on expropriation, see Jessica Einhorn, *Expropriation Politics* (Lexington, Mass.: Lexington Books, 1974).

9 The Sabbatino amendment, discussed earlier, meant that the court could not accept Chile's argument that the "act of state" doctrine protected it from suits.

10 The Kennecott Corporation published a white paper entitled *Expropriation of El Teniente* (New York: Kennecott, 1971), as well as four supplements entitled *Confiscation of El Teniente* (New York: Kennecott, 1971-1973), with documentation on the dispute. See also the account in George Ingram, *Expropriation of U.S. Property in South America* (New York: Praeger, 1974), pp. 268-90. For a description of the Kennecott "war room" in the fall of 1972, which followed the movements of Chilean copper shipments, see *Time*, November 6, 1972. See also Edmundo Vargas "La Nacionalización del Cobre y el Derecho Internacional," in Ricardo Ffrench-David and Ernesto Tironi, eds., *El Cobre en el Desarrollo Nacional* (Santiago, Chile: Nueva Universidad, 1974), pp. 159-81. Vargas defends the excess profits deduction as permissible retroactive taxation (citing examples of such taxation) but accepts the argument that the refusal of jurisdiction by the Special Copper Tribunal was a "denial of justice."

11 U.S., Senate, *Covert Action in Chile* (Washington, D.C.: Government Printing Office, 1976), pp. 128-35.

12 The 1970-72 figures are taken from Ernesto Tironi, "El Cobre en

Chile," *Mensaje*, January-February 1973, p. 40. The 1972-73 figure comes from Business School of Valparaiso, *The Chilean Economy under the Popular Unity Government* (Santiago, Chile: Gabriela Mistral, 1974), p. 63.

13   The election results are reported in Francisco Zapata, *Los Mineros de Chuquicamata: Productores o Proletarios*? (Mexico City: Colegio de Mexico, 1975), chaps. 2, 6. See also Francisco Zapata, "The Chilean Labor Movement under Salvador Allende: 1970-1973," *Latin American Perspectives,* 8 (Winter 1976), pp. 85-97. On the departures of technicians, see Zapata, *Los Mineros* p. 48; Stefan de Vylder, *Allende's Chile* (Cambridge, Eng.: Cambridge University Press), p. 131; and Tironi, "El Cobre en Chile," p. 40. On the managerial and replacement parts problems after Chileanization, see Norman Gall, "Copper is the Wage of Chile," *American Universities Field Staff Reports* 19 (1972).

14   For the application of a cost-benefit analysis to Frei's Chileanization policies, see Griffin, *Underdevelopment in Spanish America*, chap. 4. Griffin's argument was made before Frei's 1969 "nationalization by agreement." For a discussion of the issue from the viewpoint of the right, see Eric Baklanoff, *Expropriation of U.S. Investments in Cuba, Mexico, and Chile* (New York: Praeger, 1975), p. 71. Baklanoff argues that $1.5 billion in foreign exchange was foregone by Chile by not encouraging additional investment by the copper companies in 1961.

15   For the text of a plan by left militants to stimulate worker seizures in all major industries, see *El Mercurio*, 3 April 1972. *El Mercurio* originally attributed the plan to Allende's Minister of Economics, Pedro Vuskovic.

16   See Herbert E. Meyer, "Dow Picks Up the Pieces in Chile," *Fortune*, 89 (April 1974) pp. 140-57. Dow also commissioned a book-length study of its Chilean experience, which was written but never published.

17   Juan G. Espinoza and Andrew S. Zimbalist evaluate these structures in *Economic Democracy: Workers' Participation in Chilean Industry* (New York: Academic Press, 1978), pp. 155-56, 161. Based on research carried out in thirty-five enterprises in the Area of Social Property in early 1973, they conclude that worker participation resulted in increases in investment, productivity, egalitarianism, and social welfare. On the last two points, there seems to be no disagreement. In the case of investments, expenditures on machinery and equipment increased because there was no budgetary control,

and deficits were covered by advances from the state. The authors make the same point when they admit that "the rate of investment was not significantly correlated with the rate of profit. Investment was dictated in essence . . . by social priorities and political exigency." In the definition of productivity, the authors' conclusion is clearly fallacious. They define it as "product per worker" without considering the costs of labor and invested capital in relation to the goods produced; they compare production at the time of the survey with production during the period eighteen to six months before the company was taken over (a period that included the six months after the Allende election, when Chile was in a state of deep depression) in order to arrive at the conclusion that "productivity" increased or stayed the same in twenty-nine of the thirty-five firms surveyed. This kind of quantitative rather than economic definition of productivity was one of the factors that contributed to Allende's economic failure. The survey did not include the copper mines where worker participation in a highly charged political environment (dubbed by Chileans, *asembleismo*) contributed to increased costs and declining production. For an avowedly Marxist analysis that admits that Allende's brand of socialism was a failure because of insufficient attention to the importance of investment, see Barbara Stallings, *Class Conflict and Economic Development in Chile, 1958-1973* (Stanford, Calif.: Stanford University Press, 1979).

18 Mamalakis, *The Growth and Structure of the Chilean Economy*, p. 173. For an evaluation of the initially progressive and later regressive redistributive effects of the Allende program, especially the "inflation tax," see Alejandro Foxley *et al.*, *The Role of Asset Redistribution in Poverty-Focused Development Strategies*, World Employment Research Programme Working Paper No. 40 (Geneva: International Labor Office, 1976). On the difficulties facing the Allende government in both redistributing income and maintaining investment, see Alejandro Foxley, "Income Redistribution, Economic Growth, and Social Structure: The Case of Chile," in A. Foxley, ed., *Income Distribution in Latin America* (Cambridge, Eng.: Cambridge University Press, 1976), pp. 135-63. For a defense of the Allende policy, see Gonzalo Martner, "Problemas de la Producción bajo la Unidad Popular en Chile, 1970-73," *Trimestre Económico*, 42 (July–September, 1975): 695 ff. Charles Lindblom, *Politics and Markets* (New York: Basic Books, 1978), does not discuss

Chile, but the Allende case is an illustration of his basic thesis of a fundamental conflict between the equalitarian tendencies of political democracy and the special consideration that must be accorded to the private sector in an economy that is not totally state run.

19 Anaconda officials have said that they were willing to accept lower compensation for the 49 percent shares because that was to be paid in cash, rather than promissory notes. Details of the settlement are contained in Corporación del Cobre, *Negociaciones con las Empresas Americanas del Cobre Afectadas por la Nacionalización de 1971*, mimeo., (Santiago, Chile: November, 1974). Under Decree Law 788 of December 4, 1974, the junta gave itself the right to amend the constitution by decree. The copper amendment was not changed, but the Supreme Court was given the right to review all decisions of the Special Copper Tribunal, and three "transitional" articles approving the 1974 agreements were appended to the constitution. See Luz Bulnes *et al.*, *Normas Fundamentales del Estado de Chile* (Santiago, Chile: Ediciones Juridicas, 1975), pp. 157, 160–62.

20 For details see Theresa A. Einhorn and Thomas Klinker, "Overseas Private Investment Corporation," *Law and Policy in International Business* 8 (1976): 352–55. The former ambassador, Edward Korry, has argued against the OPIC compensation on the grounds that ITT and other corporations violated their OPIC contracts by bribing officials of the Allende Government (*New York Times*, 24 December 1976). A lengthy dispute between OPIC and Anaconda over whether it had been nationalized in 1969, when it was not covered by OPIC insurance, was settled in Anaconda's favor in 1977. It received $47.5 million in cash from OPIC, and OPIC guaranteed another $47.5 million of future Chilean compensation payments. Anaconda assigned OPIC another $27 million in Chilean promissory notes.

21 For the provisions of Decree Law 1748 of March 18, 1977, see *Euromoney*, July 1978, p. 26. On Chile's differences with the Andean Pact, see "Andean Pact Developments," *Chile Economic News*, 62 (May 1976): 7–8.

22 *Chile Economic News*, 86 (May 1978): 9.

23 For Chilean views of the international law aspects, see José Echeverria, "Enriquecimiento Injusto y Nacionalización," *Mensaje*, 21 (March–April 1972): 31–48, and Eduardo Novoa Monreal, *Defensa de las Nacionalizaciones ante Tribunales Extranjeros* (Mexico City: UNAM, 1976).

Chapter 6

1 For the text of the Plan Inca, see *Peruvian Times* (Lima), 22 August 1976, and the discussion in Augusto Zimmerman Zavala, *El Plan Inca, Objectivo: Revolución Peruana* (Lima: El Peruana, 1974), which claims that it was drawn up secretly in August 1968, two months before the military coup. On the other hand, government publications in 1968 and 1969 continually insisted that the IPC nationalization was unique, and there was no hint until the 1970s of plans for the establishment of the "industrial communities" and "social property sector" mentioned in Plan Inca.

2 English translations of the major documents in the IPC controversy have been published by Esso International as *The La Brea y Pariñas Controversy*, 4 vols. (Coral Gables, Fla.: 1969-1972). Useful discussions of the controversy include Adalberto J. Pinelo, *The Multinational Corporation as a Force in Latin American Politics: A Case Study of the International Petroleum Company in Peru* (New York: Praeger, 1973); Rieck B. Hannifin, *Expropriation by Peru of the International Petroleum Company* (Washington, D.C.; Library of Congress, Legislative Reference Service, 1969); Richard Goodwin, "Letter from Peru," *The New Yorker*, May 17, 1969, pp. 41-109; U.S., Congress, Senate, Foreign Relations Committee, Western Hemisphere Subcommittee, 91st Cong., 1st sess., *United States Relations with Peru* Hearings, 91st Cong., 1st sess., April 14-17, 1969 (Washington, D.C.: Government Printing Office, 1969); and Charles T. Goodsell, *American Corporations and Peruvian Politics* (Cambridge, Mass.: Harvard University Press, 1974).

3 Augusto Zimmerman, *La Historia Secreto del Petroleo* (Lima, Peru: Editorial Grafica, 1968), pp. 81-82, quoted in Pinelo, *The Multinational Corporation*, p. 76. The military was particularly concerned that a vital national resource was under foreign control. On General Juan Velasco's experience as an Army captain in 1941 in relation to Peru's dependence on IPC, see Pinelo, *The Multinational Corporation*, pp. 146-47. The modern IPC installations surrounded by barbed wire adjoined an antiquated army base where many army officers had served. See also Pedro-Pablo Kuczynski, *Peruvian Democracy Under Stress* (Princeton, N.J.: Princeton University Press, 1977), p. 110.

4 Goodwin, "Letter from Peru," quotes a United States aid official: "The idea was to put on a freeze, talk about red tape and bureaucracy, and they'd soon get the message. Unfortunately they be-

lieved we were as inefficient as we said, and it took about a year for them to get the message," p. 60.

5   For the texts of the relevant legislative provisions of the Foreign Assistance Acts of 1962 and 1967, the Sugar Act Amendment of 1962, and the Fisherman's Protective Act of 1967, see Paul E. Sigmund, ed., *Models of Political Change in Latin America* (New York: Praeger, 1970), pp. 198-211.

6   At this time, IPC in Peru does not seem to have used the embassy to bring pressure upon the Peruvians. Esso headquarters, however, despite its assertions to the contrary, was in close touch with the State Department. See Goodsell, *American Corporations and Peruvian Politics*, pp. 128-29. Kuczynski, *Peruvian Democracy*, pp. 159 ff., sees the lack of an AID program loan for budget support at this time as a contributing factor to the economic difficulties of the Belaúnde regime that helped to bring about its overthrow. Under the Belaúnde government, Peru received only 15 percent as much United States aid as its neighbor, Chile, during the same period; see Jerome Levinson and Juan de Onis, *The Alliance That Lost Its Way* (Chicago: Quadrangle Books, 1970), p. 155.

7   The text of the decree appears in Sigmund, *Models of Political Change*, pp. 206-8.

8   The figure was arrived at by using current East Texas prices for petroleum products less estimated producing and shipping costs, multiplied by the total production from 1924 until 1968.

9   This account is based on embassy dispatches to Washington between March 18 and April 8, 1969, obtained under the Freedom of Information Act. For a Peruvian version, see Zimmerman, *El Plan Inca*, pp. 177-210.

10   Estimates are drawn from Hannifin, *Expropriation by Peru*, pp. 90-92, 98.

11   See Charles Lipson, "Corporate Preferences and Public Policies: Foreign Aid Sanctions and Investment Protection," *World Politics* 28 (April 1976): 410 ff. Lipson sees the nonapplication of Hickenlooper as proof of the influence of business on United States policy — a proposition that, in view of the divisions in business attitudes, is impossible to prove or disprove. See also Daniel Sharp, ed., *U.S. Foreign Policy and Peru* (Austin: University of Texas Press, 1972), pp. 285 ff.

12   On the making of United States policy toward Peru in this period, see Jessica Einhorn, *Expropriation Politics* (Lexington, Mass.: Lexington Books, 1974), pp. 53-68.

13   Alfred Stepan, *State and Society: Peru in Comparative Perspective* (Princeton, N.J.: Princeton University Press, 1978), pp. 145–47.

14   The text of the law is translated in Sigmund, *Models of Political Change*, pp. 214–20.

15   For further details on the Grace expropriations, see Goodsell, *American Corporations*, pp. 134–38.

16   The joint statement of ITT and Peru is quoted in Goodsell, *American Corporations*, p. 152. The case was also cited in paid advertisements in the *New York Times* in 1969 and 1970. Earlier, ITT's public position had been weakened by the publication in Peru, of a telegram from its President, Harold Geneen, to Secretary of State Rusk, dated February 2, 1967, calling for "intervention of your Department at the highest level possible" against proposed legislation aimed at opening the telephone system to international bidding which Geneen said would "prepare the way for confiscation of our interests there" (Goodsell, *American Corporations*, pp. 126–27). For a detailed account of the negotiations between ITT and Peru, see Ernest McCrary, "Learning to Cope with Nationalization," *International Management*, April 1971, pp. 26–28.

17   Janet Ballantyne, *The Political Economy of the Peruvian Gran Mineria* (Ph.D. diss., Cornell University, 1976), p. 32.

18   Shane Hunt, "Direct Foreign Investment in Peru," in *The Peruvian Experiment*, ed. Abraham Lowenthal (Princeton, N.J.: Princeton University Press, 1975), p. 317. On the Industrial Community, see Peter T. Knight, "New Forms of Economic Organization in Peru," in Lowenthal, *The Peruvian Experiment*, pp. 367–73, and Giorgio Alberti *et al., Estado y Clase: La Comunidad Industrial en el Peru* (Lima, Peru: Instituto de Estudios Peruanos, 1977). The fishing, mining, and telecommunications industries had smaller percentages fixed for distribution to the workers, and they received shares in industry-wide "compensation communities," rather than in the individual companies.

19   E. V. K. Fitzgerald, *The State and Economic Development: Peru Since 1968* (Cambridge, Eng.: Cambridge University Press, 1976), pp. 23, 66, 70.

20   See Associated Press, "Peru, Dream Fades as Wells Dry Up," 30 June 1976; *ADELA Monthly Bulletin* (Lima), March 1976, p. 8.

21   The Peruvian left considered the compensation too high, because company debts were assumed by the government and the installations overvalued. See Carlos Malpica, *Anchovetas y Tiburones* (Lima, Peru: Editora Runamarka, 1976).

22 Both Cerro and the Peruvian government took out large advertisements in the *New York Times* (26 and 30 September 1973) setting forth their respective positions. On the housing conditions of the Cerro and other American-owned mines, see Goodsell, *American Corporations*, pp. 56–62. On the poor personal relations between Cerro's president and General Velasco, see Ballantyne, *Gran Mineria*, p. 271. For additional information on Cerro in Peru, see Ann Seidman, ed., *Natural Resources and National Welfare* (New York: Praeger, 1975), pt. 3.

23 *New York Times*, 31 December 1973 and 10 January 1974.

24 *The New York Times* commented editorially on 10 January 1974: "Blatant confiscation of Cerro would almost certainly dry up the international credits which have been forthcoming recently."

25 Ballantyne, *Gran Mineria*, p. 258. The full text of the agreement is published in the *Andean Times*, 22 February 1974. It is analyzed in David Grantz, "The United States-Peruvian Claims Agreement of February 19, 1974," *The International Lawyer,* 10 (Summer 1976): 389–99. Cerro declared a $135 million loss for tax purposes (*New York Times*, 12 March 1974). The Peruvian government's continuing sensitivity on the IPC question was demonstrated in August 1974, when a Peruvian magazine editor who wrote that the government had dropped its $690 million claim against the IPC was sentenced to a year in jail for "damaging the reputation of the revolutionary government." When IPC received compensation from the State Department in December, Peru sent a diplomatic protest accusing the United States of distorting "the spirit and the letter of the agreement."

26 For discussion of the experiment in Social Property, see Peter T. Knight, "New Forms of Economic Organization in Peru: Toward Workers Self-Management," in Lowenthal, *The Peruvian Experiment*, chap. 9; Peter T. Knight, Santiago Roca, J. Vanek, and F. Collazo, *Self Management in Peru*, Program on Participation and Self-Management Systems (Ithaca, N.Y.: Cornell University, 1975); Peter T. Knight, "Social Property in Peru: The Political Economy of Predominance," *Economic Analysis and Workers' Management* (Belgrade), Fall 1976. The summary of the law's provisions is taken from the text, *Ley de Empresas de Propiedad Social*, No. 20598 (April 30, 1974).

27 The texts of the 1952 contracts and their revisions in 1953, 1960, 1966, 1970, and 1971 have been published in Peru as *Contratos Marcona* (Lima, Peru: Italperu, 1971). See also Ballantyne, *Gran Min-*

eria, pp. 26–30, and John C. Connally, "The Marcona Case" (senior thesis, Princeton University, 1977). The Marcona Corporation
has published a white paper, *Nationalization of Marcona Mining
Company, Peruvian Branch* (San Francisco, Calif.: 1975).

28   "The 'Plan Inca,' " *Andean Times*, 2 August 1974, p. 12.

29   See Sven Lindquist, *The Shadow* (Baltimore, Md.: Penguin, 1972),
pp. 236–53, which also gives figures from the 1954 congressional
committee report. Diego Garcia-Sayan, *El Caso Marcona* (Lima,
Peru: DESCO, 1975), argues that the Marcona contracts were illegal from the start, because they were not approved by the Peruvian
Congress (thus providing the basis for a declaration, in the style of
IPC, that all its profits since 1952 should be returned as "unjust
enrichment").

30   The text of the decree appears in Minister of Energy and Mines,
Ahora Marcona Tambien Es Nuestra (Lima, Peru: 1975), pp. 7–14.
It also contains speeches by President Velasco and the minister of
mines.

31   See the table of Peruvian iron exports in *The Andean Report*, May
1976, p. 87.

32   The text of the agreement is published in U.S., Department of
State, *Treaties and Other International Acts Series* no. 8173 (Washington, D.C.: Government Printing Office, 1976).

33   *Business Latin America*, 27 October 1976, p. 342. See also "Peru
Claims Profit from Marcona Compensation," *Latin American Economic Report*, 4 (October 1976): 163. Other details on the negotiations have been derived from interviews with several of the participants. The connection between the loans from United States banks
and the settlement of the Marcona dispute was a personal one. A
Marcona executive sits on the board of Wells Fargo Bank, and the
chairman of Cyprus Mines, a major Marcona shareholder, is on
the board of United California Bank. See Nancy Belliveau, "What
the Peruvian Experiment Means," *The Institutional Investor*, 10
(October 1976): 145–48.

34   Stepan, *State and Society*, pp. 273, 285; E. V. Fitzgerald, *The State
and Economic Development: Peru Since 1968* (Cambridge, Eng.:
Cambridge University Press, 1976), p. 165; statistics are taken from
table 1 of John Sheahan, "Peru: International Economic Policies
and Structural Change, 1968-78" (Paper delivered at "The Peruvian
Experiment Reconsidered," Woodrow Wilson International Center
for Scholars, Washington, D.C., November 2-4, 1978).

35   On the efficiency of the state-owned enterprises in Peru, see Fitz-

gerald, *The State and Economic Development*, pp. 48-55, which argues that there was no real alternative to state ownership and evades the question of measurement. H. J. Maidenberg, "The Failures of the Peruvian Reforms," *New York Times*, 11 January 1976, estimates that the state copper mines produce at 75 cents a pound while the private mines do so at 55 cents a pound. The nationalized fishmeal industry's projected losses were estimated in July 1976 at $215 million, see "U.S. Banks to Vet Peruvian Economy," *Latin America Economic Report*, 4 (July 1976): 117. The more "realistic" pricing policy adopted in 1976 helped to reduce government deficits, but it also led to demonstrations and riots at that time and again after further price increases in May 1978. Like other problems of the state sector—the lack of responsiveness of the state steel industry to changing conditions, the inability of Centromin (ex-Cerro) to keep top managerial talent because of government restrictions on salaries, the problems of the fishmeal industry in discharging surplus workers, or the refusal of Peru to reduce copper production in cooperation with other members of the CIPEC copper cartel—these difficulties are related to the reduction or elimination of market economic criteria in decision making.

36   Richard Webb, "Government Policy and the Distribution of Income in Peru, 1963-1973," in Lowenthal, *The Peruvian Experiment*, pp. 79-127.

37   Another alternative proposed by the left involves repudiation of, or a moratorium on, foreign indebtedness—or, at least, the threat to do so to resist the stabilization programs of the banks and the IMF. The threat lacks credibility, since such a policy would destroy Peru's ability to import, among other things, 50 percent of its food supply. Three specific pieces of evidence might be cited in support of the scenario in the text: (1) the debt crisis became evident in 1975 just after the Marcona nationalization had sharply reduced Peru's revenues from iron ore exports; (2) when the Cuajone mine finally began production in 1977, it raised Peru's copper exports by 62 percent: were it not for Velasco's nationalization policies, financing and production could have come through much earlier, Peru could have taken advantage of the high copper prices of 1973 and 1974, and the international crisis of confidence in its economy might have been avoided; (3) the losses because of subsidization of prices, incurred by EPSA, the state food purchasing agency, and Petroperu, the national oil company, accounted in 1975 for 18 percent of the public sector deficit, which amounted to 54 billion *soles* or 10 per-

cent of the gross national product. See Peruvian government figures in tables 4 and 5 of Sheahan, "Peruvian International Economic Policies."

38 Quoted in Shane Hunt, "Direct Foreign Investment," in Lowenthal, *The Peruvian Experiment*, pp. 339-40.

Chapter 7

1 On the history of petroleum in Venezuela, see Edwin Lieuwen, *Petroleum in Venezuela: A History* (Berkeley: University of California Press, 1954); Anibal R. Martinez, *Chronology of Venezuelan Oil* (London: Allen and Unwin, 1969); and Luis Vallenilla, *Oil: The Making of a New Economic Order* (New York: McGraw-Hill, 1975). For the period between 1959 and 1973, the definitive treatment is Franklin Tugwell, *The Politics of Oil in Venezuela* (Stanford, Calif.: Stanford University Press, 1975).

2 Figures on production, exports, and government income are taken from Tugwell, *Politics of Oil*, pp. 182-83. On the effects of the Mexican expropriations on the strategy of the oil companies in Venezuela, see Mira Wilkins, *The Maturing of Multinational Enterprise* (Cambridge, Mass.: Harvard University Press, 1974), p. 317.

3 Tugwell, *Politics of Oil*, p. 49.

4 Tugwell, *Politics of Oil*, p. 62. For Pérez Alfonzo's own account of the development of OPEC, see *Resumen* (Caracas), 26 January 1975, pp. 19-24. He indicates that contacts were first made with the Middle East in 1949, and cites his use of the threat to nationalize "as a last resort" in order to induce the companies to comply with government controls.

5 On the 1966 tax reform conflict and the resulting division between the foreign companies and the Venezuelan private sector, see Tugwell, *Politics of Oil*, chaps. 4-5.

6 There were twelve candidates for the presidency, but Pérez and Fernandez together received 85 percent of the vote. For an analysis of the 1973 election, see John D. Martz and Enrique A. Baloyra, *Electoral Mobilization and Public Opinion: The Venezuelan Campaign of 1973* (Chapel Hill: University of North Carolina Press, 1976).

7 The relevant documents relating to the oil nationalization are published in José Agustín Catalá, ed., *Nacionalización del Petróleo en Venezuela* (Caracas, Ven.: Centauro Editores, 1975).

8 The documentation on the iron nationalization appears in José

Agustín Catalá, ed., *Nacionalización del Hierro en Venezuela 1975* (Caracas, Ven.: Ediciones Centauro, 1974).

9 Ministry of Mines, *Memoria y Cuenta, 1975* (Caracas, Ven.: 1976), pp. ix-155. The Economist Intelligence Unit reported government oil revenues for 1974 and 1975 as $8.04 and $8.45 per barrel. After nationalization the figure rose to $8.99, *Quarterly Economic Review of Oil in Latin America and the Caribbean*, 1st quarter 1978, p. 2.

10 Pérez also modified the commission's proposals for court review, inserting a provision for a compensation offer based on net book value to the companies within 45 days of the adoption of the law. Only if the companies rejected the offer was the question of compensation to be reviewed by the Supreme Court.

11 For the biographies of the principal directors of Petroven, see *Resumen* (Caracas) 7 September 1975, pp. 18-21.

12 Ministry of Mines, *Memoria y Cuenta*, pp. viii-39. The cash amounts were for oil in storage and equipment.

13 "Successful Six Months for Venezuela Oil Industry," *Latin American Economic Report*, 4 (August 1976): 126; *Resumen* (Caracas), 11 April 1976, p. 21; *El Nacional*, 11 May 1976; *Petroleum Intelligence Weekly*, January 12, 1976, p. 3; David Nott, "Venezuela, The Oil Industry, Nationalization and After," *Bank of London and South America Review*, 10 (October 1976): 544-50.

14 James F. Petras, Morris Morley, and Steven Smith, *The Nacionalization of Venezuelan Oil* (New York: Praeger, 1977), p. 168. Petras *et al.* estimated that the agreements gave the companies 700 million bolivars (about $160 million) a year in addition to nearly $1 billion in compensation; thus, over four years they would receive an additional amount equivalent to two-thirds of the compensation figure. The other sources mentioned in note 13, however, indicate payments after taxes that would add up to a lower figure.

15 In 1976, the iron miners' union was dominated by the leftist parties, which held five of the nine seats on its executive board, while centrist parties dominated the two petroleum workers' unions. See Joseph A. Mann, "Labor — the Honeymoon Is Over," *Business Venezuela*, 41 (January-February 1976): 14-20.

16 "Venezuela," *Latin American Special Report, Latin American Economic Report* Supp., January 1978, p. 11.

17 See accounts in *Wall Street Journal*, 8 April 1976; *Resumen* (Caracas), April 1976; and *Miami Herald*, 26 October 1976.

18 See the critical report on Venezuelan agriculture by the French expert, René Dumont, in *Resumen* (Caracas), 11 May 1975.

19 Kim Fuad, "The Economy: Storm Brewing?," *Business Venezuela,* 41 (January–February 1976): 7–13; Robert Bond, ed., *Contemporary Venezuela and its Role in International Affairs* (New York: New York University Press, 1977), p. 238. See also Michel Chossudovsky, *La Miseria en Venezuela* (Valencia, Ven.: Vadell, 1977).

Chapter 8

1 On the effect of nationalization in making the Third World country "the supplier of last resort," see Theodore Moran, *Multinational Corporations and the Politics of Dependence* (Princeton, N.J.: Princeton University Press, 1974), chap. 7.

2 This argument is developed in Paul Streeten, "Costs and Benefits of Multinational Enterprises in Less Developed Countries," in *The Multinational Enterprise,* ed. John H. Dunning (New York: Praeger, 1971), pp. 249 ff, and Paul Streeten, "New Approaches to Private Overseas Investment," in *Private Foreign Investment and the Developing World,* ed. P. H. Ady (New York: Praeger, 1971), p. 52. See also P. Streeten and S. Lall, *Evaluation of Methods and Main Findings of UNCTAD Study of Private Overseas Investment in Selected Less Developed Countries* (New York and Geneva: United Nations, 1973), pp. 23–26, for the argument that 40 percent of the foreign investment projects surveyed in the study could have been carried out at a lower "social" cost with domestic capital.

3 See Raymond Vernon, *Storm over the Multinationals* (Cambridge, Mass.: Harvard University Press, 1977), pp. 156–60, and Grant Reuber, *Private Foreign Investment in Development* (Oxford: Clarendon Press, 1973), pp. 43, 144–56. In 1975–77, developing country borrowers paid an average interest rate of nearly 10 percent on the international money market, according to the World Bank publication, *Borrowing in International Capital Markets.* In 1976 and 1977, after-tax profits of American investors in manufacturing in Latin America were reported as 11.3 percent and 10.5 percent, down from 14 percent in 1975. See U.S., Department of Commerce, *Survey of Current Business,* August 1977, p. 39, and August 1978, p. 22. In the computation of profits, a great deal depends on bookkeeping methods. Latin American nationalists have been able to cite unusually high profit rates since accelerated depreciation allowances have lowered book values by excessive amounts (for example,

Kennecott in Chile). Constantine Vaitsos, *Intercountry Income Distribution and Transnational Enterprises* (London and New York: Oxford University Press, 1974), examines transfer pricing practices, principally pharmaceuticals in Colombia and Argentina, to argue for the large markups within the multinational firm.

4 See Richard B. Lillich and Burns H. Weston, *International Claims: Their Settlement by Lump Sum Agreements*, 2 vols. (Charlottesville: University of Virginia Press, 1975). On the general question of compensation, see Richard B. Lillich, ed., *The Valuation of Nationalized Property in International Law* (Charlottesville: University of Virginia, 1972).

5 Geoffrey Chandler, "Private Foreign Investment and Joint Ventures," in Ady, *Private Foreign Investment*, p. 215.

6 For an incisive criticism of the abuses in the parastatal sector of Mexico, published just before the reforms introduced by President López Portillo, see David Ibarra, "Reflexiones sobre la Empresa Publica en Mexico," *Foro Internacional,* 17 (October-December 1976): 141-51. A case study of the public commodities corporation in Mexico, CONASUPO, observes that, in 1976, it received a budgetary subsidy of $300 million but only saved consumers a total of $10 million in lower prices. See Andres Gil, "CONASUPO: Observations on a Public Enterprise" (senior thesis, Princeton University, 1978). After the nationalization of the tin mines in Bolivia, production dropped by 15 percent while employment increased by 20 percent, see George M. Ingram, *Expropriation of U.S. Property in South America* (New York: Praeger, 1974), p. 143. On the measurement of the efficiency of public enterprises in Latin America see Andrew Gantt and Giuseppe Dutto, "Financial Performance of Government-owned Corporations in Less Developed Countries," *IMF Staff Papers,* March 1968, and "Public Enterprises: Their Present Significance and Their Potential Development," Economic Commission for Latin America, *Economic Bulletin for Latin America,* 16: (1971), 1-57. See also the Latin American examples in A. H. Hanson, *Public Enterprise and Economic Development*, 2d ed. (London: Routledge and Kegan Paul, 1965), and John B. Sheahan, "Public Enterprises in Developing Countries," in *Public Enterprise,* ed. William G. Shepherd (Lexington, Mass.: D.C. Heath, 1976), pp. 205-33. The structure and function of public enterprises in six Latin American countries are described in The Interamerican Development Bank, Institute of Latin American Integration, *El Regimen Legal de las Empresas Publicas Latinoamericanas y su*

Acción Internacional, 2 vols. (Buenos Aires, Argentina: Banco Interamericano de Desarrollo, 1977).

7   See Werner Baer, Richard Newfarmer, and Thomas Trebat, "On State Capitalism in Brazil," *Inter-American Economic Affairs,* 30 (1977); 69–91; Thomas J. Trebat, "The Role of Public Enterprise in Brazil" (Paper delivered at the Latin American Studies Association, November 1977); and José Roberto Mendonça de Barros and Douglas H. Graham, "The Brazilian Economic Miracle Revisited: Private and Public Sector Initiative in a Market Economy," *Latin American Research Review,* 22 (1978): 5–38. On the need for commercial autonomy and worldwide operation for successful "state enterprise capitalism," and the failure of Third World nationalized enterprises in these respects, see Douglas Lamont, *Foreign State Enterprises* (New York: Basic Books, 1979), chap. 9.

8   See Martin Bronfenbrenner, "The Appeal of Confiscation in Economic Development," *Economic Development and Cultural Change,* April 1955, pp. 201–18.

9   See the United Nations Industrial Development Organisation, *Guidelines for Project Evaluation* (New York: United Nations, 1972), especially chaps. 3, 6–8; I. M. D. Little and J. A. Murrlees, *Project Appraisal and Planning for Developing Countries* (New York: Basic Books, 1974); Louis T. Wells, Jr., "Social Cost/Benefit Analysis for MNC's," *Harvard Business Review,* 53: (March–April 1975): 40–48, 150–54; Anandarup Ray and Herman G. van der Tak, "A New Approach to Economic Analysis of Projects" *Finance and Development,* 16 (March 1979): 28–32.

10 For an attempt to provide technical formulae for an economic analysis of the costs and benefits of a decision to nationalize, based on the Allende experience, see Jorge Cauas and Marcelo Selowsky, "Potential Distributive Effects of Nationalization Policies: The Economic Aspects," in *Income Distribution and Growth in Less-Developed Countries,* ed. Charles R. Frank, Jr., and Richard C. Webb (Washington, D.C.: The Brookings Institution, 1977), pp. 535–64. On the measurement of efficiency, see Malcolm Gillis, "Allocative Efficiency and X-Efficiency in State-owned Enterprises: Some Asian and Latin American Cases in the Mining Sector," *Technical Papers Series,* no. 13 (Austin, Texas: Office for Public Sector Studies, Institute of Latin American Studies, University of Texas, 1978).

11 See the arguments developed in Reinhold Niebuhr and Paul E. Sigmund, *The Democratic Experience* (New York: Praeger, 1969).

12 See David N. Smith and Louis T. Wells, Jr., *Negotiating Third*

World Mineral Agreements (Cambridge, Mass.: Ballinger, 1975) as well as Benny Widyono, "Transnational Corporations and Export Oriented Primary Commodities," *CEPAL Review* (Santiago), 5 (1978): 135–59. For examples of assistance to host country negotiators by the UN Centre on Transnational Corporations, see "Negotiating with Transnational Corporations: Workshops for Developing Country Officials," *CTC Reporter,* (December 1977): 18–19, and "Technical Cooperation Programme: Advisory Services," *CTC Reporter,* 1 (April 1978): 10–11. The centre is developing a computerized technology index that will make information on comparative costs readily available to governments planning to import technology.

13 *Boletin do Banco Central do Brasil* 6 (December 1976): 16; Herbert Goldhamer, *The Foreign Powers in Latin America* (Princeton, N.J.: Princeton University Press, 1977), p. 41; *Documentación Venezuela Now* (Venezuelan Mission to the United Nations), 4 (October 1978): 24.

14 Richard Newfarmer and Willard Mueller, *Multinational Corporations in Brazil and Mexico,* p. 71; Fernando Fajnzylber and Trinidad Martínez Tarrago, *Las Empresas Transnacionales* (Mexico City: Fondo de Cultura Economica), p. 255.

15 See Council of the Americas, *The Andean Pact: Definition, Design, and Analysis* (New York: Council of the Americas, 1974); Richard D. Robinson, *National Control of Foreign Business Entry* (New York: Praeger, 1976), chap. 8; and Roger Fontaine, *The Andean Pact: A Political Analysis* (Beverly Hills, Calif.: Sage Publications, 1977). For a survey of the foreign investment legislation of fifty-three countries, see UN Centre on Transnational Corporations, *National Legislation and Regulations relating to Transnational Corporations* (New York: United Nations, 1978). The International Centre for the Settlement of Investment Disputes (ICSID) has also collected and published the investment laws of most of the countries of the world (7 vols.) (Dobbs Ferry, N.Y.: Oceana, 1975).

16 Lawrence G. Franko, "Joint International Business Ventures in Developing Countries," in Robert B. Williamson *et al.,* eds., *Latin American-U.S. Economic Interactions* (Washington, D.C.: American Enterprise Institute for Public Policy Research, 1974), pp. 229–43.

17 In 1976 new United States investment in manufacturing in Colombia and Venezuela was negative by $17 million while Peru and Chile only attracted $5 million. In the same year new United States in-

vestment in manufacturing in Brazil rose by $233 million. In 1977 after investment regulations were eased, new American investment began to flow into Venezuela, see *Survey of Current Business*, August 1977, pp. 46–47 and August 1978, p. 30.

18 *Survey of Current Business*, August 1978, p. 32. On the "triple alliance" of the multinationals, the Brazilian government, and local capital, see Peter Evans, *Dependent Development* (Princeton, N.J.: Princeton University Press, 1979).

19 Grant Reuber, *Private Foreign Investment in Development* (Oxford: Clarendon Press, 1973), pp. 20–21, 38.

20 See Wolfgang Friedmann and G. Kalmanoff, *Joint International Business Ventures in Developing Countries* (New York: Columbia University Press, 1971); and Lawrence G. Franko, *Joint Venture Survival in Multinational Corporations* (New York: Praeger, 1971). On public-private mixed ownership, see Lloyd D. Musolf, *Mixed Enterprise* (Lexington, Mass.: Lexington Books, 1972).

21 The use of the Overseas Private Investment Corporation (OPIC) to encourage the establishment of joint ventures was advocated in the OPIC hearings of 1973, see U.S., House, Committee on Foreign Affairs, *The Overseas Private Investment Corporation: A Critical Analysis* (Washington, D.C.: Government Printing Office, 1973), pp. 91–93. C. Fred Bergsten, Thomas Horst, and Theodore H. Moran, *American Multinationals and American Interests* (Washington, D.C.: Brookings Institution, 1978), argue that from the point of view of importing countries, such as the United States, that are interested in keeping prices down and production high, the joint venture between the multinational corporation and the raw material producing country is "the worst possible" solution. Thus, the United States government should encourage the multinational corporation to promote diversification of sources and maximization of output (p. 164).

22 In 1976 fifty-nine out of seventy-six new foreign investment projects approved by the Venezuelan government were joint ventures, see *Documentación Venezuela Now*, 4 (October 1978): 24. On the demand for a share in ownership as the "fourth stage" in the evolution of raw material concession contracts, see Stefan H. Robock *et al.*, *International Business and Multinational Enterprises* (Homewood, Ill.: Irwin, 1977), p. 165.

23 See Guy B. Meeker, "Towards a Fade-in Joint Venture Process," *Papers of the Capital Market Program, Organization of American States* (June 1974), pp. 39–99. The opposite process, a government

option to buy 49 percent ownership at a pre-established price, was included in the agreement by Chile to sell a medium-sized copper mine to the Exxon Corporation in late 1977.

24 Sanford Rose, "Why the Multinational Tide Is Ebbing," *Fortune,* 96 (August 1977): 110. The 1951 survey and a number of others with similar results are discussed in Burns H. Weston, "International Law and the Deprivation of Foreign Wealth," in *The Future of the International Legal Order,* vol. II, *Wealth and Resources* eds. Richard A. Falk and Cyril E. Black (Princeton, N.J.: Princeton University Press, 1970), p. 172.

25 Nathaniel H. Leff, "Multinationals in a Hostile World," *The Wharton Magazine* 2 (Spring 1978): 21–29. For those with substantial investments already located in the developing country, Leff recommends continuing innovation to create additional economic benefits for the host country. For a series of case studies of the movement of multinational corporations out of investment equity into the sale of technology and other services, see Jack Baranson, *Technology and the Multinationals: Corporate Strategies in a Changing World Economy* (Lexington, Mass.: D.C. Heath Lexington Books, 1978). It is estimated that the shift to "downstream" operations (refining and marketing) as a source of profits from Saudi Arabian oil has reduced company earnings from 35 cents to 21–25 cents a barrel, *Washington Post,* 15 October 1978.

26 U.S. Department of Commerce, *Survey of Current Business,* August 1977, pp. 47, 49, and August 1979, p. 27; Dale Weigel, "Private Direct Foreign Investment and Economic Development" (mimeo., Washington, D.C.: 1977), pp. 1–4; Speech by Antonio Ortiz Mena, president of the Inter-American Development Bank, 10 November 1978, in *El Mercado de Valores,* 38 (November 1978): 968.

27 W. Arthur Lewis, *The Evolution of the International Economic Order* (Princeton, N.J.: Princeton University Press, 1978), pp. 44, 46. For the Leontief predictions, see Wassily Leontief *et al., The Future of the World Economy* (New York: Oxford University Press, 1977), pp. 7–10, 62–63. On the "air-clearing" function of nationalization, see Carlos Díaz-Alejandro, "Direct Foreign Investments in Latin America," in *The International Corporation,* ed. Charles Kindleberger (Cambridge, Mass.: MIT Press, 1970), p. 336.

28 Ricardo French-Davis, "Foreign Investment in Latin America: Recent Trends and Prospects," in *Latin America in the International Economy,* ed. Victor Urquidi (New York: Wiley, 1973), pp. 170ff.

29 Gustav Ranis, "The Multinational Corporation as an Instrument of

Development," in *The Multinational Corporation and Social Change,* ed. David E. Apter and Louis Wolf Goodman (New York: Praeger, 1976), p. 101. Even in the area of raw materials, it is significant that the Jamaican government, despite its commitment to democratic socialism, has preferred taxation, production controls, and joint ventures with the aluminum companies to outright nationalization of its bauxite mining industry. For the argument for nationalization of Jamaican bauxite, see Norman Girvan, *Corporate Imperialism: Conflict and Expropriation,* pap. ed. (New York: Monthly Review Press, 1978).

Chapter 9

1   Robert Gilpin, *U.S. Power and the Multinational Corporation* (New York: Basic Books, 1975), argues that foreign investment by United States-based multinational corporations encouraged by the United States government is leading to the loss of the economic and technological lead that is responsible for American economic prosperity (pp. 199, 208). For an earlier version of Gilpin's argument made by Herbert Hoover in the 1920s, see Mira Wilkins, *The Maturing of Multinational Enterprise* (Cambridge, Mass.: Harvard University Press, 1974), pp. 52–53. U.S., Congress, Senate, Committee on Finance, *The Multinational Corporation and the World Economy* (Washington, D.C.: Government Printing Office, 1973), summarizes an analysis by the U.S. Tariff Commission that concludes that the overall net impact of American foreign investment on American exports, jobs, and earnings, is a favorable one. This conclusion is also supported by data in Robert Stobaugh, *Nine Investments Abroad and Their Impact at Home* (Cambridge, Mass.: Harvard University Press, 1976). See, however, the study by Peggy Musgrave, published as U.S., Congress, Senate, Committee on Foreign Relations, Subcommittee on Multinational Corporations, *Direct Investment Abroad and the Multinationals' Effect on the U.S. Economy* (Washington, D.C.: Government Printing Office, 1975), which estimates that, although overall national income is increased by United States foreign investment, the share going to capital has risen by 47 percent, while that going to labor has declined by 27 percent. The Musgrave argument is criticized in C. Fred Bergsten, Thomas S. Horst, and Theodore H. Moran, *American Multinationals and American Interests* (Washington, D.C.: Brookings Institution, 1978), p. 106, which concludes that the long-run impact

of investment abroad is "largely haphazard." The profits of American corporations derived from overseas investment between 1975 and 1977 averaged from 6–6.5 percent of total United States corporate profits, see, U.S., Department of Commerce, *Survey of Current Business,* 57 (December 1977): 13. The Latin American Republics account for about 0.5 percent of total profits, interest, and other payments, see U.S., Department of Commerce, *Survey of Current Business,* 58 (August 1978): 34. For a general argument that United States foreign economic policy has paid too much attention to anti-Communist ideology and not enough to "the politics of interest," see Stephen Krasner, *Defending the National Interest: Raw Materials Investment and U.S. Foreign Policy* (Princeton, N.J.: Princeton University Press, 1978).

2   On the tax credit and the petroleum industry, see John M. Blair, *The Control of Oil* (New York: Pantheon, 1977), chap. 8, as well as James C. Rosapepe, "End Oil's Foreign Tax Credit," *New York Times,* 18 August 1979, and Peter Passel, "What's the Right Tax for Foreign Oil?" *New York Times,* 7 September 1979. The Senate hearings are published in U.S., Congress, Senate, Foreign Relations Committee, Subcommittee on Multinational Corporations, *Multinational Corporations and U.S. Foreign Policy,* pt. 4: *Multinational Petroleum Companies and Foreign Policy* (Washington, D.C.: Government Printing Office, 1974), especially pp. 83–89, 114–28. For developments on the royalty tax issue in petroleum, see the summary in *Law and Policy in International Business,* 10 (1978): 309–14. On arguments against the tax credit, see Bergsten, Horst, and Moran, *American Multinationals,* pp. 208–10.

3   Bergsten, Horst, and Moran, *American Multinationals,* pp. 462–67, argue for the extension of the investment credit to overseas investment but recommend the retention of the tax credit only for nonequity investments in raw materials (such as through service contracts) and restriction of the tax deferral to investment in the neediest countries. However, they do not develop an economic argument that the latter steps are the most effective ways to promote the purposes towards which they are directed, or why one form of tax subsidy should be used for raw materials, and another for poor countries. Their position is attacked (equity investment provides capital, efficient vertical integration, and increased access to raw materials) in Timothy W. Stanley, *Raw Materials and Foreign Policy* (Washington, D.C.: International Economic Studies Institute, 1976), pp. 329–31. For further discussion of tax policy towards for-

eign investment see Peggy Brewer Richman, *Taxation of Foreign Investment Income* (Baltimore: Johns Hopkins Press, 1963); Peggy B. Musgrave, *United States Taxation of Foreign Investment Income* (Cambridge, Mass.: Harvard Law School, 1969); and G. C. Hufbauer *et al.*, *U.S. Taxation of American Business Abroad* (Washington, D.C.: American Enterprise Institute for Public Policy Research, 1975).

4   C. Fred Bergsten, "Coming Investment Wars?," *Toward a New International Economic Order* (Lexington, Mass.: Lexington Books, 1975), p. 271. The article originally appeared in *Foreign Affairs*, 53 (October 1974): 135-52.

5   "Export-Import Bank Amendments of 1978" (mimeo.), pp. 2, 6.

6   The only critical comments during the debate on the Senate floor in 1969 were by Senator Fulbright who suggested that current United States balance-of-payments problems might argue against government support for overseas investment. See the summary of the House and Senate debates in U.S., Congress, House, Foreign Affairs Committee, *The Overseas Private Investment Corporation: A Critical Analysis*, Congressional Research Service (Washington, D.C.: Government Printing Office, 1973), pp. 10-11.

7   See U.S., Congress, House, Committee on Foreign Affairs, Subcommittee on Foreign Economic Policy, *The Overseas Private Investment Corporation*, Subcommittee Report, October 21, 1973 (Washington, D.C.: Government Printing Office, 1973), and U.S., Congress, Senate, Committee on Foreign Relations, Subcommittee on Multinational Corporations, *The Overseas Private Investment Corporation*, Subcommittee Report, October 17, 1973 (Washington, D.C.: Government Printing Office, 1973).

8   U.S., Congress, Senate, Committee on Foreign Relations, Subcommittee on Foreign Assistance, *OPIC Authorization*, Testimony and prepared statement of William C. Goodfellow, Center for International Policy (Washington, D.C.: Government Printing Office, 1977), pp. 124-36.

9   See U.S., Congress, House, *Congressional Record*, 95th Cong., 1st Sess., 2 November 1977, pp. 12,051-12,065; 3 November 1977, pp. 12,109-12,128; 23 February 1978, pp. 1,438-1,454, and U.S., Congress, House, Committee on International Relations, Subcommittee on International Economic Policy and Trade, 95th Cong., 1st Sess., *Extension and Revision of Overseas Private Investment Corporation Programs*, Hearings, June-September 1977 (Washington, D.C.: Government Printing Office, 1977).

10 Overseas Private Investment Corporation, *1977 Annual Report*, pp. 14-16.

11 Bergsten, Horst, and Moran, *American Multinationals*, p. 177.

12 U.S., Department of State, "Address by the Honorable Henry A. Kissinger, Secretary of State before the Fourth Ministerial Meeting of the United Nations Conference on Trade and Development, Nairobi, Kenya, May 6, 1976" (mimeo.), pp. 5-7.

13 ICSID has now made its fact-finding facilities, but not its arbitral panels, available to nonsignatories of the convention. Besides the ICSID annual reports, the most useful sources on its activities are Paul C. Szasz, "Arbitration under the Auspices of the World Bank," *The International Lawyer,* 3 (1969): 312-19; Paul C. Szasz, "The Investment Disputes Convention and Latin America," *Virginia Journal of International Law,* 11 (March 1971): 256-65; John T. Schmidt, "Arbitration under the Auspices of the International Centre for the Settlement of Investment Disputes (ICSID): Implications of the Decision on Jurisdiction in Alcoa Minerals of Jamaica Inc. v. Government of Jamaica, *Harvard International Law Journal,* 17 (Winter 1976): 90-109; and C. F. Amerisinghe, "The International Centre for the Settlement of Investment Disputes and Development through the Multinational Corporation," *Vanderbilt Journal of Transnational Law,* 9 (Fall 1976): 793-816.

14 UN, General Assembly, 313th session, *Acceleration of the Transfer of Real Resources to Developing Countries* (A/33/28), 6 November 1978, pp. 10-12. The text of the 1962 World Bank staff report, "Multi-lateral Investment Insurance" is printed in John F. McDaniels, ed., *International Financing and Investment* (Dobbs Ferry, N.Y.: Oceana Publications, 1964), pp 170-246. See also William Conant Brewer, Jr., "The Proposal for Investment Guarantees by an International Agency," *American Journal of International Law,* 58 (January 1964): 62-87, and the documents cited and discussion in CEMLA, "Proyecto del BIRF de Creación de un Organismo Internacional de Seguros sobre las Inversiones Extranjeras," *Boletín Mensual,* 17 (March and April, 1971): 100-110, 151-62.

15 See discussion in Bergsten, Horst, and Moran, *American Multinationals*, pp. 479, 484.

16 See UN, Economic and Social Council, Commission on Transnational Corporations, Intergovernmental Working Group on a Code of Conduct, *Transnational Corporations: Code of Conduct; Formulations by the Chairman* (E/C.10/AC.2/8), December 1978, Annex (Comments on paragraph 52 on Nationalization and Compen-

sation). For the 1975 "areas of concern," see Annex 2 of "Excerpts from the Report on the First Session of the Commission on Transnational Corporations," in Karl P. Sauvant and Farid G. Lavipour, eds., *Controlling Multinational Enterprises* (Boulder, Colo.: Westview Press, 1976), pp. 238–39. For the views of American business in Latin America, see Council of the Americas, *Codes of Conduct for the Transfer for Technology* (New York: Council of the Americas, 1976).

17 The Expropriation Group is not solely concerned with the defense of large multinational corporations. Among the cases that it has considered were nationalizations by Tanzania of a United States citizen's minority interest in a coffee plantation in 1973 and of rental property owned by two Americans in 1970. The two cases were settled in 1976 by government compensation offers of $15,000 and $8,810, respectively. See U.S., Department of State, Bureau of Intelligence and Research, *Disputes Involving U.S. Foreign Direct Investment, February 1, 1975–February 28, 1977*, Report No. 855 (September 19, 1977), p. 48.

18 According to U.S., Department of Commerce figures (*Survey of Current Business*, August 1977) United States net new investment in the less developed countries dropped in 1976 by 55 percent. (If the Venezuelan and Nigerian compensation payments are disregarded the decline was still 37 percent). Disregarding the Venezuelan payment of nearly $500 million in compensation to the nationalized United States oil companies, only $1.2 billion dollars of new investment *and* reinvested profits went to Latin America in 1976 from United States investors, most of it to Brazil and to the Cuajone project in Peru. In the same year, Latin America borrowed $9 billion from the international money market, with Brazil and Mexico responsible for two-thirds of that amount; see World Bank, *Borrowing in International Capital Markets*, December 1977, table 2.2.

Selected Bibliography

Books

Agustín Catalá, José. *Nacionalización del Petroleo en Venezuela*. Caracas: Centauro Editores, 1975.

Agustín Catalá, José, ed. *Nacionalización del Hierro en Venezuela*. Caracas: Ediciones Centauro, 1974.

Alberti, Giorgio et al. *Estado y Clase: La Comunidad Industrial en el Perú*. Lima: Instituto de Estudios Peruanos, 1977.

Arévalo, Juan José. *Guatemala: La Democracia y el Imperio*. Buenos Aires: Renacimiento, 1955.

Arévalo, Juan José. *La Fábula del Tiburón y las Sardinas, America Latina estrangulada*. Buenos Aires: Ediciones Meridion, 1956.

Arévalo, Juan José. *The Shark and the Sardines*. Translated by June Cobb and Raúl Osegueda. New York: Stuart, 1961.

Baklanoff, Eric N. "International Economic Relations," In *Revolutionary Change in Cuba*, edited by Carmelo Mesa Lago. Pittsburgh: University of Pittsburgh Press, 1971.

Baklanoff, Eric N. *Expropriation of U.S. Investments in Cuba, Mexico and Chile*. New York: Praeger Publishers, 1975.

Barona Lobato, Juan. *La Expropiación Petrolera*. Tlatelolco: Secretaría de Relaciones Exteriores, 1974.

Behrman, Jack N.; Boddewyn, J. J.; and Kapoor, Ashok. *International Business-Government Communications*. Lexington, Mass.: Lexington Books, 1975.

Bemis, Samuel Flagg. *The Latin American Policy of the United States*. New York: Harcourt Brace, 1943.

Bergsten, C. Fred. *Toward a New International Economic Order: Selected Papers of C. Fred Bergsten 1972-1974*, Lexington, Mass.: Lexington Books, 1975.

Bergsten, C. Fred; Horst, Thomas; and Moran, Theodore H. *American Multinationals and American Interests.* Washington D.C.: The Brookings Institution, 1978.

Bermúdez, Antonio. *The Mexican National Petroleum Industry.* Stanford: Hispanic American Institute, 1963.

Bermúdez, Antonio. *La Política Petrolera Mexicana,* Mexico City: Joaquín Ortiz, 1976.

Bernstein, Marvin, ed. *Foreign Investment in Latin America.* New York: Knopf Inc., 1966.

Blair, John M. *The Control of Oil.* New York: Pantheon Books, 1977.

Blasier, Cole. *The Hovering Giant: U.S. Responses to Revolutionary Change in Latin America.* Pittsburgh: University of Pittsburgh Press, 1976.

Blum, John Morton. *From the Morgenthau Diaries, Years of Crisis, 1928-1938.* Boston: Houghton Mifflin, Inc., 1959.

Boarman, Patrick M., and Schollhammer, Hans, eds. *Multinational Corporations and Governments.* New York: Praeger Publishers, 1975.

Bond, Robert, ed. *Contemporary Venezuela and its Role in International Affairs.* New York: New York University Press, 1977.

Bonsal, Philip. *Castro, Cuba, and the United States.* Pittsburgh: University of Pittsburgh Press, 1971.

Boorstein, Edward. *The Economic Transformation of Cuba.* New York: Monthly Review Press, 1968.

Brothers, Dwight S. "Private Foreign Investment in Latin America: Some Implications for the Alliance for Progress." In *Constructive Change in Latin America,* edited by Cole Blasier. Pittsburgh: University of Pittsburgh Press, 1968.

Búlnes, Luz, et al. *Normas Fundamentales del Estado de Chile.* Santiago: Ediciones Jurídicas, 1975.

Business School of Valparaiso. *The Chilean Economy under the Popular Unity Government.* Santiago: Gabriela Mistral, 1974.

Cardoso, Fernando Enrique. *Dependencia y Desarrollo en América Latina.* Mexico City: Siglo Veintiuno Editores, 1969.

Cardoso, Fernando Enrique. "Associated Dependent Development." In *Authoritarian Brazil,* edited by Alfred Stepan. New Haven, Conn.: Yale University Press, 1973.

Calvo, Carlos. *Derecho Internacional,* 1st ed. Paris: D'Amyot, 1868.

Calvo, Carlos. *Le Droit International,* 5th ed. Paris: Guillaumin, 1896.

Castro, Fidel. "Why We Fight." *Coronet,* February 1958.

Cauas, Jorge and Selowsky, Marcelo. "Potential Distributive Effects of Nationalization Policies: The Economic Aspects." In *Income Distribution and Growth in Less-Developed Countries*, edited by Charles R. Frank, Jr. and Richard C. Webb. Washington, D.C.: The Brookings Institution, 1977.

Chandler, Geoffrey. "Private Foreign Investment and Joint Ventures." In *Private Foreign Investment and the Developing World*, edited by P. H. Ady, New York: Praeger Publishers, 1971.

Cohen, Benjamin. *The Question of Imperialism*. New York: Basic Books, 1973.

Cohen, Stephen D. *The Making of United States International Economic Policy*. New York: Praeger Publishers, 1977.

Commission on United States-Latin American Relations. *The Americas in a Changing World: A Report of the Commission on United States-Latin American Relations*. New York: Quadrangle/New York Times Book Co., 1975.

Connell-Smith, Gordon. *The United States and Latin America*. New York: John Wiley Co., 1974.

Coombes, David. *State Enterprise, Business or Politics?* London: George Allen and Unwin, 1971.

Corporación del Cobre, *Negociaciones con las Empresas Americanas del Cobre Afectadas por la Nacionalización de 1971*. Santiago, November 1974.

Council of the Americas. *The Andean Pact: Definition, Design, and Analysis*. New York: Council of the Americas, 1974.

Cronon, E. David. *Josephus Daniels in Mexico*. Madison: University of Wisconsin Press, 1960.

Cuellar, Alfredo B. *Expropiación y Crisis en México*. Mexico City: Universidad Autónoma, 1940.

Daniels, Josephus. *Shirt-Sleeve Diplomat*. Chapel Hill: University of North Carolina Press, 1947.

Davis, Harold C. *Latin American Thought*. Baton Rouge: Louisiana State University Press, 1972.

Díaz-Alejandro, Carlos, "Direct Foreign Investments in Latin America." In *The International Corporation*, edited by Charles Kindleberger. Cambridge, Mass.: MIT Press, 1970.

Domínguez, Jorge. *Cuba: Order and Revolution*. Cambridge, Mass.: Harvard University Press, 1978.

Draper, Theodore. *Castroism, Myth and Reality*. New York: Praeger Publishers, 1962.

Dubois, Jules. *Fidel Castro.* New York: Bobbs Merrill, Inc., 1959.

Dumont, Rene. *Cuba, Est-Il Socialiste?* Paris: Editions du Seuil, 1970.

Einhorn, Jessica. *Expropriation Politics.* Lexington, Mass.: Lexington Books, 1974.

Emmanuel, Arghiri. *Unequal Exchange.* New York: Monthly Review Press, 1972.

Espinoza, Juan G., and Zimbalist, Andrew S. *Economic Democracy: Workers' Participation in Chilean Industry.* New York: Academic Press, 1978.

Esso International. *The La Brea y Pariñas Controversy.* 4 vols. Coral Gables, Florida, 1969–1972.

Evans, Peter. *Dependent Development: The Alliance of Multinational, State, and Local Capital in Brazil.* Princeton, N.J.: Princeton University Press, 1979.

Fajnzylber, Fernando, and Martínez, Trinidad. *Las Empresas Transnacionales.* Mexico City: Fondo de Cultura Economica, 1976.

Falk, Richard A., and Black, Cyril E., eds. *The Future of the International Legal Order. Wealth and Resources,* vol. 2. Princeton, N.J.: Princeton University Press, 1970.

Fernández, José Antonio, and May, Herbert. *The Effects of Foreign Investment on Mexico.* New York: Council of the Americas, 1971.

Fishlow, Albert. "The Mature Neighbor Policy." In *Latin America and the World Economy,* edited by Joseph Grunwald. Beverly Hills, Calif.: Sage Publications, 1978.

Fitzgerald, E. V. *The State and Economic Development: Peru Since 1968.* Cambridge, Eng.: Cambridge University Press, 1976.

Fontaine, Roger. *On Negotiating with Cuba.* Washington, D.C.: American Enterprise Institute for Public Policy Research, 1975.

Frank, André Gunder. *Capitalism and Underdevelopment in Latin America.* New York: Monthly Review Press, 1967.

Franko, Lawrence G. *Joint Venture Survival in Multinational Corporations.* New York: Praeger Publishers, 1971.

Franko, Lawrence G. "Joint International Business Ventures in Developing Countries." In *Latin American-U.S. Economic Interactions,* edited by Robert B. Williamson. Washington: American Enterprise Institute for Public Policy Research, 1974.

Ffrench-Davis, Ricardo. "Foreign Investment in Latin America: Recent Trends and Prospects." In *Latin America in the International Economy,* edited by Victor Urquidi. New York: Wiley, 1973.

Friedmann, Wolfgang, ed. *Public and Private Enterprise in Mixed Economies.* New York: Columbia University Press, 1974.

Friedmann, Wolfgang, and Beguin, Jean-Pierre. *Joint International Business Ventures in Developing Countries.* New York: Columbia University Press, 1971.

Friedmann, Wolfgang, and Garner, J. F., eds. *Government Enterprise, a Comparative Study.* New York: Columbia University Press, 1970.

Friedmann, Wolfgang, and Kalmanoff, G. *Joint International Business Ventures.* New York: Columbia University Press, 1961.

Gambini, Hugo. *El Che Guevara.* Buenos Aires: Paidos, 1968.

Garcia-Sayan, Diego. *El Caso Marcona.* Lima: DESCO, 1975.

Gerassi, John, ed. *Venceremos. The Speeches and Writings of Che Guevara.* New York: Simon and Schuster, 1969.

Gilpin, Robert. *U.S. Power and the Multinational Corporation.* New York: Basic Books, 1975.

Girvan, Norman. "Las Corporaciones Multinacionales del Cobre en Chile." In *El Cobre en el Desarrollo Nacional,* edited by Ricardo Ffrench-Davis and Ernesto Tironi. Santiago: Ediciones Nueva Universidad, 1974.

Girvan, Norman. *Corporate Imperialism: Conflict and Expropriation.* New York: Monthly Review Press, 1978.

Glade, William. *The Latin American Economies.* New York: American Book, 1969.

Goldhamer, Herbert. *The Foreign Powers in Latin America.* Princeton: Princeton University Press, 1977.

González Aguayo, Leopoldo. *La Nacionalización de Bienes Extranjeros en América Latina.* vol. 2. Mexico City: Universidad Nacional Autonoma, 1969.

Goodsell, Charles T. "The Politics of Direct Foreign Investment in Latin America." In *Latin America in the 1970's,* edited by Luigi Einaudi. New York: Crane Russak Co., 1972.

Goodsell, Charles T. *American Corporations and Peruvian Politics.* Cambridge, Mass.: Harvard University Press, 1974.

Gordon, Michael W. *The Cuban Nationalizations: The Demise of Foreign Private Property.* Buffalo, N.Y.: William S. Hein, 1976.

Gordon, Wendell C. *The Expropriation of Foreign-Owned Property in Mexico.* rep. Westport, Conn.: Greenwood Press, 1975.

Griffin, Keith. *Underdevelopment in Spanish America.* London: Allen and Unwin, 1969.

The Grotius Society. Transactions for the Year 1958–1959. vol. 44. *Problems of Public and Private International Law.* London, 1959.

Hannifin, Rieck B. *Expropriation by Peru of the International Petroleum Company.* Washington, D.C.: Library of Congress, Legislative Reference Service, 1969.

Hanson, A. H. *Public Enterprise and Economic Development*, 2nd ed. London: Routledge and Kegan Paul, 1965.

Hartz, Louis, ed. *The Founding of New States*. New York: Harcourt Brace, 1964.

Haya de la Torre, Victor Raúl, *"¿A Dónde Va Indoamerica?"* (1936), In *The Ideologies of the Developing Nations*, translated and edited by Paul E. Sigmund. rev. ed. New York: Praeger, 1967.

Hirschman, Albert O. *Latin American Issues, Essays and Comments*. New York: Twentieth Century Fund, 1961.

Hirschman, Albert O. "How to Divest and Why." In *A Bias for Hope, Essays on Development and Latin America*. New Haven: Yale University Press, 1971.

Holland, Stuart, ed. *The State as Entrepreneur*. London: Weidenfeld and Nicolson, 1972.

Huberman, Leo, and Sweezy, Paul. *Socialism in Cuba*. New York: Monthly Review Press, 1969.

Hufbauer, G. F. et al. *U.S. Taxation of American Business Abroad*. Washington, D.C.: American Enterprise Institute for Public Policy Research, 1975.

Hunt, Shane. "Direct Foreign Investment in Peru." In *The Peruvian Experiment*, edited by Abraham Lowenthal. Princeton, N.J.: Princeton University Press, 1975.

Ingram, George. *Expropriation of U.S. Property in South America*. New York: Praeger Publishers, 1974.

Italperú. *Contratos Marcona*. Lima, 1971.

The Inter-American Development Bank, Institute of Latin American Integration. *El Régimen Legal de las Empresas Públicas Latinoamericanas y su Acción Internacional*. 2 vols. Buenos Aires, 1977.

Jackson, D. Bruce. *Castro, the Kremlin, and Communism in Latin America*. Baltimore, Md.: Johns Hopkins Press, 1969.

Jaguaribe, Helio. *La Dependencia Político-Económica de América Latina*. Mexico, 1970.

Johnson, Harry G., ed. *Economic Nationalism in Old and New States*. Chicago: University of Chicago Press, 1967.

Jorrín, Miguel, and Martz, John. *Latin American Political Thought and Ideology*. Chapel Hill: University of North Carolina Press, 1970.

Karol, K. S. *Guerrillas in Power*. New York: Hill and Wang, 1970.

Karst, Kenneth L. *Latin American Legal Institutions: Problems for Comparative Study*. Latin American Studies, vol. 5. Los Angeles: University of California Press, 1966.

Karst, Kenneth L., and Rosen, Keith S. *Law and Development in Latin America*. Los Angeles: University of California Press, 1975.

The Kennecott Corporation. *Expropriation of El Teniente*. New York, 1971.

The Kennecott Corporation. *Confiscation of El Teniente*. 4 supplements. New York, 1971–1973.

Keohane, Robert, and Orms, Van Doorn. "The Multinational Firm and International Regulation." In *World Politics and International Economics*. edited by C. Fred Bergsten and Lawrence B. Krause. Washington, D.C.: The Brookings Institution, 1975.

Khrushchev, Nikita. *Khrushchev Remembers*. vol. 1. Boston: Little Brown, 1970.

Knight, Peter T. "New Forms of Economic Organization in Peru." In *The Peruvian Experiment*, edited by A. Lowenthal. Princeton, N.J.: Princeton University Press, 1975.

Knight, Peter T.; Roca, Santiago; Vanek, J.; and Collazo, F. "Self Management in Peru," *Program on Participation and Self-Management Systems*, no. 10. Ithaca, N.Y.: Cornell University, 1975.

Knudson, Harold. *Expropriation of Foreign Private Investments in Latin America*. Bergen: Universitets Forlaget, 1974.

Kraus, Sidney, ed. *The Great Debates: Background, Perspective, Effects*. Gloucester, Mass.: P. Smith, 1968.

Kuczynski, Pedro-Pablo. *Peruvian Democracy Under Stress*. Princeton, N.J.: Princeton University Press, 1977.

Lall, Sanjaya, and Streeten, Paul. *Foreign Investments, Transnationals and Developing Countries*. London: Macmillan, 1977.

le Reverend, Julio, ed. *Los Monopolios Norteamericanos en Cuba*. Havana, Cuba: Instituto Cubano del Libro, 1973.

Leontief, Wassily, et al. *The Future of the World Economy*. New York: Oxford University Press, 1977.

Levinson, Jerome, and de Onis, Juan. *The Alliance That Lost Its Way*. Chicago: Quadrangle Books, 1970.

Lewis, W. Arthur. *The Evolution of the International Economic Order*. Princeton: Princeton University Press, 1978.

Lieuwen, Edwin. *Petroleum in Venezuela: A History*. Berkeley: University of California Press, 1954.

Lillich, Richard B. ed. *The Protection of Foreign Investment*. Syracuse: Syracuse University Press, 1965.

Lillich, Richard B., ed. *The Valuation of Nationalized Property in International Law*. 2 vols. Charlottesville: University of Virginia Press, 1972.

Lillich, Richard B., and Weston, Burns H. *International Claims: Their Settlement by Lump Sum Agreements*, 2 vols. Charlottesville: University of Virginia Press, 1975.

Lindblom, Charles. *Politics and Markets.* New York: Basic Books, 1978.

Lindquist, Sven. *The Shadow.* Baltimore, Md.: Penguin Books, 1972.

Locke, John. *The Second Treatise of Government and a Letter Concerning Toleration.* Edited by J. W. Gough. 3rd ed. Oxford: Blackwell, 1966.

López-Fresquet, Rufo. *My Fourteen Months with Castro.* Cleveland, Oh.: World Publishing, 1966.

McDaniels, John F., ed. *International Financing and Investment.* Dobbs Ferry, N.Y.: Oceana Publications, Inc., 1964.

Malloy, James, ed. *Authoritarianism and Corporatism in Latin America.* Pittsburgh: University of Pittsburgh Press, 1977.

Malpica, Carlos. *Anchovetas y Tiburones.* Lima: Editora Runamarka, 1976.

Mamalakis, Markos. *The Growth and Structure of the Chilean Economy,* New Haven, Conn.: Yale University Press, 1976.

Mamalakis, Markos, and Reynolds, Clark. *Essays on the Chilean Economy.* Homewood, Ill.: Richard D. Irwin, 1965.

The Marcona Corporation. *Nationalization of Marcona Mining, Peruvian Branch.* 1975.

Mariategui, José Carlos. *Seven Interpretive Essays on Peruvian Reality.* Austin: University of Texas Press, 1971.

Martínez, Anibal R. *Chronology of Venezuelan Oil.* London: Allen and Unwin, 1969.

Martner, Gonzalo, ed. *El Pensamiento Económico del Gobierno de Allende.* Santiago: Editorial Universitaria, 1971.

Martz, John D., and Baloyra, Enrique A. *Electoral Mobilization and Public Opinion: The Venezuelan Campaign of 1973.* Chapel Hill: University of North Carolina Press, 1976.

Meier, Gerald M. *International Trade and Development.* New York: Harper and Row, Publishers, 1963.

Mesa-Lago, Carmelo. *Cuba in the 1970's.* Albuquerque: University of New Mexico Press, 1974.

Mesa-Lago, Carmelo, ed. *Revolutionary Change in Cuba.* Pittsburgh: University of Pittsburgh Press, 1971.

Meyer, Lorenzo. *Mexico and the United States in the Oil Controversy, 1917-1942.* Austin: University of Texas Press, 1977.

Mill, Richard S., and Stranger, Roland J., eds. *Essays on Expropriation.* Columbus: Ohio State University Press, 1967.

Moran, Theodore. *Multinational Corporations and the Politics of De-*

pendence: Copper in Chile. Princeton, N.J.: Princeton University Press, 1974.

Morray, J. P. *The Second Revolution in Cuba,* New York: Monthly Review Press, 1962.

Niebuhr, Reinhold, and Sigmund, Paul E. *The Democratic Experience.* New York: Praeger Publishers, 1969.

Niemeyer, E. V. *The Revolution at Querétaro; The Mexican Constitutional Convention of 1916-17.* Austin: University of Texas Press, 1974.

Nixon, Richard M. *Six Crises.* New York: Pyramid, 1968.

Nove, Alec. *Efficiency Criteria for Nationalised Industries.* London: George Allen and Unwin, 1973.

Novóa Monreal, Eduardo. *La Batalla por el Cobre.* Santiago: Quimantu, 1972.

Novóa Monreal, Eduardo. *Defensa de las Nacionalizaciones ante Tribunales Extranjeros.* Mexico: UNAM, 1976.

O'Connor, James. *The Origins of Socialism in Cuba.* Ithaca, N.Y.: Cornell University Press, 1970.

Oppenheim, L. *International Law.* 8th ed. London: Longmans, 1955.

Packenham, Robert. *Liberal America and the Third World.* Princeton, N.J.: Princeton University Press, 1973.

Pastor, Robert. "Congress' Impact on Latin America: Is There Method in the Madness?" In *Report of the Commission on the Organization of the Government for the Conduct of Foreign Policy, June 1975.* vol. 3, appendix H, Washington, D.C.: Government Printing Office, 1975.

Perkins, Dexter. *The United States and the Caribbean.* Cambridge, Mass.: Harvard University Press, 1947.

Petras, James F., and Morley, Morris, *The United States and Chile.* New York: Monthly Review Press, 1975.

Petras, James F.; Morley, Morris; and Smith, Steven. *The Nationalization of Venezuelan Oil.* New York: Praeger Publishers, 1977.

Pike, Frederick, and Stritch, Thomas, eds. *The New Corporatism.* South Bend, Ill.: Notre Dame University Press, 1974.

Pinelo, Adalberto J. *The Multinational Corporation as a Force in Latin American Politics: A Case Study of the International Petroleum Company in Peru.* New York: Praeger Publishers, 1973.

Phillips, David Atlee. *The Night Watch.* New York: Atheneum, 1977.

Powell, J. Richard. *The Mexican Petroleum Industry, 1938-1950.* Berkeley: University of California Press, 1956.

Powers, Thomas. *The Man Who Kept Secrets: Richard Helms and the CIA*. New York: Knopf, 1979.

Quijano, Anibal. "Imperialism and International Relations in Latin America," In *Latin America and the United States: The Changing Political Realities*, edited by Julio Cotler and Richard Fagen. Stanford, Calif.: Stanford University Press, 1974.

Ranis, Gustav. "The Multinational Corporation as an Instrument of Development." In *The Multinational Corporation and Social Change*, edited by David E. Apter and Louis Wolf Goodman. New York: Praeger, 1976.

Reuber, Grant. *Private Foreign Investment in Development*. Oxford: Clarendon Press, 1973.

Reynolds, Clark. *The Mexican Economy*. New Haven, Conn.: Yale University Press, 1970.

Rippy, Merrill. *Oil and the Mexican Revolution*. Leiden: E. J. Brill, 1972.

Ritter, Archibald. *The Economic Development of Revolutionary Cuba*. New York: Praeger Publishers, 1974.

Robinson, Harry, and Smith, Timothy. *The Impact of Foreign Investment on the Mexican Economy*. Stanford, Calif.: Stanford Research Institute, 1976.

Robinson, Richard D. *National Control of Foreign Business Entry*. New York: Praeger Publishers, 1976.

Robock, Stefan H., et al. *International Business and Multinational Enterprises*. Homewood, Ill.: Richard N. Irwin, 1977.

Rojo, Ricardo. *My Friend Che*. New York: Dial Press. 1968.

Rosen, Steven J., and Kurth, James R., eds. *Testing Theories of Imperialism*. Lexington, Mass.: Lexington Press, 1974.

Schneider, Ronald. *Communism in Guatemala*. New York: Frederick A. Praeger, 1958.

Schwarzenberger, Georg. *Foreign Investments and International Law*. London: Stevens and Sons, 1969.

Seidman, Ann, ed. *Natural Resources and National Welfare*, New York: Praeger, 1975.

Sepulveda, B.; Pellicer, Olga; and Meyer, Lorenzo. *Las Empresas Transnacionales en México*. Mexico: El Colegio de Mexico, 1974.

Sharp, Daniel, ed. *U.S. Foreign Policy and Peru*. Austin: University of Texas Press, 1972.

Shea, Donald R. *The Calvo Clause*. Minneapolis: University of Minnesota Press, 1955.

Sheahan, John B. "Public Enterprises in Developing Countries," In

Public Enterprise, edited by William G. Shepherd. Lexington, Mass.: D. C. Heath, 1976.

Sigmund, Paul E., *The Overthrow of Allende and the Politics of Chile, 1964-1976*. Pittsburgh: University of Pittsburgh Press, 1977.

Sigmund, Paul E., ed. *Models of Political Change in Latin America*. New York: Praeger, 1970.

Sigmund, Paul E., ed. *The Ideologies of the Developing Nations*. 2nd rev. ed. New York: Praeger Publishers, 1972.

Silva Hérzog, Jesús. *Historia de la Expropiación Petrolera*. Mexico: Cuadernos Americanos, 1963.

Sinclair, Andrew. *Che Guevara*. New York: Viking, 1970.

Smith, David N., and Wells, Louis T. Jr. *Negotiating Third World Mineral Agreements*. Cambridge, Mass.: Ballinger Publishing Co., 1975.

Smith, Earle E. T. *The Fourth Floor*. New York: Random House, 1962.

Solis, Leopoldo. *La Realidad Económica Mexicana*. Mexico City: Siglo Veintiuno, 1970.

Stallings, Barbara. *Class Conflict and Economic Development in Chile, 1958-1973*. Stanford, Calif.: Stanford University Press, 1979.

Stepan, Alfred. *State and Society: Peru in Comparative Perspective*. Princeton, N.J.: Princeton University Press, 1978.

Stobaugh, Robert B. *Nine Investments Abroad and Their Impact at Home*. Cambridge, Mass.: Harvard University Press, 1976.

Streeten, Paul. "Costs and Benefits of Multinational Enterprises in Less Developed Countries." In *The Multinational Enterprise*, edited by John H. Dunning. New York: Praeger, 1971.

Streeten, Paul. "New Approaches to Private Overseas Investment." In *Private Foreign Investment and the Developing World*, edited by Peter Ady. New York: Praeger Publishers, 1971.

Streeten, Paul, and Lall, S. *Evaluation of Methods and Main Findings of UNCTAD Study of Private Overseas Investment in Selected Less Developed Countries*. New York and Geneva: United Nations, 1973.

Suárez, Andrés. *Cuba: Castroism and Communism, 1959-1966*. Cambridge, Mass.: MIT Press, 1967.

Suarez, Eduardo. *Comentarios y Recuerdos*. Mexico City: Porrua, 1977.

Swansbrough, Robert H. *The Embattled Colossus*. Gainesville: University of Florida Press, 1976.

Thomas, Hugh. *Cuba, the Pursuit of Freedom*. New York: Harper and Row, 1971.

Toriello, Guillermo. *La Batalla de Guatemala*. Mexico: Cuadernos Americanos, 1955.

Truitt, J. Frederick. *Expropriation of Private Investment*. Bloomington: Indiana Graduate School of Business, Indiana University, 1974.

Tugwell, Franklin. *The Politics of Oil in Venezuela*. Stanford, Calif.: Stanford University Press, 1975.

United Nations Centre on Transnational Corporations. *National Legislation and Regulations Relating to Transnational Corporations*. New York: United Nations, 1978.

Urquidi, Victor. *The Challenge of Development in Latin America*. New York: Praeger Publishers, 1964.

Vaitsos, Constantine. *Intercountry Income Distribution and Transnational Enterprises*. London and New York: Oxford University Press, 1974.

Vallenilla, Luis. *Oil: The Making of a New Economic Order*. New York: McGraw-Hill, 1975.

Vargas, Edmundo. "La Nacionalizacion del Cobre y el Derecho Internacional." In *El Cobre en el Desarrollo Nacional*, edited by Ricardo French-Davis and Ernesto Tironi. Santiago: Nueva Universidad, 1974.

Vattel, Emmerich de. *The Law of Nations*. London: G.G. Robinson, 1797.

Vernon, Raymond. *Sovereignty at Bay*. New York: Basic Books, 1971.

Viner, Jacob. *International Economics*. Glencoe, Ill.: The Free Press, 1952.

Wallace, Don. *International Regulation of Multinational Corporations*. New York: Praeger, 1976.

Wallender, Harvey W., et al. *The Andean Pact; Definition, Design and Analysis*. New York: Council of the Americas, 1973.

Webb, Richard. "Government Policy and the Distribution of Income in Peru, 1963–1973." In *The Peruvian Experiment*, edited by A. Lowenthal. Princeton, N.J.: Princeton University Press, 1975.

Weisband, Edward. *The Ideology of American Foreign Policy*. Beverly Hills, Calif.: Sage Publications, 1973.

West, Gerald T. and Haendel, Dan. *Overseas Investment and Political Risk*. Philadelphia: Foreign Policy Research Institute, 1975.

Weston, Burns H. "International Law and the Deprivation of Foreign Wealth." In *The Future of the International Legal Order*, edited by Richard A. Falk and Cyril E. Black, vol. 2, *Wealth and Resources*. Princeton, N.J.: Princeton University Press, 1970.

Whitman, Marina von Neumann. *The United States Investment Guaranty Program and Private Foreign Investment*. Princeton, N.J.: Princeton University Press, 1959.

Wionczek, Miguel. "A Foreign-Owned Export-Oriented Enclave in a Rapidly Industrializing Economy: Sulphur Mining in Mexico." In

Foreign Investment in the Petroleum and Mineral Industries, edited by Raymond F. Mikesell. Baltimore, Md.: Johns Hopkins, 1971.

Wright, Harry K. *Foreign Enterprise in Mexico*. Chapel Hill, N.C.: University of North Carolina Press, 1971.

Zapata, Francisco. *Las Relaciones entre el Movimiento Obrero y el Gobierno de Salvador Allende*. Mexico City: Colegio de Mexico, 1976.

Zapata, Francisco. *Los Mineros de Chuquicamata: ¿Productores o Proletarios?* Mexico City: Colegio de Mexico, 1975.

Zeitlin, Maurice, and Scheer, Robert. *Cuba, Tragedy in Our Hemisphere*. New York: Grove Press, 1963.

Zimmerman, Zavala Augusto. *El Plan Inca, Objetivo: Revolución Peruana*. Lima: El Peruano, 1974.

Zink, Dolph Warren. *The Political Risks for Multinational Enterprise in Developing Countries*. New York: Praeger Publishers, 1973.

PERIODICALS

Amerisinghe, C. F. "The International Centre for the Settlement of Investment Disputes and Development through the Multinational Corporation." *Vanderbilt Journal of Transnational Law* 9 (1976): 793–816.

The Andean Report. May, September 1976.

The Andean Times. 22 February; 2 August 1974.

Associated Press. "Peru, Dream Fades as Wells Dry Up." *ADELA Monthly Bulletin* (Lima) (1976): 8.

Baer, Werner, Newfarmer, Richard; and Trebat, Thomas. "On State Capitalism in Brazil." *Inter-American Economic Affairs* 30 (1977): 66–91.

Bath, C. Richard, and James, Dilmus D. "Dependency Analysis of Latin America." *Latin American Research Review* 6 (1976): 3–58.

Behrman, Jack N. "Foreign vs. Local Ownership." *Worldview* 17 (1974): 41.

Banco Central do Brasil. *Boletin do Banco Central do Brasil* 6 (1976).

Brewer, William Conant. "The Proposal for Investment Guarantees by an International Agency." *American Journal of International Law* 58 (1964): 62–87.

Bronfenbrenner, Martin. "The Appeal of Confiscation in Economic Development." *Economic Development and Cultural Change* (April 1955): 201–18.

Business Latin America. 30 June; 27 October 1976.

Business Week. 9 August 1976.

CEMLA. "Proyecto del BIRF de Creación de un Organismo Internacional de Seguros sobre las Inversiones Extranjeras." *Boletín Mensual* 17, (1971): 100–110; 151–162.

Chilcote, Ronald. "A Critical Synthesis of the Dependency Literature." *Latin American Perspectives* Spring 1974.

Chilcote, Ronald. "A Question of Dependency." *Latin American Research Review* 7 (1978):55–68.

Chile Economic News. 62 (1976): 7–8; 86 (1978): 9.

La Crónica (Lima). 22 May 1976.

dos Santos, Teotonio. "The Structure of Dependence." *American Economic Review* (May 1970): 231–36.

Echeverria, José. "Enriquecimiento Injusto y Nacionalización." *Menaje* 21 (1972): 31–48.

Economic Commission for Latin America. "Public Enterprises: Their Present Significance and Their Potential Development."*Economic Bulletin for Latin America* 16 (1971): 1–57.

Fuad, Kim. "The Economy: Storm Brewing?" *Business Venezuela* 41 (1976): 7–13.

Furtado, Celso. "Dependencia Externa y Teoria Economica." *Trimestre Económico* (April–June 1971).

González, Edward. "Castro's Revolution, Cuban Communist Appeals, and the Soviet Response." *World Politics* (October 1968): 39–68.

Goodwin, Richard. "Letter From Peru." *The New Yorker*, 17 May 1969.

Gantz, David. "The United States-Peruvian Claims Agreement of February 19, 1974." *The International Lawyer* 10 (1976): 389–99.

Halpern, Maurice. "Looking Back at Fidel." *Worldview* 19 (1976): 20–22.

Ibarra, David. "Reflexiones Sobre la Empresa Pública en México." *Foro Internacional* 17, (1976): 141–51.

Karst, Kenneth L. "Latin American Land Reform: The Uses of Confiscation." *Michigan Law Review* 63 (1964):327 ff.

Latin American Economic Report, 13 August; 30 July; 22 October 1976; 19 May 1978.

Latin American Special Report: "Venezuela." Supplement to *Latin American Economic Report* (January 1978).

Lipson, Charles. "Corporate Preferences and Public Policies: Foreign Aid Sanctions and Investment Protection." *World Politics* 28 (1976): 410 ff.

Mann, Joseph A. "Labor — The Honeymoon Is Over." *Business Venezuela* 41 (1976): 14–20.

Martner, Gonzalo. "Problemas de la Produccion Bajo la Unidad Popular en Chile, 1970–73." *Trimestre Economico* 42 (1975): 695 ff.

McCrary, Ernest. "Learning to Cope with Nationalization." *International Management* (April 1971): 26–28.

Meeker, Guy. "Fade-out Joint Venture: Can It Work in Latin America?" *Interamerican Economic Affairs* (Spring 1971): 25–42.

Mendonça de Barros, José Roberto, and Graham, Douglas H. "The Brazilian Economic Miracle Revisited: Private and Public Sector Initiative in a Market Economy." *Latin American Research Review* 12 (1978): 5–38.

El Mercado de Valores. 24 January 1977; 24 April 1978.

El Mercurio (Santiago). 3 April 1972.

Meyer, Herbert E. "Dow Picks Up the Pieces in Chile." *Fortune* (April 1974): 140–52.

Mexican Newsletter. 12 September 1973; 18 March; 31 December 1975.

Miami Herald. 26 October 1976.

Moran, Theodore. "Después de las nacionalizaciones." *Panorama Económico* 270 (August 1972): 27–32.

El Nacional. 20 June 1975; 11 May 1976.

The New Leader. 27 April 1964.

New York Times. 10 January; 15 October 1960; 30 September 1967; 17 September 1970; 26, 30 September; 31 December 1973; 10 January; 12 March 1974; 11 January; 24 December; 18 October 1976.

Nott, David. "Venezuela, The Oil Industry, Nationalization and After." *Bank of London and South America Review* (October 1975): 545.

Novóa Monreal, Eduardo. "Vias Legales para Avanzar Hacia el Socialismo." *Revista de Derecho Economico* 33–34 (October 1971).

Pérez-Stable, Marifeli. "Institutionalization and Workers' Response." *Cuban Studies* 6 (July 1976): 31–54.

Peruvian Times. 31 March 1972; 22 August 1976.

Petras, James, and Morley, Morris. "On the U.S. and the Overthrow of Allende: a Reply to Professor Sigmund's Criticism." *Latin American Research Review* 13 (Spring 1978).

Petroleum Intelligence Weekly. 12 January 1976.

Quarterly Economic Review of Oil in Latin America and the Caribbean. 1st quarter 1978.

Ray, David. "The Dependency Model of Latin American Development: Three Basic Fallacies." *Journal of Inter-American Studies* (February 1973): 4–20.

Resúmen (Caracas). 26 January; 11 May; 7 September 1975; 11, 18 April 1976.

Rose, Sanford. "Why the Multinational Tide is Ebbing." *Fortune* (August 1977): 110.

Schmidt, John T. "Arbitration under the Auspices of the Investment

Disputes (ICSID): Implications of the Decision on Jurisdiction in Alcoa Minerals of Jamaica Inc. vs. Government of Jamaica." *Harvard International Law Journal* 17 (1976): 90–109.

Sigmund, Paul E. "The 'Invisible Blockade' and the Overthrow of Allende." *Foreign Affairs* 52 (1974): 322–40.

Sigmund, Paul E. "U.S. Policy Towards Chile," *Latin American Research Review* 6 (1976): 121–27.

Stobaugh, Robert B. "How to Analyze Foreign Investment Climates." *Harvard Business Review* (September-October 1969).

Sunkel, Osvaldo. "Big Business and Dependencia, a Latin American View." *Foreign Affairs* (April 1972).

Sunkel, Osvaldo. "National Development Policy and External Dependence in Latin America." *The Journal of Development Studies* (October 1969).

Szasz, Paul C. "The Investment Disputes Convention and Latin America." *Virginia Journal of International Law* 11 (1971): 256–65.

Szasz, Paul C. "Arbitration under the Auspices of the World Bank." *The International Lawyer* 3 (1969): 312–19.

Time. 6 November 1972.

Tironi, Ernesto. "El Cobre en Chile." *Mensaje* 216 (1973): 40.

Trow, Clifford, "Woodrow Wilson and the Mexican Interventionist Movement of 1919." *Journal of American History* 58 (1971): 46–72.

Truitt, J. Frederick. "Expropriation of Foreign Investment." *Journal of International Business Studies* (Fall 1970): 29.

United Nations. Centre on Transnational Corporations. "Negotiating with Transnational Corporations: Workshops for Developing Country Officials." *CTC Reporter* 1 (1977): 18–19.

United Nations. Centre on Transnational Corporations. "Technical Corporations Programme: Advisory Services." *CTC Reporter*, 1 (1978): 10–11.

Vernon, Raymond. "International Investment and International Trade in the Product Cycle." *Quarterly Journal of Economics* 53 (1966): 190–207.

Visión. 13 January 1978.

Wall Street Journal. 8 April 1976.

The Washington Post. 6 March 1977.

Wells, Louis T. Jr. "Social Cost/Benefit Analysis for MNC's." *Harvard Business Review* 53 (1975): 40–48, 150–54.

U.S. News and World Report. 25 July 1977.

Zapata, Francisco. "The Chilean Labor Movement under Salvador Allende: 1970–1973." *Latin American Perspectives* 8 (1976): 85–97.

Zeitlin, Maurice. "Inside Cuba: Workers and the Revolution." *Ramparts* 8 (1970): 10-11, 66-78.

Government Sources

Connor, John M., and Mueller, Willard F. *Market Power and Profitability of Multinational Corporations in Brazil and Mexico*. Report to the Subcommittee on Foreign Economic Policy of the Senate Foreign Relations Committee. Washington, D.C.: Government Printing Office, 1977.

Musgrave, Peggy. *Direct Investment Abroad and the Multinationals' Effect on the U.S. Economy*. Report to the Subcommittee on Multinational Corporations of the U.S. Senate Foreign Relations Committee. Washington, D.C.: Government Printing Office, 1975.

Newfarmer, Richard S., and Mueller, Willard F. *Multinational Corporations in Brazil and Mexico*. Report to the Subcommittee on Multinational Corporations of the U.S. Senate Foreign Relations Committee. Washington, D.C.: Government Printing Office, 1975.

Foreign Claims Settlement Commission. *1972 Annual Report*. Washington, D.C.: Government Printing Office, 1973.

U.S., Congress. House of Representatives. Committee on Foreign Affairs. *The Overseas Private Investment Corporation: A Critical Analysis*. Congressional Research Service, 4 September 1973. Washington, D.C.: Government Printing Office, 1973.

U.S., Congress. House of Representatives. Committee on Foreign Affairs. Subcommittee on Foreign Economic Policy. *The Overseas Private Investment Corporation* 21 October 1973. Washington, D.C.: Government Printing Office, 1973.

U.S., Congress. House of Representatives. Committee on Foreign Affairs. *Chile and the Allende Years*. Washington, D.C.: Government Printing Office, 1975.

U.S., Congress. House of Representatives. Committee on International Relations. Subcommittee on International Economic Policy and Trade. *Extension and Revision of Overseas Private Investment Corporation Programs*. Hearings, June-September 1977. Washington, D.C.: Government Printing Office, 1977.

U.S., Congress. House of Representatives. Committee on International Relations. 94th Congress, 1st Session. Subcommittee on International Trade and Commerce, *U.S. Trade Embargo of Cuba*, Washington: U.S. Government Printing Office, 1976.

U.S., Congress. Joint Economic Committee. *Recent Developments in*

Mexico and their Economic Implications for the U.S. Washington, D.C.: Government Printing Office, 1977.

U.S., Congress. Senate. Committee on Finance. *The Multinational Corporation and the World Economy.* 26 February 1973. Washington, D.C.: Government Printing Office, 1973.

U.S., Congress. Senate. Committee on Foreign Relations. Subcommittee on Foreign Assistance. Testimony and prepared statement of William C. Goodfellow, Center for International Policy. *OPIC Authorization.* Washington, D.C.: Government Printing Office, 1977.

U.S., Congress. Senate. Committee on Foreign Relations. Subcommittee on Multinational Corporations. *Hearings on ITT and Chile, 1970-1971.* 2 vols. Washington, D.C.: Government Printing Office, 1973.

U.S., Congress. Senate. Committee on Foreign Relations. Subcommittee on Multinational Corporations. *Multinational Corporations and United States Foreign Policy.* Washington, D.C.: Government Printing Office, 1972-77.

U.S., Congress. Senate. Committee on Foreign Relations. Subcommittee on Multinational Corporations. *The Overseas Private Investment Corporation.* Subcommittee Report, 17 October 1973. Washington, D.C.: Government Printing Office, 1973.

U.S., Congress. Senate. Committee on Foreign Relations. Subcommittee on Western Hemisphere Affairs. *U.S. Relations with Latin America.* Washington, D.C.: Government Printing Office, 1975.

U.S., Congress. Senate. Committee on Foreign Relations. Subcommittee on Western Hemisphere Affairs. *United States Relations with Peru.* Washington, D.C.: Government Printing Office, 1969.

U.S., Congress. Senate. Select Committee on Intelligence Activities, 94th Congress, 1st session. *Alleged Assassination Plots Involving Foreign Leaders.* Washington, D.C.: Government Printing Office, 1975.

U.S., Congress. Senate. Select Committee on Intelligence Activities. *Covert Action in Chile, 1963-1973.* Washington, D.C.: Government Printing Office, 1975.

U.S., Congress. Senate. Select Committee on Intelligence Activities. *Intelligence Activities and Covert Action.* Washington, D.C.: Government Printing Office, 1976.

U.S., Department of Commerce. Bureau of East-West Trade. *United States Commercial Relations with Cuba, A Survey.* Washington, D.C.: Government Printing Office, 1975.

U.S., Department of Commerce. Bureau of Foreign and Domestic Commerce. *Commerce and Navigation of the United States for The*

Calendar Year 1937. Washington, D.C.: Government Printing Office, 1938.

U.S., Department of Commerce. Bureau of Foreign and Domestic Commerce. *Commerce and Navigation of the United States for The Calendar Year 1938.* Washington, D.C.: U.S. Government Printing Office, 1940.

U.S., Department of Commerce. *Survey of Current Business.* September 1967; August 1977; September 1977; August 1978; August 1979.

U.S., Department of State. *Address by the Honorable Henry A. Kissinger, Secretary of State before the Fourth Ministerial Meeting of the United Nations Conference on Trade and Development, Nairobi, Kenya, May 6, 1976.* (mimeo.)

U.S., Department of State. *Bulletin.* 28 August 1953; 14 September 1953; 29 June 1959; February 1960.

U.S., Department of State. *Foreign Relations of the United States, 1938.* vol. 5. Washington, D.C.: U.S. Government Printing Office.

U.S., Department of State. *Treaties and Other International Acts Series.* no. 8173.

Pamphlets, Reports, and Conference Papers

Blasier, Cole. "The USSR in the Cuban-American Conflict." Paper presented at "The Role of Cuba in World Affairs." University of Pittsburgh, 15–17 November 1976.

Dominguez, Jorge. "The Cuban Armed Forces and International Order." Paper presented at "The Role of Cuba in World Affairs" University of Pittsburgh, 15–17 November 1976.

Foxley, Alejandro, et al. *The Role of Asset Redistribution in Poverty-Focused Development Strategies.* World Employment Research Programme Working Paper No. 40. Geneva: International Labor Office, 1976.

Gall, Norman. "Copper is the Wage of Chile." *American Universities Field Staff Reports* 19 (1972).

Gantt, Andrew, and Dutto, Giuseppe. "Financial Performance of Government-Owned Corporations in Less Developed Countries." *IMF Staff Papers* March 1968.

Gillis, Malcolm. "Allocative Efficiency and X-Efficiency in State-Owned Enterprises: Some Asian and Latin American Cases in the Mining Sector." *Technical Papers Series* no. 13. Austin, Texas: Office for Public Sector Studies, Institute of Latin American Studies, University of Texas, 1978.

Meeker, Guy B. "Toward a Fade-In Joint Venture Process." *Papers of the Capital Markets Development Program* Organization of American States, June, 1974.

Mesa-Lago, Carmelo. "Present and Future of Cuba's Economy and International Economic Relations." Paper presented at "The Role of Cuba in World Affairs." University of Pittsburgh, 15–17 November 1976.

Overseas Private Investment Corporation. *1977 Annual Report.*

Pérez-López, Jorge. "Cuban-Soviet Terms of Trade: Sugar and Petroleum." Paper presented at "The Role of Cuba in World Affairs." University of Pittsburgh, 15–17 November 1976.

Trebat, Thomas J. "The Role of Public Enterprise in Brazil." Paper read at Latin American Studies Association. November 1977.

Walters, Alan A. *The Politicization of Economic Decisions.* Reprint paper no. 1. Los Angeles: International Institute for Economic Research, 1976.

Weigel, Dale. "Private Direct Foreign Investment and Economic Development." (Mimeo.) 1977.

Unpublished Theses and Other Papers

Ballantyne, Janet. "The Political Economy of the Peruvian Gran Mineria." Ph.D. dissertation, Cornell University, 1976.

Connally, John C. "The Marcona Case." Senior thesis, Princeton University, 1977.

Gil, Andrés. "CONASUPO: Observations on a Public Enterprise." Senior thesis, Princeton University, 1978.

Speeches

Castro, Fidel. Printed in *Granma,* 25 August 1968.

Castro, Fidel. Speech of 26 July 1970. Printed in *The New York Review of Books,* 24 September 1970.

Cooper, Richard N., undersecretary of state for economic affairs. Speech to the Council of the Americas, 27 June 1977.

Index

DESIGNED BY IRVING PERKINS
COMPOSED BY METRICOMP, GRUNDY CENTER, IOWA
MANUFACTURED BY BANTA DIVISION
GEORGE BANTA COMPANY, INC., MENASHA, WISCONSIN
TEXT AND DISPLAY LINES ARE SET IN TIMES ROMAN

Library of Congress Cataloging in Publication Data
Sigmund, Paul E
Multinationals in Latin America.
"A Twentieth Century Fund study."
Bibliography: p. 383. Includes index.
1. International business enterprises — Government
ownership — Latin America. 2. Corporations, American —
Latin America. 3. Latin America — Foreign economic
relations — United States. 4. United States — Foreign
economic relations — Latin America. I. Title.
HD2755.5.S54   338.8'888   80-5115
ISBN 0-299-08260-1
ISBN 0-299-08264-4 (pbk.)